COMMANDER

★ ★ ★ ★ ★ IN ★ ★ ★ ★ ★

CHEAT

COMMANDER

★ ★ ★ ★ ★ IN ★ ★ ★ ★ ★

CHEAT

RICK REILLY

HEADLINE

The right of Rick Reilly to be identified as the Author of
the Work has been asserted by him in accordance with the
Copyright, Designs and Patents Act 1988.

First published in the US by Hachette Books 2019
First published in Great Britain in 2019
by HEADLINE PUBLISHING GROUP

7

Cataloguing in Publication Data is available from the British Library

Hardback ISBN 9781472266101

Jacket design by Carlos Esparza
Jacket photograph © Ian MacNicol/Getty Images
Jacket copyright © 2019 Hachette Book Group, Inc.

Printed and bound in Great Britain by Clays Ltd, Elcograf S.p.A.

Headline's policy is to use papers that are natural, renewable and recyclable
products and made from wood grown in well-managed forests and other
controlled sources. The logging and manufacturing processes are expected
to conform to the environmental regulations of the country of origin.

HEADLINE PUBLISHING GROUP
An Hachette UK Company
Carmelite House
50 Victoria Embankment
London EC4Y 0DZ

www.headline.co.uk
www.hachette.co.uk

This book is dedicated to the truth. It's still a thing.

Contents

1

THE BIG LIE

To find a man's true character, play golf with him.
—P. G. Wodehouse

IN THE 30 YEARS I've known Donald Trump, I never believed anything he said, but the *wink-wink* of it was that I never thought he believed any of it either. He was like your crazy uncle at Thanksgiving who sits in the living room telling the kids whoppers about punching Sinatra while the parents all roll their eyes in the kitchen. He was a fun, full-of-it fabulist.

One time, for instance, I was in his office in Trump Tower. He pulled a yellow laminated card out of his wallet and slapped it down on his massive desk like a fourth ace.

"Look at that!" he said. "Only nine people in the world have that!"

The card read: *Bearer Eats Free at Any McDonald's Worldwide.*

"It's only me, Mother Teresa, and Michael Jordan!" he crowed.

I pictured Mother Teresa, at that very moment, pulling into the drive-thru at the Calcutta McDonald's, rolling down the window, leaning her habit out, and saying, "I need 10,000 double cheeseburgers, please."

I liked Trump the way I liked Batman. He was what eight-year-old me thought a gazillionaire *should* be like—his name in 10-foot-high letters on skyscrapers and on giant jets, hot and cold running blondes hanging on each arm, $1,000 bills sticking out of his socks.

So I knew the whole "running for president" thing had to have an angle. There's always an angle. The trick was figuring out what it was.

The first time I met Donald Trump, way back when, I was the back-page columnist at *Sports Illustrated*. I was playing in the AT&T Pebble Beach Pro-Am when he came at me with a bible-salesman grin and a short-fingered hand to shake. His wife, Marla Maples, was smiling at me, too.

Uh-oh, I thought. *What's this?*

"You're my favorite writer!" Trump bellowed. "I love your stuff. Tell him, Marla!"

"He does!" she said. "Look!" And she pulled out of her purse a column I'd written. Okay, there was the set-up. What was the hook?

"So," he said, "when are you going to write about ME?"

Ahh, there it was.

No problem. Trump was the most accessible, bombastic, and quotable businessman in the world. Why would I turn that down? So when I set out to write my golf book *Who's Your Caddy?*—in

which I would caddy for 12 golf legends, celebrities, and oddballs—I asked if he wanted to be a chapter. "Absolutely!" he said.

When the day came, he didn't have anybody to play with, so he announced that I wouldn't be caddying for him, I'd be playing with him. Okay, you take what you can get. We played his Trump National Golf Club Westchester in Briarcliff Manor, New York, and it was like spending the day in a hyperbole hurricane.

Trump didn't just lie nonstop about himself that day. He lied nonstop about ME. He'd go up to some member and say, "This is Rick. He's the president of *Sports Illustrated*." The guy would reach out to shake my hesitant hand, but by then Trump had dragged me forward to the next member. Or secretary. Or chef. "This is Rick. He publishes *Sports Illustrated*." Before I could object, he'd go, "And this is Chef. He was voted Best Hamburger Chef in the world!" And the poor chef would look at me and shake his head with a helpless "no," same as me.

When we were alone, I finally said, "Donald, why are you lying about me?"

"Sounds better," he said.

Sounding better is Trump's m.o. It colors everything he says and does. The truth doesn't break an egg with Trump. It's all about how it sounds, how it looks, and the fact checkers can go run a 100-yard dash in a 50-yard gym.

A friend of mine had dinner with Trump and his wife, Melania, in 2015, when this whole presidential thing was starting to simmer. The husbands and wives had veered off into separate conversations. The wife said, "You have a lovely accent, Melania. Where are you from?"

"Slovenia," she said.

Trump, in mid-sentence, turned to her and interjected: "Say Austria. Sounds better."

But when I read The Big Lie, it nearly made me spit out my Cheerios. It was a tweet he'd originally posted in 2013, but I hadn't read it until his campaign began. Trump was embroiled in one of his hundreds of celebrity feuds, this one with somebody in his weight class—Dallas Mavericks owner and billionaire sports fan Mark Cuban. Cuban had dissed him on some forgettable TV show years before. "I think I said, 'I can write a bigger check than Trump right now and not even know it was missing,'" Cuban remembers.

Trump seethed about it. Trump can dish out the insults by the steam shovel but he can't take a teaspoonful back. His rule is: "When I'm attacked, I fight back 10 times harder." He vowed lifetime revenge on Cuban that day.

That's when he challenged Cuban.

> **Golf match? I've won 18 Club Championships including this weekend. @mcuban swings like a little girl with no power or talent. Mark's a loser**
>
> **—Donald J. Trump, Twitter, March 19, 2013**

Eighteen championships? That's like an NFL quarterback telling you he's won 18 Super Bowls. It's preposterous. It's a Macy's Thanksgiving Day float of a lie. Besides, Trump had already given away his little secret of how he does it that day at Westchester. "Whenever I open a new golf course," he told me, "I play the official opening round and then I just call *that* the first club

championship. There you go! I'm the first club champion!...
That's off the record, of course."

You gotta admit: It's sleazy, it's morally bankrupt, but it's
pretty clever.

I did keep it off the record, for years. But then he *kept* blud-
geoning people over the head with it.

"You know, I've won 18 club championships," he said half a
dozen times during campaign stops. "I'm a winner." As though
the trunk of his Rolls-Royce is so full of golf trophies that he can't
even get it shut.

In an interview with the *Washington Post*, he said, humbly,
"My life has been about victories. I've won a lot. I win a lot. I
win—when I do something, I win. And even in sports, I always
won. I was always a good athlete. And I always won. In golf, I've
won many club championships. Many, many club championships. And I have people that can play golf great, but they can't
win under pressure. So, I've always won."

After a big primary win, he bragged at the podium, "I know
how to win. I've won...these people will tell you. Have I won
many club championships? Does Trump know how to close?"

At another campaign stump: "Winning is winning. It's not
easy to win club championships, believe me. And I'm not talking
about with strokes. I'm talking with no strokes."

Winning 18 club championships is a lie that's so over-the-top
Crazytown it loses all credibility among golfers the second it's
out of his mouth. To double-check, I called the only guy who
could come close: George "Buddy" Marucci, of Philadelphia. Like
Trump, Marucci belongs to more clubs than you can fit in your

bag. Like Trump, he's in the right age bracket, at six years younger than Trump. Like Trump, he's got all the money he needs to play as many club championships as he can fly to. Unlike Trump, he's as fine a golfing businessman as you can find. Marucci took 19-year-old Tiger Woods—24 years his junior—to the last hole of the 1995 U.S. Amateur final before finally losing.

So, Buddy Marucci, do YOU have 18 club championships?

"Ha!" he laughed. "No way. I have a few, but nowhere near that many. It's hard to win a club championship. I might have eight. Tops."

This is a guy who's been breaking par for the past 45 years. He belongs to nearly every creamy course in the world—Winged Foot, Seminole, Pine Valley, Cypress Point. If it's on a top 10 in the world list, Marucci probably has a locker there.

"Eighteen?" he said. "I don't see how anybody could do that." When I explained to him how Trump did it, he said, "You know, I'm not sure even doing THAT I could get to 18."

When Trump told Gary Player he'd won 18 championships, Player scoffed. "I told him that if anyone beats him, he kicks them out. So, he had to win."

Was Trump's name on the wall of any clubs he *didn't* own? Nope. Was it on the walls at Trump Washington, D.C., in Virginia, a course that was already up and running when he bought it? Nope. Or Trump Jupiter, which was a Ritz Carlton course when he bought it? Nope. Was it on the wall at any of his own courses he'd opened? Oh, yes.

Trump International in West Palm Beach, Florida, has a plaque on the wall that lists all the men who've won the men's club championship. Trump appears three times: 1999, 2001, and 2009. But hold on. The course wasn't even *open* in 1999. Turns out, then White House spokesperson Hope Hicks admitted to the *Washington Post*, Trump played in a "soft opening" round on November 1 of that year with "a group of the early members" and declared it the club championship.

Congratulations?

On March 17, 2013, Trump tweeted he'd won the club championship again at Trump International. This is the one he was gloating to Cuban about.

Just won The Club Championship at Trump International Golf Club in Palm Beach-lots of very good golfers-never easy to win a C.C.

But the plaque for that year lists the winner as "Tom Roush." The catch? It wasn't really the club championship at all. Trump won the "Super Seniors Club Championship," which at most clubs is reserved for players 60 and older. Something to be proud of, sure, but not within a Super Walmart of beating the best young players in the club. The difference between "Club Champion" and "Super Senior Club Champion" is the difference between Vanna White and Betty White.

"I remember Melania used to ask us, 'What is this 'Super Seniors'?'" recalls former Trump Westchester exec Ian Gillule. "And Mr. Trump would say, 'Oh, Super Seniors is *better* than just a regular club championship, honey.' He was saying it tongue in cheek but she didn't know the difference."

I called golf writer Michael Bamberger of Golf.com. He once did a story for *Sports Illustrated* on playing every Trump course *with* Trump. Had he heard about these 18 club championships? He had.

Bamberger: "We were at Trump Westchester and Trump says, 'Michael, I just won the club championship here.' And I'm thinking, 'Wow, that's a little hard to believe, since he's about a 9 or 10 [handicap] and you don't get any strokes in the club championship.' So I said, 'Who'd you beat?' And he said, 'This guy!'" Trump was pointing to his longtime cement contractor, Lou Rinaldi, who's a zero handicap and a terrific player. Bamberger looked at Rinaldi, who shrugged his shoulders as if to say, "I'm gonna argue with my boss?"

Later, Bamberger found out that, too, was the senior club championship. "Then I found out even later," Bamberger says, "that it wasn't that year at all. It was a different year."

At Trump Bedminster in New Jersey, Trump once won a senior club championship from 87 miles away. He'd declared that the club should start having senior club championships for those 50 and up, but he forgot that one of the best players at the club had just turned 50. Having zero chance at beating the guy, he went up to his Trump Philadelphia course on the day of the tournament and played with a friend there. Afterward, according to a source inside the Bedminster club, he called the Bedminster pro shop and announced he'd shot 73 and should be declared the winner. The pro, wanting to stay employed, agreed. His name went up on the plaque. "But then," says the source, "somebody talked to the caddy up in Philly and asked him what Trump shot that day. The caddy goes, 'Maybe 82. And that might be generous.' He pulls that kind of sh*t all the time around here."

More than one source described another time when Trump happened to walk into the Bedminster clubhouse just as a worker was putting up the name of the newly crowned senior club championship winner on a wooden plaque. Trump had been out of town and hadn't played in the tournament, but when he saw the player's name, he stopped the employee. "Hey, I beat that guy all the time. Put my name up there instead." The worker was flummoxed.

"Really, sir?"

"Yeah, yeah. I beat that guy constantly. I would've beaten him. Put my name up."

Of the 18 club championship "wins" that Trump listed for *Golf Digest*, 12 are actually senior or super senior club championships. To repeat: senior and super senior club championships are not men's club championships. They're like bowling with bumpers. Besides, as I say, most of those smell like three-day-old halibut. So that leaves six *real* club championships. One of the six he lists was Trump Westchester 2001, when the club wasn't officially open yet. That leaves five. The next was Westchester 2002, when the club was only nine holes. If it really happened, you can't count that. That leaves four, one of them being Westchester in 2004. Could he have actually won that?

"Well, no, I know for a fact that's not true," Gillule says. "He never won any in the eight years I worked there. I mean, I loved working for Mr. Trump, but you know, some people take a certain license with the truth."

We do know that Trump played in the 2007 Westchester Men's Club Championship and was knocked out in the first round by a 15-year-old named Adam Levin. Trump was four-up with five holes to play, helped greatly by the 60-year-old calling two ticky-tack rule violations on the kid, one for accidentally touching the grass inside a hazard and one for fixing a small ball mark off the green, both loss-of-hole penalties.

That's when, according to Levin, Trump said to the small gallery, "The kid put up a good fight, didn't he?" A small bonfire lit under Levin, who wound up winning hole after hole, tying Trump up through 18 and then winning on the second playoff hole.

"He didn't even say 'Congratulations' or 'Good match,'" remembers Levin, now a data analyst. "He didn't look me in the eye. He just shook my hand and walked off. He'd kind of been a dick the whole day. We were together for five or six hours, so there was plenty of time for conversation with me or my parents, but all he ever said was, 'Isn't this course fantastic?' and 'Aren't these facilities the best?' He's a total asshole with no character."

That leaves three possible club championship wins, all at one course—Trump International in West Palm Beach. But we already know the 1999 win there is a lie, since the course wasn't open. That leaves two. Of those two—2001 and 2009—I have never seen a signed scorecard or spoken to any objective person who remembers him winning or not winning.

Final score on the "18 club championships": Lies 16, Incompletes 2, Confirms 0. By this time, Trump's nose has grown so long he could putt with it.

The whole thing bugged me so much I started to itch. I wasn't offended as a voter. I was offended as a *golfer*. You can't *get away* with that. You want to make political promises you can't keep? Great, knock yourself out. You want to invent tales of your cut-throat savvy in business deals? Live it up. But golf *means* something to me. I've played it my whole life. It's kept me sane and happy and found me more friends than I can count.

One of the things I love the most about golf is that you're your own referee. You call fouls on yourself. Integrity is built into the fabric of the game. Honesty is more precious in golf than the little white dimples. As Ben Crenshaw likes to say, "Golf is a game with a conscience."

For golfers, the stain of cheating is so much graver than winning or losing that we live in mortal fear of being called a cheater. Tom Watson accused Gary Player of illegally moving a leaf away from his ball at the Skins Game in 1983 and they've hardly spoken since. *One leaf.* Vijay Singh could win 10 majors and never lose his label as a cheater, based on a tiny incident that may or may not have happened once years ago in Indonesia.

So here was Trump caterwauling about 18 golf championships that were faker than Cheez Whiz, and it started to make me think. How much of what Trump says about his golf brilliance does the country believe? During the campaign, when Trump stood up in front of 30,000 red hats and bloviated, "When it comes to golf, very few people can beat me," did people buy that? Because 50 guys at every course in America can beat him.

When Trump turned his back on Puerto Rico after Hurricane Maria, did anybody know that he'd abandoned his "fabulous"

11

golf project there the year before, a bankruptcy that left the tiny territory with a $32 million debt?

When Trump held endless 18-hole meetings at his Florida courses with this prime minister and that emperor, were these leaders returning home to laugh at OUR president the way they laughed at him at the United Nations? Would they think all Americans cheat at golf?

It got me thinking...

Somebody should point out that the way Trump does golf is sort of the way he does a presidency, which is to operate as though the rules are for other people.

Somebody should explain that facts and truth are to Trump what golf scores and crowd sizes are—"feelings"—malleable and negotiable, flitting this way and that like an arm-waving inflatable car-lot balloon man.

Somebody should write that the way Trump cheats at golf, lies about his courses, and stiffs his golf contractors isn't that far from how he cheats on his wives, lies about his misdeeds, and stiffs the world on agreements America has already made on everything from Iran to climate change.

"Golf is like bicycle shorts," I once wrote. "It reveals a lot about a man."

You could write a book about what Trump's golf reveals about him.

Here it is.

2

YOU AIN'T NO BALLERINA

Golf is fatal.
—THEODORE ROOSEVELT

FOR PRESIDENTS, THE WHITE House is a kind of prison with butlers. You can't go anywhere without a squadron of Secret Service people and a week of planning. You sleep above your office, where a desk full of the world's biggest problems silently screams for you. That's why golf is perfect for presidents. With no skyscraper windows, no streets for people to line up on, no intersections, no passing cars, presidents can stay relatively safe.

Where they play, how they play, how often and why they play can sometimes tell you more about a president than a room full of historians.

Golf didn't become trendy in America until the turn of the 20th century, and one of the first to get bit was William Howard Taft, a man who topped 300 pounds. He loved the game so much that he once blew off the president of Chile, who was waiting for him back in the White House, to keep his tee time.

Woodrow Wilson was such a worrier that his doctor *ordered* him to play golf to relieve his indigestion, even though Wilson couldn't play dead in a cowboy movie. He rarely broke 110. He'd putt hunched over 90 degrees, like a man talking to a pet mouse, with a putter that couldn't have been much taller than a toilet plunger. Wilson played only with his wife and his doctor, fearing that anybody else would want to talk about the League of Nations or somesuch. He became hopelessly addicted to the game. He even painted his golf balls black so he could play in the snow. Wilson makes Trump look like a newbie. Presidential golf historian Don Van Natta estimates Wilson might have played as many as 1,600 times during his eight years, about every other day, always first thing in the morning. He played faster than the morning train and was usually back at his desk by 9 am.

The swashbuckling Warren Harding was just the opposite. Golf to him was a kind of party with spikes. Why hurry? He loved all celebrities, but especially golf stars. He hosted the legendary night owl Walter Hagen often. One day, Hagen presented Harding with one of his favorite drivers.

"What can I do for you in return?" Harding asked, tickled.

The habitually late Hagen said it sure would be convenient to have a Secret Service badge to get him out of speeding tickets. He got it.

Harding was the first in a long line of presidents who fudged the rules. He was great fun on the golf course, long on laughs, always in plus fours and a bow tie. He wasn't above having a few belts between green and tee, which, coupled with his big off-balance lash, kept him from scoring well. Still, he was devoted to it. He was in San Francisco, on a vacation that included boat loads of golf, when he suddenly shuddered and died, probably of congestive heart failure. To commemorate him, San Francisco is now home to a terrific public golf course, Harding Park.

Calvin Coolidge wasn't good or fun or loose with golf at all and, in fact, was a chop's chop, which is to say he was so bad he couldn't even shoot his weight. When he left the White House for good, he left his clubs there.

Our most talented golfing president, by far, was Franklin Delano Roosevelt. A big hitter with a fine iron game and a diamond cutter's touch around the greens, he won many golf medals as a teen and, at 18, won the men's club championship (no, *really*) at Canada's Campobello Golf Club. But polio hit him at age 39, 12 years before he became president, and he never played again. Still, his work projects gave us dozens of terrific public tracks, including Bethpage in New York, site of the 2019 PGA Championship.

Harry Truman played piano, not golf, but his successor, Dwight Eisenhower loved it like dogs love bones. He could hardly stand to be away from his clubs. In fact, he'd stroll the halls of the White House with an iron, taking half-swings while he pondered what to do about the postwar world. He and his idol—a permanently tan heartthrob named Arnold Palmer—fueled the 1960s golf boom in this country that didn't slow down until the Great Recession of 2007.

Ike loved golf but it didn't love him. His Achilles' heel was putting. He'd approach the ball as if it were a snake, freeze like a statue over it, then jab at it and jump back fast. He seemed to have 11 kinds of yips. To practice, he built a putting green outside the Oval Office. Sometimes, upon re-entering the office, he'd forget to take off his spikes. I once crouched down there and felt the holes he left in the wooden floor.

Were it not for his bad back, President Kennedy could've been terrific. He played on the Harvard freshman golf team but hurt his back playing football and didn't go out the next year. His swing was elegant and upright, with a perfectly balanced finish, his slim right shoulder facing perfectly toward the target, his hatless hair tossed back with the wind, a kind of Gatsby in cashmere. Unlike Trump, JFK didn't want to talk about his golf, didn't want cameras around while he played it, and didn't want to announce what he shot. After his election but before his inauguration, Kennedy rattled his tee shot in and out of the cup on the 16th at Cypress Point, the most famous par 3 in the world. Kennedy breathed a sigh of relief. "You're yelling for the damn ball to go in," he said to his playing partners, "and I'm seeing a promising political career coming to an end!"

LBJ played miserably and mostly as a way to cajole congressmen to vote for this bill or that. They say he wrangled the votes he needed for his landmark Civil Rights Act on the golf course. He was fond of swear words and mulligans, taking sometimes five, six, and seven of each in a single nine holes, always reminding his opponents, "It's not nice to beat the president." After he was out of the office, he found out how true that was.

Nixon played, but never looked natural at it, always smiling too big, wearing his pants too high. His friends said he did it just to suck up to Ike as his vice president. Nixon was about an 18 handicap, but after resigning over Watergate, golf became a refuge and he got down to 12. So, you know, Watergate wasn't *all* bad.

Nixon's resignation, coupled with the resignation of his veep Spiro Agnew, shoehorned into the Oval Office the only bona-fide college sports star we've ever had, former Michigan lineman Gerald Ford. A natural athlete, President Ford loved golf, but it didn't love him. Still, he'd play as much as he could. He'd even play in the PGA Tour's Pebble Beach Pro-Am, a nightmare for the Secret Service, not to mention the galleries. Ford hit far more people with golf balls than ever voted for him for president (that number is zero), mostly because his driver was long and wrong. But he did make a hole in one once, at Colonial Country Club in Fort Worth, playing with Crenshaw in the Pro-Am. "The place went crazy," Crenshaw remembers. "He was beside himself. He turned to me said, 'I can't believe I just did that!'"

Golf went dark for a while after Ford. Jimmy Carter fished. Reagan could take golf or leave it, preferring horses. He was about a 13. You can still see his locker at Los Angeles Country Club.

There can't be a more golfy family than the Bushes. Bush 41's grandfather, George Herbert Walker Bush, was the president of the U.S. Golf Association (USGA) and invented the Walker Cup, the amateur version of the Ryder Cup. Bush 41's father, Prescott Bush, was scratch (a 0 handicap) and also president of the USGA for a year. Bush 41 was the fastest golfer I've ever seen. He was an 18 handicap with elbows flying every which way. He looked like a man trying to swat a horsefly. What he cared about more than score was finishing in less than two hours. The best-selling author James Patterson played with him once. "It was a blur," Patterson says. "The whole thing seemed to be a rush to get to the end. It was a feeling like, 'Wow, are we done now?' But he was very nice, very kind, and very down to earth."

Bush 41 loved the Texas pros like Crenshaw and Tom Kite as if they were his sons. In fact, any writer who dared criticize either of them would hear it from him personally, including yours truly. After Kite got out-captained by Seve Ballesteros in Spain at the 1997 Ryder Cup, despite having 8 of the top 14 players in the world (Europe had one), I poked a little fun at Kite. He was squiring Bush and Michael Jordan around in his plodding four-man cart while Seve was zipping hither and yon in some sort of turbo cart by Maserati, seemingly showing up at every hole, shouting instructions in Spanish, telling players which greens had been mowed *during* the round, and generally driving circles around Kite. Europe beat the United States, 14.5 to 13.5. The next week, Bush sent *Sports Illustrated* a hand-typed letter:

Was Rick Reilly even there? Didn't he sense the comeback in the air on Sunday?...Tom Kite and the American players don't deserve the cynical, subtle put down Reilly lays on them.

An America fan,

a Tom Kite fan,

G.B.

Yes, I was there. In fact, I perched next to Bush half a dozen times that day. Apparently, I didn't make much of an impression.

Bob Hope once said, "I've always enjoyed playing golf with a president. The only problem is that there are so many Secret Service men around there's not much chance to cheat." Hope would've loved playing with Bill Clinton.

When I played with Clinton in 1995 at Congressional Country Club for a story, he cheated with the *help* of the Secret Service. He didn't take mulligans, though, which are complete do-overs of a shot. No, he took what the press called "Billigans." He'd hit his first ball and tell everybody he was going to play that one. But then he'd take three, four, even five practice shots from the same place—Billigans. (Wholly illegal.) Of course, with so many balls on the hole, it started to look like an Easter egg hunt. It was hard to figure out which was his first ball. Luckily, the Secret Service seemed to always know: the one near the pin. What agent doesn't want to be ambassador to Sweden?

Clinton didn't seem to give a fig about the four SWAT guys in the trees or the six agents walking with us, all of them Uzi'd up under their sport coats. We also had 13 golf carts following us, one of which held the red phone, one the assistant to the chief of staff, and one the chief of protocol. I don't know how the chief of protocol would've liked what Clinton said to me as we walked past a balcony full of people waving to us. He was waving with his right hand and elbowing me in the ribs with the left.

"What?" I said out of the side of the mouth.

"You see the blond on the left?"

"Yeah?"

"I just got a wink from her."

I wanted to say, "They *did* mention I was a reporter, right?"

Like Trump, Clinton was fabulous golf company. Unlike Trump, he wanted the round to last as long as humanly possible. A six-hour round was delirium for Clinton: more cigars, more laughing, less Bosnia. He zinged you, slapped you on the back, and praised you, sometimes all in one par 3. He was oddly conversant on anything golf. "You like that new bubble shaft?" he asked me. (I didn't even realize I *had* one.) He had a complicated swing you'd never be able to find parts for—moving here and there, up and down, left and right. At impact, he'd jump up on the balls of his feet, like Andre Agassi hitting a forehand, and it produced a big cutting slice. This, plus the 24 clubs he had in his bag (the limit is 14), plus all the chasing down of the errant Billigans, was more than the caddy, a 70-year-old black gentlemen, could handle.

"Get off your toes!" he finally said. "You ain't no damn ballerina!"

The chief of protocol's mouth fell open like a drawbridge. The necks of the Secret Service agents snapped. There was an awkward pause. Then Clinton just said, "You're right. My bad." With all the Billigans and craziness, it was hard to tell what he shot, but the card said 82, which he told me later was the best of his life.

(Quick story about Trump and the Clintons: One time, Hillary gets her brother, Hugh Rodham, on at Winged Foot, even though neither are members. Rodham shows up wearing shorts. That's a no-no at Winged Foot. Pants only. Hugh Rodham is a man of large girth, so there weren't any pants in the pro shop that fit. The valet says to a caddy, "Go in and get Mr. Rodham a pair of rain pants to wear." The caddy goes in, tries to think of a guy near to Rodham's size, goes to Trump's locker, gets his rain pants, and runs out. Rodham plays in the rain pants. When this story gets back to Trump, he flips out. He makes Winged Foot buy him an entirely new rain suit. *Clinton cooties*.)

The greatest day for presidential golf buffs was February 15, 1995, the only time three presidents have played in one group. It was at the Bob Hope Desert Classic—standing president Clinton, Bush 41, and Ford, with Hope thrown in as a foursome filler. It was a unique moment. I always fantasize that at one point Hope said, "You're on the tee, Mr. President," and three guys knocked heads trying to tee up their ball.

Bush shot 93, Clinton 95, and Ford 103. And we know those scores are real. It was on NBC. Bush, though, was a menace to the gallery. On the first hole, he ricocheted one off a tree and hit an elderly woman on her nose, breaking her glasses and splattering blood everywhere. On the 14th, he hit a man on the back of the leg. His wife Barbara shook her head and said, "As if we don't have enough violence on television."

Bush 43 was a fair golfer—about a 15—but he stopped playing golf in 2003 out of "solidarity" with soldiers in the war. No, he actually did. What would it take to get Trump to stop playing? Nuclear winter?

"The Bushes don't cheat," Crenshaw avers. "Forty-three will get to the first tee and say, 'Now look, I'm not moving this ball today. I'm playing it honestly all the way through.' And he would."

Crenshaw became so close with Bush 43 that one year, when he was playing the PGA Tour's Kemper Open near Washington,

43 insisted he stay at the White House. After the first round, though, Crenshaw, famously awful at directions, got lost coming back to the White House and ended up parked on the side of the highway, wrestling a map. A patrolman pulled up and asked where he was trying to go.

"Well, uh, you're not gonna believe this," Crenshaw stammered, red-faced. "But I'm stayin' at the White House."

When the cop stopped laughing, he escorted him there personally.

Obama loved golf and liked to play it with—are you ready for this?—sportswriters. I kid you not. He played dozens of times with ESPN *Pardon the Interruption* hosts Michael Wilbon and Tony Kornheiser. Obama is a feverish sports nut, so it was a good fit. I know, because he was my fantasy football partner for an ESPN column once. He knew more than I imagined.

"We need a wide receiver," I'd say. "Let's pick (so and so)."

"No way," he'd say. "They just lost their receivers coach."

You could've put Obama's golf on a USGA poster—no cheating, no mulligans, no do-overs. He also kept it very private. He rarely played with politicians or world leaders, mostly guys from his travel advance team, especially as he was trying to get better. After a year and a half out of office, he was down to an 11 handicap, according to Wilbon. "I'm not a hack, but I'm not quitting my day job," he likes to say now. Off the tee he's "very straight," Tiger Woods says, but "not long." His chipping is salty, but he's a disaster in the bunkers. Like Saddam Hussein, he may someday get in a bunker and never get out.

Which brings us to Trump.

No president has been as up to his clavicles in golf as Donald Trump. None has been woven so deeply into the world of golf. Trump doesn't just play courses; he builds them, buys them, owns them, operates them, sues over them, lies about them, bullies with them, and brags about them. From the people he knows, to the businesses he runs, to the favors he hands out, to the access he grants, to the trouble he gets into, to the places he goes, to the money he makes, to the money he loses, to the opinions it informs in his brain, Trump's soul is practically dimpled.

But keep on your toes, ballerinas, because it's a wild dance.

3

THE KID WITH THE BIG SHEKELS

You gotta watch those guys at Cobbs Creek. They'll take your teeth.
—DONALD J. TRUMP

IF YOU WERE BORN a son of Fred Trump, you heard one thing over and over: *Win, win, and then win some more. Whatever you have to do, be a winner.* Fred Trump constantly urged his boys to be "killers." Life as a Trump was not about hugs or picnics or bedtime reading. It was about winning. Nothing else mattered.

"The stories you hear about Fred," says Jack O'Donnell, vice president of Trump Plaza Casino from 1987 to 1990, "he was pretty rough on the boys—win, win, win, strict, strict, strict—always finish on top. That's not easy."

Donald took to sports and no wonder. Every day, sports gave young Donald the chance to prove to his father he was a winner. A naturally good athlete—"I was always the best athlete," he once boasted, "Nobody ever talks about that"—Trump likes to say that at one time he could've been a pro baseball player. "But those weren't good times for baseball in terms of, you make $2," he told golf podcaster David Feherty. So he chose a career in real estate instead. So, to recap: Major League Baseball was dying to get Donald Trump, but they weren't paying enough to suit him, so he broke their heart and joined his dad's business.

It's no wonder Trump fell in love with golf. Every round of golf comes with 18 chances to win, plus the 19th chance—my final score versus yours. *I beat you. I win. You're a loser.* Trump's love affair with golf has far outlasted any romance he's had with any woman or career or party affiliation.

Fred, a second-generation German, played, but only rarely. One day when Trump was young, his dad took him out to a golf course called Forest Park near Queens. Young Donald didn't play that day but says his father "was, potentially, a very good golfer. He probably only played 10 times in his life, but he had a beautiful swing."

Donald himself didn't take up the game with passion until college in the late 1960s, and I could give you 1,000 guesses where and you'd never get it.

It was Philadelphia's scruffy Cobbs Creek, aka "The Crick," a goulash of gamblers and hustlers and out-of-work steelworkers. It was a public track, full of $2 weekend hacks and $100/hole sharpies and Penn students. One of those students was Trump, who'd drive the 10 minutes from Penn's Wharton School of Business to play it with his buddies. "I remember Trump," says Bob Steele, 76, a Cobbs "Cricker" since 1962. "He didn't sneak on. He paid. You could tell the kid came from big shekels. I remember he was always yakkin'. Good-lookin' guy, though. He stood out from the rest of 'em. Well dressed, you know? When he ran for president, I saw him on TV and I said, 'Hey! That guy was a Cricker!'"

If you were a true Cricker, you bet on everything before, during, and after the round, and then bought a cold beer from out of the trunk of Cornbread's car, sat under the trees, and laughed and argued about it until dark. They played for knee-knocking amounts for the time—$50 Nassaus. Carry-over skins. Pig and Wolf. Vegas. If you could think of a bet, somebody would give you action. And not just golf bets. One time, a guy named Lou bet he could carry two guys and their bags on his back up the 100-yard hill at 17—and did.

So it was that the millionaire's son learned the game among the carpenters and bus drivers and spike-shoed grifters on a course that needed a shave and a clean shirt. "I had friends that were golfers," Trump told *Golf Digest*. "I'd never played golf—I always played baseball and football and stuff. And so I'd go out to Cobbs Creak...a public course, a rough course, no grass on the tees, no nothing, but it was good, and great people. All hustlers out there. I mean, more hustlers than any place I've seen to this day. I played golf with my friends, and then I started to play with the hustlers. And I learned a lot. I learned about golf, I learned about gambling. I learned about everything."

They were expensive lessons. Says Steele: "The hustlers here, man, they'd see some yokel show up in a panama hat asking for a game and they'd send the poor guy home without even hamburger money."

There were Row Boat and Frankie and a dozen other guys, unafraid to break the rules to break your wallet. Even pioneering black pro and consummate hustler Charlie Sifford would show up now and then. This was a place full of guys with holes in their pockets, the better to drop an extra ball when nobody was looking. And when they were out of sheep to fleece, they'd fleece each other.

"One time, Frankie was playing another hustler for $50," remembers Steele. "So it's tied up on 18. The guy Frankie is playing hooks it left into the long gunch and can't find it. All of a sudden, the hustler goes, 'Hey! I found it!' Frankie comes running over, pissed. 'You slob! How you gonna find your ball when it's in my pocket?!?'"

As a Cricker, Trump learned (a) it's not cheating if you don't get caught; (b) if you trash talk enough, your opponent might choke; and (c) the best stroke in golf is the one where your opponent writes you a check.

At the Crick, he honed a swing with a powerful move through the ball. It starts way, way inside and so flat it's almost parallel to the ground. But on the downswing, he gets it back on plane, then slams violently through the ball, propelled by a furious turn of the hips, the kind of hip turn you rarely see in amateurs, nearly Sam Snead-like, with a big follow through. He's a president who gets off bombs. "He outdrove me every time," Bill Clinton once lamented.

"For me, it's all about the hips," he once told *Golf Digest's* Jaime Diaz. "Just get them out of the way as fast and as hard as I can and let the arms really swing through. I read about the hips a long time ago in Ben Hogan's book, and it became my simple key, and I've stayed with it. It might look a little crazy, but the more I clear, the straighter I hit it."

"What most impressed me," Tiger Woods blogged after playing him, "was how far he hits the ball at 70 years old. He takes a pretty good lash."

Unfortunately, the rest of his game isn't nearly as good. Former tour star and now Fox golf analyst Brad Faxon played with Trump in West Palm Beach. "He's good off the tee, hits this nice draw every time," Faxon says. "His irons are OK. He's a poor chipper. He'll do anything not to chip, so he'll putt anytime he can, even out of bunkers if he can, around water. He's an OK putter. He's a 4 [handicap] tee to green and a 20 [handicap] chipper."

"I'm pretty much a natural golfer," Trump has said, humbly.

Golf + Trump is an odd couple, because in golf the most revered thing is not winning but honor. Jack Nicklaus may be the game's greatest winner, but The King will always be Arnold Palmer, for the way he showed kindness to princes and plumbers alike. Bobby Jones was so taken with the idea of honor that he refused to turn pro, despite winning seven majors. Wasn't gentlemanly. It wasn't until Tiger Woods that the idea of scorched-earth winning came along. Woods' father, Earl, once told me they used to have a mantra they repeated after every victory: "We came. We saw. We won. We got the fuck out of town."

Still, Woods would rather finish last than cheat. Every day, in every tournament, in every state, players report violations on themselves that nobody else saw. Hale Irwin once missed the playoff at the 1983 British Open by one shot because he says he whiffed a one-inch putt on the final day. Nobody saw it but Irwin. In golf, that's enough. Not long ago, a South Dakota high schooler named Kate Wynja was about to win the state championship in a rout when she realized she'd signed for a 4 on a hole when she'd actually made a 5. Nobody else knew. Wouldn't have made a lick of difference in the outcome. But she immediately told officials, who had no choice but to disqualify her. She lost not only the individual title but her team's state title. Even Jack Nicklaus himself was impressed. He tweeted:

Congrats to this young lady for using golf as a vehicle to teach us all life lessons on honesty and integrity.

In golf, you don't cheat your opponent. You don't cheat your friends. You don't cheat, period. But somehow—either from his father drilling into his brain or the Crickers drilling into his wallet—this was lost on Trump. "Win or else" flattened "honor of the game" in a one-round knockout. Trump had to win, no matter what, and those great spaces of golf allowed him the cover to do it.

"He found a game that suits him to a T," says O'Donnell. "He has such a short attention span that makes golf perfect for him. You stand on the tee box for a minute and chat, then you hit, then you go your own way. It's very short periods of concentration.

But the best part is that it's all self-regulated. He can cheat any time he wants."

When college was over, he took all that to the country clubs, where Trump figured out that not only could he pencil-whip his very un-Crick opponents even easier, but his quick charm and solid game could also help him grease the rails to the top.

"There was this [New York] banker who was really going to do bad numbers on me," Trump told Golf Channel's David Feherty on a podcast, referring to his Atlantic City casino bankruptcies. "I was playing one day and we needed another person. Here's this [banker] at the course. They said to him, 'Would you like to join the group?'...He was a terrible golfer, terrible....Now, I'm in deep trouble. I owe this man tens of tens of millions of dollars. So he topped his first ball, topped his second ball. This goes on for two or three more holes. I finally said, 'Do me a favor. Take your hands in a V, point the V to the shoulder. Strengthen your grip.' He had a terrible weak grip. The guy winds up hitting the nicest ball of his life. It goes out to the right and hooks back into the fairway. He says, 'I've never hit a shot like that! That's the nicest shot I've ever hit!' He ends up playing the best he's ever played.... So he sees me the next day and says, 'Hey, can we work this out over lunch?' And I worked it out with him in about 10 minutes. So, who knows, without golf, maybe I wouldn't be sitting here!"

No other sport captivated Trump like golf. He became addicted to the constant competition, hole by hole, day by day. And not just the bets. He came to see his handicap as a kind of contest, too, one he has to win daily.

"I'd say he's a solid 7," says Trump's permanent caddy at his Washington course, A.J. (He prefers I don't give his last name.) "He really gets through it. He can drive it a long way. For a 72-year-old man, he's amazing. He has a little trouble around the greens, but he can flop it [hit a very high and soft chip] from anywhere. He's amazing with the flop. He can have his hot putting days, too. Sometimes, not so much."

"I'd say he's a legit 10," Faxon says. "He'll probably get mad at me for that, but I think that's about right." Four-time major winner Ernie Els played with him and declared him to be "an 8 or a 9." LPGA great Annika Sörenstam has played with him at least twice and says, "I would say he's a 9 or 10."

So the caddy and the pros who make a living in the game estimate his handicap to be somewhere between a 7 and a 10. The only problem with all that is Trump *insists* his handicap is a 2.8. In the world of golf handicaps, that difference is huge. If Trump is a 2.8, Queen Elizabeth is a pole vaulter. No possible way. It would take a 9 handicap five good years of hard practice to get to a 2.8 and Donald Trump doesn't practice.

Former Republican Speaker of the Florida House Will Weatherford played with Trump in 2015 at Southern Highlands Golf Club in Las Vegas, the day of the Floyd Mayweather–Manny Pacquiao fight. "He was a lot of fun," Weatherford recalls. "When you play with Donald, you do a lot of listening. He was telling stories, entertaining us the whole way around."

Was he a stickler about the rules?

"Not so much. I remember on one par 3, he hit his first shot way out of bounds. Teed up another and I think that one was lost, too. The third one landed about 12 feet from the hole. He made that putt. I'm pretty sure he gave himself a 2 on that hole. Look, I take mulligans, too. I'm not judging....But then later, he was apparently telling people he was a 2 or a 3 and that they should call Will Weatherford and I'd confirm what a great golfer he is. I mean, if he's a 2, that's news to me. I've played with 2s and that didn't look anything like a 2."

What was he then?

"Well, I'm about a 12 or 13 and I wouldn't say he was any better than me."

When you look up Trump on GHIN.com—the USGA's online handicap search site—he's listed as a 2.8. But, as of press time, he'd only posted 20 times in the past seven years. Seven years? For an avid golfer like Trump, that's preposterous. In golf, honor demands that you post every round, good or bad, high or low, so that the bets are fair. You finish your round, shake hands, go straight to the computer, post your score, pay off the bet, and then drink your beer, in that order. If people see that you don't post your scores, your phone is going to stop ringing. Even the people Trump plays with post their scores. In 2016 alone, Rudy Giuliani posted 16 times. Tony Russo, a noted Washington lobbyist, posted 20 times just in the summer of 2018. Anybody who only plays three times a year would be a 22.8, not a 2.8. We know the 2.8 is a lie because, as president, he's averaging about 80 rounds a year, according to TrumpGolfCount.com, a slavish accounting of Trump's golf activity. If he's playing an average of

80 rounds a year, and only posting 3 rounds, that means he's leaving 95% of them off.

So what's he doing? He's cherry picking. He's only putting in his showiest rounds. Even with the scores he posts, he's either shaving multiple shots off his total or inflating the difficulty of the courses he played. The GHIN system takes your 20 most recent scores, throws out the worst 10, and averages the best 10, factoring in course rating and course slope. But take a look at those 20 scores:

- He posted only one score in all of 2016, and two in 2015. So which do you believe? The Trump who says he's great at golf, who wants you to vote for him because he's a golf champion, who tweets about playing golf all the time? Or this Trump, who apparently only plays every time Germany wins a war?

- Look at the "slopes" of his scores. Slope is the relative difficulty of a course. The computer is much more impressed with the 100 you shot on a 130 slope course than the 100 you shot on a 115 course. The average course slope is about 120. Fifteen of the 20 scores Trump posted were on courses with slopes of over 140. Anything over 140 is insanely hard. That's like a skier who only goes down double black diamonds. Only the most sadistic courses in America are over 140. Just to give you an idea, Augusta National is a 137. Bethpage Black in New York is harder than Chinese algebra, and it's only 144. I play once a week on some pretty good courses, and the highest slope out of my last 20 is 135. So Trump could be tricking the GHIN computer by plugging in the slope of the way-back pro tees—even though everyone says he plays the normal tees—to make whatever score he shot look more impressive to the computer, which drives his handicap lower. Again, it's dirty and unscrupulous but—you gotta admit—kind of genius.

- He posted a 68 in October of 2017, and then deleted it. Now, do you know any golfers who would delete a 68? Most would get the scorecard blown up and make wallpaper.

So why go to such lengths to gin up a fake 2.8 handicap? What's so bad about being a 9? According to the National Golf Foundation, only around 3% of men over 70 are single-digit handicaps. Most 70-somethings would give their dentures for that. Why must he pretend he's a 3, a phony number he can't

Date	Score	Course Rating/ Slope	Differential
6/16	77	72.4/134	3.9
5/15	85	73.0/144	9.4
5/15	81	71.6/140	7.6
10/14	86	74.7/149	8.6
10/14	84	74.7/149	7.1
7/14	75	69.5/137	4.5
7/14	83	71.8/135	9.4
6/14	78	72.2/137	4.8
6/14	77	73.1/143	3.1
6/14	76	71.9/139	3.3
8/13	70	72.3/147	-1.8
7/13	76	70.2/132	5.0
6/13	79	73.0/144	4.7
6/13	79	71.6/140	6.0
7/12	76	73.9/144	1.6
6/11	74	73.0/144	0.8
5/11	83	74.7/149	6.3
5/11	83	74.7/149	6.3
4/11	84	74.7/149	7.1
9/09	85	74.7/149	7.8

*Self-reported

play to from the red tees? Put it this way: Jack Nicklaus is a 3.4 on GHIN.com. If you needed a partner for a death match, loser cleans the Fallujah Denny's with a toothbrush for the rest of his life, would you take Trump or Jack Nicklaus?

So why isn't being a 9 good enough for Trump?

Because, as you're about to find out, "good enough" is never good enough for Donald Trump.

4

PELE

He cheats like hell.
—SUZANN PETTERSEN, LPGA GOLFER

I USED TO HAVE this coach who told us, "How you do one thing is how you do everything. You loaf in practice, you're gonna loaf in the game. You cheat on your tests, you're gonna cheat on your wife."

I've found that to be true with golf. The guy who plays slowly on the course is going to be molasses in meetings. The guy who's generous with compliments on the course is going to do the same at dinner. And the guy who cheats on the course is going to cheat in business, or on his taxes or, say, in politics.

Jack O'Donnell worked with Trump for four years as vice president of Trump Plaza Casino in Atlantic City. O'Donnell's dad was one of the founders of Sawgrass, the iconic Pete Dye golf course near Jacksonville, Florida. "My dad always told us to respect the game," O'Donnell says. "That's the one part of the game that tells me what kind of person you are. You play the ball where it lies." So when O'Donnell's office colleague, the late Mark Eddis, came back after his first round with Trump, O'Donnell couldn't resist asking.

"So, does he improve his lie?"

Eddis looked at him and threw his head back in laughter. "Every shot but the tee shot."

Trump doesn't just cheat at golf. He cheats like a three-card Monte dealer. He throws it, boots it, and moves it. He lies about his lies. He fudges and foozles and fluffs. At Winged Foot where Trump is a member, the caddies got so used to seeing him kick his ball back onto the fairway they came up with a nickname for him: "Pele."

"I played with him once," says Bryan Marsal, longtime Winged Foot member and chair of the coming 2020 Men's U.S. Open. "It was a Saturday morning game. We go to the first tee and he couldn't have been nicer. But then he said, 'You see those two guys? They cheat. See me? I cheat. And I expect *you* to cheat because we're going to beat those two guys today.'... So, yes, it's true, he's going to cheat you. But I think Donald, in his heart of hearts, believes that *you're gonna cheat him*, too. So if it's the same, if everybody's cheating, he doesn't see it as really cheating."

Okay, but...

a) Everybody *isn't* cheating. Except for an occasional mulligan on the first tee and accepting a gimme (a short conceded putt) from an opponent, 85% of casual golfers play by the rules, according to the National Golf Foundation.

b) To say "Donald Trump cheats" is like saying "Michael Phelps swims." He cheats at the highest level. He cheats when people are watching, and he cheats when they aren't. He cheats whether you like it or not. He cheats because that's *how* he plays golf, that's how he learned it, that's how he needs it, and whether you're his pharmacist or Tiger Woods, if you're playing golf with him, he's going to cheat.

In fact, he *did* cheat with Tiger Woods. Not long after becoming president, he invited Woods, Dustin Johnson (the No. 1 player in the world at the time), and longtime Tour pro and Fox golf analyst Brad Faxon to play.

They set up a bet: Faxon and Trump against Woods and Johnson. But because Woods and Johnson are so preposterously long off the tee, they decided Faxon and Trump could tee off the middle tees. Trump would get a stroke subtracted on the eight hardest holes; everybody else would play scratch. Off they went.

"On this one hole, Donald hits his second and fats it into the water," Faxon remembers. "But he quickly says to me, 'Hey, throw me another ball; they weren't looking.' So I do. But he fats that one into the water, too. So he drives up and drops where he should've dropped the first time and hits it on the green."

Meanwhile, on the other side of the fairway, Woods, being Woods, has hit his approach to a foot from the hole for a kick-in birdie. Everybody's on the green now, with Trump about 20 feet from the hole, and getting a stroke. Trump said, "So, where does everybody stand here?"

FAXON: "Well, Tiger just made a three. What's that [putt] for, Mr. President?"

TRUMP: "Four for a three."

Faxon had to laugh because Trump was actually putting for a seven, but he was claiming it was for a four, which would've worked out to a three with his free stroke on the hole.

"How great is that?" Faxon recalled. "Four for a three! But he missed it anyway. It was really fun to play with him. He rakes [picks up] every putt [as if it's conceded], but you kind of want him to. You've heard so much about it, it's almost like you want to witness it so you can tell the stories."

One time an old country singer/songwriter friend of mine played golf with Trump in L.A. for the first time. On the very first hole, Trump kicked his ball from the rough onto the fairway. This stopped the singer cold.

"Wait a second," he yelled. "So this is how it's going to be today, Donald?"

"Oh," Trump explained. "All the guys I play with throw it out of the rough. You have to do it just to keep up with them."

Just for the record, I've played for 50 years and only know one guy who does that. His picture is on the cover.

Once, Trump hosted three famous ESPN football announcers—Mike Tirico (now with NBC), Jon Gruden (now the Raiders coach), and Ron (Jaws) Jaworski, the old Eagles quarterback—at one of his courses. Trump loves to show off his courses to celebrities, and the more celebrated you are, the more he wants you to see them and the more he wants his members to see you. Trump arrived as the other three were warming up and he picked the teams immediately. "It's gonna be me and Gruden, 'cause I like winners."

Off they went. At one point, they were playing a blind par 5, and Tirico, who's a 12.3 handicap, had 230 yards into the green.

He hit the 3-wood of his life. "Oh my god!" his caddy said, open-mouthed. The thing had the flag covered from the start. It crested the hill perfectly and was going to be tight to the pin. Shocked at his sudden skill, Tirico high-fived his caddie and strode toward the green, his shoes barely touching the grass.

But, somehow, when they got there, the ball wasn't near the pin. It wasn't even on the green. It was 50 feet *left* of the pin, in the bunker. Unless it hit a drone and ricocheted sideways, there was no physical way it could've ended up there.

"Lousy break," Trump said to Tirico, who checked the marking on the ball to be sure it was his. It was. Befuddled, it took Tirico two swipes to escape the bunker on the way to a 7.

"Afterwards," Tirico remembers, "Trump's caddy came up to me and said, 'You know that shot you hit on the par 5? It was about 10 feet from the hole. Trump threw it into the bunker. I watched him do it.'"

What did Tirico do? He laughed, shook his head, went inside, and paid Trump his money. When it comes to golf, Trump is the tornado and you are the trailer.

But why? Why does Trump cheat so much when he's already a decent player? And how can he be so shameless as to cheat right in front of people? They call him on it, but he just shrugs and cheats some more. It's ruined his reputation in the golf world. Ninety percent of the people I interviewed—on and off the record—say he openly cheats. A lot of them said they stopped playing with him because of it. So why? Why cheat? Why lie? Why exaggerate his handicap, his scores, his club championships?

"Because he has to," says Harvard psychiatrist Dr. Lance

Dodes, co-author of *The Dangerous Case of Donald Trump*. "He *needs* to be the best at everything. He can't stand not winning, not being the best. It had to have started very early in his development. To him, not being the best is like fingernails on the blackboard to you. He can't live with it.... He exaggerates his golf scores and his handicap for the same reason he exaggerates everything. He has to. He exhibits all the traits of a narcissistic personality disorder. People with his disorder have no conscience about it. He has no sense of morality about things. He lacks empathy towards others. He's a very ill man. He doesn't get that other people have rights and feelings. Other people just don't matter to him."

Trump consistently says he doesn't cheat. "I never touch the ball," he says. That's sort of true, maintains actor Anthony Anderson. "I'm not going to say Trump cheats. But if Trump's caddy cheats for him, is *that* cheating?"

"We clearly saw him hook a ball into a lake at Trump National [Bedminster]," actor Samuel L. Jackson once recalled, "and his caddy told him he found it!"

LPGA player Suzann Pettersen, a friend of Trump's, thinks he must pay his caddy extremely well "since no matter how far into the woods he hits the ball, it's in the middle of the fairway when we get there."

You can try to fight against it, but you'll fail. The first time L.A. Clippers coach Doc Rivers played with him, Trump was on the other team and his buddy was going to be Trump's partner. The buddy came over to console him. "He's like, 'Well, that's it. You've got no chance of winning today.' I figured he was trash talking. I'm like, 'Okay, let's see what you got!' But then I saw the way

Trump cheats. About the fifth or sixth hole, I went up to my buddy and said, 'I finally see what you mean. I've got no chance.'"

Boxer Oscar De La Hoya says he witnessed him cheat. Rocker Alice Cooper, too. New Jersey native Bill Rayburn wrote to me on Facebook about it. "I caddied for him once at a celebrity thing. Even with a gallery, marshals and me standing there, he openly cheated at least 10 times in the round. I finally stopped counting around the 15th hole.... He kicked his ball away from tree stumps, improved his lie, grounded his club in traps, and on the green repeatedly cheated on his ball marking, making sure to get his ball closer to the cup.... Trump walked off the 18th hole trumpeting his score, 74. Which easily was closer to 90 in the real world. Then he tipped me $10."

It's so brazen you almost admire it. When Trump and I played together that day at Westchester for *Who's Your Caddy?*, he took "floating mulligans" and re-dos, and simply subtracted shots when it came time for me to write his score down. "I have to take a newspaper 4 once in awhile," he said.

I also heard "I'm-taking-a-mulligan" excuses like:

"You distracted me."

"That bird flew over just as I was about to hit."

"My foot slipped."

The man even took a gimme chip-in that day. A "gimme" is usually a putt that your opponent concedes you will make. He says, "That's good," meaning, "I concede that you'll make that putt, so just pick it up." Gimmes are illegal under the rules of golf but as common on the course as hot dogs. Still, a gimme should not be longer than two feet, three feet tops.

Gimmes are supposed to be like gifts: they can only be given, never taken. Except for Trump. When you're playing with Trump, he has the only gimme vote. He'll declare any putt he has under five or six or eight feet a "gimme" and scoop it up. But as *you* go to pick your shorter putt up, too, he stops you and warns that "you better brush that in." He's the conductor of the Trump Train and you're just hanging on to the caboose.

The Olympic hockey star Mike Eruzione played with Trump in Palm Beach the day of Barbara Bush's funeral, an event Trump was uninvited to. Eruzione says Trump is "so much fun" to play golf with partly because you can needle him. "We're playing along," Eruzione recalls, "and I finally said, 'Mr. President, you're a very talkative guy, but I haven't once heard you say, 'That one's good, Mike.'"

But never in the history of golf has anyone taken a gimme *chip-in* until Trump did that day with me. I was in the hole for a 5 and he was lying OFF the green in 5, and he said, casually, "Well, I guess that makes this good," and he scooped the ball up.

I was gobsmacked. We were playing a $10 medal bet—i.e., a total-score bet—so every shot counted. Even if he could've chipped it close—which he wouldn't have—he'd have made a 7.

"Did you just take a gimme chip-in?" I asked, dumbfounded.

"Well, yeah, 'cause you were already in for 5."

By the time I got my jaw refastened, he was driving off in the cart. I put the scene in my book. When he was running for president, the *Washington Post* asked him about that gimme chip-in. Trump had a very odd answer: "I don't do gimme chip shots. If I asked his approval, that's not cheating, number one. Number two, I never took one."

So that clears THAT up.

In the end, the scorecard said he beat me. The rules had been pulverized into Gerber's pea puree by then, so I paid up the $10. Then he bought lunch. It's not the money; it's the winning.

"I played with him once at Trump L.A.," says Ken Slutsky, a golf executive and investor. "At the end he said, 'You owe me $27.' I said, 'Donald, you cheated on every single hole. I'm not paying you a dime.' He just kind of shrugged and left. He didn't seem to care."

Trump's cheating during a round is legendary, but his cheating after the round is just as sharp. His score always gets what I call the Trump Bump. He may wrap up a very sketchy 77 at noon. On the ride home, it'll be 75. By dinner, 72.

It's not just his score that gets the Trump Bump. It's anybody's score he likes. The legendary golfer Lee Trevino tells about the time he played one of Trump's courses, shot a 72, and then ran into Trump in the locker room.

"What'd you fire?" Trump asks.

"Seventy-two," Trevino says.

Trump is delighted and wants to start introducing the legend around his clubhouse. "This is the great Lee Trevino. He just shot a 70!" For the next person, it was, "You know who this is? Lee Trevino! He just shot a 68!" Then it was, "He just shot a 66!"

Says Trevino, "I had to get out of there before I broke the course record!"

It's not just golf scores that get the Trump Bump. It's also net worth, crowd sizes, body weight—up or down—whatever makes him the winner.

Even his buildings. His 68-story Trump Tower in New York City, for instance, isn't really 68 stories. It's 58. There's a story in the stories. When Trump Tower was finished, his 664-foot building came up 41 feet shorter than the nearby 705-foot GM Building. Trump thought, well, his first 19 floors are commercial, what was to keep him from listing the first residential floor as the 30th, instead of the 20th? If he did that, he could add 10 floors instantly, and the top floor would be listed as the 68th, which would make it at least sound taller than the 50-floor GM Building. So that's what he did. He liked the idea so much he did it for his 90-story Trump World Tower (actually 70 stories), too.

It seems a harmless kind of lie, but it caused a problem for NYC firemen in April of 2018, when a Trump Tower apartment caught fire. The information the 911 operator was getting was that the fire was on the 50th floor. But firemen on the street counted only 40 floors up to the flames. Were there two fires? What the hell was going on?

I'm 6-foot-1. I've stood next to Trump many times and we're always eye to eye. I also stand eye to eye with Barack Obama. When you look at pictures of Obama and Trump together, they're about eye to eye. It all jibes. Yet when the White House doctor announced Trump's size and weight in January of 2018, Trump was suddenly "6-3, 239 pounds." That height and weight conveniently kept Trump one-tenth of one body mass index point from being categorized as "obese." At his true 6-1 height, he'd have had to weigh 12 pounds less to avoid The Big O. Now, it's possible that Trump grew two inches since the last time I stood with him, but, since he's in his 70s, it seems unlikely.

Sometimes, the White House Trump Bumps for him. Remember short-lived White House Director of Communications Anthony Scaramucci? On his first day on the job, The Mooch was trying to illustrate how competitive Trump is. "I have seen him throw a dead spiral through a tire," Scaramucci said, according to reporters who recorded the session. "I've seen him at Madison Square Garden, with a topcoat on, standing in the key and he's hitting foul shots and swishing them. He sinks three-foot putts. I don't see this guy as a guy that's ever under siege. This is a very, very competitive person." All that was fine until the White House released the transcript of Scaramucci's briefing. Somehow, the "three-foot putts" had turned into "thirty-foot putts."

Trump often ballyhoos the 68 he says he shot once at a famous and difficult Los Angeles country club course, which would be some incredible feat, even for a vanity 3-handicap like Trump. It's a course that's tighter than Chris Christie's underwear, full of peril, tricky greens, and bunkers deep enough to hide a Mack truck. So when Trump came barreling up to the clubhouse one afternoon bragging he'd just shot a 68, it was instantly met with swimming pools of skepticism. "No way," members sitting on the porch at 18 said to him.

But there's a reason Trump's friends call him Double Down.

"Yes, I did," he said. "And it was a *legit* 68, too."

Is there any other kind?

The head pro at this particular club is a rules stickler. He serves as a rules official for the PGA of America. He would sooner play in five-inch marabou heels than commit a rules violation. As soon as Trump left, he immediately summoned the two caddies for the group into his office. The two caddies, still in their white overalls, came in and sat down. The pro closed the door.

"So," he said. "Mr. Trump says he shot 68 here today. Is that true?"

The two caddies looked at each other.

"No way," said one.

"No f*cking way," said the other.

"Seventy-nine at BEST," said the first.

The 68, they said, came with tosses, kicks, and golf balls getting free rides back to the short grass. It came with do-overs, takeovers, and floating mulligans. It came with very little sounds of plastic balls actually going into little plastic cups. "He played really well that day, but I don't think he shot a 68," says longtime NBA and college basketball coach Mike Dunleavy, who was in the group. "There was some moving of balls around, some other stuff." There was so much trickery and fraud, it was impossible to know what he'd really shot. Somewhere in the high 70s, they'd give him. For anybody else, high 70s on that course would've been a save-the-scorecard kind of day. For Trump, it wasn't nearly enough.

Longtime Los Angeles player and caddy Greg Puga, the 2000 U.S. Mid-Amateur champion, has had Trump in his group plenty. He's heard about the 68—it's a staple of L.A. caddy rooms—and he isn't buying a thimble of it. "Sixty-eight?" Puga says. "There? You gotta be kidding me. I could take him to the Long Beach Putt-Putt and he's not shooting 68. No way. No how. Not ever."

To turn a 78 into a 68, you need some clever tricks. Trump has two sleeves full.

*The Invisible Dunk

"I've played with him a lot," says a frequent guest in Trump's foursomes. "This one time, I was in the fairway and he was right of the green but a little bit down the hill. He didn't think anybody was watching, but I was. I saw him make a chipping motion from the side of the hill but no ball came up. Then he walked up the hill, stuck his hand in the hole and pulled a ball out. It must've been a ball he had in his hand the whole time. Then he looked up and yelled, 'I chipped in!' I mean, who does that?"

*The Quick Rake

This is a sneaky little move in which you hit your approach putt and then quickly walk up and rake up what's left of it, no matter the length, before your opponents can stop you or think to holler, "Hey, wait a minute!" Trump has mastered this move. He does it sometimes before the ball has even stopped rolling. MSNBC cameras caught him doing it once to a ball that had sped five feet past the hole and was gaining speed. By the time anybody can object, the ball is already in his pocket.

*The Ball Switch

"Whenever I've caddied in Trump's group," says Puga, "he always gets his own cart. He makes sure to hit first off every tee box and then jumps in the cart, so he's halfway down the fairway before the other three are done driving. That way he can get up there quick and mess with his ball. So this one time—we were on the 18th—he hits first, kind of blocks it right, and jumps in his cart and starts driving away. My guy pures one right down the middle. I mean, I SAW it go right down the middle. One of his best drives of the day. But by the time we get to my guy's ball, it's not there. We can't find it anywhere. And Trump is now ON the green already putting! Where's our ball? And then Trump starts yelling back at us, "Hey guys! I made a birdie!" He's hold-ing up his ball and celebrating. And that's when we realized. That fucker stole our ball! He got up here early, hit OUR ball, and then hurried up and pretended like he made the putt for a birdie. I mean, what the hell?"

Once, Trump played a course with one of L.A.'s more famous holes—a par 5 where Howard Hughes once landed his plane to pick up Katherine Hepburn for a date—that has a pond just left of the green. "I saw Trump's ball go in the lake," one of the caddies told me. "I mean, I saw the ripples! But by the time we caught up to him and his cart, the ball was back on the fairway. When we asked him what happened, he said, 'Must've been the tide.'"

Proof Trump cheats is that whenever he plays in front of TV cameras, he goes from hero to hack.

The famous Pebble Beach Pro-Am is a four-day, three-course pro-celebrity clam bake started by Bing Crosby and televised yearly by CBS. This is the one Bill Murray always enters. At the Pebble event, there are really two tournaments going on—the pro one and the team one. Each tournament has a separate cut.

In the team one, you make the cut as a team—you and your pro—but Trump's team never did. He played in it seven times and never made the cut. The closest he came was in 1998 when the whole thing was cancelled for weather. You might say, "Well, there you have it. Trump had terrible pro partners."

TRUMP SCORES IN TELEVISED TOURNAMENTS

AT&T Pebble Beach Pro-Am (Pebble Beach, CA)

Year	Trump's Pro	Team Finish	Pro Finish
1993	Paul Goydos	Missed Cut	Missed Cut
1998	Fulton Allem	Weather Cancellation	Tie 45th
2001	Jim McGovern	Missed Cut	Tie 63rd
2002	Brad Elder	Missed Cut	Missed Cut
2003	Brian Claar	Missed Cut	Tie 42nd
2005	David Frost	Missed Cut	Missed Cut
2006	John Cook	Missed Cut	Tie 53rd

American Century Celebrity Championship (Lake Tahoe, NV)

Year	Finish	Score	# of Players	Winner	Winning Score
2004	56th	−12*	80	Dan Quinn (hockey)	74*
2005	42nd	26*	80	Billy Joe Tolliver (football)	76*
2006	62nd	268	80	Jack Wagner (actor)	213

*Stableford point system.

Not true. His pro partners for those seven years were solid Tour players—Paul Goydos, Fulton Allem, Jim McGovern, Brad Elder, Brian Claar, David Frost, and John Cook. But in the six tourneys that finished, Trump's pro went on to make the pro cut four times. Take a typical year, 2006: The Cook/Trump team finished 111th, but Cook made the pro cut. The weak link was Trump.

The other true measure of Trump's golf game was the American Century Celebrity Championship at Lake Tahoe, a woodsy course on the California-Nevada border. Tahoe gets a stellar, raucous field of celebs most years—ex-athletes, actors, singers, scratch players, and duffers. Trump played the Tahoe event three times—2004, 2005, and 2006.

In those three Tahoe tries, he never finished in the top half of the field. The first year, he was 56th out of 80, which is not stellar when you consider the field includes players like the famously golf-plagued Charles Barkley. The next time, he finished 42nd out of 80. Finally, in that calamitous 2006 Tahoe tournament, he finished 62nd out of 80 and averaged 89.3 per round, and that's with Tahoe's rule that no player can take worse than a double bogey. Then again, Trump may have been exhausted. According to lawsuits raging as this book went to press, he had affairs with two different women at that one single tournament—porn star Stormy Daniels and *Playboy* model Karen McDougal.

So, just to recap, in those three Tahoe tries alone, the man who once said, "When it comes to golf, there are very few people who can beat me," was beaten by 157 people, or more than 60% of those who tried.

* * *

So how is Clinton's cheating different than Trump's?

It isn't. It's still cheating. But Clinton's methods were less diabolical and more goofy. Trump's are often so over-the-top it verges on sad. Clinton wasn't trying to pretend he was six shots better than he really was. With Trump, the cheating was a path to something more important: I win again. With Clinton, the cheating was more like, "Doggone it. I know I can do this! Let me try again." (And again. And again.) It's like the difference between a guy who goes to the bank and steals the pen versus the guy who steals the vault.

Trump's friends defend his cheating, but in a way you might not expect. "My rounds with him have been some of the most fun days I've ever had playing golf," says Coach Dunleavy. "Yeah, he moves it and kicks it and all that, but no money changes hands at the end. There's a wager, yeah, but then nobody pays anybody. So that's not really cheating to me. It's just fun."

To show how much fun, Dunleavy tells a story about he and Trump as partners in a game against two of their buddies. Dunleavy hits his approach shot onto the corner of a kidney-shaped green that left him no possible putt. He was going to have to chip it off the green or somehow try to putt through the fringe and hope it came out back onto the green. Trump, his partner, came over and secretly knocked the ball on to a part of the green where Dunleavy could putt it. Dunleavy picked it up and put it back where it was.

"That's when Donald starts yelling to the other two," Dunleavy recalls. "He goes, 'Guys, guys! I wanna tell you how great a guy Coach is. I knocked his ball over here so he could have a putt at it. But then he put it back! And that's why he's an unemployed coach and I'm worth $13 billion."

5

BUY, LIE, AND CRY

Owning a great golf course gives you great power.
—Donald J. Trump

ONE CHRISTMAS, WHEN DONALD Trump was small, he and his younger brother Robert got building blocks. The next day, Donald asked Robert if he could borrow his blocks to build something big. His brother was happy to lend them. Donald used the blocks to build a huge building that almost reached the ceiling.

"He was so proud of it," his late mother recalled. The next day, Robert asked for his blocks back. But Donald couldn't do it. He'd glued them all together.

If Donald Trump could glue together every great golf course in the world and slap his name on them, he would. But he doesn't. Instead, he takes the ones he owns and *pretends* they're the best. As of late 2018, he owned 14 golf courses and operated or will operate another five. The Trump name is on golf courses in America, the UAE, Scotland, Ireland, and, soon, Indonesia.

Trump Golf Courses and Golf Resorts

America

Course	Location	Access
Trump National Golf Club, Westchester	Briarcliff Manor, NY	private
Trump National Golf Club, Bedminster, NJ	Bedminster Township, NJ	private
Trump National Golf Club Hudson Valley	Hopewell Junction, NY	private
Trump National Golf Club Philadelphia	Pine Hill, NJ	private
Trump National Golf Club Colts Neck	Colts Neck, NJ	private
*Trump Golf Links at Ferry Point	New York City, the Bronx	public
Trump National Golf Club Washington, D.C.	Sterling, VA	private
Trump National Doral Golf Club	Miami, FL	public
Trump National Golf Club Jupiter	Jupiter, FL	private
Trump International Golf Club	West Palm Beach, FL	private
Trump National Golf Club Charlotte	Mooresville, NC	private
Trump National Golf Club Los Angeles	Rancho Palos Verdes, CA	public

Overseas

Course	Location	Access
Trump International Golf Links, Aberdeen	Balmedie, Scotland	public
Trump Turnberry	Ayrshire, Scotland	public
Trump International Golf Links & Hotel	Doonbeg, Ireland	public
*Trump International Golf Club, Dubai	Dubai, UAE	public
*Trump World Golf Club	Dubai, UAE	public

In Development

Course	Location
*Trump International Golf Club & Resort	Bali (Indonesia)
*Lido City	Indonesia

*Operates only.

"Somebody made the statement that Donald Trump has built or owns the greatest collection of golf courses, ever, in the history of golf," Trump once said. "And I believe that is 100% true."

Would that somebody be Trump? Because nobody who knows golf would say that. His lineup of courses is nice, but since he always buys properties that are in default or bankrupt at, as he often says, "10 or 15 cents on the dollar," he's often trying to put rouge on a cadaver. One he bought—Trump Los Angeles—had just fallen into the Pacific. He does not have a single course in the 2019–2020 *Golf Digest*'s Top 100 American courses, the bible of all golf rankings. In fact, he doesn't have a single course in the top 175. The best he can do is Trump International in West Palm Beach (178). He does much better overseas, though. Of the three courses he owns in Europe, two are on *Golf Digest*'s Top 100 World (outside the U.S.) list: Trump Turnberry (10) and Trump International at Aberdeen (64).

His other courses—Trump Los Angeles (CA), Trump Washington (VA), National Hudson (NY), Trump Colts Neck (NY), Trump Philadelphia (NJ), Trump Charlotte (NC), Trump Ferry Links (the Bronx), Trump Doral (FL), Trump Jupiter (FL), and Doonbeg in Ireland—are all bologna sandwiches on white bread. They'll fill you with golf for the day, but you'll never salivate about them later.

So that isn't "the greatest collection of golf courses ever, in the history of golf." It's not even the best collection owned by any American now. That would be Trump's rival, Chicago greeting-card tycoon Mike Keiser, who owns Bandon Dunes resort in Oregon. All four of his courses there are in the Top 100 American list. Keiser also owns Cabot Cliffs in Nova Scotia (9), Barnbougle Dunes in Tasmania (11), and Barnbougle Lost Farm in Australia (23). So the Top 100 list score would be Keiser 7, Trump 2. Although Trump has gotten one bite of revenge: Keiser backed Jeb Bush for president.

But one thing is true of all of Trump's courses: the attention to detail is immaculate. Everything must be perfect. The man will spend an hour looking at every green on *the practice range*. The problem is that golf is not a game of perfect. It's meant to be like nature, played over stream and stones. That's what makes it better than tennis. Every golf course is different and new and you never know what kind of lie you're going to get. But Trump golf is stuffy, all too combed and primped, with way too many cart paths and waterfalls and fairways your Foot Joys sink into. Trump doesn't build golf courses so much as financial statements.

Trump's first course was Trump International Golf Club in West Palm Beach, Florida, an 11-minute drive from his Mar-a-Lago social club and hotel. He built the course in 1999 from scratch. He might have given it such a $50 name because it was such a 50-cent piece of property. It was 300 grungy acres of weedy vacant lots, surrounded on one side by the county jail, on the other by the airport, on another by a string of bail bonds houses and immigration passport/visa joints, and on the final side by a strip joint.

How Trump got Trump International in the first place was pure Trumpaliciousness. It started with the purchase of Mar-a-Lago Club, the gold-dripping mansion Trump bought in 1985. He began complaining that the jets at nearby Palm Beach International Airport were making too much noise over his bedroom. Very unfair. But was that new? Did planes suddenly start diverting over Mar-a-Lago just to spite Trump? Nope. Nothing had changed much in the flight paths for 60 years. In fact, Mar-a-Lago has had a red flashing light on top of it as far back as anybody can remember. Didn't matter to Trump. It was violating his sensitive ears. He sued.

The first suit went nowhere. Undaunted, he sued then-airport director Bruce Pelley, personally, three times. One time he sued him for assault, complaining that it was as if Pelley were "standing in front of Mar-a-Lago with a noise gun." The court didn't buy it. Trump even sued Pelley for fraud, saying that Pelley was purposely sending airplanes to get even with him. Pelley, of course, didn't control the path of the airplanes. That was done by the FAA and the tower. All three suits died slow deaths.

The truth is Trump wasn't really after peace and solitude. He was after the scrubby wasteland *next* to the airport. He was hoping one of the lawsuits would go through and he could get that land in a settlement to build a golf course for his swanky Mar-a-Lago crowd to play. It didn't work, but when he was out of lawsuits, he pitched the West Palm Beach County Commissioners the idea of him leasing the land anyway. What good was it doing them? They struck a deal.

(Note: Despite what you see in articles over and over again, Trump did not "win the land in a settlement." That's what he told reporters once he signed the lease, but it's a lie. "Absolutely not true," says one Palm Beach official who didn't want to be identified because...well...you know. "His noise lawsuits went nowhere. This was a business deal, pure and simple. But as soon as he signed the lease, he went to the *Palm Beach Post* and told them he'd won it in a settlement. They wrote it, and it keeps getting repeated over and over.")

But why would the county want to get in bed with a guy who'd sued them so many times? Because Trump could charm an elephant into doing an arabesque. Just to protect themselves, the county included a clause: Trump could never sue them again. (He would anyway.)

Trump poured millions into that flat-as-a-tortilla land. To

make a course that he promised would be "the best in America," there was only one architect to hire: Tom Fazio. Fazio not only built Steve Wynn's Shadow Creek in Las Vegas, a course Trump lusted after for its majestic fake waterfall, but Fazio has landed more courses on *Golf Digest*'s Top 100 list than any living American architect. Trump had to have Tom Fazio.

But Fazio was too expensive, so Trump hired his brother, Jim Fazio. This is a little like wanting Michael Jackson to play at your bar mitzvah but getting Tito instead. At Trump's order, Jim put in massive dunes where there were no dunes, a 75-foot-high 18th tee box, and a faux waterfall big enough to turn Steve Wynn green. He sodded it with lush grass and posted 889 canary date palms around the perimeter. He bathed his clubhouse interior in gold and put the whole thing behind big, black, screw-you gilded gates that screamed "Keep Out"—even though the whole place was set on leased public land.

Now all he had to do was talk Trump International up. Nobody on earth better at that. His course was going to be "the best course anywhere in America," he said. It was going to be "incredible" and "amazing," and there was "going to be nothing like it in the world." And it *was* pretty good, if your taste runs to fake Eiffel Towers in front of your hotel. But it's like a woman who's late to the beauty stylist. After a while, you just can't hide your roots. Unseemly things kept happening.

Take, for instance, the Palm Beach County Jail, which stands nine stories high and looms over one of the holes. In the first couple of years the course opened, the exercise yard was on one of the higher floors, so inmates would climb up the fencing and yell awful things at the well-heeled players. "It used to be you went past there and the guys in the exercise yard could see you," says a man who played there often as a guest. "And man, they'd get on you. 'Hey, white boy! You come in here and I'd have you for lunch!'" As author and member James Patterson likes to say, "Little criminals up there, big criminals down here."

Then there was the infamous Black Swan Murder. In 2001, a man named Cyril Wagner—the guest of a Palm Beach doctor—was playing the 17th when a big black swan known as "Alex" came at him with menace. Mr. Wagner swung an iron at it. Alex didn't duck and was struck dead. Wagner said it was the swan or him, self-defense. Trump banned Mr. Wagner forever. "But I probably sold 20 memberships out of that," Trump told me. *Man, you talk about lucky!*

Then there was the topper, the night in April 2018 when the strip joint that sits on the corner of this seedy area, Ultra, hosted none other than porn star Stormy Daniels. As part of her "Make America Horny Again" tour, Ms. Daniels stormed Ultra, dancing to Tom Petty's "American Girl" and coming undressed as Wonder Woman. She performed to a sardined house, some of whom paid as much as $1,000 to see her, all within a 9-iron of Trump's golf club. It's unclear whether Trump International members got a discount.

The president wasn't there, but almost everybody else was. People stopped their cars in the parking lot just to get their picture taken in front of the marquee. The parking lot was jammed with limos and pickups, the kind of event that could unite both sides of the aisle.

"I'd pay $35 to see what the big guy got his hands on," one limo driver said. One gentleman said he was only there to "support the First Amendment."

A true patriot.

Ready for a little quiz?

Okay...

1. Trump National Golf Club Washington, D.C., is in what city? (Hint: It's not Washington.)
2. Trump National Golf Club Los Angeles is where? (Hint: It's not Los Angeles.)
3. Trump National Golf Club Charlotte is in what town? (Hint: It's not Charlotte.)
4. Where is Trump National Golf Club Philadelphia located? (Hint: It's not even in Pennsylvania.)
5. What's so international about Trump International Golf Club West Palm Beach? (Hint: Not much.)

Answers:

1. Trump Washington is in Sterling, Virginia, a 45-minute drive from the White House.
2. Trump Los Angeles is in Rancho Palos Verdes, California, 75 minutes south of L.A.
3. Trump Charlotte is in Mooresville, North Carolina, an hour from Charlotte.

4. Trump Philadelphia is in Pine Hill, New Jersey, about 45 minutes from Philly.
5. Trump International is in West Palm Beach, Florida, which
   isn't very international at all. The vast majority of members
   are American citizens.

And if that little subterfuge bothers you, you haven't seen
anything yet.

Trump's m.o. when he buys a golf course is always the same:
Buy, Lie, and Cry.

Buy: Trump always buys at the bottom. He gets deals, whether
it's a decrepit hotel, abandoned land, or a golf course that's gone
bust. Then he pours money into it, just never as much as he says.
Whenever you hear Trump talk about how much money he poured
into a golf course—"$200 million" "$250 million"—you can divide
that at least by 10. Then he slaps his name on it and begins to…

Lie: Because Trump is the greatest press wrangler in American business history, he immediately begins talking up his
courses so big you'd think he'd just put 18 holes inside the Taj
Mahal. Every course is set "on the greatest piece of property anyone's ever seen. And that's not me saying that." (Yes, it's usually
just him saying that.) Every course is "way better" than (insert
name of famous course in the same state). "And that's guys at
(insert same course name here) telling me that." He needs to talk
it up so he can convince people to pay $200,000 to join a course
that two years before was a goat track.

Now it's time to...

Cry: At the very same time he's telling the world how awesome his piece of property is, he's suing the cities they're in for overvaluing it.

Take Trump Westchester (NY), his second course. Trump bought it in 1996 when it was a vanilla sort of course known as Briar Hall Golf and Country Club in Ossining, New York. It was owned by the bank, which sold it to him for $7.5 million. Trump immediately bulldozed it and put Fazio the Lesser on it. He built a typically immaculate and overwrought course—the waterfall on No. 13 is over 101 feet high and is so fake looking you're sure you saw it on *Fantasy Island*. Trump started talking it up like it was the greatest thing since the Vardon grip. "This will be the best course in New York," he crowed, fully aware that New York has Shinnecock, Friar's Head, and a dozen other showstoppers. He signed up celebs—for free, of course—Yankees skipper Joe Torre, Jack Nicholson, and Hugh Grant. Trump even gave Bill Clinton a freebie. It was a hit.

On his financial-disclosure declaration during the presidential campaign, he valued it at $50 million. In fact, he valued ALL of his golf courses at $50 million, for a whopping total of $700 million. That's a statement that belongs in a padded room. No way. Never. Fifty million for a golf course like Trump West Palm Beach with no hotel and no land to build homes on? Preposterous. The golf world howled at that canard.

"I've evaluated over 3,500 courses in America, Canada, the Caribbean, all over," says Larry Hirsh, a golf course value analyst for Golf Property Analysts near Philadelphia. "And I can only recall one property that we appraised anywhere near $50 million."

Which course?

"I can't say. But it was a very well-known multi-course golf resort that most every American golfer knows. It has more than two courses, I can tell you that."

Was it a Trump course?

"No."

(My guess: It's got to be Pebble Beach, Pinehurst, or Bandon Dunes.)

What's the most expensive 18-holes-only course you've ever evaluated?

"Somewhere in the $20 millions," Hirsh said.

Okay, so Trump's $50 million value for each of his courses is just a flat-out Double Whopper with extra cheese. But get this: At the same time Trump was saying Westchester was worth $50 million, he was suing Ossining for its $11 million tax valuation of it. His lawyer said that was way too high. Trump insisted it was only worth $1.4 million. That's a $48 million difference, if you're scoring at home.

Says Patterson, "I'll give him $1.6 million for it right now."

With two under his belt, Trump started thinking even bigger. He bought the 450-acre Bedminster, New Jersey, hunting and horse estate of the former car tycoon John DeLorean, whose *Back to the Future* car company had gone belly up and who had personally gone broke in a cocaine scandal. Trump got it for a song—$35 million. Trump started interviewing course designers, but this time with a twist.

He started with one of America's best golf designers, Bobby Jones, Jr., the son of the legendary architect Robert Trent Jones. Jones is from New Jersey, so it piqued his interest. But when he sat down in Trump's office for the interview, Trump had a surprise.

"You'll design and build the course, but your name won't be on it," Trump said.

Jones had to blink a few times.

"Excuse me?" he said. "Whose name will be on it?"

"Mine."

More blinking.

"Wait. You want me to ghostwrite your golf course?"

"Yes. Exactly."

Jones passed. Trump got Fazio instead, the real one this time, Tom. Turns out Fazio loves Trump. "He's just so much fun," Fazio says. "I love the guy. He's crazy. He's nonstop. He has so much energy. He's so funny and he never stops. The guy never sleeps. He calls you at all hours. Good thing he doesn't drink. Can you imagine all that on booze? Oh man."

Fazio took the job, but only if his name *was* on it. Even then, he had his regrets. "Donald would constantly chopper out (from New York City), wanting to talk details. Details, details, so many details. So, finally, my son just moved onto the grounds for the entire project. No way I was going to deal with Donald every single day. Besides, I don't work weekends and the guy never stops working."

Eventually, Tom stopped working for Trump and stuck to just being friends. "He uses Jim," Fazio says. "He does good work and he's much cheaper. And it doesn't matter to Donald. He just tells people, 'This is by Tom Fazio' anyway."

Bedminster—which now has 36 holes—is also a hit. It's already held a woman's major, the 2017 U.S. Women's Open, and will hold the 2022 PGA Championship.

After Bedminster, Trump went on a buying spree. In 2002, he bought the partially ocean-swallowed Ocean Trails in Rancho Palos Verdes and called it Trump National Golf Club Los Angeles. In 2009, he bought a course in Pine Hill, New Jersey, and called it Trump Philadelphia. He bought a course called Branton Woods in New York and called it Trump National Golf Club Hudson Valley. That was an adventure in itself.

The contact point for the sale was longtime golf executive Ian Gillule, who was working for the seller, Eric Bergstol. Gillule got Trump interested in the course, and Trump suggested they go up and see it that Saturday. But that wasn't going to work for Bergstol. "No, no, no, definitely not Saturday," Bergstol said. "I have to be discreet. We're having a member–member (tournament) on Saturday. None of the members know I'm selling it. Tell him Monday. We're closed Monday. He'll have the whole place to himself."

Trump wasn't budging. "I'll never forget what he said on the phone that day," Gillule remembers. "He said, 'You tell Eric that on weekends I make million-dollar deals. On weekdays, I make *billion-dollar* deals. You tell him I'll be there Saturday, but I'll be discreet. Nobody will know I'm there.' "

"Discreet" and "Trump" go together like "gasoline" and "soup." Trump and Gillule drove from Manhattan up to Hudson Valley in Trump's white Rolls-Royce. "As we pull up, I see that the carts are all staged, dozens and dozens of them, all in a row," Gillule recalls. "All the players are gathered there and the pro is giving everybody instructions. And it was literally like Rodney Dangerfield showing up in *Caddyshack*. He pulls that big white Rolls-Royce right up on the curb in front, gets out, and yells, 'Hey everybody! How you doing? I'm buying this place!' "

In 2012, Trump bought the former The Point Lake and called it Trump National Golf Club Charlotte. Trump made a ton of changes on that one, not all of which pleased the course's original designer, the golfing legend Greg Norman. Trump was playing with Norman and two writers and Norman seemed pissed the whole round, they say. Might have been because Trump told Norman he wouldn't change anything, and on the first three holes they played, Norman saw that he'd changed something on *every hole*. He was frying. He'd hit his shot, get back in the cart, glare at Trump, and speak to nobody. Trump came over to *Golf Digest*'s Jaime Diaz and said, "Greg is behaving very poorly. He should be better. The fans should be entertained by him."

If you think Norman was pissed that day, you should hear him talk about what Trump did to one of his next purchases— Doonbeg in Ireland.

"That was my favorite course I ever built by hand," Norman

remembers. (A "by-hand" golf course is one that is built almost entirely without bulldozers or tractors, one that threads itself through the natural landscape without moving much earth.) "It was just my baby. We worked with the environmentalists, hand in glove, to build a course that they wanted, the developer wanted, and the community wanted. It was my passion, my labor of love."

Trump bought it, kept the clubhouse, and practically redid the entire course. Most Irish golf critics have panned the Trump version. "Usually, there's an unwritten code," Norman says. "You call the architect and talk over any changes. But, not in this case, I guess....To have somebody else come in and change it all around, that really bothered me. So I just switched off. I haven't gone back. I don't want to go back. I'll never go back."

When an architect agrees to work for Trump, he needs to understand the "for" part. It's Trump's course and he'll get it the way he wants, even if it makes no sense. You just draw it up. "He's the boss," Tom Fazio says. "What are you gonna do? He writes the checks."

But here's the crazy thing: Trump is actually a pretty good golf architect. At his 36-hole Trump Washington, he worked nothing short of a miracle, without Fazio's input, stealing holes from the lesser 18, rerouting the course to better showcase the Potomac River, and building a couple world-class par 3s. "It's a much, much better facility than it was prior to him buying it," says member Gary Newman. "And it was all him doing the work."

So if Trump was the architect for Trump Washington, did

Trump stiff Trump? Because he's famous for short-changing architects. One prominent American architect refuses to work for him. "He called me about doing a course, so I asked around. All the references I got were the same. He does a lot of jerking you around, trying to sucker you."

Architect Gil Hanse has worked a lot with Trump. Not long ago, though, Hanse got up at a corporate dinner, gave his speech, and then said, "I'll take any questions you have, except ones about Donald Trump."

It's not so much the promises Trump breaks or the lies he tells, it's the sheer volume of them. For three years, freelance documentary maker Matt Howley and his crew followed Trump everywhere for Golf Channel's *Donald J. Trump's Fabulous World of Golf*. The idea was to showcase Trump's burgeoning golf-course empire. They had *carte blanche* access to Trump, who loved the attention. It meant more sizzle, and more sizzle means more members, and more members means more initiation fees in his pocket.

"Donald Trump really treated us well," Howley says. "He was great. He knew everybody's name, asked a million questions. He was very kind."

There was only one problem. "I was always introduced as the president of the Golf Channel," Howley says with a laugh. "One time, he introduced me as the president of Golf Channel and this whole Japanese table of businessmen got up and bowed to me. I didn't know what to do, so I bowed back."

If Howley wasn't the president of Golf Channel, then he and his crew were suddenly from *60 Minutes*, especially if they were walking through the dining room at Mar-a-Lago. "He'd go from table to table, shaking people's hands and saying, 'Yeah, *60 Minutes* is with me.'"

Why wasn't the truth good enough? Why wasn't, "This is a crew from Golf Channel. They're documenting me for my show," impressive enough for Trump?

"Because that's his gold standard for TV—*60 Minutes*," Howley says. "He always goes for his gold standard. I got used to it. After a while, I started to *believe* I was with *60 Minutes*. Honestly, just from spending so much time around him, I found myself lying much more than I used to. My friends started getting on me about it. They'd be like, 'Dude, that didn't happen that way. Why are you lying about it?' You tell enough lies and you sort of forget after a while."

When you toss that much bullshit around, it's hard to remember where the piles are. For instance, Trump once said of the former Lowes Island Club he turned into Trump Washington, "This place, when it's finished, will be the finest club anywhere in the country. There will be nothing like it."

But, wait. That's almost exactly what he said about Trump Los Angeles when it opened: "No one has ever seen anything like this. There is nothing that you can compare it to.... It's going to be the greatest, most spectacular golf course that you've ever seen."

But that can't be, because that's almost exactly what he said about Trump Jupiter: "It doesn't get any finer."

But how can that be when he promised Trump Doral would be "the finest resort and golf club in the country"?

Now you're completely confused, because he declared Trump Turnberry to be, "The greatest golf course anywhere in the world. Everybody knows it."

Speaking of manure, Trump also says, repeatedly, "I've been given more golf environmentalism awards than anybody." That's the Moby Dick of fibs. He hasn't been given one legitimate golf environmental award. Not one. Zero.

He is proud of the great numbers of people he employs at his golf properties, but, as ever, those numbers get the Trump Bump. "I employ thousands of people," he told Golf Channel's David Feherty. "I take care of their kids' educations...[pause]...well, indirectly."

Wait, indirectly?

If that's true, can Trump say he fights fires because some of his taxes go to the fire department? Does he save people's lives because the city hospital gets subsidized?

Sometimes the gap between the truth and the Trumps is so great you couldn't cross it with a Cessna. Take Trump Golf Links at Ferry Point in the Bronx, New York.

The Truth: In the early 1980s, the City of New York decided to build a golf course on a condemned garbage dump. They got Jack Nicklaus to design it and went through two or three developers trying to get it made. Finally, they gave up and did it themselves. By 2008, it was almost done. They hired the Trump Organization to operate it, as long as it agreed to build a $10 million clubhouse and handle the grow-in of the greens, which usually takes a year and a half. Sweet deal for Trump, who didn't have to pay the city a cent the first four years it was open. It finally did open in 2015—with 15-foot-high letters that read: TRUMP LINKS.

The Trump: "*That course would not have been open for 10 years more had I not gotten involved,*" *Trump told* Crain's New York Business. "*It wasn't getting built. Nobody could get it open....I was able to do it. I got it open.*" *Ivanka Trump even went so far as to blog that* "*My family was able to do in two years what the city hadn't been able to do in two decades....My father went out to the construction site, where he saw a bunch of guys literally moving sand from one end of the course to the other. He essentially looked at them and said, 'You guys have made a lot of money pushing sand around for the last 20 years, but that stops with me. It's time to get this done.' And they did.*"

The Truth: No. The course was almost done except for the greens, a few cart paths, and a couple lightning shelters. Adrian Benepe, who was the NYC parks commissioner at the time, still shudders about it. "That was the first time I realized the whole family was pathological liars," Benepe says. "Ivanka just made her story up. Just invented it. He didn't bring that course in. We finished it."

The Trump: When Trump became POTUS, his son Eric became the mouthpiece for all the golf properties, and a new generation of fable telling began. Ten years after Trump signed on, they finally opened the clubhouse. (Although it wasn't really ready to open. They did it to coincide with the 2018 U.S. Open on Long Island.) Eric came to the ribbon-cutting ceremony and said, "You literally cannot get on the course, it's so packed."

The Truth: It definitely is *not* hard to get on Ferry Point. On June 30, 2018—a Saturday—I went to their website to book a tee time for the next morning. A Sunday summer morning tee time in New York, on a course that's "packed"? That would be hard, right? All they had left for a foursome was 9:40 a.m., 11:30, 11:40, 11:50, noon, 12:10 p.m., 12:30, 12:40, 12:50, 1:00, 1:10, 1:20, 1:40, 2:00, 2:10, 2:20, 2:40, 2:50, 3:00, 3:10...you get the idea.

The Trump: Eric Trump said business at Ferry Point is "spectacular."

The Truth: Business is not spectacular. In 2016, gross receipts were down 9% from 2015. In 2017, they were down 17% from 2016. That's been true across all of golf, but it's particularly grating when a city is trying to make back the whopping $127 million it sunk into a course.

The Trump: Eric and Ivanka speak of Ferry Point as some kind of city-beautification project that the family sacrificed to build, out of their civic hearts, like they ought to be on a United Way poster.

The Truth: The Trumps have been paid and paid well for operating the place. As for brightening the lives of Bronx golfers, they haven't. At $175 a round for a resident, almost nobody from the Bronx can play it. The patrons are mostly Wall Street guys and midtown execs and Yankees pitchers with the day off. By far, the biggest winners in the deal have been the Trumps.

The Trump: When it opened, Trump tweeted:

TrumpGolf Links at Ferry Point will host many major championships over the years. Great thing for NYC—congratulations to all!

The Truth: It has yet to have one.

6

THE GREAT MUCKLE GYPE

I think his mother would be horrified.
—MAIRI STERLAND, TRUMP'S COUSIN

IN SCOTLAND, DONALD TRUMP is less popular than tipping. They hated him before he was president, and now they hate him more than the English. They don't hide it. I saw one guy who held up a giant sign that read: "Keep Scotland Great—Get Trump Out."

Since I speak a little Scottish, allow me to translate a few others:

- Trump You Great Muckle Gype! (Trump You Big Lumpy Fool!)
- Trump You Tangerine Roaster! (Trump You Orange Idiot!)
- Clackwanker! (Douche!)
- You Weapons-Grade Wanker! (You Very Large Jagoff!)
- Trump Is a Witless Cocksplat! (Trump Is a Dummy Head!)

- Trump You Clueless Numpty! (Trump You Stupid Know-Nothing!)
- You Wankmaggot! (Doesn't translate.)
- What a Gobshite! (What a Useless Prick!)
- Trump You Orange Bawbag! (Trump You Orange Testicle Sack!)
- Get Out, King Fucktwaddle (Self-explanatory.)

That's a lot of animus for a guy whose mother was *born* in Scotland. If anybody else with a Scottish-born mother had been elected U.S. president, Scotland might have given him Dundee and half of Edinburgh. "It's hard to put into words how big that would be here," says John Huggan, the longtime Scottish golf writer. "A half-Scottish president? Oh my god. But now it's just completely the opposite. He is genuinely hated here. I haven't met anybody who wants him here. He's an arse. He's the walking caricature of what some Scots think Americans are like—loud, brash, and obnoxious."

Among the things they hate about him is that everything he seems to know about the UK you could fit on the head of a golf tee. For instance, Trump owns a golf course in Ireland called Doonbeg. At the press conference Trump held before his July 2018 trip to the British Isles, a reporter asked Trump if he was worried about the high level of venom the UK spits his way. "I believe the people in the UK—Scotland, Ireland, I have property in Ireland, as you know—those people they like me a lot." The only problem with that answer is that Ireland isn't in the UK. That's Northern Ireland.

His White House staff doesn't seem to know where Scotland is, either. As he was leaving England to go visit his Trump Turnberry golf resort on the west coast of Scotland, the official White House Twitter page announced:

Today, @realDonaldTrump and @FLOTUS had tea with Her Majesty Queen Elizabeth II at Windsor Castle before departing the UK.

The only problem with that tweet is that Turnberry is very much in the UK, as is Scotland, come to think of it.

On June 24, 2016—the day after the UK's Brexit vote—Trump happened to be in Turnberry. He tweeted:

Just arrived in Scotland. Place is going wild over the vote. They took their country back, just like we will take America back.

The only problem with that tweet is that Scotland voted 62% *against* Brexit.

He then went to a raucous ribbon-cutting press conference, set in front of the Turnberry lighthouse, escorted by bagpipers in kilts and was confronted by a comedian who threw Nazi-logo golf balls at him.

It got worse. He returned home and started telling reporters that he'd predicted Brexit. "I was in Turnberry the day before," he said more than a few times. "I saw it coming." The only problem with that is he was there the day *after*, and every UK newspaper has proof.

Then, somehow, it got worse than that. On his 2018 UK visit, Double Down doubled down. "I predicted Brexit," he told the *Sun* newspaper of London. "I was cutting a ribbon for the opening of Turnberry—you know they totally did a whole renovation, it is beautiful—the day before the Brexit vote...I said, 'Brexit will happen.' The vote is going to go positive, because people don't want to be faced with the horrible immigration problems." Then he REPEATED it.

Finally, just to add a little seasoning to the whole bouillabaisse of naked lies, bonehead errors, and cultural insults, Trump said, "You know, my mother is from here. I'm Scotch."

The only problem with that is nobody's "Scotch." They're Scottish.

Blue-eyed Maryanne MacLeod was born on the Isle of Lewis, about as far north in Scotland as you can go, in a tiny town called Tong, near Stornoway, youngest of 10 children of peasant parents. In 1930, at age 17, she boarded the ship *Transylvania* out of Glasgow, bound for New York, to live with a sister. All but one of her siblings would do the same—chain migration, as Trump calls it. She worked as a maid until she happened to meet a rich German-born New York apartment tycoon name Fred Trump and married him in 1936.

But what kind of story is that? Young Donald Trump went to work making it sound better. "She was on vacation in America when she met my dad," he tells people.

Trump's mother had five kids—Maryanne, Frederick Jr.,

Elizabeth, Donald, and Robert—and returned to Tong every year, still speaking fluent Scottish Gaelic despite her fancy Bloomingdale's dresses. She returned every year until late into the 1990s, but Donald only went with her once, as a toddler, and never went again. Maybe it's what the Scottish wind does to that hairdo, which makes it look like a snapping red wolverine.

Never went again, that is, until 2006, when he wanted to build a luxury public golf resort near Balmedie, just north of Aberdeen on the east coast. For $11 million, he'd purchased an old shooting ranch called the Menie Estate, perched on a delicate stretch of dunes land designated SSSI—Site of Special Scientific Interest—Scotland's most sensitive grade. Environmental groups were breathless with anger over the idea. They pointed out, over and over, how much damage building a golf course could do to the giant, fragile, constantly moving dunes, much less Trump's two courses, not to mention an eight-story, five-star, 450-room hotel, a sports complex, 950 time-share apartments, and 36 villas. Made no difference to Trump. He wanted it, and he was going to get it.

So the day before he was to plead his case in front of the Aberdeenshire Council, he landed his jet in nearby Stornoway and visited his cousin, who still lives in the childhood home of his dear Scottish mother.

For 96 seconds.

He came up the walk, cameras clicking, waved a few times, went into the house, looked around, and came briskly out. Then he held a press conference that was two hours, or 75 times longer than the visit, mentioning more than once that he was "Scotch" and he was going to build "the greatest golf course in the world" and that he would create 6,000 jobs and bring $1.2 billion to the local economy. That figure, of course, was flubberdeegook. He'd started with $300 million and lathered his way up as he went.

Later, a Trump cousin, Mairi Sterland, told a Scottish blogger: "I used to laugh about [being related to] Donald Trump. Now I hardly dare mention him....He is outrageous. You quail at the thought of what he's capable of."

The "Hey, I'm Scotch, too" gambit didn't work. In November 2007, the council turned him down.

No problem. Trump went over their heads. He started wining and dining the head of the nation, Scotland First Minister Alex Salmond, a pro-business stalwart. "Salmond believed Trump's crap," says Suzanne Kelly, a reporter for the *Aberdeen Voice*. "He enjoyed flying back and forth to New York, eating Trump's steak and lobster dinners. He got the Trump mojo put on him." A year later, Salmond decided to override the environmentalists and the locals and the Aberdeenshire Council and grant Trump permission to build his golf resort, dunes be damned.

"Six thousand jobs across Scotland, 1,400 local and permanent jobs in the northeast of Scotland," Salmond reasoned. "That outweighs the environmental concerns."

Construction of the greatest course in the world was ready to start.

First thing Trump needed was an architect.

"First of all, he told me right away he never wanted to build any 36 holes," says American architect Tom Doak. "He told me, 'I asked for 36, hoping to get permitted for 18. All I wanted was the 18.' But then the Scottish government stepped in and gave him 36. 'And I don't even WANT 36!'" That was a problem for any architect to have to build an extra 18 boring "resort" holes and a problem for Trump to have to build them. "There were a ton of problems. I turned him down." Finally, on reportedly his fifth try, he got a respected English designer, Martin Hawtree.

Cue the bulldozers, accompanied by the screaming of the dunes huggers, who abhorred the flattening and pinning down of giant dunes that migrate 11 meters per year. In Scotland, moving dunes is akin to cementing over Walden Pond. Trump argued that by preventing sand movement he was "preserving the dunes." That's like saying a T-bone preserves the cow.

"That's a live dune system," says renowned Scottish designer David McLay Kidd. "When you stop them from moving, they're effectively dead."

Kidd would know. He was the last architect to build a golf course in an ultra-sensitive dunes site—the first to try in 100 years—in Machrihanish, which you drive to by taking Paul McCartney's long and winding road. They were so careful with the dunes, they might as well have been wearing oven mitts. "We used no heavy equipment at all," reports David Southworth, the American developer of the project. "Nothing. We did it with shovels, by hand. We couldn't disturb the orchids. We worked hand-in-hand with the environmentalists and the local people. It was a real challenge." What they gave them is a course called Machrihanish Dunes, which has been called "the most natural course on earth." What they gave him back is no protesters, no lawsuits, and no pissed-off locals.

Back to Trump. Reporters started digging in on the deal. Turns out, before Trump had shown official interest in the Menie Estate, he'd secretly tried to buy the neighboring houses and farms he thought were ugly, houses he didn't want his customers to have to look at. He sent his project director, Neil Hobday, knocking on doors, pretending to be an innocent passerby named "Peter White" (Hobday's middle names), inquiring cheerily if their homes were for sale. None were.

Would they want to sell them anyway, for a good price?

No, they wouldn't.

Trump bought the estate anyway and began brooding about those "ugly" houses.

Plan B: Trump had his lawyers apply to have the local government use eminent domain to buy the houses or, as they say in Scotland, "compulsory purchase." Didn't matter that this isn't at all how compulsory purchase works. It's meant for homes that are blighted, homes that stand in the way of a highway or a park. It's not a way for one neighbor to force out another because they don't like how his crabgrass looks. Again: Denied. (Trump's publicity people later claimed the "compulsory purchase" story was made up to build sympathy for the dunes residents. The only problem with that claim is that nearly every paper in Scotland has copies of Trump's application.)

Plan C: Start making life hell for the holdouts. Trump declared that one property, owned by a farmer named Michael Forbes, was a "slum" and that Forbes lived like a "pig." Then, just for seasoning, he added, "My mother was born in Stornoway. She was the most clean woman I've ever seen, immaculate. The people of Scotland are that way....Maybe his heritage is from somewhere other than Scotland."

Forbes didn't go punch Trump and he didn't sue him. Instead, he put up a Mexican flag—in solidarity with other Trump insultees—and told Trump to "take his money and shove it up his arse." Not long after, Forbes and his elderly mother, Molly, who lives nearby, started having trouble with their water lines. She didn't sue, either. Instead, she just started trapping rain water in old paint buckets and getting water from a stream via wheelbarrow. She wouldn't move, either.

A neighbor named David Milne woke up one day to find that Trump had planted a row of giant trees blocking his 40-mile view of the coastline. He also found new 20-foot-high, 70-foot-long earth berms starting three feet from his property line, plus a new fence on two sides of his property, for which Trump sent him a $3,500 bill. Milne didn't sue. Instead, he threw away the bill, put up a Mexican flag, and waited for the trees to die. "Trump planted the wrong kind," Milne says. "Sitka spruces. Sitkas don't do well in our high winds and sea air." They did die. Trump's crews replaced those with more Sitkas, fronted by cypresses this time. "They'll die, too," Milne told me in July of 2018. "We can already see the sea through the gaps."

None of them moved. In fact, they moved others. They became local heroes. When a documentary came out about the whole mess—*You've Been Trumped*—they became national heroes. In fact, Michael Forbes was named "Scot of the Year" by Glenfiddich scotch. That fried Trump's brain. He immediately banned Glenfiddich from all his properties, tweeting...

Michael Forbes lives in a pigsty and bad liquor company Glenfiddich gave him Scot of the Year award....Does anyone smell publicity stunt?

...thus giving Glenfiddich more publicity than it could have ever dreamed.

It all amounted to a Scottish standoff. At press time, the second course still hadn't come, nor the hotel, nor the time-share condos, nor the 6,000 new jobs, nor the $1.28 billion for the economy. There was some talk about Trump trying again to build homes—500 of them—but when a Scotland Natural Heritage report came out in late summer 2018 showing that some of the dunes and much of the marine terraces had been damaged beyond repair, chances looked dismal for that, too.

"Donald Trump didn't do what he promised," admitted a sheepish Alex Salmond. "Balmedie got 10 cents on the dollar."

One golf course *was* built, though—Trump International Golf Links Scotland—and it's pretty good, if you like links courses that seemed to have been dreamed up by an interior designer. Links courses are supposed to be watered by the rain and cut by the wind. They're supposed to be a wrestling match between brown and green, with brown ahead on points. Bathed in wind, you play them along the ground, the kind of places where you putt from 100 yards out. Trump's course is much too lush, greener than the lawn of the Kentucky governor, so green it's blue-green. It doesn't thump. It swishes. Your feet sink.

The other problem is nobody plays it. I spent two days walking on it (under Scotland's Right to Roam laws) and never saw much of anybody—no Trump, no guards, and only one foursome each day. It was empty. For one, it's too expensive (almost $370 per round). For another, it's too Trump. "There might be people who would like to play it," says Martin Ford, an Aberdeenshire official who voted against the course, "but they don't want to give Trump their money."

Trump Aberdeen is a money pit. According to the required tax papers the club had to file, it lost $4.5 million in 2017. Remember those 6,000 people Trump was going to hire? It employed just 85 in 2017. Salmond now refers to Trump as "a complete and utter nincompoop."

"It was almost like the whole thing was a dry run for his campaign as president," Ford says. "He bullied everybody. He started false rumors. Established alternative truths by repetition. Then we watched the [presidential] campaign and it was everything he had done up here in Aberdeen."

It got worse. Trump found out 11 power-generating windmills were to be placed in the sea half a mile or so from his course and blew a gasket. He said they were so ugly they would spoil his guests' rounds of golf. Besides, he said, windmills are noisy, don't work, and kill birds. Salmond was a stone this time. Trump wrote more than a dozen letters to him excoriating him, threatening him, and begging him to kill the windmills. "Your country will become a third world wasteland that global investors will avoid," he wrote. Salmond didn't so much as wiggle a toe.

Trump sued. He lost. The windmills are churning out there now. You can't hear them, but you can see them from the beach, and he's right, they're not pretty. Of course, since you can't see the ocean much from his course, does it matter?

It did to Trump. "I doubt if I'll ever do business in Scotland again," he harrumphed.

Two years later, he bought another Scottish course.

In a land where you can't throw a bucket of birdseed without hitting a great golf course, Trump Turnberry stands out. Since Trump took over in 2014, it's twice as good as it was. When you throw in the magnificent par-5-length hotel that sits elegantly and high above it, it might be the best golf resort in the entire country. Nearly everything Trump botched in Aberdeen, he's done perfectly in Turnberry.

A true links course, Turnberry sits on the rocky site of Robert the Bruce's castle, guarded by a postcard white-and-yellow lighthouse where Robert Louis Stevenson roamed as a child (his dad was the keeper). Turnberry was just fine before Trump, of course. It delivered some of the greatest golf in history, including The Duel in the Sun in 1977 between Jack Nicklaus and Tom Watson. Turnberry is a beauty that's been unlucky in marriage. It's been owned by the Japanese, the Westin hotel chain, Arabs, just about everybody. "Trump is the first guy who's made promises to us and then actually delivered," says Clive Douglas, a former captain of the club. "He came in and bang, bang, bang. He did everything he said he'd do."

What? No lies, no lawsuits, no feuds?

"No, nothing at all."

His only mistake? Naming the place after himself. In Scotland, "Trump Turnberry" goes over like "Trump Versailles" would in France or "Trump Rushmore" in America. The name pisses Scots off. "I refuse to say it that way," says Huggan. "I refuse to put those two words together in my mouth and nobody can make me say it that way."

When Trump changed the famous lighthouse logo to his own crest and slapped a big "Trump Turnberry" above it, the pro shop merchandise sold like anthrax cupcakes. Finally, somebody convinced Trump to get rid of his logo and go back to the old one without his name. That worked. You go in the pro shop now and you can hardly find a stitch of Trump stuff. "It all hit the clearance sale table," one Turnberry employee told me. "I got a 200-quid bag for 40!"

That's just one reason Trump is bleeding money at Turnberry. According to Bloomberg, Trump Turnberry lost $36 million in 2016 against revenues of only $12 million. That debt load doubled from the previous year.

It's too bad. Turnberry is so much better under Trump. Take the lighthouse. It used to just sit there by the 9th tee, looking a lot like Melania, gorgeous and lonely. There's even a splendid halfway house at the base of it now and two luxurious guest suites in the top half. I was sitting on the porch of it on the day Trump was to arrive from his chaotic meeting with British prime minister Theresa May in July of 2018. Word was, Eric Trump was ensconced in the suite for the weekend. There were snipers in the turret above. I saw somebody I recognized: Keith Thomas, one of the president's military aides who carries the "nuclear football," the satchel that contains the codes for the president to launch a nuclear attack. He didn't have the satchel with him, though, he had a lemonade. He was admiring the Firth of Clyde and, in the distance, Northern Ireland.

"Sorry about the view," I said.

He jumped up and practically saluted. "Yes, sir, it is! Never been here before."

I asked him if his boss would be arriving by Marine One.

"No, sir," he said. "We're trying to be low key in Scotland, so he's coming in by motorcade."

Well, "low key" is in the eye of the beholder. Trump would be landing in Air Force One at nearby Prestwick Airport, along with a C-17, which carries The Beast presidential limo and other security vehicles, and a third plane full of press and officials, plus a military fighter jet escort or two, plus God knows what else. When they arrived, they'd also find Eric Trump's helicopter parked garishly on the hotel lawn, with giant letters spelling "TRUMP" on the side.

I couldn't resist asking Thomas about "the green box," the Port-O-Let-sized container that's always with the president—a bombproof, bulletproof tiny fortress they can shove him into if things get hairy. "Does it have food and water inside?" I asked.

He laughed. "Hmmmm. I don't know, sir. I'll have to find that out for you."

Yes, get back to me first thing in the morning.

I asked him how he thought the planned anti-Trump protests would go the next morning. There'd already been some that morning on the road in front ("You're Not Welcome Here"), and there were more planned all over the nation, including giant ones in Edinburgh, Glasgow, and, of course, Aberdeen and Balmedie.

"I think it will be fine," Thomas said. "These Scottish people are so nice. Even the protesters are nice. It's kind of hard to hate them."

He's right. Protests in Scotland are just a notch below a picnic. For a solid week in 2016, there was a comedian named Janey Godley who would stand on the road that runs in front of the Turnberry hotel holding up a sign that read: "Trump Is a Cunt." Each day, the hotel staff would invite her in for lunch and tea. One time, on a freezing, rainy winter day, a man kept marching back and forth on the street, holding up his anti-Trump sign. The guys in the bag room insisted he come inside, warm up, and eat a cheeseburger.

That early evening, the motorcade arrived. There was heavy security everywhere. Trump was having his picture taken on the grand front steps of the hotel with patrons and family when—stunningly—a Greenpeace protester flying a microlight flew right over him, not even 30 feet above, making three loops. How he got past all the military and Secret Service and security aircraft, who knows. He was flying a flag behind him that read: "Trump—Well Below Par."

"I couldn't believe it," said Tim Size, an American from St. Louis who was standing right there. "It was right above us. I thought sure the snipers would shoot him down. He could've had a bomb or a gun—anything. But they didn't. He just flew away. We asked one of the Secret Service guys later why they didn't shoot. He said, 'If we'd been back home, we would've. But not in Scotland.'"

After a long pause, Secret Service rushed Trump inside the hotel. Once inside, according to two sources who were there, Trump later asked his wife, "What'd the banner say?"

" 'Well below par'," Melania answered.

"Beautiful!" Trump exulted. "I WANT to be below par!"

Greenpeace protesters do not play a lot of golf.

The next morning, as Thomas predicted, the protesters were everywhere, in the sheep fields and on the roads leading in and out, as they were all over the Scottish nation, with a rage they hadn't shown to an American president since Nixon, if that. They even wrote messages in the sand at Balmedie in hopes Trump would fly over ("Putin's Pussy"). He never did.

Trump saw them as he began his golf round. They chanted and yelled at him: "Racist!" "Cunt!" and "Fuckhead!" And what did he do? He waved at them as though they were fans. Gave them the big hi hello.

Admit it. The guy is clever.

As usual, Trump was playing that day in a cart. Trump always plays in a cart. The only problem with that is that, at both Aberdeen and Turnberry, you must have a signed doctor's letter to take a cart. They want you to walk. Yet there he was.

Despite all the people, protesters, and press around, Trump still cheated.

"I'm shooting him on the second fairway," says Scottish photographer Stuart Wallace. "And I see a Secret Service agent kick his ball out of the rough. The [agent] was in a buggy up ahead of him and [Trump's] drive ended up in the rough and he got out of his buggy and kicked it out on the short stuff. Unbelievable."

Afterward, a Turnberry caddy emailed me. He'd never seen Trump play before. "He had 4 or 5 hacks out of one bunker before hand-wedging it onto the green!"

The next day, after the Trump circus left town, a very pro-Trump Texan came to Turnberry. He took at a look at the obligatory massive flag flapping from the trademark 100-foot pole by the first tee and wrinkled his nose. He was expecting the stars and stripes and wasn't seeing it, only the white and blue of the Scottish flag.

"Hey," the Texan asked a caddy, "Is that a new Trump flag or somethin'?"

Give him time.

7

TACKY IS AS TACKY DOES

I only do 10s.
—Donald J. Trump

TRUMP IS NOT JUST a political outlier. He's a golf outlier. Forget how he plays the game. Just in the simplest politeness of the game, the timeless etiquette of it, Trump seems to have come from another planet.

For instance, he never takes off his hat for the traditional end-of-round handshake, which is considered gentlemanly. He doesn't take it off inside the clubhouse, either, which is a little golf-gauche. He doesn't care whose honor it is on the tee box, either. He just steps up first and hits it. He's not what you'd call a good loser, either.

"I played with him once," says *Los Angeles Times* NFL writer Sam Farmer. "And I actually beat him out of $10. He handed me the two fives, but they wouldn't quite come out of his hand. He held onto them and made me pull. I thought they were going to rip. When I finally got them, he goes, 'It's all right. I've got a supermodel girlfriend and my own 727, so I'm okay.'"

There's a famous story about the time Trump lost $50 to a guy at Winged Foot. Trump said he didn't have any cash. "That's okay," the guy said. "I'll take a check."

Trump said he didn't have any checks on him.

"That's okay, I'll take a bank draft. I'll go get it." So the guy gets in his car and gets a bank draft for $50, brings it back, and Trump signs it. Weeks later, Trump sees him, pissed off.

"You cashed my check!"

"Of course I did."

"Nobody *ever* cashes my checks. They frame them!"

This is a man who famously drives his golf cart on greens. To repeat: He drives ON THE GREEN. There is video of him doing it at Trump Bedminster. In golf, that's the unholiest-of-unholies. Driving your cart on the green is like hanging your laundry in the Sistine Chapel. A green is a tender and delicate thing. Caddies don't even set their bags on it. Driving on the green leaves tire tracks on the perfect surface that can send your partner's putt careening off line, not to mention the putts of the 100 players behind you. I've met people who were 100% for Trump politically but vow they'll never vote for him again because he drove on the green. Says one woman, "That's such a violation!"

"He did it all the time at Doral," says Joe Santilli, a former member there. "He'd come along with five or six people and play through us, never asking permission, just playing through. And he'd drive his cart right on the green."

I hear you: *It's his course. He gets to do what he wants.* But there's a line, and driving a cart on a green is about three national parks past it. If you go to a friend's house for dinner, does that mean he has the right to come out of his bedroom drunk in his half-open bathrobe and plunk himself down on your wife's lap?

"He drives across tees, too," says a source inside Bedminster. "The guy walks as little as possible. He gets out, walks two feet, hits, and gets back in the cart."

Very hard to get your 10,000 steps that way.

Chefs don't call Michelin asking for an extra star. Actors don't go on TV saying they deserve an Oscar. And golf course developers don't beg to be on Top 100 golf course lists.

Except Trump. He begs, bullies, and badgers the magazines that do the ratings. When he's not happy with the ratings he gets, he'll rip them out of the magazine, scrawl something nasty on them with a Sharpie—"DISHONEST!"—and mail them to the editor.

Since he unveiled his first course in 1999, Trump International in West Palm Beach, Trump has wheedled, lobbied, and lied ceaselessly hyping them. The higher the rankings, the more he can charge for memberships and guest fees. Rankings, though, are a number he can't Trump Bump and it drives him crazy.

For instance, he's said repeatedly that Trump Los Angeles is better than Pebble Beach. Now, understand, Pebble Beach is universally thought of as one of the most beautiful courses in the world. It's been ranked the best course in the world hundreds of times. It's held five U.S. Opens, which have been won by no less than Jack Nicklaus, Tom Watson, and Tiger Woods. For many touring pros, it's the place they'd play if they only had one round left. So to say Trump Los Angeles is better than Pebble Beach is a family-sized jar of stupid sauce.

Yes, Trump Los Angeles has stunning views of the Pacific, but that's all it's got. "It's a plate of sausages," says architect Robert Trent Jones, Jr. In golf-design lingo, a "plate of sausages" means it's laid out like somebody laying sausages all in the same direction, packed onto the platter. I've played it. Once was enough. Seventeen holes run parallel to the ocean, back and forth, over and over again, until you feel like you're on a boot camp march. Only one hole, the first, goes perpendicular. Says golf architect Tom Doak, "Nobody in the world thinks his course is better than Pebble—except Donald Trump."

It gets so ridiculous at Trump Los Angeles that, no joke, they don't even like to see the Pebble Beach logo. "I walked in there once wearing a Pebble Beach shirt," says L.A. golf marketer Robert Ward. "The general manager says, 'Is there any way you can change your shirt? Mr. Trump really doesn't like to see that logo.' I'm not kidding. And Trump wasn't even around."

Trump was never on the Wharton debating team, but he employs some masterful rhetorical tricks when flogging his courses. For instance, when Trump lies, he doubles down by making his enemies complicit in his side of the argument. Take, for instance, what he says about his Trump Philadelphia course in Pine Hill, New Jersey, which has the misfortune to be a 10-minute drive from the universally acknowledged and current No. 1 course in the world—Pine Valley (NJ). Being next door to Pine Valley is sort of like being Penelope Cruz's foster sister. Still, Trump has said, repeatedly, "It is as good as Pine Valley, if not better....I really believe it. A lot of the people there are saying so. And if you went there, you would say it, too. Everybody that goes there says it."

(Let's pause here for the world's golfers to slap their foreheads in unison.)

I went to Trump Philadelphia and...no, no, a million times no. It's not in the same galaxy as Pine Valley. Since *Golf Digest* began ranking courses, no other property has finished No. 1 in America as many times as Pine Valley. Trump Philadelphia, meanwhile, has never made their top 200. It isn't even ranked in the top 15 courses in the state of New Jersey.

"It's the same soil!" Trump insists.

BUYER: Why are you charging Park Ave prices for this Hell's Kitchen tenement building?

TRUMP: Same soil!

Even his buddy Tom Fazio giggles at this one. "He tells reporters, 'People are telling me this is better than Pine Valley.' But he never says who those people are. Do you know who the people are? They're the people who work for him, like his caddies. He will be like, 'Hey Mario, don't you think this is better than Pine Valley?' And Mario will go, 'Oh yeah! Much better!'...I honestly think he believes the things he says. He hears himself say it and pretty soon he completely believes it."

Put it this way, Trump keeps a locker there, but, according to the members and employees I spoke to, hadn't been there since 2015. If it were better than the No. 1 ranked course in the world, you think he might swing by now and again?

It drives Trump out of his brain when other courses are ranked above his or when his courses don't make the lists at all. He lies and tells people the reason his courses go unranked is because, "I don't let the raters on my courses. I don't want to bother the membership." But that's a fat lie. The truth is, he's dying to get on the lists. It's a game he can't control and can't fudge and can't buy, so it vexes his sleep.

One night, in March of 2014, an editor and writer at *Golfweek* named Jeff Babineau answered his home phone. It was Larry Glick, Trump's right-hand golf man, saying Trump would be calling in five minutes. "Take the call," Glick instructed.

Trump called. He was hot. *Golfweek* has two lists: Top 100 Classic (pre-1960) and Top 100 Modern (post-1960). Trump's new Doral makeover had finished just after the deadline for *Golfweek's* 700 to 800 raters to see it. But Trump begged *Golfweek* to extend the deadline and they gave in. A group of raters were rushed through as a favor for one of the biggest golf developers in the country. So the raters hurried over, heard Trump say, "Doral is the greatest course in Florida!," played it, huddled together, and ranked it No. 99 on the Modern list. Now, for perspective, there are 15,000-plus golf courses in the United States, and to be recognized in the top 100 is really good. But good is not nearly good enough for Donald Trump. He heard about the 99 and was fried about it.

Rrrrring, rrrrring.

"Hello?" Babineau said.

"You need to take Doral out of your rankings," Trump barked, skipping the customary opening greetings. "Take it out now."

"Is this Mr. Trump?"

"Yes. Take it out."

"Well, first of all," Babineau tried to explain, "the rankings are already in print. They'll be in the next magazine."

"Doral needs to come out," Trump insisted. "Take the course out."

Babineau said he couldn't do that and wouldn't do that. Trump then began to harp on the *Golfweek* writer in charge of the ratings, Bradley Klein.

"Klein's an idiot," Trump kept saying. "You have an idiot in charge of your rankings."

Trump insisted this was more order than request. Doral had to come out of their rankings because...just because. He was hinting at removing all his advertising from *Golfweek*, and...who knows what?

Babineau sighed and finally said, "Then I suppose you want ALL of the Trump properties out of the rankings, right?"

"Such as?"

"Well, for one, Trump International Scotland is in our Great Britain and Ireland Modern rankings."

"Where do you have that ranked?"

"No. 1."

Pause.

"Well, at least you got SOMETHING right."

Doral stayed in at 99.

The long-suffering Klein is used to this from Trump. "He [Trump] started calling me about eight or nine years ago," Klein says. "I was driving in Phoenix, and Donald calls me, and all of a sudden he starts yelling at me because Trump National [Bedminster] Old Course [wasn't] high enough. 'It's the greatest course,' 'It's better than this, better than that,' on and on and on. He's ranting and raving. At one point, he says, 'I don't know what I have to do. I'll do anything you want me to do. I'll call up the publisher and if you want me to, I'll buy ads.'"

Klein finally had to get him off the line. He said, "Mr. Trump, I can't have this conversation. You're fired."

When Trump can't get what he wants from editors, he starts hammering the salespeople. "He'd say, 'If I'm not No. 1, then I don't want to be in at all,'" says one golf magazine salesperson who asked not to be identified. "Then he'd call and say the Trump properties were too exclusive to be ranked. Don't rank them. He called me once and said, 'You make my course No. 1, and you don't have to work anymore.' To which I answered, 'Well, I'm going to have to work tomorrow. That's just not possible.'"

If you simply agree that Trump courses should all be ranked

No. 1, you'll get along really well with him. Once, in discussing Trump Washington, he told *Golf Digest's* David Owen that it "blows away Congressional [a famous D.C. club that has hosted two U.S. Opens] like nobody ever blew it away. They say it's not even a contest."

Congressional is ranked 80th by *Golf Digest* among U.S. courses. Trump Washington is good but unranked. It's not in their Top 200 list either. It doesn't even make their Best 10 Courses in Virginia. So he's right. It's not even a contest.

Trump once tweeted that he was about to go play Trump International (West Palm Beach), "the number-one rated golf course in the State of Florida."

Okay...no. I've never seen a reputable ranking of Trump International as the best in Florida. It's not within a par 5 of the best course in Florida, a state with so many great golf courses it should count as its own country. Seminole, for instance, is a gem and unrivaled in the state. It's ranked 12 in America. The unforgettable TPC Sawgrass (Stadium) and its first-ever island green is ranked 49. I could go on. "I can probably name 25 courses in South Florida alone that are better," says longtime PGA Tour star Mark Calcavecchia. "I mean, there's nothing wrong with [Trump International], but it's nothing amazing." It's ranked 156th by *Golf Digest*.

To be sure, Trump has some fine courses. Trump Bedminster is very good. It's already held a U.S. Women's Open and will hold the 2022 PGA Championship, a major. Trump's course in Aberdeen, Scotland, is sensational to look at, albeit a bastardization of a links course. His Turnberry is so much better under Trump that it's crazy it's currently not scheduled to hold another Open Championship.

The problem is, Trump insists they're ALL wonderful. "Every one of my courses is, like, amazing," Trump said once. Really? Because if you're speaking of your Trump National Hudson Valley, it isn't even America's best golf course named Hudson. (Hudson National is 81st.) If you're talking about Trump Colts Neck, that's just a muni with a fancy clubhouse and high dues. If you're talking about Doonbeg in Ireland, you must be, as the Irish say, "thick as a plank."

Course raters for magazines are not allowed to give interviews, but I got a major American golf magazine rater to explain why Trump's American courses don't break an egg with them.

"They're mostly big boring Fazios," the rater says. "Whether it's Tom or Jim or the nephew (Tommy). But that's what Trump wants. He's a maximalist. The bigger, the better, the waterfalls. The other problem is the land they sit on isn't interesting. So when really new, interesting courses come along, like Bandon Dunes or Friar's Head, they're going to push the big, boring courses off the list. I mean, you look at his courses and there's not one that deserves it. Doral is only for the big Tour bombers now. Trump Jupiter is his best course in Florida, but it's not good enough. Trump Philadelphia is crap—way too steep. His courses in Charlotte, Washington, Hudson Valley, Colts Neck—those are all big yawners. Trump invited as many raters as he could get to Trump L.A. and that backfired because that course is a real piece of sh*t. Trump Ferry Point, though, is really good for a public course (95th on *Golf Digest*'s Top 100 Public Courses), but otherwise, no. No way."

There are a lot of lists, though, and as we've seen, sometimes a Trump course will find its way on one. The first time Bedminster made a list, there happened to be a press event there and his then-chairman of Bedminster, Ashley Cooper, stood up with a secret that he just couldn't contain any longer. With great pride, dressed in a beautiful summer suit, Cooper revealed that Bedminster would be showing up at No. 47 in the upcoming top American course rankings for *Golf* magazine. Cooper was practically bursting with pride.

Then Trump stepped up. "I know Ashley's happy we're 47th," Trump grumbled, "but I think 47th sucks."

Once, Trump was asked to make his own ranking. Which were the top 10 courses in the country, did he think? It read:

1. Trump Bedminster
2. Winged Foot
3. Trump Westchester
4. Trump West Palm Beach
5. Augusta National
6. Cypress Point
7. Trump Los Angeles
8. Oakmont
9. Trump Philadelphia
10. Pebble Beach

What? No Trump Ferry Point?

Trump's rankings-grubbing strategy has two prongs: (1) Lie about the greatness of his courses and (2) Rip everybody else's.

To wit:

Bandon Dunes in Oregon is America's purest golf destination. Set in the wilderness against breathtaking cliffs, waves, and sand dunes, it's all caddies and no carts, flabbergasting beauty, steak and whiskey and cigars around the outdoor fireplaces afterward. It might even have America's best par-3 course, a 13-hole jewel designed by Ben Crenshaw and Bill Coore, plus it has the Punchbowl, a rolling, football-sized putting course with waitresses in long gowns serving you cocktails as you gamble, laugh, and savor another perfect sunset.

Trump despises Bandon Dunes, saying it's set in a "vast wasteland." Up against his Aberdeen and Turnberry courses, he called it "a toy by comparison." Some toy. All four of Bandon Dunes courses were ranked in *Golf Digest*'s 2019–2020 America's Top 100 Courses: Pacific Dunes is 17, Bandon Dunes 36, Old McDonald 50, and Bandon Trails 69. There are zero Trump courses on the latest list.

But here's the funny thing: By all accounts, Trump has never *been* to Bandon Dunes. "I checked with a bunch of my guys up there," says architect Doak, "and not one of them had ever heard of him coming." I did the same. I go to Bandon once a year, and nobody I know who works there had ever seen Trump, either. "We have no record of him ever being here," says Michael Chupka, Bandon's director of communications.

Doak took it a step further. "I called a friend of mine who knows [Trump] and said, 'Hey, next time you see Trump, ask him if he's been to Bandon Dunes?' " The friend called back and reported, "Donald said, 'No,' but some of his friends have and 'they say it's nowhere near as good as Aberdeen.' So that tells you everything you need to know."

Trump doesn't do golf trips with buddies, and he rarely builds golf courses outside of the northeast or Florida or L.A. He's only got one American course outside of those areas—Charlotte—and anybody who lives in Charlotte will tell you he almost never goes there. You could tell that when he got up at a rally in Charlotte in the summer of 2018 and said that his golf course sat along the "largest man-made lake in the world, by far." Wrong, by far. His course sits along Lake Norman, which is not only *not* the world's largest man-made lake, it's not even among the top 10 biggest reservoirs in the U.S.

Trump likes golf courses the way he builds them and everybody else can turn theirs into parking lots. He likes lush green grass, big water features—"the more water, the better for Donald," Fazio says—and Pentagon-sized clubhouses anchored by 80-foot flagpoles. Nothing else will do.

Exhibit A: When they played the 2014 U.S. Open at the classic Pinehurst (NC) No. 2, Trump excoriated it in a tweetstorm:

I have numerous courses that are far superior to Pinehurst.

I'd bet the horrible look of Pinehurst translates into poor television ratings. This is not what golf is about!

To which longtime *USA Today* golf writer Steve DiMeglio added, wryly:

Maybe needs 1 of your waterfalls.

But here's the thing: Trump wasn't AT the U.S. Open. He was watching it on TV. He complained that the greens "looked terrible" on TV and it was a disservice to the game to have the Open on such a dump. But if you were there, you knew how sensational the setup was. The best greens do not necessarily look great on TV. The best greens are a patchwork of different grasses, a combination that produces the purest surface that rewards the truest putters. Sometimes that gives a green that looks a little brown on TV. It's the kind of linksy land golf was invented on, watered by the rain, mowed by hungry sheep, natural and true. But Trump hates it. What can brown do for Trump? Nothing.

Exhibit B: His waterfalls.

"Jesus, the waterfalls," says architect Jones. "I like waterfalls if they're natural. But the kind of phony waterfall he builds, I hate. It's artificial. It's in your face. It's Las Vegas. It's clownish. But it IS in keeping with his character."

As you stand next to Trump's 101-foot waterfall at Westchester, trying to putt, you find out it's very, very loud.

YOU: I think you're away.
FRIEND: What???
YOU: I THINK YOU'RE AWAY!!!
FRIEND: YES, IT IS A NICE DAY!

When Trump Los Angeles opened, it had a giant fake waterfall behind the first hole, thundering so loudly you wondered if a tsunami was coming. Worse, when you were done with the hole, the cart path brought you within inches of it, getting the passenger wet, as though you were playing Trump Splash Mountain. Yeah, you're wet, but you only have 17 more holes to go.

Trump insisted on a waterfall at West Palm Beach, too. He also has one at Trump Washington, an otherwise wonderful course, wandering as it does along the Potomac and among the ponds and bogs near it. It's just you, the eagles, and the wind on a really good golf course. Until, that is, you make the turn back to the clubhouse at 18, when, out of nowhere, a giant mountainous waterfall rears up behind the green. This thing is the Iguazu of Trump waterfalls. It pumps 25 gallons a minute and is so huge and fake that on the flattened top of it there's room for 200 guests to fit comfortably for weddings, of which there are dozens and dozens, members say.

"He's got a thing for the waterfalls," chuckles Fazio, who designed Trump Washington, D.C., with lots of input from Trump. "I remember he and I were on the site one day. There's a ravine behind the 18th green. And Donald hollers at [his contractor], 'Frank! Frank! I need a big waterfall here!'" Later, some of my people said, 'Tom you can't let him do this! It's going to look ridiculous!' And I told them, 'Are you nuts? He's the boss. As long as I get paid, I don't care.'"

Trump's taste is Early Whatever Reminds You He's Rich. When he gave me a tour of his Trump Tower apartment in New York City, the views were incredible, 270 degrees. But it all looked a little like Liberace's bathroom. Everything was dripping in gold, crystal, or white gold–trimmed crystal. I sat down at a beautiful white grand piano and asked if I could play. It was hopelessly out of tune. Clearly, nobody had played it in years. "Oh, man, he was SO pissed you said his piano was out of tune," reports *Sports Illustrated* writer Michael Bamberger, who has played golf nine times with Trump. "He was like, 'That sonofabitch Reilly said my piano was out of tune! That piano is NOT out of tune!'" He's probably right. I only play piano an hour a day. What would I know?

There was a huge, gold telescope in the corner of the apartment, pointing downtown. I looked through it and was amazed at its power.

"I watched the Twin Towers come down through that," Trump said over my shoulder.

I pulled my head away from the telescope and looked at him in shock. "Oh, my god," I said.

Trump nodded with pride and said, "Solid gold."

Greeting arrivals at nearly every Trump course is an Italian marble–belching over-the-top fountain, featuring four Poseidons, seven growling lions, and gallons of spouting water. It looks like it should be on Mike Tyson's lawn. "When he first put that in, we were all like, 'Oh, my god, how gaudy can you get?'" says Trump Washington member Gary Newman. "But now we don't even see it."

One thing you can't help seeing at Trump Washington is a Civil War memorial near the 14th hole, which overlooks the Potomac River. It reads:

The River of Blood

Many great American soldiers, both of the North and South, died at this spot, "The Rapids," on the Potomac River. The casualties were so great that the water would turn red and thus became known as "The River of Blood." It is my great honor to have preserved this important section of the Potomac River!

—DONALD JOHN TRUMP

It's a very nice monument except for one little problem: It didn't happen. No battle like that occurred anywhere near the monument. Three different Civil War historians confirmed the lie. That's when the fun started.

"How would they know that?" Trump replied when confronted by the *New York Times*. "Were they there?"

He's right, of course. Were you at Gettysburg? Then how do you know what Lincoln said? When the *Times* trotted out the names of its three prominent Civil War historians, Trump trotted out his own vague army of them. "I was told that by numerous historians," Trump said.

Fine. Names please?

Uh, well, he couldn't remember their names. Besides, he said, he hadn't talked to the historians himself. His team had.

Fine. Give us your staff names and we'll get their sources.

Trump refused. "Write your story the way you want to," he said. "But many people were shot there. It makes sense."

No, it's bullshit. I checked with Loudon County spokesman Glen Barbour, who looked into it and emailed that "the county was not aware of any historical significance on the property." That was just immoral. What Trump did next was illegal. He cut down 450 trees along the Potomac River, the better for his members to see it. That's illegal in Loudon County without permission, and nobody gave it to him, according to Barbour. He says the county was on a simple inspection there in 2010 when they discovered the tree-asco. They issued a stop-work order on any more changes, not to be lifted until Trump paid a hefty fine for cutting down all those trees, and restabilized the river bank. Bottom line? Trump got what he wanted without waiting and let his people sweep up the mess, as usual.

That little trick caused even more upheaval, though. By removing the trees, the Secret Service decided it gave snipers a clear shot. So they decided nobody could boat or canoe on the river while the president was on the course, which angered fisherman, companies that transport goods on the river, and local canoeists, who sued.

But the fibbing doesn't end there. Keep looking at that Civil War memorial for a second. Below you can see the Trump family coat of arms, which sports three lions and two chevrons on a shield below a gloved hand gripping an arrow. The motto reads, "Numquam Concedere"—latin for "Never Concede," truly Trump's philosophy.

It's a beautiful coat of arms, except for one small problem: Trump stole it.

It's actually the 80-year-old family crest granted by British authorities in 1939 to Joseph Edward Davies, the third husband of Marjorie Merriweather Post, the socialite who built Mar-a-Lago, now Trump's combo Winter White House/social and golf club. Trump made only one small adjustment to it—replacing the word "integritas" (Latin for "integrity") with "Trump." (Yes, he took out "integrity" and replaced it with "Trump." Some of this stuff writes itself.)

Mr. Davies was ambassador to Belgium and served as a special envoy for President Truman. Trump liked the Davies family crest and began passing it off as his own. He now uses it everywhere, on Trump golf towels, on Trump golf balls, even on the toilet paper in the luxurious men's room stalls at his clubs. Yes, the toilet paper has his name on it. Not sure he thought that one all the way through.

Trump never asked permission to take the Davies family coat of arms. If he had, he'd have had to call Davies' grandson, lawyer Joseph D. Tydings, a Democrat and former U.S. senator from Maryland. And what would Tydings have said? Take it. "You don't sue Trump," Tydings explains, "because you'll be in court for years and years and years." He talked his family out of suing Trump over the whole mess years ago. He told them it would be an endless and costly exercise. Still, he admits, his grandfather "would be rolling over in his grave to think Trump was using his crest."

Free to fly the fake family flag, Trump figured, "Why not take it to Scotland?" So he did. It turns out the Scots don't take family crests so lightly. It's a criminal offense to steal another family's coat of arms. Scots do not bullshit around about family crests. Scotland heritage authorities ordered Trump to cease and desist or face criminal charges. Trump sued, naturally, in 2007. Five years later, he lost and finally gave up, motto or no motto. He changed enough things on the crest to get around the law, including replacing the lions with a two-headed eagle (representing his Scottish and German roots) clutching golf balls. The two-headed eagle also happens to be the official crest of Russia.

Of course, Trump's European heritage isn't all that regal. His grandfather once owned a hotel in Canada that dabbled in prostitution.

Now *that* would be a family crest.

8

YOUR DAY IN TRUMPLAND

He who has the fastest golf cart never has a bad lie.
—MICKEY MANTLE

REALLY? YOU HAVE A tee time with the President of the Freaking United States?

Okay, brace yourself, because what you're about to experience isn't really golf. It's more of a para-military heavily armed exercise with odd-shaped sticks, using a vague set of rules that requires you to lose, and it will all be over very quickly so put your memory on "save."

First of all, you'll play at one of Trump's courses—since he's been president, he's played *only* at his own courses. He hasn't played once anywhere else, even at the only un-Trump course where he's a member: Winged Foot Golf Club in Mamaroneck, New York.

Me, I'd rent a car. Yours could get egged by protesters. With Trump spending so much time at his courses, thousands of Trump resisters have come to realize it's a great place to remind him how much they loathe him. As a result, the police blotters in Trump golf towns make fabulous Cheerios reading. For instance:

- A woman wrote a Spanish slur in lipstick on the entrance sign to Trump Los Angeles. The man she was with peed on it.
- About 200 activists laid down on the front lawn of Trump Los Angeles and formed a human-body message reading: "RESIST!"
- A woman took a cornfield near Trump Bedminster and carved into it the words "VOTE" and "TRUTH" in letters 60 feet high and 75 feet wide.
- Video posted by the *Washington Post* appeared to show at least four individuals in dark clothing using gardening tools to carve six-foot-tall letters into the green at Trump Los Angeles spelling out: "NO MORE TIGERS, NO MORE WOODS."
- A 61-year-old man named Cliff Tillotson, owner of a successful construction firm in Hawaii, was charged with turning Trump golf greens into a kind of giant message board. At four different Trump courses, Tillotson allegedly used a chemical to write into dozens of greens things like, "If Jesus came back tomorrow he wouldn't be an evangelical," "Product of too much Propecia" (a slap at Trump's use of a hair-loss drug), and an entire soliloquy from *Macbeth*. Personally, I've never had a putt over an entire Shakespearian soliloquy, but it has to be a *bitch* to read.

Every Saturday, the "People's Motorcade," as they call themselves, drives up and down outside the Bedminster gates carrying on with all kinds of anti-Trump signs and hijinks. There's the truck with an effigy of Trump in the back complete with a Pinocchio nose. Oh, and for the trips when Trump choppers in, they've laid out a giant "FU45" near the landing pad for his viewing pleasure.

Because Trump once planned to build a family mausoleum on his Bedminster property (he now wants to be buried at Mar-a-Lago), protesters are dying all over the place. One day, at a major intersection near the front gates, about 30 people held a "die in," laying on the ground, holding tombstones labeled with pre-existing conditions. A group called INDECLINE built an elaborate and extraordinary "Trump Cemetery" with realistic tombstones marking the deaths of "Decency," "The American Dream," and "The Last Snowman."

Anyway, I hope you get to play Trump Bedminster, in New Jersey, because there's nothing quite like it. Just to become a member can cost you up to $300,000. It was once the country estate of car tycoon John DeLorean, who would let his friend Jackie O ride her horse there among the pastoral hither and yon. It's 45 minutes from Manhattan and 10 exits past the fanciest place you've ever been. Its two courses are pretty good, the service is immaculate, and the interiors are just slightly more lavish than a sultan's dream. Enjoy the one-mile tree-lined driveway that takes you to a place that's a cross between Augusta National and the Paris Ritz, only with sniper towers.

It's literally true. When the 2017 U.S. Women's Open finished at Trump Bedminster that summer, Fox started dismantling its camera towers. *Hold on,* the Secret Service said. *We'd like to buy that tower.* Now, whenever Trump is at Bedminster, there are two snipers in that tower, one looking out toward the course, the other watching over the swanky compound that includes Trump's cottage (read: mansion), Ivanka's cottage (ditto), and eight other actual rental cottages (luxurious), all surrounding a fabulous pool, lounge, and, one imagines, people in togas peeling grapes for you.

Bedminster might be Trump's favorite place in the world. It has 36 holes, and unlike Mar-a-Lago, he doesn't have to drag the 10 SUVs, the Beast presidential limo, and the SWAT team over to Trump International to play. It's all right outside his front door. Ivanka and husband Jared Kushner spend lots of weekends at their cottage for the same reason. On Shabbat, they can simply walk the 100 yards to dinner without driving. Trump Bedminster is one of three official residences of the president—along with Trump Tower and Mar-a-Lago—which means Congress allotted $41 million in 2017 to its official protection. His 17-day vacation there in August of 2018 cost taxpayers over $3 million.

"Gotta be 300 Secret Service, Marines, SWAT, everything," the Bedminster car valet told me. "You know he's coming because you hear the choppers. There's always three—Marine One, Marine Two, and a Blackhawk—so nobody knows which one he's in. They land right over there." He pointed to a helicopter pad near the compound.

Q: Why doesn't Trump ever go to the legendary Camp David

in Maryland, traditionally the summer getaway spot for presidents and a place pre-set for security?

A: Because Camp David is for suckers. "Camp David is very rustic, it's nice, you'd like it," Trump said in an interview with a European journalist in 2017. "You know how long you'd like it? For about 30 minutes."

Okay, you're here. You'll be directed to the locker room to change shoes. With golf carts, almost nobody sweats anymore playing golf, so golf locker rooms are pointless except as a way to feel rich, and Trump very much wants you to feel rich. Trump locker rooms are spectacular. When you walk, the marble squeaks under your feet. Drink the Trump coffee (out of business) or the Trump vodka (out of business) or the Trump water (out of business). Sink deeply into the leather couches and eat some Trump nuts (out of business). Go find his locker. At every American Trump course I visited, he had one, sometimes full size, sometimes half, always locked. Sometimes, the clubhouse guys get so sick of guests taking selfies in front of it, they tape over the nameplate.

Now it's time to go hit a few warm-up shots on the practice range. This is where you'll see Trump for the first time. He'll greet you like a nephew greets his Lotto-winning uncle. He'll give you the big 20-second, pull-you-in handshake. The left hand will be on your right shoulder. He'll make you feel like a visiting king.

Trump is not big on practice. He'll whack a few and want to go to the first tee. If you're playing the Old Course at Bedminster, check out the cool plaque there. It reads:

This is the best design I've ever done.
—TOM FAZIO

Turns out the plaque misquoted him. "I don't believe I said it exactly like that," Fazio texted me. "It's kinda like him calling you the publisher of *Sports Illustrated*. Sounds better."

Bring your A game because you'll be playing with decent golfers. Trump doesn't suffer hacks. They take too long. If there's a politician in the group, he will almost certainly be a Republican. Through 2018, Trump hadn't played with a single Democratic member of Congress or state governor, despite reaming out Obama in a 2012 tweet for the same thing:

Obama should play golf with Republicans & opponents rather than his small group of friends. That way maybe the terrible gridlock would end.

You will not believe the security around you. There can be as many as 60 Secret Service agents, six SWAT guys, and 30 carts following along as you play, holding, among other things:

- The nuclear football
- The assistant chief of staff
- A doctor with vials of Trump's blood
- A communications staff member
- The secure satellite phone
- The one-man portable bomb shelter

- An entire supply of gas masks, machine guns, and weapons
- A small missile, which really speeds up play

"I couldn't believe what has to happen to get him around the course," says 1989 Open Championship winner Mark Calcavec-chia, who was teeing off one day at Trump International in Florida around the same time as Trump. "Just in front of the club, there was a fire truck, an ambulance, 10 black SUVs, police cars, dogs, everything. On the course, there were at least two Secret Service guys and at least one cart on every hole.

"Anyway, we finally teed off and he was about two or three groups behind us. We've got four holes left and now here he is, coming through us. They basically strip-searched us in the middle of the fairway. We all got patted down in case we had a gun out there. Anyway, we go into the dining room after. He was in there eating. I had to go through two or three detectors just to get to the dining room. I'm like, 'Hey, man, we were just searched on the course. What do you think happened in five holes?'"

The story goes that one day when Trump was playing Bedminster, a member hit an unspeakable hook not just deep into the woods but bound for I-78. As the caddy was looking for it, he suddenly found four machine gun barrels in his face, all held by camouflaged Marines. So, the perimeter is covered, in case you were wondering.

Yes, other groups can still play when the president is playing, as long as they're willing to stand down when he comes through, and he will come through. Trump plays breathtakingly fast—"When you pick up every putt within six feet, you can do that," says one caddy—and it means the vanguard of the Secret Service has to work faster. You'll be playing along at Bedminster when two Secret Service golf carts will come up quickly and stop you mid-6 iron.

"Gentlemen," the agent will say. "Will you please step to the side of the fairway? The president is coming through."

PLAYER: Sure. What hole is he on?
AGENT: 8.
PLAYER: But we're on 11.
AGENT, LOUDER: Yes. Will you please stand aside?

You won't have to wait long. Soon enough, Trump will come barreling through, charming and friendly, shaking everybody's hand, thanking them for waiting, asking them how their round is going. He'll even take pictures with you. "Just don't post it on social media," he'll say, and they've almost all complied.

Okay, time to quiet the knocking of your knees and hit that first shot. Not to worry, Trump will make it fun. Playing with Trump, everybody has fun. He'll pay attention to you. He'll ask a thousand questions. *How's business? How much you pay for that putter? You wanna sell it?* He'll give you tips and he'll know what he's talking about. *You gotta come more from underneath, like this!* You'll be answering his questions and working on his lesson and trying to keep up, and it will all be a big bowl of crazy.

Bill Clinton once said, "I love playing with him. He outdrives me on every single hole, but I forgive him."

Don't expect a lot of in-depth conversation with the president, though. Trump's golf conversations go about 7,000 yards long and one inch deep. Often, Trump and his caddy ride in their own cart and will always be way ahead of you, the better to kick, foozle, or throw his ball out of the cabbage.

"It's like a roller coaster ride," says author James Patterson, who belongs to both Trump Westchester and Trump International in West Palm Beach. "He's a good golfer. He's a real golfer. But we rushed around more than I would've loved. We were playing through people all the time. I hate playing through people. You're like, 'Sorry about this. Won't be but a minute. Excuse me.' I don't play well doing that."

Eruzione got to play with him on the day of Barbara Bush's funeral, the one Trump was or wasn't invited to, depending on which network you watch. Eruzione was just standing around the pro shop at Trump Jupiter when the president called up looking to see which celebrities might be hanging around. Trump loves playing with celebrities. David Trout, the Jupiter pro, named Eruzione. "Great!" Trump said.

Eruzione had a ball. "It was great. We played fairly quickly. We went through five or six foursomes." I've been playing golf 45 years and have never played through more than two foursomes in one round in my life. So five or six groups is triple warp speed.

Three and a half hours later—sometimes less—the round will be over and you'll have no idea what he shot or you shot but it'll be fun. I asked Eruzione how Trump played the day he played with him. "I don't really know. We only putted out on a few holes. He had a couple of presidential mulligans. He said that was his right.

He picked up putts. He's the president; he can do whatever he wants to do. We really played fast and then he left. He had to get right out of there and go watch the Barbara Bush service. So I have no idea what he shot. He'd play four or five holes even, then make a double bogey and then he'd pick up. His tee ball was a little erratic that day. He'd push it to the right. He's pretty good, though."

Now he'll invite you to the grill room for lunch. I wasn't with Trump, though, the day I played Bedminster, so I skipped lunch and went straight to the caddyshack.

It's actually not a shack at all, but a stately white one-story cottage near the first tee that's a doppelganger for the Eisenhower cottage at Augusta. Trump hasn't been invited to join Augusta, so perhaps this is his reasonable facsimile. Inside, a dozen guys in white overalls (also very Augusta) were watching a huge TV and eating free cheeseburgers whipped up by the resident caddy/cook, Scotty.

I love caddies because caddies will tell you the truth and use very few words doing it. A buddy of mine played awful one day in Ireland. He hit it all over the map. At the end of 18, he said to his caddy, "What do I owe you?" The caddy scowled at him and said, "A fucking apology."

I sat at the Bedminster caddy house kitchen table and threw out a question to nobody and everybody:

So what's it like working for Trump?

That sat them straight up in their seats.

"No cheating stories!" one caddy hollered out and everybody laughed.

"Mr. Trump is really generous," one caddy began. "Every time he comes in here, [he asks] how we're all doing, are we doing good, stuff like that. And he hands everybody a $100. Guys who aren't here are always like, 'Damn! I missed that?'"

A caddy over by the fridge wrinkled his nose.

FRIDGE CADDY: "Wait. You're saying every single time he comes in here he hands everybody hundreds? Because I've never once seen that."

FIRST CADDY: "Well, okay, not *every* time."

FRIDGE CADDY: "I mean, how many times has he even *been* in here?"

FIRST CADDY: "Well, at least once."

Everybody agreed Trump was a good player, an "8 or 9," they all said, knowing full well that he tells the world he's a 3.

Does he cheat?

There was a lot of sudden interest in birds out the window. One caddy held his hand up while looking me right in the eye. His expression was flat, but his eyes were very wide, like he was about to give me a clue on *Password*.

"Donald Trump never cheats," he said, slowly and sternly.

He stared at me.

Blink. Stare. Blink.

"Ohhh!" I said. "His caddy cheats FOR him?"

The entire room howled. What followed was a dozen or so stories about just HOW he cheats.

- "He's always got four balls in his pocket, if that tells you anything."
- "He foozles his ball on every hole. All 18. I promise you. Every hole."
- "He wants you to throw it out of the woods, kick it out of the rough, fluff up his lie. We all know the deal."

Most of them said they didn't mind doing it but felt a little bad when there was money on the line or a tournament going on.

"I have a friend at his course in Palm Beach," one caddy said, "a really, really good player. He's a +3 or +4 [that means he averages three or four strokes *under par*]. It kills him to do what you gotta do when you caddy for Trump. It absolutely *kills* him."

All the cheating Trump's caddies do for him actually hurts Trump's game. His only real weakness, besides the ethics bypass he seems to have undergone, is chipping around the greens, where he's just awful. That's why his caddies fluff up nasty lies, take his balls out of bunkers, and kick his ball onto the green out of the cabbage. But if you never have those lies, you never learn how to hit them. "Because of the caddies, he never gets to practice those hard shots around the green," says Ned Scherer, who has played with Trump at least 10 times and belongs to both Trump D.C. and Trump Jupiter. "Golf is all about practice, but he never even gets to try them."

Trump's caddy at Bedminster is almost always a very friendly Jamaican gentleman. People like to tell about the time Trump hit one in the pond. Everybody saw it splash a good 30 feet from shore. The Jamaican gentleman was forecaddying. When the group got up to the pond, the caddy says, "Boss, your ball is right here." It was sitting safely on grass. Somebody in the group yelled at the caddy, "What did you do with your mask and flippers?"

Like so much of what happens with Trump, the caddies were revolted by the immorality of the cheating but impressed by the genius of it.

"For a while he kept a can of red spray paint in his cart," one caddy said. "Whenever his ball hit a tree that he didn't think was fair, he'd go up and paint a big X on it. The next day, it was gone."

"That's true!" somebody else yelled. "It's like the mafia with him. You get the red X, you're dead."

It's a great gig, caddying at Bedminster, and none of them want to wreck it, which is why they're smart enough to keep their names out of this. They're also smart enough to keep up with the main two Trump caddy rules.

1. If you're caddying *for* Trump, keep the hell up.

The caddies say his golf cart—the #1—is rigged to go twice as fast as the rest. Keep up with him or put in your application at Chili's. "You gotta run. I mean you gotta sprint. Especially if you're forecaddying. We used to have this guy, he'd come in from 18 with Mr. Trump, run straight into that bathroom, and throw up. But he always made it."

2. If you're caddying *against* Trump, lose.

"Mr. Trump always takes the best caddy," an older caddy explained, "and he makes sure the guy he's playing against gets a shitty caddy or a brand-new caddy. We had this one guy, it was his first week, and it was a match with Mr. Trump and one of our best players versus these two guys from another club. The visitors got the new kid. But somehow, this kid got them around pretty good and it's all tied going into 18. Now, Mr. Trump is fuming. The kid has no idea he's about to get fired. No clue he's got a noose around his neck. But Mr. Trump's partner pulls it out and they end up winning, but, man, that kid came close."

Funny, though, the best Trump story I heard wasn't from a caddy but from a member who came up to me as I was looking at the tournament plaques on the locker room wall. Trump was listed as winner of the "Super Seniors Club Championship" three times, which, naturally, Trump counts in his 18 club championships. Super Seniors is usually defined as age 60 and over. He was also listed as the winner of the "Senior Club Championship" one time—50 and over. But on the regular "Club Championship" plaque, he wasn't listed at all. But there was another plaque, the "Bedminster Member-Member," and Trump's name was on that three times. A "member-member" is a two-man team tournament. It's usually a one-day deal, the team with the lowest best-ball score wins.

Anyway, this barrel-chested guy came up to me.

"You know how Donald got one of those?" he said.

No, but I'd sure like to.

"Okay, you'll love this. One year we were playing the Member-Member on the Old Course. But Trump wasn't in it. He and his buddy were just playing by themselves at the New Course. When they were done, he came in to the pro shop and asked what score won the Member-Member. They told him some number, net 61 or something. Whatever. And Trump goes, 'Oh, me and so-and-so played better than that today. So we actually won.' And the pro is like, 'I'm sorry?' And Trump tells them that he and his buddy should be the winners and the guy should put their names on the plaque instead. And that's how he won one of those Member-Members. Can you believe that?"

Yes. Yes, I can.

But you? You should definitely go to lunch with him, because it's the most unforgettable burger you'll ever have.

Take his lunches at Trump Washington. According to a waiter I spoke to there, the Secret Service always puts him at the corner table, a six-top. There are agents everywhere. There's an agent standing in each corner of the grill, too, with more scattered around the restaurant. There's even one with the chef, all morning, to watch where he gets the food and how he cooks it. "Mr. Trump always has a burger, every time," the waiter said. "He also likes to come for breakfast before his round."

Trump will order up a ton of fries, cheeseburgers, maybe some hot dogs, and lots of Diet Cokes. Anybody can come up and sit down. Yes, you heard that right. Anybody can come up to the president's table and have a seat, ask questions, shoot the breeze. Is this a great country or what?

Keep your ears open, because Trump will say nearly anything. It was at a post-round lunch early in his presidency when Trump told a group of Bedminster members the White House was "a fucking dump," a quote that made it into Alan Shipnuck's story on Trump in *Sports Illustrated*, caused a bit of a dustup, and was renounced by Trump in a tweet:

I love the White House, one of the most beautiful buildings (homes) I have ever seen. But Fake News said I called it a dump—TOTALLY UNTRUE

But a source inside Bedminster corroborates it. "This was just after he'd been elected," the source said. "He was having lunch and pontificating on this and that, about Paris (climate change) and how he'd kicked Hillary's ass and just everything. And then he goes, 'I can't believe I gotta live in the White House. What a fucking dump.'"

Keep your head on a swivel, too, because there's always insanity that comes with Trump on a golf day. Remember when Trump greeted 180 Harley Davidson cyclists as part of a bizarre pro-Trump anti-Harley Davidson rally? That happened outside the clubhouse at Bedminster. Remember that whole incident when a Breitbart reporter alleged that Trump campaign manager Corey Lewandowski grabbed her violently by the arm while she was trying to ask Trump a question? That happened at Trump Jupiter. Remember all those Cabinet-post interviewees who kept pouring in and out of meetings with Trump? That happened a lob wedge away from the first tee at Trump Bedminster.

Also, as long as you're on property, would you keep an eye out for the famous painting?

It's of Trump. It's six feet tall and was won by Melania at a charity auction for $20,000 (outbidding LPGA star Paula Creamer). It was one of those speed paintings. You know, it takes the guy six minutes and you think he's terrible and then he flips it right side up and there's—Jimi Hendrix! Except this one, painted in

September of 2016 by Michael Israel, was of Trump. The problem was Trump paid for it with $10,000 out of the Trump Foundation, according to the New York Attorney General's office, which is very illegal. If you buy a painting with charity money, it has to be used for charitable purposes—like for the wall of a hospital. But Melania bought it and hung it at Doral, according to the New York Attorney General's office.

There's another famous Trump painting that was never painted at all but still caused some teeth gnashing. After Trump won the election, three members of Winged Foot—where Trump has belonged since 1969—wanted to honor their member/president with a huge painting, to be hung in the clubhouse. "Three members out of 900, by the way," says Thomas Leslie, Winged Foot's president. "They wrote a letter to me saying they thought it was appropriate that the club put up a painting of Mr. Trump now that he was president." Leslie said thanks but no thanks. "I said that without taking any kind of political view on this, we only hang pictures of golfers who've won major championships here or those who were pros here." Left unsaid was that with the Men's U.S. Open coming to Winged Foot in 2020, the less ammo you can give the protesters, the better.

Okay. It's time to say goodbye. But before you go, look around for the famous American Academy of Hospitality Sciences Five-Star Diamond Award plaques every Trump club usually has. I've probably seen them at five different Trump courses.

These plaques are quite a rare honor—"another feather in our cap," as Trump told Mar-a-Lago members in an email once. Except the American Academy of Hospitality Sciences isn't really an academy and it isn't a science. It's just a guy named Joey (No Socks) Cinque and his secretary/girlfriend (No Nylons?) working out of Joey's apartment in New York.

Joey No Socks is quite a character. *New York* magazine says he survived a mob hit and was friends with mob capo John Gotti. New York police nabbed him selling stolen paintings and sculpture, to which Joey pleaded guilty but served no time. After his conviction, Joey bounced around until he came up with this academy beauty and started handing out these awards. Lo and behold, he struck up a friendship with Trump. Along the way, Trump has been named as a trustee, along with three Trump staffers, Trump's two sons, plus Joey's gal, and labor leader Ed Malloy, according to the *Chicago Tribune*. That could win you a lot of five-star diamond awards.

> JOEY NO SOCKS: OK, this meeting will come to order. First item of business: who should get our famed American Academy of Hospitality Sciences Five-Star Diamond Award this month? The chair recognizes Mr. Trump.
>
> TRUMP: I name Mr. Donald Trump!
>
> DONALD JR.: I second it!
>
> JOEY NO SOCKS: Done!

As of November 2017, former White House press secretary Anthony Scaramucci and Trump Bedminster General Manager David Schutzenhofer were still listed as "trustees."

Joey No Socks even stood next to Trump at his big 2017 New

Year's Eve election-win party at Mar-a-Lago. "There's nobody like him," Trump said back in 2009. "He's a special guy."

When asked about socializing with a convicted mobster, Trump said, "Hey, if a guy's going to give you an award, you take it. You don't tend to look up his whole life story."

Right. Why would a president want to do that?

Anyway, now it's *really* time for you to go. Hope you didn't steal anything. That's Joey No Socks in your rearview mirror.

9

MO TRUMP MO PROBLEMS

I like having friends, but I like having enemies more.
—DONALD J. TRUMP

THERE WAS ONCE A sleepy little town about an hour south of Los Angeles perched on palm-sweaty cliffs overlooking the blue Pacific called Rancho Palos Verdes. It was a wonderful place to take a nap. Most of the bars closed at 11:30—in the morning. With mostly rich, retired, Republican seniors living in it, Rancho Palos Verdes was about the most peaceful burg you might ever find in all of southern California.

Was, that is, until Donald Trump showed up.

It all started with a thunderous roar. "It sounded like this massive incredible rumbling," remembers singer Tom Sullivan, who lives there. "The ground was shaking under us."

But it wasn't an earthquake. It was the sound of a golf hole sliding into the sea. It was June 2, 1999, six weeks before the much-ballyhooed Pete Dye–designed Ocean Trails Golf Club was supposed to open. Most of the 496-yard, cliff-hanging 18th hole was just...gone. The project built by two brothers—Ken and Bob Zuckerman—was now officially screwed.

Eventually, they'd file for bankruptcy. A few years after that, riding to the rescue, came the new buyer, Donald J. Trump.

The town was delighted. This was 2002 and Trump wasn't a TV star then. All they knew was that he was an East Coast tycoon who jetted around on a 737 with his name on it, had fine spun-red hair, and was usually standing next to his latest knockout wife. They also knew he had a very thick checkbook and a love of golf and would probably rebuild the course in a swanky way. They immediately invited him to town to celebrate this wonderful new relationship. Only Rancho Palos Verdes had no idea they'd just gotten in the ring with a brawler.

Even as a kid, Donald Trump relished a good fight, sought them out, thrived on them. He was that very bad combination: very big and thin-skinned. He'd pull girls' hair. He'd pound his baseball bat into the ground. He'd bully smaller kids. "In the second grade I actually gave a teacher a black eye," he wrote in *The Art of the Deal.* "I didn't think he knew anything about music and I almost got expelled." He spent so much time in detention, he got the nickname "DT." Worse, no matter how much trouble he got in, Double Down always came back for twice as much.

At 13, his parents sent him to New York Military Academy, hoping it might smooth him out. It didn't. Donald came out of military school fists up. His thirst for scrapping can't be quenched. "My rule is when attacked, fire back 10 times harder," he once said. And he's not talking about for a while. He's talking forever.

Trump likes talking tough. Likes to tweet about kicking Joe Biden's ass. Likes to poo-poo NFL anti-spearing rules to protect players' brains as "ruining the game." Likes telling 1980 U.S. Olympic hockey hero Mike Eruzione that he liked the NHL better "when they didn't wear helmets." (To which Eruzione replied, "Without helmets, a lot of players you watch would be in the hospital today.")

Fistfights in golf are rare, but Trump likes telling about the time he punched a guy out at Winged Foot. "It was this big handsome asshole," Trump told me. "And he was just being a complete jerk! So I sink this putt on the ninth hole to win the match and then I turn and just coldcock him, just knock him out right there on the green!... They ended up suspending both of us. I was back off suspension after two weeks and he never got back in."

A couple questions: (a) How do you win a match on the ninth hole? (b) If Trump just suddenly swung and punched, why did the other guy get booted? (c) And why for good?

Besides, that's not how some people at Winged Foot tell it. "First of all, Trump is not well liked at Winged Foot," says member Bill Fugazy, who has known Trump for years and whose late father also knew him there. "He's just bad news to be around, a weird guy. It's hard for him to get a game. So when it happened, he was playing by himself.

"The turn there is on 10, not 9. So he goes into the bar to have a quick soda, then goes to the 11th hole. But the guys ahead of him were just getting on the tee. One of them goes, 'Donald, what do you think you're doing?' Trump goes, 'Playing through.' The guy goes, 'Yeah? Well, usually you ask permission for that. That's kinda rude.' Words were exchanged. Trump goes, 'Get the fuck out of my way.' This guy goes, 'Who you talking to?' Trump shoves him and leaves the course. He was brought in and suspended. The other guy wasn't suspended. Why should he be? He didn't do anything."

So no punch-out?

"Who's he gonna punch?" Fugazy says. "He's got tiny spongey hands. He couldn't punch anybody."

As Trump got older and started making too many millions to go around punching people, he decided suing them in court was the next best thing. It's another chance to fight and win. Even better, if he loses, he can always say it was rigged, or the judge was crooked, or Hispanic. Or he can settle and not have to admit he lost at all.

Trump loves suing like he loves red ties. He'll sue over anything: flagpoles, trees, hedges, fences, berms, neighbors' yards, roads, streets, sidewalks, taxes, fees, airplane noise, helicopter pads, property lines, university scams, water, drainage, unpaid bills, half-paid bills, too much rent, not enough rent, stolen deposits, zoning, the environment, courses he's built, courses he didn't, deals he made, deals he didn't, paintings of himself, donations, schools, his announced net worth, and his *actual* net worth. He's sued friends, enemies, partners, and rivals. Trump has sued and been sued by just about everybody. According to *USA Today*, as of mid-2016, Trump had been part of more than 3,500 lawsuits in his life. That's almost 50 lawsuits a year, since birth.

Don't most sports billionaires tangle themselves up in that many lawsuits? Isn't that just part of the game at that level? "Not me," says Mark Cuban. "In my whole life, I've been sued twice, I think."

Poor little Rancho Palos Verdes had no idea about any of that when Trump showed up to their packed town hall to celebrate this new and imperfect union of town and golf course. Trump walked to the podium to cheers and immediately gave the citizens a hint of the fuckery to come.

He started with a reference to the last course he'd rebuilt—Trump Westchester in New York. "If you had called the mayor of Briarcliff Manor five years ago and asked him, 'Whaddya think of Trump?' his answer probably wouldn't have been not so great [*sic*]. We were fighting them really hard. But if you call him now, he'd say it's the finest relationship they've ever had....Everybody in the town loves us."

That would've been news that day to then-mayor of Briarcliff Manor, Bill Vescio, considering Trump has barely ever stopped suing his 38,000-person town, or insulting him on Twitter, or telling people not to vote for him since the day he bought the place. As I write this, Trump is suing the town again, this time over taxes.

That moment at the podium in Rancho Palos Verdes was the start of 16 years of chaos—Trump versus Rancho Palos Verdes, a 10-round knockout fight.

Round 1: Trump v. Schools

Turns out, much to Trump's surprise, he hadn't quite bought the entire golf course. Some of it—basically the 15th hole—still belonged to the Rancho Palos Verdes (RPV) school district. Without it, Trump would have a back eight.

Trump flipped. He started calling the superintendent of schools at the time, Ira Toibin, to tell him how unfair it was and how they'd hidden this information from him and how he might sue and how they needed to fix this immediately, if not sooner. He'd call Toibin at home, work, everywhere. "I must've had six personal phone calls with Mr. Trump," says Toibin, a very buttoned-up sort of man who, at press time, was again the RPV school superintendent. "He hadn't read the paperwork. It was such a lucrative deal, he hadn't really read it. He didn't know who we were at all. He kept wanting to negotiate [a buyout] with me. But I kept saying, 'I don't negotiate, Mr. Trump. I have our attorney do that for us.'"

That attorney would become a pain in Trump's famous neck. He was the school district's very determined Milan Smith, who wound up publicly calling Trump "arrogant" and "pompous."

"I have never had any contact with any human being who appears to be so self-absorbed and so impressed with himself," Smith told a tiny beach paper called *The Easy Reader*. "He's kind of like a big bag of wind."

One time, Trump got up at an RPV town meeting and called Smith an "obnoxious asshole." In this sedate little town, these were words that you just never heard. Wait until the book clubs heard about it! But calling Smith an "obnoxious asshole" turned out to be a very bad idea for Trump, since The Obnoxious Asshole is now a federal judge on the Ninth Circuit Court of Appeals, the body that overturned Trump's first Muslim-country travel ban.

Trump's complaint was that Smith wanted too much for the missing land—$5 million. Trump wanted to pay $1 million. Smith was as immovable as an Easter Island statue. So Trump kept calling Toibin.

"He'd call and yell at me, using a lot of swear words. [Toibin doesn't swear, so you'll have to fill in with your imagination.] 'You _____ guys are trying to rip me off! It's not worth _____ $5 million! Come to New York and _____ negotiate with me!' I kept telling him, 'Donald, this money will go to kids' educations, to kids' facilities. Plus, the state will match it. So it's $10 million for the kids. Think of it as a donation."

"This is 'Trump-change' for him," Smith said, knowing perhaps that nobody can run a golf course shaped like a donut. In the end, Trump paid the $5 million. But he never forgot it.

Round 2: Trump v. Patriotism

Trying to stiff school kids will get you some nasty PR in a small town, but Trump bounced back with a great idea: patriotism. Trump is very good at clubbing people over the head with his patriotism. (*See: NFL.*) He immediately put up a 70-foot flagpole in front of his clubhouse with a flag that could nicely cover Mount Rushmore. Giant flag poles are a standard trick Trump uses at his clubs. When he first tried it, at Mar-a-Lago, he complained that he absolutely had to have a massive flagpole because, as his attorneys wrote, a smaller one "would fail to appropriately express the magnitude of Donald J. Trump's...patriotism." Just so you know, Donald J. Trump's patriotism is exactly 100 feet high. One hundred and ten feet? No.

Rancho Palos Verdes was almost entirely Republican, but this mother of all flagpoles was just way too much and well over the city's allowed limit. The city told him to cut it down to 26 feet or get rid of it. Trump refused. It went to the city council for debate.

That sound you just heard was the trap door slamming. Trump ran, not walked, to the papers to complain that the city was infringing on his patriotism. *What kind of country is this where they make a man feel bad for putting up an American flag?* And it's true, nobody is more patriotic than Donald Trump, except for perhaps when there's a military draft going on. The city looked bad. The town split in two over it, with the giant-flag crowd far outweighing the but-that's-ridiculous crowd. They let Trump keep the pole, and the flag, just like it was.

Only RPV city councilman Steve Wolowicz, a lifetime Republican, seemed to get what was happening. "I have to offer congratulations to all of us," he said, "for providing the very type of publicity that a real estate developer seeks."

Round 3: Trump v. Laundry

It started with Tiger Woods. In 2007, the actor Michael Douglas was holding an annual celebrity pro-am tournament and schmoozefest at Trump Los Angeles, and they said Woods was going to show up. That's when Trump took a look at the distant houses 360 yards from the tees at his practice range and decided they were very ugly. He had a long row of 10-foot-high ficus trees planted in front of them so nobody would have to look at the houses while hitting their practice shots—not Tiger, not Douglas, not Catherine Zeta-Jones, nobody. The problem with the trees is that they blocked the homeowners' views of the ocean, a view they'd paid dearly to have. Trump's people said it was just temporary, but long after the tournament, the ficus trees were still there.

Complaints started pouring into the city. The council decided to meet with Trump about it—at the "ugly" houses themselves. Yes, Trump would be going *inside* these homes.

The whole gaggle walked from the Trump Los Angeles driving range to the eye-offending abodes and the view-blocking trees. Along the way, Trump called these very expensive, ocean-front, gated homes "horrendous" and "ugly" and "awful." Then he walked into the backyard of the one belonging to a resident named Jessica Leeds. There were towels drying on the balcony railing from a recent trip to the beach. With Ms. Leeds standing there, Trump said, "Your house looks like shit." Also: "This house is ugly. My customers shouldn't have to look at your ugly house." I don't know about you, but if I ever talked that way to somebody inside their house, my mom would've whacked me with a frying pan. Yet nobody stopped Trump, nobody upbraided him, nobody made him apologize. It was all too awkward for polite little Rancho Palos Verdes.

They said a lot more at the next council meeting. One man got up at the meeting and said, "Since purchasing this property, the Trump Organization has done what they want, how they want and when they want it with complete disregard for its governing authorities."

The council voted unanimously to force Trump to take down the trees. Even Trump's Winnebago full of lawyers couldn't fix it. Trump lost and issued his standard quote for such occasions: "We've been treated very unfairly."

The whole tree trick is SOP for Trump golf. At his Doral resort, more than 2,500 residents complained that Trump had put up high trees that blocked their views. Some of them got so mad they started ripping them apart at night. Trump sued five middle-class Doral homeowners who bordered his property for $15,000 each.

"There are behaviors in people's backyards that are inconsistent with a world-class set of golf courses like Donald Trump is attempting to create," a Trump spokesman said. That must've been a great surprise to the neighbors. They had no idea they were part of a world-class set of golf courses. Come to think of it, they weren't. They had zero to do with it. Most of them didn't even play golf. What were their horrible behaviors? "Playing music, drinking alcohol, and hanging out undergarments on their clotheslines."

The nerve.

Round 4: Trump v. Dead People

The way Trump sees it, you can't very well play Trump National Golf Club Los Angeles and drink Trump bottled water and buy Trump golf balls unless you drive up Donald Trump National

Drive first. He wanted to rename the road leading to his club from Ocean Trails Drive to that name, but the city had rules about that kind of thing. You had to be dead to get a street named after you, and by all accounts, Trump was not dead. Trump sued, because Trump is very serious about putting his name on things.

The squabble over the street was stirred into a whole other bubbling cauldron of trouble...

Round 5: Trump v. Homes

Trump had a desire to start building lots of homes on his property, which wasn't part of the deal. The city rejected him. Trump sued for $100 million, accusing the city council of fraud and violating his due process. The council, exhausted and Trump-weary, decided to try a new tactic. Give in on half his demands and hold fast to the ones that really matter, and maybe, somehow, he'll take that as a win. On this case, he did. He got his eponymous road, but lost on the houses.

Round 6: Trump v. Time

When you go to any Trump golf property, you'll notice there are always a gazillion framed articles and magazine covers about...(wait for it)...Trump. But not long after Trump Los Angeles opened, a *Washington Post* reporter noticed something odd at the club. There was a *Time* magazine Man of the Year cover with Trump's picture on it. Except it was fake. The date on it was March 1, 2009, a date *Time* didn't publish a magazine. The closest magazine to that date had Kate Winslet on the cover. Trump had never been Man of the Year. It seemed very unfair. He tweeted:

The Time Magazine list of the 100 Most Influential People is a joke and stunt of a magazine that will, like Newsweek, soon be dead. Bad list!

Once the fake Man of the Year cover was discovered at Trump Los Angeles, people started reporting fake Man of the Year covers at other courses—five of his clubs in all, including clubs in Scotland and Ireland. Trump's people ended up taking them all down, but why? Shouldn't winning 18 fake club championships automatically win you fake *Time* Man of the Year?

Round 7: Trump v. Taxes

Some people like to drive to Cape Canaveral for rocket launches. I like to watch Trump tell people what he's put into his golf courses. It's classic Trump Bump.

It usually starts at $100 million. "I'm putting $100 million into this course," he'll say. "By the time I'm done, it'll be the most expensive course in the world." Then it will balloon. Soon it will be "$150 million," then "$200 million," and eventually it'll top out at "$250 million," although he once said he put "$325 million" into Trump Aberdeen. If you paved every fairway in gold, and lined the cups with diamonds, you couldn't spend $325 million on a golf course.

At Trump Los Angeles, Trump worked his way up to "$264

million" sunk into the course. That's a lie so full of hot air it could float the *Queen Mary*. Course appraiser Larry Hirsh actually LOL'd when I told him the $264 million figure. "I guess anything is possible," he said. "But for somebody to put $264 million into a golf course would be a very, very big challenge." Saying you put $264 million into a golf course is like saying you went to the fridge and made yourself a $50,000 sandwich. We know it's a lie because not long after Trump announced the $264 million figure, his lawyers were suing the L.A. County Assessor's office for its assessment of the course. They said it was only worth $10 million. So, Trump was only off by $254 million.

Round 8: Trump v. Dye

The only problem with Trump Los Angeles is that it sucks. It's a monotonous layout. It's back and forth, forth and back, every hole but one running parallel to the ocean, every ball bouncing toward the ocean, every putt breaking toward the ocean, until, eventually, you want to jump in the ocean. And that doesn't even count the three horrid waterfalls it opened with. Once you play it, you'll see why the LPGA only played one year on it and bolted.

"I only played 14 holes of it," says Scottish golf architect David McLay Kidd, who designed Bandon Dunes. "I got so tediously bored that I walked in. It's narrow. It's blind. It's contrived.... Donald Trump's answer is always spend more money, build more, more cart paths, more waterfalls. Sometimes what's required is restraint."

That might be why Pete Dye, the original designer, made Trump take his name off the course.

"I met with Mr. Trump and we discussed his branding and redesign concepts for Ocean Trails," says Perry Dye, Pete's son. "We 'agreed to disagree'—as is now very hard to do with President Trump....He wanted waterfalls....We felt that...was unnecessary, as all 18 holes already look at the Pacific Ocean and Catalina Island."

It doesn't help, either, that a single round at Trump Los Angeles costs $300.

Trump is right though: The views of the Pacific are incredible. Luckily, the California Coastal Commission forced Trump to keep the hiking trails in and around the course open, so you can see it all for free.

Round 9: Trump v. Charity

On the official website for Trump Los Angeles, there used to be a page telling you how Trump Los Angeles had given over $5 million to charity since their opening. There was a list of over 200 causes it had donated to, and, hey, wouldn't the world be a better place if we all opened our hearts and wallets like Trump L.A.?

The only problem was they actually hadn't donated anywhere near $5 million. In a lengthy investigation, NPR could only document $800,000 in donations, and most of that was free rounds and free brunches.

In fact, of the 200 organizations the club listed, 17 said they couldn't find any record of a donation of any kind from the club, and 26 others couldn't be proven one way or the other. Many of them weren't even charities at all, like the LAPD Homicide Bureau.

Here you go, boys—free fingerprint kits. On us!

Some didn't exist at all—Downed Officers Fund, Sing for the Heart, Simply Not Simple. Those were listed, but they were all fake. So somebody was zooming somebody.

The Trump Organization did not return calls to NPR or to me on this subject, but did take out the bogus $5 million claim and 86'd the list.

Round 10: Trump v. Women

Like his golf courses and clubhouses, Trump wants everything to be a 10, including the women he employs at them, according to a lawsuit filed by women who worked at his course in Rancho Palos Verdes.

According to them, Trump insisted on "good-looking women" to hold down his hostess stands and his waitress jobs. "I had witnessed Donald Trump tell managers many times while he was visiting the club that restaurant hostesses were 'not pretty enough' and that they should be fired and replaced with more attractive women," swore Hayley Strozier, who was the director of catering at the club until 2008. That was backed up by restaurant manager Sue Kwiatkowski, who said that one time, he took her aside and said, "I want you to get some good-looking hostesses here. People like to see good-looking people when they come in."

He likes them to be young, too, according to Lucy Messer-schmidt, a then-hostess who said she got yanked from the schedule whenever Trump was on the premises. Stacia Solis testified that younger, prettier waitresses would be assigned to serve Trump's table, even if they weren't the best. One male employee testified he never saw a male waiter serve Trump. One female supervisor refused to fire a female employee even though her boss said Trump wanted her gone because she was "fat."

Trump settled that mess for $475,000, though he admitted no guilt.

So, 15 years later, after all the lawsuits, nastiness, and Excedrin headaches, how does the very Republican enclave of Rancho Palos Verdes, California, feel *now* about Donald Trump?

Well, in 2008, it voted for John McCain, in 2012 for Mitt Romney, and in 2016, overwhelmingly, for Hillary Clinton.

10

ONE GOOD PUNCH

My whole life is about winning. I don't lose.
—DONALD J. TRUMP

FOR DECADES NOW, THE golf world has known something about Trump that the rest of the world is just finding out. Yes, Trump is a very big dealmaker, but he's an even bigger deal breaker. Doesn't matter what he's said to the press or what he's signed or what he's shaken on, when it comes time to pay up, he can flip like a weathervane.

That moment will be the crucible for you. That's when you'll find out if you can be shaken down or find the guts to stand up to him. Whether you're the chancellor of Germany or a wallpaper guy, that moment with Trump can make or break your company, your career, your life. It's happened in golf a hundred times. Some rise to it, others get buried by it.

At Trump Westchester, the architect who designed the

55,000-square-foot clubhouse, Andrew Tesoro, had it happen to him, and it threatened to kick a very big hole in his life.

Tesoro was a 50-something architect on Columbus Circle in New York City, a single dad of an adopted son. At first, he thought it was kind of cool to be working for Trump. "I can remember one time, I brought my son out with me to the course," Tesoro said. "He was maybe five. Donald saw Victor and was kind enough to give him a lesson. He put a little kiddie club in his hand—you know, a cut-down regular golf club for kids—and showed him how to swing it. Victor was so excited. But then Trump took the club back. Victor started crying. He wanted to swing the club. I tried to tell him, 'He was only loaning the club to you, son'—but five-year-olds aren't that good at understanding loans. It really irritated Trump, my son crying. He turned away from us, handed the club to one of his lackeys, and walked off. I learned that about him. He's not patient with kids."

Pretty soon, Tesoro noticed that Trump wasn't all that patient with bills either. Trump kept paying $10,000 invoices with checks for $6,000. Tesoro just figured it was some kind of accounting system he didn't understand and kept working. "Many people told me, 'Inflate your bills because Trump will chisel you.' I didn't do that because I'm a fair and honest guy. My way of doing business is to treat people with decency and figure they'll treat you that way back."

Big mistake.

By the time he got to the end of the job, Trump still owed him well over $100,000 in unpaid bills. Tesoro went to Trump's main point man on the golf project and complained. The man told him to come to the clubhouse the next day and meet with two of the managers Tesoro knew well and they'd settle up. "They'll chisel you down, but they'll settle," the guy said.

So the next day, Tesoro came by himself and walked into the clubhouse he'd designed. But it wasn't just Tesoro meeting with two staffers. There were 40 people in the lobby. All the vendors were there, from the tile guy, to the electrician, to the landscaper. "And it wasn't two people we were going to meet with, it was 15 administrators and lawyers, all there to gang up on the little guys."

Tesoro put his name on the clipboard and waited. At last, he was called into a big boardroom with all the suits around a big table, 30 eyebrows furrowed. He took his chair. They got out a big stack of papers and went through all his bills, one by one. "I remember one bill was for something like $2,147 for bathrooms. The guy looks at it and goes, 'Well, you should've known a bill for that much wasn't going to please him.'"

Hey Visa, why'd you send my husband a bill for $2,147? You must've known that wasn't going to please him.

In the end, Trump's people offered him 40 cents on the dollar—$56,000 on a bill of over $141,000—take it or leave it. They said he could sue, sure, but they'd tie him up in court for seven or eight years and he still might not get it. Welcome to Trumpland. Tesoro said he needed time to think. He went home and stewed about it. He wondered how he could keep his business going if he was fighting Donald J. Trump in court for the next seven years.

"I didn't want to fight. I wanted to be an architect." A few days later, he sent Trump a bill for a flat $50,000. He still didn't get paid.

This time Tesoro went straight to Trump himself. Trump greeted him in his Trump Tower office like a returning astronaut. "How's the best architect in the world?" Trump said with a big handshake and smile. "Have a seat!"

Finally, Tesoro asked him, flat out, "Why don't you pay me?" Trump explained to Tesoro how the project cost too much and took too long. Tesoro wondered how that was his problem. Trump stood up, offered his handshake, and said he'd give him $25,000, and otherwise, he could go talk to Bernie, his lawyer, down the hall.

In the end, Tesoro took the $25,000—18% of what he was owed.

"I got snookered," Tesoro says. "I'm pretty savvy, but I got conned and snookered. When I see [Senator] Lindsey Graham and members of Congress kissing his ass over stuff they know isn't right for the country, I don't blame them. He makes fools of people. I know how persuasive that man is now."

It was all rancid water under the bridge until Tesoro was taking Victor to school one day and a mother said, "You should go public with your story." Tesoro wanted no part of it, but she kept bugging him. Finally, he agreed. Next thing you know, he was on a "Hillary Clinton for President" TV ad—the architect who got stiffed by the Republican nominee for president.

"I got thousands of emails, Facebook comments, phone calls from strangers, everything, mostly supportive and sympathetic," Tesoro says. "Maybe 10% were like, 'Oh, you were probably trying to rip him off.' That's what some people think. People would call me to say they were still going to vote for Trump. Some called to say they weren't going to vote for Trump. But I wasn't paid a dime to do it and, what's more, I never got an ounce of work out of it."

The money Trump shorted him not only robbed young Victor of money that would've sent him to a school he wanted to go to—Yale or Princeton—but time, too. "He [Victor] didn't get much attention from me through all of this," Tesoro says, a little regretfully. "I spent so much time trying to fight Trump that I had a terrible year in business and didn't get to pay much attention to my son in his last year of high school. But Victor understands. He gets it. At one point, he said, 'You know, Dad, that Trump guy is kind of like Hitler.' And I said, 'No. That's taking it too far.' But now, after seeing him as president, I think my son might be closer to the truth than I thought."

Then there was a young lawyer named Brad Edwards.

In a tiny office, in a gentrifying section of Fort Lauderdale, Edwards was handed a case that made his eyes bug. It involved Trump Jupiter golf club and, to Edwards, it seemed too good to be true.

It all started when Trump bought the debt-plagued Ritz-Carlton Jupiter golf resort and transformed it into Trump National Golf Club Jupiter. It was a killer buy—$5 million for a nice Jack Nicklaus course and clubhouse with 400 members in America's ritziest golf address.

There was only one tricky part—Trump also got $51 million in an odd kind of debt—deposits the club owed to members, who had each put up whopping initiation fees, some up to $200,000, for an equity membership. (An equity club means the members own it. A nonequity club means the developer owns it.) That means they could get their money back when they quit, as long as there was a buyer to take their place, and there was always going to be a buyer, everybody figured. After all, it's Jupiter.

Now that $51 million is absolutely untouchable to the new owner of an equity club. You can put it in a CD and get 1% or 2% interest, but you are not ethically allowed to speculate with it, use it for your own purposes, borrow it, spend it, use it for condos, put it into your jet, nothing. Hands off, as written in the contract.

Except in TrumpWorld.

In his first big meeting with his Jupiter members, Trump held a town hall, laid on the charm, and fired up the boaster oven. He said he was going to create the "best club in America" on the "best piece of land" in all of Florida, and pretty soon you'll be at the most "sought-after" so on and so forth. Oh, and one more little thing, you're not going to get your initiation fee back. I'm putting all $51 million into the course.

That one sentence made the members sit up straight in their chairs. There were about 150 in that room who were already on the list to sell their memberships. They'd signed a deal saying they could. And now this billionaire was just going to walk away with their $51 million?

It got worse. Trump then wrote everybody a letter: "If you

choose to remain on the resignation list—you're out [of the club]." Not only were you out—meaning you couldn't play golf at the club, eat at the club, drink at the club, set foot on the grounds, or even look over the hedges—but you'd STILL have to pay your monthly dues until your membership could be replaced. Most private golf clubs add 25 or 30 new members a year, so that meant the last guy on that list might wait five years to get his money back and still have to pay his dues every month—for nothing.

No way that would stand up in court. It was just an empty threat. They had a written contract, and nowhere did it say they were out of the club for getting on the resignation list. Who would be scared by that?

Answer: Most of them.

The thought of having to sue Donald Trump and his small stadium of lawyers scared the pee out of them. Most went along with Trump's shakedown. They forked over their huge deposits and joined Hurricane Trump.

The remaining 65 lawyered up in the form of a class-action suit brought by Edwards, who not only didn't flinch at having to go up against Trump, he licked his lips.

"I try a lot of cases," Edwards said. "A lot of really difficult cases. But it's rare when you get such a slam-dunk. It just looked—impossible to lose."

Trump's coterie of lawyers tried the usual stall tactics, paper threats, and time-wasting motions. None of it worked. These 65 members had enough money they weren't going to run and hide. It went to a hearing. Edwards flew to New York and deposed pre-president Trump, who said, basically, "Nope. I'm reading

the contract differently. I read these deposits as nonrefundable."
This would be like looking at a cow and saying, "Nope. I see a
chicken." How was that possible when it read right in the contract that they got their money back?

"I really don't know," Edwards says.

He deposed Eric Trump, the titular president of the Trump
Organization, who said no, no, no, he hadn't revoked their membership, that they were still allowed to use the club. That was not
true. They all had emails from the club telling them they couldn't
be on the property. Their gate transponders were turned off. Their
head pro told them they couldn't play the course. The only part
of the club they still had access to was their monthly bill. Besides,
Eric's father had already said in deposition that these members
were banned. He described them as "angry people."

Donald reasoned that these members couldn't be around
because, "You're probably not going to be a very good club member. You're not going to be so happy." Apparently, seeing somebody else walking around with $200,000 of your money puts
people in a bad mood.

With all those emails and letters as evidence, Trump was
deader than Bob Hope on this case, and yet he kept fighting. But
why? For a lousy $6 million in dues? When he'd already pock-
eted $45 million in one meeting? That's a pretty good deal, right?

Nope. Good was not good enough for Trump.

Edwards didn't just beat him. He beat him twice. A judge
ruled in February 2017, and again on appeal in January 2018,
that Trump owed the members $4.7 million in dues, plus interest
and legal fees, for a total of $5.4 million. That's not a settlement.

Edwards won a verdict. A young lawyer from a tiny firm next to a taco stand in Fort Lauderdale had just won $5.4 million from the standing president of the United States.

"In the long run, though, Trump had already won," Edwards says, looking back on it all. "He bought this gorgeous club for $5 million. He snapped his fingers and turned $45 million of debt into an asset. It was a great business move. But he just wouldn't quit. And it just taught everybody that even when there's a class of people who were right—and they were clearly right—Trump is a fighter who's gonna fight to the very bitter end, no matter what. You don't just have to beat him, you have to beat him three or four times. You have to keep beating him even as he's laying on the ground because he'll get up and fight some more. The guy will never, ever quit."

Meet Juan Carlos Enriquez.

The bulk of the painting for Trump's re-do of the Doral golf resort in Miami was done by his small mom-and-pop business, The Paint Spot, run by Enriquez and his family. It was a monster job, worth well into six figures.

When he was done, Trump still owed him the final payment, about $30,000. It didn't come and it kept not coming. Enriquez wore out the little door on his mailbox looking for it. Two years went by—no $30,000. You think when Trump talked about the Forgotten Man, he meant Enriquez?

Now, Trump could find $30,000 in the cushions of his 757, but for Enriquez, that was a big chunk of his yearly gross. It was an eight-month job and people had to get paid. "I got three girls, a wife, 10 employees, my brother. I had to get my money," says Enriquez, the son of Cuban immigrants. "People who don't pay leave a bad taste in my mouth."

But Trump wouldn't cough it up. "I've paid enough," Trump told him.

Dear First National,

Stop sending me notices on my car loan. I've paid enough.

Enriquez offered to settle for $26,000. "I don't settle," Trump said.

So the painter took a big gulp and sued Donald J. Trump, soon to be president of the United States.

"I mean, if you're right, you're right," Enriquez says. "So I was 95% sure I was going to win. But the lawsuit kept dragging on and on. The legal bills grew to be 10 times the disputed amount. If I lost, I was going to have to close up shop. It would've been over $400,000. Where am I gonna get $400,000?"

Finally, in 2017, after three years, Enriquez won. Naturally, Trump's lawyers appealed. More sleepless months. Finally, Trump lost the appeal, too, and Enriquez pocketed well over $300,000, most of which went to his lawyer.

But get this. In between, Enriquez actually voted for Trump. "Hey, business and politics are two different things," he says. "I think he's doing what he said he was going to do."

Painters weren't the only people who were stiffed at Doral. There were also the 48 servers who worked a Passover event there and were stiffed between $800 and $3,000 each for over-time. Trump, who "never settles," settled.

"That's nothing new," says former Palm Beach County commissioner Shelley Vana. "We heard of so many vendors who said he didn't pay them. Everybody was saying it. 'Watch out. He doesn't pay his vendors. Be careful.'"

Trump even tried to stiff a guy who made a $1 million hole in one. At a charity tournament at Trump Westchester, a Wall Street tycoon named Marty Greenberg stepped to a tee box that was advertising a $1 million prize to anybody that made an ace there. Greenberg did it. Except Trump's insurance company said, "Nope. The hole had to be at least 150 yards. It was 139." They refused to pay. Trump refused to pay. Greenberg sued. Trump settled for $158,000.

This is where it gets worse. Trump still wouldn't pay it. Instead, he paid it out of the Donald J. Trump Foundation account. What does the Trump Foundation have to do with this, you ask? Absolutely nothing. That was self-dealing and illegal and incurred the Trumps a fat fine, on top of the $158,000, and a few years later, became one of the reasons the Trump Foundation was shut down for good by the New York Attorney General's Office.

But surely lots of golf course/real estate tycoons must have to stop payment and sue constantly, right? With so many contractors to deal with?

"Never," says David Southworth, an American golf course developer in the same league with Trump. "Not once."

Not once? In how many years?

"Twenty-seven," he says. "We've never not paid someone. We've never stiffed anyone. We've certainly had discussions over time with people, we've never just stopped paying them."

Have you ever heard of any other developer doing it?

"No," he says. "But I've been hearing that about Donald for a long time. There must be some merit to it. I hear it enough."

Mike Meldman is on Trump's level. He's the owner of Discovery Land Company, a fantabulous collection of more than 20 fun, unusual, and hip golf courses where rock music is played at the practice range, the snack shack might be a surfboard with legs, and a tequila shot comes just before your tee shot on 18. Places like Gozzer Ranch in Idaho (Wayne Gretzky is a member), Madison Club in La Quinta, California (John Elway), and El Dorado in Cabo San Lucas (George Clooney and Cindy Crawford). Not only does he always pay up, but sometimes he forgets to *stop* paying. His golf-architect bonuses are happy legend. Tom Fazio completely stopped working for Trump a long time ago, but he almost never turns down Meldman. Fazio has a set handshake deal with him: $1.5 million to design a course in the U.S., $3 million to design one out of the U.S., and zero interference from the boss. No muss, no fuss, no weekends.

(The first time Meldman met Trump, he was introduced by Fazio. Trump was just starting to get into golf development. The ever-needling Fazio said, "Donald, this is Mike Meldman, the Donald Trump of golf. This is who you think you are and who you wanna be. But you'll never be him.")

So, Mike Meldman, in your 30-plus years of building golf resorts, have you ever stopped paying anybody?

"No, not once. Not ever."

Ever sue or been sued?

"Maybe...twice?"

"Look, Donald is Donald," says Southworth. "He was always like this. He was like that before and he's like that now. It's like there's a kid with a stick and an ant farm. He's the kid and we're the ant farm."

Finally, there was the tiny, lone-wolf entrepreneur named Andy Batkin.

In 2006, Batkin had the notion of a Million Dollar Golf Challenge. The idea was that 100 PGA Tour hopefuls—guys who hadn't yet made it—would put up $15,000 of their own cash for a chance to win $1 million.

Catchy hook, but Batkin needed a big name to give it sizzle, so he flew to Trump Tower to pitch The King of Deals. All Trump had to do, Batkin said, was add his glitzy name to it, do a few interviews, watch it all unfold in a one-hour special on ESPN, and he'd get a big flat fee.

"Just think," Batkin told Trump. "Someday, [NBC golf analyst] Johnny Miller might be saying, 'This guy got his start on Donald Trump's Million Dollar Challenge!'"

That excited Trump. "Really? Johnny Miller might say that?"

"Sure!"

Plus, Trump's people had an idea. If Batkin agreed to hold it at a Trump-branded golf course in the Caribbean, it would kill two birds with one stone. "Mr. Trump had to get down there anyway," says Ashley Cooper, who ran Trump's golf businesses at the time. "He owed them one trip down there [as part of a licensing deal] and he'd never seen the course. So it was a win-win on all sides."

Sold. Trump scrawled his seismometer autograph on the contract, and they were in business.

Fast forward...months later, to Trump's office, 10 minutes before the giant press conference to announce the big challenge. It was about to take place below in the giant, gilded lobby of Trump Tower.

Every local TV station in New York was there, plus over 50 photographers and reporters. Upstairs, Trump and Batkin waited to go down. The plan was that Trump would descend on his magnificent gold lobby escalator, wave, smile, get to the mic, and tell the world about the "incredible, really spectacular, amazing" million-dollar event that was coming to their lucky TV sets and how it would be "like nothing we've ever seen in golf."

Except as he sat in his office, Trump had a bomb sitting in his vest pocket, lit.

He turned to one of his underlings and said, "Tell me again why the fuck I'm doing this?"

Batkin's heart stopped for a second. What was this? With nine minutes to go?

The underling stammered a bit until Batkin interjected, "Well, because it's going to be great. And you get your fee, plus you have to go down there anyway."

"How much are you getting?" Trump barked.

Keep in mind, financially, Batkin was no *S.S. Trump*. He was a dinghy bobbing in the open sea. He'd taken out a $1.5 million personal loan to guarantee Trump the three-day event would come off. He desperately needed Trump and this press conference to beat the wannabe mini-tour golfers out of the bushes. The golfers would then pony up $15,000 to play for a chance at a cool million. "For a lot of them, they were going to have to borrow it from their uncles or their brothers," Batkin says. "But I didn't know if we'd really get guys to do it. I had everything I owned on the line."

With no Trump, he was a dead man.

Batkin tried to breathe.

If all went well, he told Trump, he was going to gross in the high six figures, but then he was going to have to start paying all kinds of people. A small bead of sweat trickled down his brow.

Trump chewed on that like it was an aspirin tablet.

"Fuck it," Trump said. "I'm not going down there until I get half."

Batkin just stared at him.

"I was glad I was wearing a dark suit," Batkin recalls. "Because I really thought I was about to soil it."

This is when Cooper, Trump's golf guy, tried to step in and douse the fire. "No, no, we're all right. Andy, tell him again your vision for this."

Batkin explained how this million-dollar challenge idea didn't have to stop at golf. It could be done with tennis, sailing, bowling, lots of things. "And you'd be in for all of it," he said to Trump.

That seemed to make Trump even madder. "Half," he said. "Otherwise, fuck it."

Batkin couldn't believe this was happening. He felt like he might puke. He checked his watch. Seven minutes. He swallowed hard and stared at the most famous business tycoon in the world.

"Donald, why should I change the deal?" Batkin said, firmly. "We have a signed contract."

Trump, in full scowl, stared at his shoes. Batkin felt like somebody had knitted sweaters for each of his teeth.

In TrumpWorld, this is the moment where the little guy knuckles under. Trump has the money, the lawyers, and the poker face to make you break. It always worked.

Except this time.

"Okay, fine," Batkin said. He got up to leave.

"Where are you going?" Trump said.

"Downstairs," Batkin said. "And when they ask me, 'Where's Donald?' I'm just going to say, 'Oh, five minutes ago, upstairs, he reneged on the deal. Tried to hold me up for half my company.' And then I'll take out these papers in my right hand and show them your signature."

Trump seethed but stayed put. Batkin got in the elevator. Trump's assistant, Carolyn Kepcher, ran into it with him.

"Andy, you can't do this! This is bad for everybody. Please don't do this!"

Batkin held up the papers and said, "Carolyn, we have a signed deal."

They descended, Carolyn trying to talk him out of it as they dropped. Batkin wasn't budging. This was a titanic risk he was taking. Why?

"Going into high school," Batkin recalls, "I was 4-foot-11. I knew all about bullies. My dad taught me how to box. He'd say, 'You get one good punch on their nose, that'll do it. You'll probably get way worse from them, but they won't come back.' And that's what I was thinking about. This guy is just another bully. I mean, it's Trump, so it was scary. But I knew I couldn't allow it, or I'd be sunk."

The elevator opened and they walked into the gilded Trump Tower lobby. Two minutes to go. It was almost time to start the press conference. Batkin was praying for a power blackout.

Finally, with 30 seconds left, he saw Trump's polished shoes coming down the escalator, like a god descending from Olympus. Trump was giving the packed lobby crowd his half-grin, waving at them, like nothing had happened.

Batkin finally inhaled again.

Trump came to the stage and shook Batkin's hand. They turned for pictures, all smiles. "I'd never seen that many flash-bulbs in my life," Batkin remembers.

Out of the side of his smile, Trump said, "You think anybody would be here without *me*?"

Batkin kept smiling and murmured back, "You think anybody would be here if you weren't holding my million-dollar check?"

11

TRUMP V. OBAMA

Obama ought to get off the golf course.
—DONALD J. TRUMP

I HAVE A BUDDY who has to hide his golf from his wife. She thinks he plays too much, which he probably does, so he can't post his scores. He can't talk about his round. He has to make up excuses for why he wasn't at his desk when she calls.

Trump has the same problem. Not with his wife. With the country. In his first 22 months as president, he played a documented 149 rounds, or about 1 every 4 days, according to TrumpGolfCount .com. He's taken so much heat about playing too much golf that he tries to hide it. Unlike my buddy, he's not very good at it.

For instance, one March, he said he was going to be working all day at Mar-a-Lago. But then Trump friend Chris Ruddy posted a picture of him shaking hands with somebody. On Trump's left hand was a golf glove.

Busted.

One summer day in 2018, as he was getting ready to leave for 10 days in Bedminster, he announced that he was going to be working and taking meetings the entire time. "This is not a golf trip!" The only problem was that when he left the White House, he was wearing a pair of FootJoy golf shoes.

What's strange is that, before he became president, he said he would do no such thing, ever, never. "I love golf," he told a crowd at a February 2016 campaign stop in Portsmouth, New Hampshire, "but if I were in the White House, I don't think I'd ever see Turnberry again. I don't think I'd ever see Doral again....I don't think I'd ever see many of the places that I have. I don't ever think I'd see anything—I just wanna stay in the White House and work my ass off, make great deals, right? Who's gonna leave?"

Who? Him. According to NBC News, in his first 579 days in office, he'd spent exactly one-third at one of his properties.

Trump threw gallons of shade at President Obama for allegedly neglecting his duties in favor of the golf course. He criticized him 27 times on Twitter alone for playing too much golf as president. Obama did play a lot of golf. In fact, halfway through his eighth year, Obama had played 250 rounds of golf in his presidency, a figure that astonished Trump. He nearly sprained his tweeting thumbs:

250 rounds...that's more golf than a guy on the PGA Tour plays!

Well, no. A PGA Tour player plays about 250 rounds per year. Over seven years, that would be 1,750 rounds, not 250. But get this: Over the 2018 Thanksgiving weekend, in Palm Beach, Trump played five straight days, more than anybody on the PGA Tour played that week.

Can you believe that, with all of the problems and difficulties facing the U.S., President Obama spent the day playing golf. Worse than Carter

Well, Carter didn't play golf. Obama also took one-third as many vacation days in his first year as Trump did in his (111). In fact, no modern president took as many vacation days in their first year as Trump. The only one to come close to Trump's vacation bonanza was Bush 43, who took about 70, mostly to his ranch in Texas, but in much bigger clumps, so the costs were far less.

We pay for Obama's travel so he can fundraise millions so Democrats can run on lies. Then we pay for his golf.

True, but some golf is more expensive than other golf. Obama played 61% of his rounds at nearby military courses like the one at Andrews Air Force Base, 35 minutes away from the White House. Trump never plays military or public courses. The only local course he plays is Trump Washington in Sterling, Virginia. Mostly, though, he prefers taking Air Force One down to Trump

International in West Palm Beach at a cost of $3.6 million per trip. To put that in perspective, Obama's yearly Martha's Vineyard vacations cost Americans $450,000, according to Judicial Watch.

Trump relished ripping Obama whenever he played on a big news day. When ISIS beheaded American photojournalist James Foley, Obama was playing in Martha's Vineyard. Trump even posted a video on Instagram of Obama smiling in a golf cart mixed with footage of the decapitation. In an ice-cold rebuke, he wrote:

Not under my watch.

When Trump became president, he'd see his golf clubs less than he'd see the White House basketball court. Who would have time? He'd be busy fixing the nation's problems, seven days a week. Except just the opposite happened. Trump is on a pace to play almost triple the amount of golf Obama played. Obama wound up playing 306 rounds in his 2,920 total days in office, or once every 9.5 days. Trump is on pace, over eight years, to obliterate Obama's number—at 759 rounds, which goes to show you that bone spurs do heal very nicely.

That 759 rounds would be third all-time, behind the record set by Woodrow Wilson's estimated 1,600 rounds and just a smidgen behind Eisenhower's estimated 800. Ike played so much golf, in fact, that a bumper sticker got popular: "BEN HOGAN

FOR PRESIDENT. IF WE'RE GOING TO HAVE A GOLFER, LET'S HAVE A GOOD ONE."

Anybody want to put Tiger Woods on a bumper sticker?

Much more importantly, to Trump critics, is that Trump's golf is exponentially more expensive. Through September 2018—19 months into his presidency—Trump's far-flung golf trips had cost American taxpayers an estimated $77 million. Just the Secret Service's cost of renting golf carts alone to protect him cost over $300,000, according to documents obtained by TMZ.

This might be why one American, Kathy Rentz, a Republican from Pennsylvania, scrawled across her IRS federal tax return, "Not for Trump's Golf Trips!"

It's not just the cost, it's the optics. On May 11, 2018, Trump's lawyer, Rudy Giuliani, declared that Trump was too busy to meet with FBI special investigator Robert Mueller. The next day, Trump played golf.

One February, Trump encouraged people to celebrate Martin Luther King Jr. Day with acts of kindness. "It's not a day to hang out in the park or pull out the barbecue grill," he said. "It's a day to do something to help someone else, and that can be as simple as…picking up the newspaper for that elderly person who can't get to the end of the driveway." Then he went out and played golf at Trump International. Maybe he was looking for newspapers?

In March of 2018, as 800,000 people were marching all over the country to protest the lack of gun control in America just after the Stoneman Douglas High School mass murders, he played golf.

Remember that round Trump played with pros Woods, Johnson, and Faxon in November of '17? As they made the turn that day, an aide took Trump aside and told him militants had just shot up and bombed an Egyptian mosque, an attack which would leave 311 dead. Wouldn't the president want to issue a statement immediately?

"I was in a golf cart with Trump," Faxon recalled to Medium .com. "I thought he'd have to go back to Mar-a-Lago and make a statement. There were hundreds of lives lost."

But Trump kept on playing. "The optics are going to look bad," Faxon remembered Trump telling the pro players. "I'm on a golf course and we have a disaster. The media will take this that I don't care, I'm gallivanting around with celebrity golfers. In reality, whether I'm in the White House, Mar-a-Lago, or on the golf course, my statement is not going to change."

FYI: Obama did *not* post a fake video on Instagram that day of Trump toodling along in a golf cart mixed with footage of bloody mosque murders.

But maybe the most tin-eared moment of his golfing annals was when he tweeted:

Heading to the Southern White House to watch the Funeral Service of Barbara Bush. First Lady Melania has arrived in Houston to pay our respects. Will be a beautiful day!

A day filled with grief and mourning? Let's play 36!
Sadly, he only got in 18.
What if Obama and Trump played *against each other*?
Please?
It's probably never going to happen, but for a time, Trump

wanted it to. "His swing looks like it's coming along beautiful," he once told the *New York Post*. "His game looks much better. I'd love to play him for the presidency." When Trump bought Virginia's Lowes Island golf course in 2009 and turned it into Trump Washington, D.C., he said he was hoping it would replace Congressional as the home course for Tiger Woods' annual PGA Tour event (it didn't) and that he was looking forward to playing it with President Obama. (He didn't.)

He could've. One time, in 2014, Obama was in Westchester and asked his staff to set up a game at Trump Westchester. It's unclear what happened, but some say Trump wouldn't allow it because it meant closing down his course for his members for part of the day. He did, however, club Obama over the head with a tweet:

> **If Obama resigns from office NOW, thereby doing a great service to the country—I will give him free lifetime golf at any one of my courses!**

Let's say there is a god for golf writers and it's on—Obama v. Trump—18 holes, loser has to wash the other's limo in a Speedo.

Who would win?

Wait! Before you lay down your bets, let's consider...

*Cheating...

If Trump is playing, he's cheating. Apart from conceding short gimmes, Obama does not cheat. Trump always shoots in the

70s whether he did or not. He's 80 proof. For The Donald, golf is never about improving or the exercise or enjoying the day. It's about beating you, no matter what it takes to do it. Obama plays like he sleeps with the USGA rule book under his pillow. He's a stickler. Everything is by the book.

"I can definitely vouch for #44 in his integrity on the course," emails basketball star Stephen Curry of the Golden State Warriors. "The man knows how to enjoy the game and do it the right way for sure. Except we only played for $1 so the stakes weren't that high."

Wait. No mulligans, no my foot slipped's, no gimme chip-ins?

"No," Curry writes.

So if we're playing this match with five USGA rules officials following each president with cameras, then Trump won't be able to cheat, which means he'll be out of his element, doing something new, and that's never good in a pressure match.

Advantage: Obama.

*Putting...

Trump picks up every putt within six feet and, if you're not a threat, will pick up yours, too. You could park an Airstream trailer in Trump's Friendship Zone. He gives so many putts, it gets a little emasculating. "A month or so ago I gave a guy a 10-footer," Trump told *Golf* magazine in 2010, "and it was more insulting giving it to him then *not* giving it to him. You don't want him to think you feel sorry for him. It's a very fine line."

You heard that right. Trump *gives* 10-foot putts. If this were basketball, it'd be the equivalent of saying, "Don't even bother taking that 3. You'll never miss that."

Still, Trump is an excellent putter. Obama not so much.

Advantage: Trump.

*Handicaps...

Obama came into office as a 17 handicap and left as about a 13—"an honest 13," he says. The ESPN sportscaster Michael Wilbon, a frequent partner of Obama's on the course, estimates him to be an 11 now. Trump's 2.8 is a bigger lie than Clinton's "I did not have sex with that woman," but he brags about it so he'd be stuck giving Obama eight shots. That means on the eight hardest holes, Obama could take one shot off his true score for purposes of the bet. To win any of those eight holes, Trump would have to beat him by two shots.

Giant advantage: Obama.

But let's say they played straight up, with no shots given.

Advantage: Trump.

So who would win?

"I would win," Trump said at a rally in Bluffton, South Carolina, once. "No, seriously, I would."

If they had to walk? Obama by 20.

But let's say they get to arguing. Let's say Obama catches Trump cheating and fronts him, and Trump throws his phantom Winged Foot punch again. Who wins the fight?

Well, they're about the same height, no matter what the White House doctor says, but Trump outweighs Obama by a good 75 pounds. Obama, though, is 15 years younger, is light years faster, and works out constantly. Trump's idea of exercise is, as he told the *New York Times*, standing in front of a podium for an hour. "That's exercise," he says.

Advantage: Obama.

Plus, Obama is left-handed, so if he could slip that first Trump haymaker, he could surprise the big ginger with a hard left and maybe knock him out cold.

At which point, Obama could lean over him and say, "Not on my watch."

12

PROFESSIONAL PEST

He's not as smart as we thought he was.

—ARNOLD PALMER

THE WORLD OF PROFESSIONAL golf is just slightly more Republican than a Cabela's grand opening. In a poll done by Golf.com, players were asked if the USGA and PGA should move their tournaments off of Trump's courses as a reaction to his incendiary comments about Mexicans and immigrants. A fat 88% said no. Only 4% said yes. A full 42% of them said they'd vote for him again, compared to 20% who wouldn't. The Philadelphia Eagles and the Golden State Warriors might refuse to come to the White House, but 90% of Tour players would be on the first NetJet there.

Caddies? Not so much.

In October of 2017, at Liberty National Golf Club in Jersey City, New Jersey, Trump became the first standing president to attend the President's Cup, a Ryder-Cup-wannabe event that pits the 12 best American players against the world's 12 best players not from Europe, if that makes any sense. It's that age-old America versus Australia-South Africa-Fiji-Asia-Latin America-And-A-Few-Others battle. That year, America swamped the ASAFALAAAFOs, 19–11. When it was time for the trophy presentation, Trump and his massive entourage of Secret Service, SWAT guys, press ops, and assistants were all flowing out of his luxury box to the 18th green, when swimming against the tide was a caddy of one of the winning American players. He was stopped cold by two agents, who put big hands on each of his shoulders.

"Sir, where are you going?"

"I'm just walking," the caddy said. "Can't I walk?"

"Sir, you're the only one going this direction. Where are you going?"

Their grips got tighter. They weren't blinking.

The caddy looked at both of them and sighed. "Look, guys, I appreciate you have a job to do and I mean no disrespect, but I just can't stand to be anywhere near that motherfucker you work for."

The agents loosed tiny smiles and let him go. A few minutes later, Trump gathered with the best golfers on the planet, raised the trophy high, and dedicated it to a very surprising group of people.

"On behalf of all the people of Texas, and all of the people of...Puerto Rico and the people of Florida, that have really suffered over this last short period of time with the hurricanes, I want to just remember them and we're going to dedicate this trophy to all of those people who went through so much."

It was a bizarre choice. At that moment, Puerto Rico was begging for U.S. help to restore electricity and water and not getting much. The entire $300 million contract to get the electricity turned back on had been handed to a tiny company out of Whitefish, Montana, the hometown of Trump's then Interior Secretary Ryan Zinke, whose son worked for a time for the company. With thousands of people trapped in their homes without power or water—filling out a grisly death toll that would eventually rise to 3,000 people—a golf trophy didn't seem all that helpful.

Just then, a fan hollered out: "You don't give a sh*t about Puerto Rico!"

Golf takes long hours, piles of money, and manicured acres to play, so it mostly leans toward the rich, except when it leans to the very rich. The people who watch it on TV are the toniest demographic of any sport, which is why the products being pitched are usually luxury cars, Wall Street companies, and watches that cost more than some people's houses. Those corporate boards lean politically the same way as the players, but they need rich Democrat fans to buy, too, so Trump has been an uncaged lion for them.

Take, for instance, Cadillac.

Cadillac's Trump problems began with an idle promise Trump made to the Palm Beach County commissioners long before he was president, back when he was trying to get the land near

Mar-a-Lago to build Trump International (West Palm Beach). He told them, "If you lease me the land, I promise you I'll get you a Tour stop." The commissioner of the PGA Tour then was an achingly quiet guy named Tim Finchem, who would rather administer gallbladder surgery on himself than rock the corporate boat. He knew Trump could rock a cruise liner, and he wanted no part of him as a business partner. So Trump wasn't getting any Tour stop. No way. That idea was dead. Still, when Trump gets his heart set on something, he will turn oceans into deserts to get it. He wanted a Tour stop no matter what, which meant there was only one other way—buy a course that already HAD a Tour stop.

Enter Doral.

Since 1962, Doral's Blue Monster course in Miami had been a classic stop on the PGA Tour's Florida swing, a straw-hat old-school tourney won by no less than Jack Nicklaus and Nick Faldo. Only the Masters, Pebble Beach, and the Colonial had been Tour stops longer than Doral. So, in 2012, Trump bought the entire Doral resort out of bankruptcy for $150 million—lock, stock, and all four courses, plus the hotel, by far his largest golf purchase ever. He changed the signs immediately, calling it Trump National Doral Miami. He declared Doral's Tour stop "a major," which it most assuredly wasn't, and told the press he now had "the greatest site in Florida," which he absolutely didn't. Still, Trump had his wish. Finchem and the PGA Tour would now be coming to *him*, at *his* course, and *he* could take center stage for one week as the New God of Golf. That's when the trouble started.

The sponsor of the Doral stop was Cadillac, and suddenly,

Cadillac was having to share top billing with Trump and his King Kong personality and his shooting-gallery press conferences and his helicopter flying in from West Palm with the giant TRUMP painted on its side, the TV cameras lapping it up. There is only one star at any Trump event and it's the Donald.

"Trump was getting more commercial air time than Cadillac," said a person involved in the sponsorship. "He parked his damn helicopter in the middle of the golf course. Here was Cadillac, paying all that money, and the whole tournament was suddenly all about Trump." Said another, "They were getting dwarfed. No way were they going to get their money's worth with Trump there."

Trump loved the attention, driving his supercharged cart up behind golfers (a no-no), interrupting players during practice rounds (not cool), and being sure to be seen whenever and wherever possible (as you'd expect).

"You should've seen him," says one caddy of an American player. "He'd come out to the (practice) range and go down the line with the same script for each guy. He'd come up to the first guy and go, 'Hey, you're lookin' really good!' Then he'd point to the guy hitting balls next to him and go, "But I don't know if you can beat THIS guy!' So then he'd go to that guy and say, 'Hey, you're looking really good! But I don't think you can beat THIS guy' and so on. Made me wanna hurl."

Cadillac asked Trump if he could please tone it down and stop flying his chopper in during the tournament. "Maybe you could fly in before play starts?" they asked. He owned the hotel; could he maybe just stay put at Doral for the four days? Trump said he'd consider it, but he kept choppering in during play, a killer cutaway shot for any TV director. *Here comes The Man himself!*

Worse, the players were starting to grumble about the course. Not long after he bought it, Trump had architect Gil Hanse re-do the Blue Monster. Hanse, with Trump by his side at every step, somehow gave Doral a charm bypass. He added length and difficulty but took out the character. Doral became nothing but a Big Bangers Ball—only long hitters invited. A tournament that had been won by smaller, crafty players like Lee Trevino, Tom Kite, and Ben Crenshaw was now only winnable by the beasts, like Tiger Woods and Dustin Johnson (twice). Cue the grousing and grumbling in the locker room. After he finished that first week, a reporter asked four-time major winner Rory McIlroy what his takeaway was on the new Doral.

"My takeaway?" McIlroy said. "Maybe it's time for me to reconsider my schedule."

"They made it too long," says architect Bobby Jones. "Dick Wilson [the original designer] had already made a terrific course, a tough course, but you know Gil [Hanse] was gonna do whatever Donald said." Says that caddy, "Doral is a disaster now. Way too long. It's just a slog now. Only 15 guys can win it—the 15 longest guys."

That, of course, delighted Trump. He loved seeing the best players in the world shoot 78s on his Monster. It was somehow a reflection on his own golf skill. "He's one of a kind," Tour star Rickie Fowler said of Trump with a laugh. "He likes seeing us get beat up by his golf course."

It all became too much for Cadillac. They bailed out. Two months before the election, the Tour moved the tournament from Doral to Mexico. After 55 years at Doral, Trump's ached-for Tour stop up and emigrated to Mexico on him. "It's quite ironic that we're going to Mexico after being at Doral," McIlroy said with a grin. "We just jump over the wall."

Today, Doral isn't half the place it used to be. I visited it in May of 2018 and found it...empty. "Doral is a conference resort," said the now-late general manager of The Breakers hotel, David Burke. "Big groups, corporate events. But Trump is so controversial now, corporations don't want to risk pissing their clients off by staying at a property with 'Trump' in the title. My buddy runs it and he says they're empty."

Forbes confirms this. They report that Doral lost 100,000 booked room nights since Trump took over the White House. Worse, *Forbes* reports that revenue at Trump's U.S. golf properties fell by an estimated 9% in 2017. When Trump broke tradition with every modern president and refused to sell his businesses or at least put them in a blind trust, he must've figured he'd make much more money his way. Turned out just the opposite. Most financial experts say if he'd have sold it all and put everything into America's bull market, he'd be worth $500 million more today.

When I visited Doral in May of 2018, it was like somebody had pulled a fire alarm. I stood outside the pro shop at a spot where I could see half a dozen golf holes but only saw one (1) golf cart. The practice range had room for 50 people, but only two were there. There was one kid taking a tennis lesson. There were the standard 100-foot poles waving flags the size of a Chili's, miles of marble and gold and plush carpet, the standard belching Venetian fountain, just nobody gawking at them. It was so empty that an oddly serendipitous thing happened. Twelve hours after I checked out in the main lobby, a gunman entered that lobby, draped a massive American flag over the front desk, started screaming that he wanted to see Trump, and began shooting the joint up with a machine gun. He shot everywhere—shattering the gilded mirrors, the massive chandeliers, and the huge windows. He was eventually shot in the leg by Miami police and apprehended. But here's the good thing: The place was so empty nobody got hit. Zero deaths, zero injuries.

It was the rarest event for Trump: A loss even he couldn't spin into a win. Though he did come up with a pretty good line. "I hope they have kidnapping insurance," Trump said.

So the next time you hear somebody say, "Name one good thing Trump has ever done for people," you can point out that he saved a lot of lives that day.

(A note from our Irony Dept.: Trump Doral has managed to sign a pro tour golf event again, but it's on the PGA's Latin American Tour. Hope they have machine-gun insurance.)

Dumping the Doral Tour stop wasn't the first time pro golf ran from Trump. For 36 years, there existed a silly-season event called the PGA Grand Slam. It was a fabricated event, usually played in exotic places, pitting the winners of the four majors against each other, for no apparent reason. In 2015, it was supposed to move to Trump Los Angeles in Rancho Palos Verdes,

California. But then Trump opened up his presidential campaign by declaring that Mexican immigrants to the U.S. were "bringing drugs. They're bringing crime. They're rapists. And some, I assume, are good people."

Golf buried its head and groaned, but Trump didn't apologize. Double Down doubled down. He told the Golf Channel he'd received "tremendous support" from the golf world because "they all know I'm right."

That was too much. The PGA Tour, LPGA Tour, USGA, and PGA of America rose up to yell, "It's not true." They issued this statement:

> In response to Mr. Trump's comments about the golf industry "knowing he is right" in regards to his recent statements about Mexican immigrants, we feel compelled to clarify that those remarks do not reflect the views of our organizations....Mr. Trump's comments are inconsistent with our strong commitment to an inclusive and welcoming environment in the game of golf.

It's a triple blue moon when the stodgy world of golf takes a stance on anything political, but this time, it was pissed enough to not just speak but act. The PGA of America refused to play the Grand Slam at Trump's course and then canceled the Grand Slam altogether. It hasn't come back since. What do you know about that? A golf-crazy presidential candidate killed two pro golf tournaments in two years.

It hurts Trump deeply when pro golf rejects him this way.

He knows pro golf like a blind man knows his room. He knows who's who, even down to the golf writers.

Once, during the presidential campaign, a pro from Trump Bedminster, Jim Herman, won the 2016 Houston Open. Trump had staked him on Tour to help him get his start, and Herman's win was a huge surprise. Steve DiMeglio, the longtime golf writer from *USA Today*, called the campaign in hopes they could fetch him one quote from Trump about Herman. It was a long shot. Trump was stumping in Milwaukee, where it was madness. Every political writer was dying for time with the primary-gobbling phenomenon.

All of a sudden, DiMeglio was on the phone with Trump, who was going on and on about Herman, what a great guy he is, what a great player, "I always believed in him," and "We're so proud," etc., nonstop. Finally, in the background, DiMeglio heard, "Can somebody get him the fuck off the phone? He's supposed to be on stage! Who's he talking to anyway?" Then DiMeglio heard, "Some golf writer from *USA Today*."

"I heard about that from our political writers for a while afterward," DiMeglio remembers with a laugh. " 'How the *hell* did you get Trump again?' "

Now that he's president, Trump can get some of America's most famous team-sport pro athletes to play with him. According to TrumpGolfCount.com, he has a pro athlete in his foursome 45% of the time. And why not? Trump is a good player, and athletes are usually good, too, which allows the whole parade to fly along in under three and a half hours, the way he likes it. Among the dozens of athletes he's played with are Peyton Manning, Tom Brady, Kirk Cousins, and John Elway.

He's always been able to get games with the most famous golfers in the world: Jack Nicklaus, Arnold Palmer, Gary Player, and Greg Norman. As president, that hasn't changed. So far, he's teed it up with Tiger Woods, Rory McIlroy, Dustin Johnson (twice), Rickie Fowler, and more. Bryson DeChambeau gave him a golf bag. Trump's most frequent pro partner since he's been president has been David Frost (four times), not the deceased talk-show host but the journeyman South African.

They all say the same thing: He's great fun and they have no idea what he shot. Only Rory McIlroy guessed at it. "He probably shot around 80. He's a decent player for a guy in his 70s.... Sometimes he will give himself some putts, but that's fine, he's the president, he can have that luxury."

Woods: "Our discussion topics were wide-ranging; it was fun. We both enjoyed the bantering, bickering, and needling.... We didn't have a match and played for fun." (This, of course, turned out to be a fib, as innocently revealed by Brad Faxon to me in Chapter 4.)

Justin Thomas: "I've never seen that many golf carts on one hole in my life."

Japanese star Hideki Matsuyama got to play one day not only with Trump but also with Japanese prime minister Shinzō Abe. Through an interpreter, he said: "I had no idea what it would be like, only what I'd read in the media, but he wasn't like they say he is at all. He was fun. It was enjoyable. We chatted the whole day. He asked me so many questions. About Japan. About how I like America. He offered me whatever help I needed. I was really nervous, but at least my first drive went straight."

Did either leader cheat?

"Well, we weren't betting. There was nothing riding on it. They weren't professional golfers. They were just trying to have fun, so it was a very easy and enjoyable day."

(In other words: *Hai.*)

Jack Nicklaus likes Trump and stands up for him against critics, but then again, Trump has given him good work at his golf courses, especially Trump Ferry Point in the Bronx.

Trump used to like to tell people he was tight with the late, great Arnold Palmer, too. Once, the golf writer James Dodson was leaving an interview with Trump to go to one with Palmer. Dodson says Trump "crossed one finger over the other and he said, 'Arnold and I are like that.'" Dodson remembered, "And I told Arnold that the next night at dinner, and he laughed and said, 'Really? It's more like this.' And he crossed his hands and put them at his own throat."

"One moment stands out in my mind," Palmer's daughter, Peg, recounted recently to writer Thomas Hauser of the *Sporting News*. "My dad and I were at home in Latrobe. He died in September [2016], so this was before the election. The television was on. Trump was talking. And my dad made a sound of disgust—like 'uck' or 'ugg'—like he couldn't believe the arrogance and crudeness of this man who was the nominee of the political party that he believed in. Then he said, 'He's not as smart as we thought he was,' and walked out of the room. What would my dad think of Donald Trump today? I think he'd cringe."

Trump often calls Tiger his "good friend," but it seems to be a one-way friendship. Woods did design Trump World Dubai, though it's not owned by Trump, only operated by him. Still, Eric Trump—who seems to have gone to the Donald Trump School of Fabulousness—thinks it's just another sign that they're super bros. "They've been very, very close," Eric said. "When you combine Trump and Tiger, it's a match made in heaven. It's a very amazing combination."

Yet every time we ask Tiger about Trump, it's like we asked him about an uncle who's in Leavenworth. "Well, he's the president of the United States. You have to respect the office. No matter who is in the office, you may like, dislike personality or the politics, but we all must respect the office." If that's true, then why did Woods' spokesman Glenn Greenspan try to build an O'Hare runway between the two of them? "Tiger is not in partnership with Mr. Trump or his organization and stating otherwise is absolutely wrong. Tiger Woods Design's contract and obligation is to the developer, DAMAC Properties. Our association ends there. I can't put it any clearer that Tiger Woods Design does *not* have an agreement with Mr. Trump."

When Trump eliminated protection for the 800,000 DACA "Dreamers," putting American-born young people at risk of being deported to countries they'd never even seen, Woods was in a pickle. The Tiger Woods Foundation is very involved in funding the educations of underprivileged kids from immigrant families. This was everything they didn't believe in. Its own foundation kids were terrified. The Tiger Woods Foundation had to tweet out:

We are committed to and in full support of our #DACA scholars and alumni. Join us in urging Congress to pass the #DREAMAct. #DefendDREAMers.

All doubt was removed the night Tiger went on *The Late Show with Stephen Colbert*, where Colbert asked him about the presidents with whom he'd played. Tiger recalled Bush 41 ("We played in about two hours"), Clinton ("lotsa cuts," which is to say, "sliced shots"), and Obama ("very competitive").

"What about Trump?" Colbert asked.

Woods got a big grin on his face and replied, "You said 'presidents,'" getting a big laugh from the crowd.

Trump does seem to be friends with Dustin Johnson, who lives in Palm Beach Gardens—20 minutes from Mar-a-Lago—and his grandfather, Art Whisnant (who was once drafted by the Minneapolis Lakers) lives in West Palm Beach. Trump once asked Johnson to come have Thanksgiving dinner with him, according to Whisnant. "They're tight," the grandfather says. So tight that on Tuesday of the 2018 U.S. Open week at Shinnecock Hills, New York, Johnson drove clear back into the city to appear at the opening of Trump's new clubhouse at Trump Ferry Point in the Bronx. Tiger wouldn't do a Tuesday appearance on Open week if you gave him Queens.

But playing golf with Trump can cause some serious blowback. Take what happened to McIlroy. He got pilloried for it.

"History will brutally judge [McIlroy's] golfing buddy Trump," wrote Ewan MacKenna in *The Irish Independent*. "But we ought to judge Rory right now."

McIlroy was so rattled by the reaction, he jumped on Twitter and vented.

I don't agree with everything my friends or family say or do, but I still play golf with them. To be called a fascist and a bigot by some people because I spent time in someone's company is just ridiculous. I hope, to some degree, this clarifies my decision to accept the invitation.

He also said he'd "think twice" about doing it again.

Trump really is tight with the one and only Long John Daly, who calls him his "great friend" and who came to the White House three months into Trump's reign with no less than Sarah Palin, Kid Rock, and ultra-right-wing rocker Ted Nugent. There, the foursome gleefully posed for a mocking photo in front of a painting of Hillary Clinton. Seems right that Daly would be one of the first celebrities Trump invited. Between them, Trump and Daly have fathered eight children and married seven different women.

Then there was the night a gaggle of Tour players and officials visited the White House. Among the Tour players were DeChambeau, Jason Bohn, Kevin Streelman, and Billy Hurley. Tour commissioner Jay Monahan was there, too.

"We walk into the Oval Office about 8 p.m. and there he is at the desk, still in his suit," Streelman recalls. "He jumps up and goes, 'My golf guys!' He seemed happy to see us and he couldn't have been more friendly. He let us take pictures, showed us around, and then he goes, 'You guys want to see the Lincoln Bedroom?' Next thing you know we're in the Lincoln Bedroom.... Then he says, 'Come with me.' We're in the Private Residence! He knocks on this one door, pretty loud, and goes, 'Melania? Are you decent? I got some guys I want you to meet.' After a while, she came out and we got to meet her, too! I mean, it was awesome! It was like we were his golf buddies and he was just showing us around his house! Just like a normal guy!"

(Trump also has a fun little trick he likes to play with visitors. He'll show people a button under his desk. It looks important. "You want me to push it?" he'll say. Before they can holler, "No!!!" he hits it. Instantly, a butler brings him another Diet Coke.)

Trump also calls Tour superstar Phil Mickelson "a good friend." They've played a couple times together, plus Mickelson is scheduled to design a Trump-operated course in Bali. But since the election, Mickelson has gone stone-cold mum on the subject. When I asked Mickelson about his friendship with Trump, he looked me right in the eye for about 10 seconds, smiled, and walked away.

Then there's Bernhard Langer, the sensational German who's dominated the Senior Tour. Trump says Langer is a "friend" and even offered a story about Langer to defend his own outrageous lie that "3 to 5 million people voted illegally" to help Hillary Clinton win the popular vote tally. Trump declared that Langer, a Florida resident, had been unable to vote at his usual polling place while several people "who did not look as if they should be allowed to vote" were ushered through.

It's a lovely story except for one small fact: Langer is a German citizen. He can't vote here.

One of Trump's goals when he got into the golf business was to someday see a golf major played on one of his courses. Since the Masters is permanently held at Augusta National (GA), that left him three options: the U.S. Open, the Open Championship (formerly the British Open), and the PGA Championship. It took him about 20 years, but the dream is about to become real. In 2022, the 104th PGA Championship will be held at Trump Bedminster.

The PGA announced the selection years before even Trump himself thought he'd ever be president. When Trump started running and began insulting everybody from Muslims to McCain, the PGA czars started getting nauseous. "What could we do?" says one PGA official. "We had a signed contract. We couldn't back out." If Trump is re-elected in 2020, that PGA would be in the middle of his fifth year.

A U.S. Open, though, might be out of the question. Even Trump admits that if he really wants a U.S. Open he's going to have to take his name off Trump Bedminster, which is his best chance to land one. "But my courses are all booming," he explained. "Without the name, they don't boom." Which is an odd thing to hear from a man who has declared that all his courses are the greatest layouts on the best pieces of property with the best members in the world. Why would they need the name?

U.S. Open sites are set through 2027, and none of them are

at Trump properties. Eight of those next nine will be in states where Trump has courses, and most of them will be played on tracks that he's said are inferior to his, including two at the "highly overrated" Pebble Beach.

Nobody better buy a damn shirt.

As to a Trump overseas course hosting an Open Championship in Europe, it's remotely possible, just not anytime soon. His course in Aberdeen is getting passed over left and right. Word was it would host three years of Scottish Opens beginning in 2019, but now the Scottish Open will go to a rival course two hours away, The Renaissance Club, designed by American Tom Doak. If it weren't for his name on it, Trump Turnberry would absolutely get the Open Championship. Since Trump bought the course, he's improved it so much it'd be a joke not to have one there. But the R&A has announced its Open schedule through 2022, with no Trump Turnberry in sight.

"He'll never get an Open Championship as long as he's the president," says John Huggan, the Scottish golf writer. "And, for sure, not as long as his name is on the course." Huggan says it's a bad match: Trump plus the walking dandruff balls that run the Royal and Ancient, the governing body that runs the Open. "All those R&A stiffs—'Oh, jolly good,' 'More tea?', and all that—and here comes this extroverted blowhard. No way. They'd never do it."

Would it help if he dedicated a trophy to them?

13

E W W W W W

*It doesn't really matter what [they] write as long as you've
got a young and beautiful piece of ass.*
—Donald J. Trump

AMONG THE INVITED AT the opening of Trump Bedminster in
2004 was the former owner of the estate, bankrupt car legend
John DeLorean, then 79. Trump was standing with a gaggle of
golf writers when DeLorean drove up in a golf cart with his girlfriend in tow.

"Trump introduced them to everybody," remembers Eamon
Lynch, a columnist and Golf Channel personality. "He and
Trump visited for a while. Then DeLorean left. Trump turned to
us and said, 'The poor guy. He's a very old, sad figure. He's lost all
his money. And worst of all, his girlfriend is a solid 4.'"

Trump looks at women the same way he looks at golf trophies.

They're fun to collect and it's okay to cheat to get them. When he introduced me to Melania the first time, he said, "Look at her."

"What do you mean?"

"Look at her!"

"I just did look at her."

"No, look at her! Up and down. It's okay."

"Donald, I'm *not* going to look at her like that."

"Look at her! She likes it!"

So, red-faced, I quickly looked down at her shoes and back up in 1/10th of a second. He was grinning.

"All real."

As his women employees at Trump Los Angeles found out, he's not particularly interested in women for their SAT scores. This is how he's always been. Even at military school, he was called "ladies' man." The idea that women are individual human beings with brains and goals and ideas doesn't register much under the big orange canopy. At Trump Turnberry, it came out that the men get more than twice the bonus the women get, according to *The Scotsman*.

The most important quality in a Trump wife is that she be a 10 who doesn't play golf, doesn't care much about business, and doesn't watch too carefully. At that same Bedminster opening where Trump was holding court with that same gaggle of writers, a man in a suit came up with news. "Guess what? The Trump family has been selected Golf Family of the Year!"

Lynch remembers Trump thanking the guy, who then drove off. "Then Trump turns and says to us, 'Well, that tells me I can't get caught having an affair for the next year.'"

That's not easy. To Trump, women are like French fries. He knows he should stay away from them, but he can't keep his hands off. That can cause trouble for a man as famous as he is. A TV producer who spent time around him remembers Trump's infamous security guy, Keith Schiller, standing behind them during certain shoots. "He'd say, 'Don't shoot the redhead' or 'Stay off the blonde.' So I'm trying to frame the shots in these weird ways to keep these women out of the shot. It was nuts."

Someday, at the Smithsonian Museum, they should have an exhibit on the 2006 weekend Trump spent at the American Century Celebrity Challenge in Lake Tahoe, California, perhaps with a vat of Purell for afterward.

Despite the fact that he'd just turned 60, Trump, who was married at the time, not only played three full days of golf, he managed to bed a porn star, sleep with a Playmate of the Year, and grope a second porn star, as alleged by her two female friends. You talk about stamina.

NBC's golfapalooza, held at the Edgewood Tahoe resort in Lake Tahoe, is a boozy soup of golf and groupies and celebrities, many of them A-list pro athletes. That July, Aaron Rodgers, Drew Brees, and Ben Roethlisberger played. They also sprinkled in a few golfing nonathlete celebs, like actor Anthony Anderson, broadcaster Al Michaels, and comedian Ray Romano. Trump, with a hot NBC show called *The Apprentice* in its second year, was as sought after as any of them.

The presence of all those celebrities is why so many eligible women end up congregating for the wild nights at the official tournament hotel, Harrah's Casino. It's a *Guys Gone Wild* kind of weekend. Adult-film studio porn-house Wicked Pictures even had a booth in the gifting room to hype its latest, uh, releases. It stocked the room with swag and stars, including two of its leading ladies: Stephanie Clifford, aka "Stormy Daniels," and Jessica Drake. Cleavage and lipstick ready, the XXX stars lured plenty of male celebs in, including a certain amorous real estate owner in a red hat named Donald J. Trump, who'd seen Daniels earlier that day on the golf course. He came in and got a very famous photo with her, much to his regret 11 years later.

But it didn't stop at the photo. They got to talking, flirting, dining, and, finally, according to Daniels, having sex that night in Trump's suite.

Judging just on virility, you'd have to agree a 60-year-old man bedding a famous porn star is something of an achievement. But it wasn't good enough for Trump. He apparently went for seconds. According to Jessica Drake, Trump came *back* the next morning to the Wicked booth and began flirting with her, too. He invited her to walk with him during his round that day, which she did. He got her number and invited her up to his suite that night. That made her a little queasy. She'd heard stories from Daniels about Trump "chasing her" around his room "in his tighty-whities." So she brought two female friends as backup.

"When we entered the room," Drake recalled at a Gloria Allred–run press conference, "he grabbed each of us tightly in a hug and kissed each one of us without asking permission. He was wearing pajamas." Trump asked them a lot of questions about life as a porn star, and then they left "30 or 45 minutes later," Drake said. She says Trump called her later and offered her $10,000 for sex. As a form of seduction, Drake wasn't impressed. In fact, she said it wasn't "acceptable behavior for anyone, much less a presidential candidate" and tagged him a "sexual assault apologist."

Even two porn stars didn't do the trick. Somewhere in the middle of all that, Trump allegedly fit in a bedding of Playmate Karen McDougal, whom he'd been having an affair with and had flown in for the occasion. How's that for depth of douchery? When you're cheating on the mistress with whom you're cheating on your wife, you've entered a kind of infidelity *Inception*.

And where was his new bride of six months, Melania, during these Mattress Olympics? Back in New York with their new four-month-old baby, Barron.

This wasn't the first time Trump cheated at a golf tournament. He cheated on his then-girlfriend soon-to-be wife Marla Maples at the 1993 AT&T Pebble Beach Pro-Am, according to *San Francisco Chronicle* society columnist Pat Steger. She wrote in her column:

> Donald Trump had a great time at...Pebble Beach, but not such a great time was had by Marla Maples who joined him mid-tournament—which meant that the gorgeous blond model he brought with him, who does Frederick's of Hollywood catalogs, had to go home to L.A.

Stranger still, Maples had flown in with a wedding dress in her suitcase, expecting to marry Trump that Saturday afternoon, but Trump 86'd it at the last minute, Steger wrote. True to form, Maples was pregnant with daughter Tiffany at the time.

And now let's all break for a shower.

* * *

The irony is Trump has been one of the best friends the Ladies Professional Golf Association (LPGA) Tour ever had. He knows the players, knows the tournaments, and loves being involved. And, yes, it's probably just coincidence that his favorite LPGA star is also one of its most photogenic players, its blond bombshell, Natalie Gulbis.

Gulbis, a four-time tournament winner, first met Trump at the LPGA's season-ending ADT Championship, at Trump International in West Palm Beach, Florida. The ADT was as fancy as it got in the LPGA, a crescendo that featured only the Tour's 30 best players. It even allowed Trump to show off Mar-a-Lago—where the players and top officials stayed. Trump relished the idea of 30 female golf pros at his disposal. He'd come down every morning of the tournament and weave through the omelettes.

"Natalie!" he roared one morning in 2005. "Congratulations on making it to your first Tour championship. I see you're leading the tour in birdies this year. What do you think of the course?"

Gulbis was amazed. "How did he even *know* that?" She loved how he seemed to care about her, asking so many questions, inquiring about her love life, advising her on agents and corporate sponsor and moves to make in her career.

"He believed any notion that I should accept less money than a PGA Tour player for appearances or endorsement contracts was just plain wrong," she told a reporter. He even tried to help her love life. At the time, Gulbis was dating the aforementioned Roethlisberger, the 6-foot-5 Pittsburgh Steelers quarterback, but he'd eventually break it off with her, leaving Gulbis publicly heartbroken. Trump told more than one friend that Roethlisberger broke up with her because she had "no tits," according to golf writer Kevin Cook. What was Trump's love advice to Gulbis? Lie. "From now on I want to read that you dumped him," he insisted.

Trump was lavishly generous at the ADT, and the players loved it. But it wasn't long before they experienced some Trump trickery. In fact, it was the first year, 2001. The players had torn it up in Round 1 with some low scores. Trump wasn't having that. A Trump course is not a welcome mat. He sent his crew out that evening to shave lake banks and speed the greens up to faster than the hood of a Buick, and had them stop cutting the rough, according to players. As a result, nearly every player in the field scored worse from Round 1 to Round 2, which is unheard of in pro golf unless there's suddenly bad weather, which there wasn't. The winner, Hall of Famer Karrie Webb, was six shots worse that second day. The redoubtable Annika Sörenstam, who finished second, was also six worse. Major-winner Grace Park was nine.

The Trumpster was delighted. He kept driving around in his turbo cart, asking players, "How about this course, huh? Tough, huh? When's the last time you shot this high?"

"When I was nine," one said.

"He definitely instructed his staff to change the preparation of the golf course," says LPGA Hall of Famer Dottie Pepper, now an on-course reporter for NBC. "How do you prepare for one course on Thursday and then have to play a completely different course Friday? The players were ticked off. But there was nothing we could do. And the LPGA wouldn't stand up to him. They'd just say, 'It's Donald Trump. We're lucky to have him.'"

But were they? Letting Donald Trump host a women's golf tournament is like letting Justin Bieber babysit. There's bound to be trouble. For one thing, Trump would kick off the pro-am by having his 727 buzz the course, causing panic in Palm Beach. The West Palm Beach airport switchboard would light up with people sure a plane was crashing. "People would be freaking out," says one airport official. "Are we getting bombed?'"

"Everything he does to the country now, as president, he did to us beforehand, in golf," says a then-high-ranking LPGA official who doesn't particularly want the most powerful man in the world knowing who she is. "Like, he sent us this astronomical bill for the media hospitality. He charged us for more media than you could've possibly crammed in that room. There weren't even that many there to begin with, but he charged us for way, way more that weren't there. And he kept unloading merchandise he didn't want from his pro shop right out in front.

"One of my closest friends came and brought a group of people to see the tournament. So I said, great, let's all have dinner at Mar-a-Lago. We sat behind a big door, totally hidden, so Donald wouldn't bother us. After a while, I looked up and saw him coming in. I'm like, 'Uh-oh.' He sees us, pulls up a chair, without even asking, takes off his jacket and says, 'Well now I know why Oprah is such a big fat slob.' Well, my friend is from the south. She's *very* proper. I thought she was going to swallow her fork. Why was he bringing up Oprah around us? We weren't even talking about Oprah. 'You know, she was here last weekend; she couldn't stop stuffing kiwi tarts in her face!' We just sat there, silent."

If you think that was awkward, you should've heard what was happening at the nine-story Palm Beach County jail that overlooks the third hole. "It hangs over that green," Pepper recalls. "Their rec area was on one of the upper floors. There was this one inmate who would climb up on the netting above. This guy was like Spiderman, just hanging way up on it. And he'd taunt the players the whole time, cat calls and all the usual gross stuff. I think they finally changed their P.T. time." Trump says this absolutely never happened, and then put up some very expensive tall trees to block the prison views.

No current or former LPGA commissioner would talk about Trump for this chapter, but when Trump was tweeting angrily on the day of Senator John McCain's dramatic Washington, D.C. funeral, former LPGA commissioner Carolyn Bivens (2005–2009) tweeted:

**The depths of depravity know no bounds with Trump.
Clueless and classless**

Eventually, all good things must come to an end. After five years, the ADT tournament announced they'd be switching venues. Naturally, Trump sent them off with all best wishes.

"Just think," he said to a group of them that year, "next year at this time you'll be in a freaking Holiday Inn outside Houston."

When 33-time Tour winner Amy Alcott met Trump the first time, she was in the hotel elevator at the now-defunct Trump

Marina casino in New Jersey. She'd made an ace that day at an LPGA event and was beaming. Trump got in the elevator and recognized her.

"Are you a golfer?" he asked.

"Yeah, I'm Amy Alcott."

"Of course you are! I'm a big fan."

"Thanks! I actually had a hole in one today."

"Wow. That's fantastic. I'm going to have some champagne sent up."

"Wow. Thank you!"'

"Are you paying for your room?"

"Well, yes, of course."

"Well, you shouldn't be. We'll take care of it."

Alcott was flattered and thankful. Except no champagne ever arrived. And nobody ever took care of the room but her. "But I did see him leave in his helicopter," Alcott says.

They'd meet again when the LPGA held an event at his one-and-done Trump Los Angeles in Rancho Palos Verdes, California. "He'd put me in his cart," says Alcott. "And since it's Donald's cart, it goes twice as fast as any cart. We're driving down the middle of the freaking fairway DURING the tournament. One time, he goes, 'Oh, there goes Lorena Ochoa!' and he drove right down the middle of the fairway and up to the green. There was Ochoa trying to line up a birdie putt and he's waving and going, 'Hi Lorena! How you playing?'"

Longtime LPGA touring pro Kris Tschetter was even less impressed than Alcott. She and Trump played together in a

Wednesday Pro-Am once at the ShopRite Classic in New Jersey. "In my 25 years being a Tour pro," Tschetter says, "that was the worst experience I ever had playing golf."

Trump leered at her, spoke suggestively, and was "gross," Tschetter says. "He was just a pig. He hit on me, but in a kind of creepy way. I was SO not interested. I guess the fact I was married didn't matter to him. I was just like, 'Ewwwww' the rest of the round."

One of the other players in the group that day, a sales executive named Rob (he prefers not to give his last name), says it was worse than that. "Not only was he hitting on Kris, but Kris's husband was caddying! Trump would take me aside and go, 'What do you know about Kris and her husband?' I'm like, 'How should I know? He's right over there.'"

Since it was a tournament, he played by the rules, right?

"No, he kept taking all these extra shots," Tschetter says. "You can't do that in a Pro-Am. At one point, we made a 5 (as a team) and he said to write down a 4 because 'everybody cheats in Pro-Ams.' I mean, he couldn't be stopped. There was no way to say 'no' to him."

Rob: "I kept saying to him, 'Why are you cheating? To win an umbrella?' I wouldn't do it, so he took over the scorecard."

But here's the amazing thing about that day. After all the boorishness, Trump sent his helicopter to take them on a tour of New York, land on the roof of one of his buildings, wait while they ate dinner below, and bring them back to New Jersey, all on him. He wasn't even there.

It's not the money, it's the winning.

*　　*　　*

Just because the LPGA was done with him didn't mean Trump was done with the ladies. He lobbied for and got the 2017 U.S. Women's Open at Bedminster. The deal was signed long before he ran for president, and when he did, his first comment accused Mexico of sending us mostly rapists. Then came the *Access Hollywood* tape in which he boasts to Billy Bush about "grabbing women by the pussy." Then came the debate question from Fox's Megyn Kelly asking him why he has called women "slobs," "dogs," and "fat pigs."

LPGA and USGA officials stewed. How could they hold a women's Open hosted by a man whose idea of women came from *Porky's 6*? It was like riding a lion. They'd get eaten alive if they stayed on, but they'd get eaten alive if they didn't. They decided to just hold the tournament and hope for the best.

Immediately, women's groups started applying heat. A month before it was to start, a group called UltraViolet rented a plane and flew a banner over the *men's* U.S. Open that year that read: "USGA/LPGA: TAKE A MULLIGAN, DUMP TRUMP."

(*Aside to Greenpeace: Please call UltraViolet from now on for all golf-banner wording.*)

Women's pro golf was finally getting some press, just all the wrong kind. Media rooms at normally ignored LPGA events were filling up with reporters, all wanting to ask the players, "How do you feel about playing the Open at Donald Trump's golf course?"

American Brittany Lincicome shrugged and said, "Hopefully maybe he doesn't show up."

It'd be a great slogan, wouldn't it?

The 2017 U.S. Women's Open: Hopefully, Trump won't show up.

But he did show up. He drove past hundreds of protesters outside the gate and became the first U.S. president to ever attend a U.S. Women's Open. He sat in a corporate tent on the 18th green behind bulletproof glass and waved a lot. The Open was won by South Korean Park Sung-hyun, as if anybody remembers in the midst of the Trump Tornado.

When it was over, he tweeted:

Thank you to all of the supporters, who far out-numbered the protesters, yesterday at the Women's U.S. Open. Very cool!

One last note: Through the first 22 months of his presidency, there wasn't a single documented round when he'd played golf with a woman.

14

WHO'S YOUR CADDIES?

If a caddy can help you, you don't know how to play golf.
—DAN JENKINS

THE MOST LOYAL EMPLOYEE Donald J. Trump has doesn't work in the White House or on his campaign or on his legal team. The most faithful man in the president's life is his caddy at Trump Washington, a 60-something ex-Marine named A.J.

A.J. (he'd prefer we not use his last name) is so loyal that if you criticize Trump, he'll fight you—and has. One day, when the 2017 Senior PGA Championship was being held at Trump Washington, he overhead one of the Tour pro's caddies—Brian "Sully" Sullivan—dissing Trump.

"He was running his mouth, sir," says A.J., who calls everybody "sir" or "ma'am." "Yellin' about Mr. Trump. He was sayin' to somebody, 'Don't tell me how I have to feel about him! I hate that motherfucker!'"

A.J. says he came up on Sully from behind and put him in a full military choke hold, yelling, "Now, you listen to me, fucker! You're not gonna come to Mr. Trump's course and eat Mr. Trump's food and then use the word 'hate' about my president. I won't have it, you got me?"

That's not quite the way the story is told by Sullivan, who caddies for Senior Tour player Joe Durant, but his memory is a little fuzzy. "It's possible I was hungover," Sullivan recalls. "I don't like D.C. anyway and I sure as hell didn't want to be on a Trump course. Some guys started talking about Trump. I mentioned that I can't stand the son of a bitch. I said he was the biggest jerk in the world. A.J. got all worked up and said, 'That man pays my rent. He puts food on my table!' I said if he has to take money from that horse's ass, then he ought to find a different loop. He kind of just grumbled off. Of course, as luck would have it, he and I got paired for the first two days. We buried the hatchet."

Tensions were high because, for seniors, it was a big tournament and Trump's name was attached to it. There were protesters by the entrance every day that week, and A.J. always made sure to drive his car right by them. "There'd be a bunch a women out front with all their stupid signs, sir. So I go real slow by 'em, see, hit the window button—*zzzzzzzttt*—toss 'em the bird and I yell, 'Fuck you!' They'd start yelling at me and I'm like—*zzzzttttt*—right back up. And I laughed, sir."

A.J. sticks with Trump no matter how much it costs him. "I used to caddy for a lot of the ladies here, sir," he says. "But once Mr. Trump won the election, that all ended. Now I hardly do it at all, sir. I guess they don't like him. I'm the president's caddy and they're not gonna ask for me, sir. So that's it."

One time, after a bad drive, Trump slammed his driver back in his bag, as guys will do, and wasn't really watching what he was doing, and the driver ricocheted back and hit Trump in the head. "A.J.?" Trump asked, pissed. "Did you just hit me in the head with my own driver?"

"Sir, Mr. Trump, why would I do that?" A.J. said. "You're my president!"

There are more than a few members at Trump Washington who'd love to hit Trump in the head. A valet told me, "We had a bunch of them quit when he won." Most of the anti-Trump crowd stayed, but they resist in their own small ways. Every time one member sees A.J., he says, "Is this the day, A.J.? Is this the day?"

"Is this the day for what, sir?"

"Is this the day you take him out for me?"

"This one time, we're playing through, sir, like we do and, you know, usually the Secret Service has the people standing on the side in plenty of time for us. But this one guy, sir, young guy by the name of Jonathan Wallace, he was taking his sweet time getting out of the way. He was just moseying along, sir, doing it on purpose. Then he gives it one of these (A.J. flips the bird), right to Mr. Trump. Sir, that really made me mad. Mr. Trump just asked me who it was. I told him. He said, 'Let's go say hello.' Not me, sir. I went the other way. But Mr. Trump went over there and talked to him. Right away, this Wallace guy caved, sir. He caved." (I couldn't get Jonathan Wallace to call me back to hear his side of it.)

None of this used to be A.J.'s life. His Trump days used to be filled with pro athletes or businessmen. Now it's Congressmen and Fox hosts. Among his favorite these days is South Carolina senator Lindsey Graham, a Republican. "I love hearing that accent of his, sir. Mr. Trump plays pretty good with him. One time, he taught Mr. Trump a game called 'Hogan.' A Hogan is when you hit the fairway and the green and then two-putt. You do that, you get one Hogan point. So we played it, and, bam, Mr. Trump gets a Hogan on the first hole. And he just keeps going. Mr. Trump got 11 Hogans, sir! Shot 73 that day, I kid you not, sir. He made about four 15- to 20-foot putts on the back and shot 73. Coulda been even lower."

A one-over par 73 on a "wet and windy day" as Graham described it, for a 72-year-old overweight man? That's freaking unbelievable. How unbelievable? Well, at that same Senior PGA Championship, at the same course, from the same blue tees, Tom Watson never shot better than 74. Tom Kite put up a 75 and an 80. Corey Pavin had an 82. Between them, those three men have won nine majors.

When asked by a reporter how many gimmes there were in that 73, Graham allowed that they didn't really putt out that often and that "the president is better at receiving than giving." So, in other words, that 73 had more sugar in it than a family pack of Butterfingers. Now why would Graham resort to telling the truth about Trump's scorekeeping skills? Perhaps because of the vitriol Trump tweeted about him during the 2016 campaign, calling him "nasty" and "so easy to beat" and a man with "no honor."

Now, though, Graham is No. 1 on Trump's golf speed dial.

Graham remembers legendary Republican Senator John McCain asking him why he kept playing golf with someone like Trump. "I told him, 'I hope you understand. . . . The best place to talk to him is in his world.'"

A.J. had Trump and Tennessee Republican senator Bob Corker in his world one day—along with no less than QB Peyton Manning—but it didn't seem to grease any wheels for his boss in Congress. Not long afterward, Corker said Trump needed "adult daycare."

A.J. has no time for another Republican senator, Kentucky's Rand Paul, whom he calls "a real chooch."

A chooch?

"Yeah, I don't know how to translate it, sir. A chooch. He treated me like a peon. Never even tried to fix a ballmark. Treated me like dirt, sir. He's a rich guy who thinks he's above everybody. A real chooch, sir." (Paul didn't return calls.)

Paul didn't sound like he had that much fun playing with Trump and A.J., either. When asked who won the golf match, Paul said, "The President never loses, didn't you know?"

Actually, yes, that's been mentioned.

In my 18 holes with A.J., he didn't say a single negative thing about Trump. He didn't even say a neutral thing about Trump. To hear A.J. tell it, Trump has Einstein's brain, Lincoln's wit, and Nightingale's heart. A.J. is smart that way. A loyal caddy can go a long, long way with Donald Trump.

Take Dan Scavino.

Scavino was a 16-year-old summer caddy when he got Trump's bag one day in 1990 at Briar Hall Golf and Country Club (NY), which was to become Trump Westchester. "I'll never forget the day his limo first pulled up," Scavino told *Westchester Magazine*. "I was star-struck. I remember his first gratuity. It was two bills—two hundred-dollar bills. I said, 'I am never spending this money.' I still have both bills."

The two hit it off. Trump told him, "You're gonna work for me one day." Scavino graduated from State University of New York (Plattsburgh) in 1998 and went to work for Coca-Cola, but Trump brought him back soon enough to be the assistant general manager at Westchester. Then Scavino became executive vice president. When Trump decided to run for president, Scavino asked if he could be part of it. Trump made him social media director of the campaign.

A billionaire and a caddy is a friendship that could only be made in golf, where kings take orders from cobblers and lifetime allegiances are sealed over 6 irons. It was the perfect match. Scavino is Trump's Mini Me. They both speak fluent golf. They both love stirring up liberals. They are both often very short on details and understanding, but long on Atomic Pile Driver slams and face-first personal takedowns. "They share thumbs," former campaign advisor Barry Bennett says. "They complete each other's tweets." Neither is well read nor a particularly good speller. Doesn't matter. As a two-man Twitter team, they shout from the rooftops anyway. They find a phrase—"fake news" or "enemy of the people" or "Crooked Hillary"—and repeat it so many times, people start to accept it.

With Scavino running Trump's feed, Trump's tweets became

even more bombastic, ultra-opinionated, and, often, a par 5 over the line. Former White House communications czar Hope Hicks called Scavino "the conductor of the Trump Train." One day, the train jumped the tracks. Trump tweeted out an image of Hillary Clinton, with a Star of David, against a background of money and the line "Most corrupt candidate ever!" It was a Scavino special, cobbled together with cut-and-paste images from the Internet and no thought of maybe asking somebody, "Hey, is this too much?"

Within seconds, Trump was blasted as antisemitic. Scavino had to issue a statement taking responsibility. He tweeted:

> **The social media graphic used this weekend was not created by the campaign. It was lifted from an Anti-Hillary Twitter user. The sheriff's badge, which is available under Microsoft shapes, fit the theme of corrupt Hillary and that is why I selected it.**

Except it wasn't a sheriff's badge, it was a Jewish star. (It was probably a mistake on Scavino's part, since his wife is Jewish.) The more Scavino pumped up Trump's tweets, the more it sounded like the Twitter feed of somebody else—Scavino's. For instance, on March 2, 2016, Scavino tweeted on his own account:

> **@MittRomney, You will not stop the #TrumpTrain You look like a complete LOSER. Very DESPERATE attempt. #Fail**

Hmmm. That's got a certain ring to it. Another time, just days before the election, Scavino tweeted:

NBC news is #FakeNews and more dishonest than even CNN. They are a disgrace to good reporting. No wonder their news ratings are way down!

A minute later, the same message, word for word, was posted on Trump's account as his original tweet. Scavino hastily deleted his, but in a world of screenshots, it was too late.

Robert Draper, of the *New York Times Magazine,* conducted an exhaustive study of Trump's tweets and estimated that Scavino was "responsible for—at least as a 'co-conspirator' "—about half of Trump's 37,000 tweets. The late-night and early-morning tweets seem to be 100% Trump, but the daytime stuff has the patina of Scavino. Whichever it is, neither of them particularly knows what they're doing. Scavino violated the Hatch Act by tweeting support for a candidate. Scavino also got Trump dragged to Federal District Court by blocking some followers, which, it turns out, is unconstitutional for an American president.

Still, he's put Trump's Twitter rants on a kind of steroid regimen. Fox News host Megyn Kelly accused Scavino of rabble-rousing against her: "The vast majority of Donald Trump supporters are not at all this way," Kelly told an audience in Washington. "It's that far corner of the Internet that really enjoys nastiness and threats and unfortunately there is a man who works for Donald Trump whose job it is to stir these people up and that man needs to stop doing that. His name is Dan Scavino."

But just think of it: Trump's Twitter feed is the most powerful pulpit on the globe, and a caddy has his hands on it, daily. It's full-throated Trumpness, even Trumpier than Trump, sent without censure or concern and teeming with what Bush 41 called Trump's "casual cruelty." It's a flamethrower that sometimes winds up setting the Oval Office curtains on fire. During his 2012 campaign, Mitt Romney had 22 people approve each tweet before it went out. During the day, Trump has two—himself and his caddy. At night, just one. That's not going to change. CNN asked Scavino, who is now the White House Director of Communications, if there was anything Trump could do or say that would make him leave Trump's side. He answered with an unequivocal "no."

Scavino refused my requests to interview him, but we know he's a Catholic who once kissed the pope's ring. He was about 40 when Trump was elected. Scavino's wife, Jennifer, became sick with Lyme disease, and the couple says they spent so much money trying to get her well, they went bankrupt in 2015. Some people say this is why they got divorced after 18 years. "Dan was a great husband, though," says Ian Gillule, who worked with him at Westchester. "He's very gregarious, a big personality, a people pleaser, and very political." Also, apparently, not a guy who will ask his billionaire boss for a loan.

In a way, A.J. and Scavino are the same guy. A.J. is Trump's outdoor caddy and Scavino his indoor one. They're both mostly unknown, yet they know all the secrets. They both do the same job: They give their man the right club to take shots with. These two work for a human flamethrower and yet somehow haven't been torched. Cabinet members, attorneys general, chiefs of staff come and go like the Wendy's drive-thru and yet they stay employed. What's their secret? It might be the Caddy Code: Show Up, Keep Up, Shut Up. It only takes one bad read or one bad club to get fired as a caddy, but A.J. has been Trump's loop for years now. Scavino has survived Trump's well-oiled guillotine and remains one of the few staffers who's lasted since the beginning. A president who trusts nobody trusts Scavino. "The president has zero concern that Dan has any interest in anything but serving him," the *New York Times* quoted a top administrator as saying. When you're the only other person who has the president's Twitter password, you're trusted.

All of which proves one thing. Jeff Sessions should've learned to caddy.

15

LITTLE BALL, BIG BALL

I'm not a schmuck. Even if the world goes to hell
in a handbasket, I won't lose a penny.
—Donald J. Trump

ONE DAY I WAS playing with my friend Lenny "Two Down" O'Connor. He kept hitting his irons "fat"—hitting the ground before he hit the ball. A good iron shot is just the opposite—the club traps the ball against the earth and sends it soaring.

"Two, you idiot!" he yelled at himself. "Little ball first, THEN big ball!"

That's been part of the problem with Donald Trump as president. In his brain, the big ball keeps getting in the way of the little ball and vice versa.

So many of the problems, controversies, and conflicts Trump has gotten into as president started with golf. Conversely, his golf has twisted how he makes decisions about this great, big, troubled blue ball he's supposed to be running.

Take, for instance, Puerto Rico.

Why did Trump seem to turn his back on our own people during the devastating 2017 hurricane that would leave almost 3,000 dead and the island without water and power for eight months?

Why? Golf might be why.

It started in 2008, when the Trump Organization agreed to operate a course called Coco Beach Golf & Country Club, about 30 minutes from San Juan. It was in trouble and needed a big name to get it some publicity. So, for a fat fee and part of the deal, Trump agreed to operate the course and let them call it Trump International Golf Club Puerto Rico. In his pitch to get the deal, Trump guaranteed the course would start turning a profit. Bigly. Puerto Ricans were thrilled.

But Trump only sunk it deeper. Before Trump, the course was losing about $5.4 million a year. With Trump—$6.3 million. Some of that was the $600,000 Trump took out for his fee over those years. Within three years, the Coco Beach company defaulted on $26 million in government bonds and had to get $33 million more in government financing, which they also couldn't repay. Trump finally declared bankruptcy on his end of the project in 2015, and the Coco group went belly up, too, leaving the Puerto Ricans with a $33 million hole.

Fast forward two years to the worst hurricane to hit Puerto Rico in 85 years. It was a catastrophe. Yet, as American citizens were dying for water, medicine, and power in Puerto Rico, their president seemed to not give a damn. He made jokes. "See, there's this big thing called the Atlantic Ocean," he said. He mused about how to pronounce the name "Puerto Rico." Then he decided they only had themselves to blame. He tweeted:

> **Texas & Florida are doing great but Puerto Rico, which was already suffering from broken infrastructure & massive debt, is in deep trouble.**

That was too much for Lainie Green, a Puerto Rican marketing executive who threw an epic tweetstorm back at him:

> **Massive debt you and your sons helped when you bankrupted your golf course & never paid back the $33 mil bond you left Puerto Ricans with.**

> **You remember because you filed for the bankruptcy a month after you started running for president in 2015.**

> **So how much are you going to give back of that $600,000 paycheck you got for sticking Puerto Rico with a $33 million debt?**

"He came down here and was so obnoxious," says Green. "He said, 'We're gonna pour $600 million into the course.' That was bullsh*t. They didn't put any of their own money into it. He and his sons were here for seven years and every year they lost

218

more and more money. The [Coco] owners went to the [Puerto Rican] tourism bureau and asked for a $33 million bond. The government said no....But Trump's sons kept saying, 'No, Donald Trump will be here all the time! He knows what he's doing! Trust us!' So they loaned the money. By 2015, they had to declare bankruptcy and the Trumps left us holding the bag."

When Trump visited the devastated island in late September, he seemed cavalier about it all, almost flip, visiting only the mostly untouched ritzy part of the island, where he shot rolls of paper towels like 3-pointers at a room full of dismayed Puerto Ricans and then left.

"That was disgusting," Green remembers. (She was crying by now as she spoke.) "These are human beings. American citizens! The people he's responsible for! He had absolutely no empathy for our people. There's something psychotic and wrong about that. He had every opportunity to say, 'Hey, I love Puerto Rico. I don't want to fail them.' Instead he took swipes at my people and threw paper towels to his f*cking rich friends. I'd love to see Trump Tower without power for eight hours, much less eight months."

If she could get face-to-face with Trump, what would she say?

"I'd say, 'Would you ever leave your grandkids alone in the dark with no power, no water, and nothing to help them? Because that's what you did to these people.'...He let them die."

Take, for instance, immigration.

When Trump first tried banning U.S. travel to people from seven different Muslim countries—Iran, Iraq, Libya, Somalia,

Sudan, Syria, and Yemen—some Americans wondered, "Why those seven? Why not the UAE or Saudi Arabia? After all, the UAE helped fund the Taliban and may have been a backer of 9/11. Saudi Arabia has been the breeding ground for hundreds of terrorists, not to mention Osama Bin Laden."

Why? Golf might be why.

Even now, Trump is up to his clavicles in golf deals with the UAE, specifically controversial UAE tycoon Hussain Sajwani, sometimes called "The Donald of Dubai." Sajwani, a devout Muslim, even came to Trump's post-election party at Mar-a-Lago, earning a shout out from the man of the hour. "Hussain and the whole family, the most beautiful people, are here from Dubai tonight!" Sajwani owns two courses with Trump's name—Trump International Golf Club Dubai and Trump World Golf Club Dubai. The latter was designed by no less than Tiger Woods. Trump wasn't going to screw that up with a travel ban. What if Tiger needs to meet with his concrete guy?

Then there's China. Trump's relationship with China is fickle, but in June of 2018, Trump threw a lifeline to shady Chinese telecom giant ZTE. It got both aisles of Congress leaping out of their chairs in protest. "China...uses these telecom companies to spy & steal from us," Republican senator Marco Rubio pointed out. So why did Trump grease the skids for a company that America wants to see burn?

Why? Golf might be why.

At Trump Dubai, Sajwani awarded a $32 million infrastructure construction contract to the mostly state-owned China State Construction Engineering Corporation to build a road that would lead to the golf course. In other words, Trump was suddenly in bed with China. So when China's Xi Jinping person-ally asked Trump for help with ZTE, Trump might've thought, "Would helping ZTE make working with Xi really easy? Yes. Yes, it would." So he did it, against the advice of nearly everybody.

And why, you ask, wasn't Indonesia on the travel-ban list, since there are more Muslims in Indonesia than any country in the world (227 million) and, in just the first three weeks of May 2018, 49 people died in multiple ISIS attacks there committed by Indone-sian Muslims?

Why? Golf might be why.

Trump has two courses about to open in Indonesia, one in Bali, to be redesigned by Phil Mickelson, and the other in Jakarta, by four-time major winner Ernie Els. Remember when Trump's lawyers announced they'd be suspending all unfinished projects now that he was president? Not so much. He's moved forward in Indonesia. Should an American president be in business at all in a country like Indonesia, whose citizens committed almost twice as many terrorist acts as Iran in 2016? Depends. Will this coun-try put up a golf course with his name on it?

When Trump made "Buy American, Hire American" one of his campaign slogans, he was at the same time issuing an execu-tive order that greatly increased the amount of foreign H-2B tem-porary visa workers coming to this country. But why would he do that when an H-2B could come here and join a terrorist cell as easily as somebody who hopped a fence or faked a passport?

Why? Golf might be why.

Trump needs H-2B visa workers to make his golf courses and hotels work. He knows this country doesn't have an unemployment problem. It has an employment problem. It can't find enough people to do jobs most Americans won't do—mowing fairways, cleaning hotel rooms, washing gold-rimmed soup bowls. So nobody in golf was surprised that three days after the Trump administration raised the H-2B visa cap from 66,000 per year to 81,000, the Trump Organization applied for and got an additional 76 of them to use at its properties.

You ask, "Does Trump employ illegal immigrants at his golf courses?"

I answer, "Did Liz Taylor own a wedding dress?"

In December of 2018, Trump Bedminster got caught employing an illegal maid, to almost nobody's surprise. "They had all kinds of illegal immigrants working at Doral," says Joe Santilli, a former member there. "I know because I'd talk to them. I speak Spanish. They would be hired through a contractor so Trump wasn't on the line if they got caught. But they had tons of illegals working on crews there."

There's almost no conceivable way not to. I don't know many golf clubs that don't use them. The day I played with Trump at Westchester, he stopped three laborers who were finishing up a cart path and gave them each $100 bills for their good work. Then he got back in the cart and said, "Now they're the Donald Trumps of Chile!"

Take, for instance, Cuba.

When Trump got into office, he immediately started reversing Obama orders that would finally allow Americans to travel to Cuba, calling it a "bad deal" for Americans. In one iteration of the travel ban, Cuba was even named to his hit list. Some Americans thought, "Why? Why come down against Cuba now after all the progress the two countries have made?"

Why? Golf might be why.

In 1998, according to *Newsweek*, Trump secretly looked into building a hotel and golf course in Cuba. He paid an American consulting firm called Seven Arrows Investment to travel to Cuba to explore his options there, in direct violation of the embargo on Americans doing business in Cuba. Seven Arrows charged Trump $68,000 for the trip but, to disguise its illegality, made it look like a charity trip.

It went deeper. According to *Bloomberg*, more than a few Trump Organization people went down to Cuba to explore golf course and hotel possibilities more recently, too. When *Bloomberg* found out, it asked Eric Trump about it. He emailed back: "While we are not sure whether Cuba represents an opportunity for us, it is important for us to understand the dynamics of the markets that our competitors are exploring."

Wait, is that a denial?

There's paperwork for all this—lying to the IRS, repeatedly violating the embargo—but the statute of limitations has passed, so why let a bunch of snoopy American reporters in there to dig up new stuff? Trump may have thought, "Let's just keep everybody out of Cuba altogether."

Take, for instance, the wall.

Not *that* wall—the wall he wants to build in Ireland to keep the Atlantic Ocean off his Irish golf course, Doonbeg.

"The sea water is clearly rising," Trump's attorneys argued in a planning application in Doonbeg, a little burg on the southwest coast of Ireland. "Mr. Trump's property stands to be forever damaged without the wall." It said it right there in the application. The Trump Organization was asking for permission to build a giant wall because the effects of "climate change" were wrecking Trump's course.

Imagine that. Trump, who has said climate change is "a hoax," "fictional," and "a canard," was asking for the right to protect himself against rising sea water. The man who pulled the U.S. out of the Paris Agreement on climate change believes climate change is damaging his property.

"In our view, it could reasonably be expected that the rate of sea level rise might become twice of that presently occurring," the application said. Trump actually wanted two "flood defense walls," as his lawyers called them. Combined, they'd run about 3,000 feet along the coast, protecting three golf holes.

The Council gave permission. Irish environmentalists flipped out. They agreed the sea was rising, but said a wall could open a Pandora's box of ecological problems. For one thing, it would push all the water onto nearby farms, ruining their crops. The beach and dunes could be destroyed. Surfer groups opposed it. As of the start of 2019, the application was still under appeal.

A bit of advice to the world's leaders: If you want to get in good with Trump, take golf lessons.

Japan's prime minister Shinzō Abe gets golf. He gave Trump

a $3,755 gold-plated driver. They play together often. Chinese president Xi Jinping, though, hates golf. He's shut down 111 golf courses in China already and forbids any of the 88 million members of his Communist Party to play it. He thinks golf is a waste of water and land. Whatever good Trump did for their relationship with ZTE, Xi's disgust for golf hurts it. Would Trump start a trade war with China out of the blue, just to get even?

If you run a country but don't play golf, you're pretty much dead to Trump. German chancellor Angela Merkel always seems to be on the outside, her nose pressed to the grill room window, looking in at Trump and the day's foursome. One German official publicly suggested she should learn to play golf.

Playing golf hasn't hurt members of Trump's golf clubs any. Trump has put at least five of his members into senior roles in his administration, including Newt Gingrich's wife, Callista, America's new ambassador to the Vatican, and Adolfo Marzol—member at Trump Washington—who is now the senior adviser at the Department of Housing and Urban Development.

Andrew Giuliani, son of Trump's lawyer Rudy Giuliani, was named in March to a White House post as public liaison assistant. He's a scratch golfer and member at Trump Westchester. Robin Bernstein might seem an odd choice to be the ambassador to the Dominican Republic, seeing as she only speaks "basic Spanish," until you realize she was a campaign donor, sells insurance to Trump, and is a founding member at Mar-a-Lago. Whenever she's in the D.R., she can check in on Trump's proposed golf courses as Cap Cana, another unfinished project he was supposedly going to suspend and didn't.

Doesn't every president appoint their friends to sweet jobs? Yes, but unlike any president before him, Trump never divested his businesses before becoming president. Every single decision he makes as POTUS can affect his own wallet. When you can get up to $350,000 from people for joining your club, it helps to make membership attractive.

Hey, how would you like to be ambassador to Sweden? Just sign here!

The lines get blurred. In 2018, Trump visited the factory of avid golfer Robert Mehmel, a man who sells millions of dollars' worth of radars and electronics to the U.S. military and who also happens to be a member of Trump's Bedminster golf club.

CSPAN captured Kevin Burke, a lobbyist for airports, mentioning to Trump at a White House meeting, "I'm a member of your club, by the way."

"Very good, very good," Trump replied.

The word is out. If you're a lobbyist, a special-interest dealer, a foreign intermediary who needs Trump's ear, pony up the initiation fee and join one of his clubs. The access is fantastic. Can't afford that? Have a wedding there. As advertised for a time on a Trump Bedminster brochure, if you hold your wedding there, Trump might even show up, say hello, and pose for pictures, at no additional charge. ("We ask you and your guests to be respectful of his time & privacy," the brochure asked.) Lots of people have posted videos of him doing exactly that. On July 2, 2018, Trump surprised a wedding, posed for pictures, and even kissed the bride. Then he walked off to applause and a cry of "We love you!"

Somewhere, a tiny tear trickled down Angela Merkel's cheek.

*　　*　　*

For most people, it's the goats.

When I try to explain how Trump constantly hot-foots his golf cart down the line between illegal and immoral, I always bring up the goats.

"Did you know," I say, "that on Trump's Bedminster course there's a small herd of eight goats?"

Goats?

"Goats," I say. "He keeps eight goats on his golf course in order to get a farmland tax break, saving him about $80,000 in taxes per year. He also has a tiny hay-making enterprise at Trump Colts Neck in New York, just enough to get another farmland write-off."

Wait. Our current president keeps goats on a golf course as a tax dodge?

"Yes. Goats. To get an $80,000 tax dodge. A man who costs Americans nearly $4 million every time he goes to visit his golf course in Florida has found a way to save $80,000 in taxes."

That is so...genius!

They don't know the half of it. Even as president, Trump and his family have mixed shrewdness and self-dealing, politics and golf into a kind of not-quite-illegal but odorous machine that lets them get what they want.

Take the helicopter pad Trump uses at Mar-a-Lago, his winter refuge. Trump pestered and yelled and bullied the powers that be in West Palm Beach to let him land his helicopter on his property, but he was always denied. Hell, in West Palm Beach, the waiters have helicopters. But when Trump became president, he insisted he needed the pad to land Marine One. National security. The town said okay, but only for as long as he was president and only for Marine One. Great. Trump built the chopper pad. One week later, Trump's personal chopper, with a giant TRUMP painted on the side of it, was parked on the pad.

Before he entered office, LBJ put his radio and TV stations into a blind trust. Jimmy Carter sold his peanut farm. Both Clinton and Bush 43 put their businesses in blind trusts. Obama took his entire stock portfolio and put it in Treasury bonds. Not Trump. He didn't change a thing except to say that "Don and Eric and Ivanka will be running things." As a result, every time Trump plays golf at his courses in West Palm, Bedminster, or Washington, he's putting money in his own pocket with free advertising, not to mention the cost of housing and feeding all that staff. (Staff even gets a discount in his pro shops.)

If you thought Trump wouldn't dare use the Office of the President to try to get what he wants for his golf courses, you don't know Trump. It took only a few days after the election to prove it. That's when he took a congratulatory meeting in Trump Tower with four Brits—two money guys who'd backed Brexit, a journalist from the right-wing journalist site Breitbart UK, and the very vocal pro-Brexit activist Nigel Farage. One of the Brits, Andy Wigmore, returned to London and told the BBC that Trump kept complaining about the windmills Scotland was putting up in the sea next to his Aberdeen course. (Maybe you heard: Trump really hates those windmills.)

Wigmore quoted Trump as saying, over and over again, "They offend me." He said Trump begged them all to go back to the UK and try to do something "about getting rid of the wind farms."

It got worse. When the BBC interview aired, the journalist from Breitbart, Raheem Kassam, immediately emailed Wigmore, according to CNN, and flipped out:

WHY DID YOU GIVE THOSE QUOTES. This was a PRIVATE MEETING AND YOU HAVE F***** ALL OF US NOW.

Kassam insisted Wigmore say the conversation "never happened," an odd demand coming from a journalist. White House Spokeswoman Hope Hicks said Trump never brought up wind farms at all. Then CNN showed her the emails. Ooops.

Try as they have, nobody has been able to get Trump to divorce his golf businesses interests from the country's interests. In fact, Trump mixes them all the time. Since he has stayed at one of his properties roughly one-third of his days as president, American taxpayer dollars stuff his pockets, unchecked. In pursuit of them, he has no problem doling out free advertising for his golf properties. In an address to the South Korean National Assembly, Trump managed to get in a plug for how great his Bedminster course was. In an address of the U.S. Coast Guard, he made sure to mention that his Trump International is "one of the great courses of the world." On his 55-million-follower Twitter feed, he's raved about how "amazing" this course is or "magical" that one is or "spectacular" a third one is. A woman named

Dani Bostick, a schoolteacher and Army wife from Winchester, Virginia, noticed it, too. On July 15, 2017, she called him out on it via Twitter:

> **Nice job sneaking Bedminster into the caption of the picture. Nothing like free advertising on your huge social media account.**

Apparently, Trump didn't appreciate that. She got blocked.

Trump has found a way to cash in on the presidency like nobody who came before him. For instance, just in golf:

- Did it seem unusual to you that a few weeks after Trump was inaugurated, he doubled the initiation fee at Mar-a-Lago from $100,000 to $200,000? Then again, why wouldn't he? Suddenly, hanging around places like Mar-a-Lago, Bedminster, and Trump Washington gives an ambitious CEO or lobbyist fabulous access to the most powerful man in the world. Using the GHIN handicap system and membership rolls, *USA Today* found that at least 50 executives of companies that have federal contracts, plus 21 lobbyists and trade-group officials, are members at the clubs Trump visits the most often in Florida, Virginia, and New Jersey. Two-thirds of them played on one of the 58 days the president was there, *USA Today* reported.

- Does it seem odd that a guy who promised to have "absolutely no conflict of interest with his businesses" continues to lord over those businesses? Former hockey star Mike Eruzione belongs to Trump Jupiter and sees it. "I talk to our pro [David

Trout] a lot," Eruzione says. "He [Trump] is very hands on. He calls and checks on how it's doing, asks about certain greens, how the fairways are, where to move this or that, even though he's the president. He's a very hands-on guy."

Oops. Five minutes for blabbing.

- Did it seem funny that the very day he met with the Queen of England at Windsor Castle, he flew directly to his Trump Turnberry golf course in Scotland, plugging it shamelessly on Twitter? "This place is incredible!" he wrote. He only had two days to prepare for his historic meeting with Russian president Vladimir Putin in Helsinki. Why wouldn't he go there and start cramming? Maybe because Helsinki doesn't have a Trump golf course to market?

Trump gets a lot of deserved credit for what he did in the world of golf during The Great Recession of 2007. Then, golf was radioactive. People were leaving the game by the busload. A bank would rather help you buy a yacht than buy a golf course. But Trump went out and started buying golf courses with cash everywhere—five along the American east coast and three more in Scotland and Ireland. But where would a guy coming off four bankruptcies get that much cash to buy all those courses? And why was the self-proclaimed King of Debt paying cash?

Some thought it had to be the Russians. They might've gotten that idea from his son, Eric, who, in 2014, told golf writer James Dodson, "We don't rely on American banks. We have all the funding we need out of Russia.... We've got some guys that really, really love golf, and they're really invested in our programs. We just go there all the time."

Congress followed up on those comments but never came up with anything. Since Trump won't release his tax returns, it's nearly impossible to know. So whence then?

Allow me to take an educated guess.

When you join any private golf club owned by one person—like Trump's are—you must plunk down a fat initiation fee, which can run from $50,000 to $500,000. Trump Westchester gets $200,000. Trump Bedminster gets $350,000. You get your money back when you leave, as long as there's a new person in line willing to take your place and pay the going initiation fee. (Don't get ahead of me here.)

Let's say, just for the math, Trump Covfefe has 500 members, all of whom have put down $75,000 each. That's $37.5 million in cash sitting in the bank. Most course owners save that money in case there's a disaster at the course, i.e., moto-cross vandals hold an impromptu night-time event on your fairways or a massive flood hits that you're not covered for. But not Trump. He keeps those fat fees. When you look at the contracts that Trump has his members sign, you notice the fine print says, "Membership deposits and all other club revenues are the property of the owner of the club and may be used for any purpose, in its sole discretion."

It means Trump can legally take that $37.5 million of those Covfefe dues and do whatever he wants to with it. He can buy hair dye with it. He can corner the ketchup market. Or he can buy golf courses. Lots and lots of golf courses.

According to the *Washington Post*, Trump spent $400 million on golf courses, wineries, and hotels between 2006 and 2015, all in cash. "It's not unethical," says National Golf Course Owners Association CEO Jay Karen. "It's in the contract. But to me, it's a risk. If something happens and you need that money for the course, it's not there."

Sorry, folks. I know the Bolivian wombats ate the entire course, but all your money is in my fabulous course in Ireland. You should come see it!

Or let's say the bottom falls out of the economy and Trump wants to sell Trump Covfefe for $50 million, but he can't get anywhere near that. Let's say he can only get $5 million for it. The new owner buys the club AND the initiation fees, so they better be there.

Remember when he informed the Trump Jupiter members that their refundable deposits were suddenly nonrefundable? Is it possible he'd already used their deposits to buy another course and he didn't have it?

Could this little maneuver also be what Trump referred to throughout 2018 when he alleged that special counsel Robert Mueller was "horribly conflicted" in his investigation of Trump and Russia? Mueller, then the FBI director, quit Trump D.C. in 2011—two years after Trump bought it—with no hard feelings, Mueller's spokesman says. But the *Washington Post* reported Mueller quit the club and then "sent a letter requesting a dues refund in accordance with normal club practice and never heard back." Trump said this was "a huge conflict of interest" and meant the investigation was tainted. It wasn't much money. Most people paid about $40,000 to get in. "He probably didn't get his money back," says Trump D.C. member Ned Scherer, "but I don't know anybody that's gotten their money back since Trump bought it."

It's all legal, but it also means he's got a kind of golfing Ponzi scheme going: The money could be long spent, but it doesn't matter because Mr. X, who is leaving, gets his deposit back from Mr. Y, who is coming. Trump never has to reach into his pocket. It all works great—until something really bad happens, like an infestation of glowworms ruins all your greens and you didn't buy glowworm insurance.

Whenever I talk to people who belong to Trump courses but hate Trump, they always say the same thing: "I'm just here to play golf. It's got nothing to do with Trump. I'd never support him personally."

Memo to them: When you forked over your $200,000, it went right in his pocket.

Trump as president is baffling to the political world, but to we golfers, he speaks our language. Often, he speaks it at the excruciatingly wrong time, but he speaks it.

For instance, when 17 people were murdered at Stoneman Douglas High School in Florida, Trump wanted teachers to start packing guns in class. But not just any teachers. "I want highly trained people that have a natural talent...like hitting a golf ball...or putting....How come some people always make the 4-footer and some people, under pressure, can't even take their club back!"

STAFFER: Mr. President, there's been yet another mass murder in our schools!

TRUMP: Find me a good putter!

Of his dalliances with the Kremlin, Trump once said, "This Russia stuff is nasty business. Much nastier than trying to make a three-foot putt."

For the rest of the world, it's an ethical horror show, but for his golf buddies, Trump as president is a hoot. A friend of mine is tight with Trump. Has been forever. Talks to him once a week. He wouldn't speak on the record, but he summed it up like this: "Look, The Donald is The Donald. He's fun. He's nuts. He's full of shit. He'll probably go down as the worst president of all time, but he'll always be a friend of mine."

Trump's pal, architect Tom Fazio, says the world takes Trump way too seriously. "I love that Donald will say anything. I mean, anything! He just shoots from the hip and crazy stuff comes out. He's always been like that. But the press thinks he's serious. He's usually not serious."

But...but...but...we're talking about nukes, climate change, refugees, guns, Russia, China, war, the future of the nation, and the future of life on this big ball. Maybe it's time he got a little serious?

Neither Trump nor anybody with the Trump Organization would talk to me or take my questions for this book. But maybe the whole problem with Trump's presidency is golf itself. Golf is a solitary game. In golf, it's just you and that great big course waiting with all its perils and traps. But to run the world, you need teammates. Trump hates teammates. That's one reason he loves golf so much. He's always in a cart by himself, 100 yards ahead of everybody else, just Him and his caddy, the better to kick and throw and foozle. But you can't kick and throw and foozle your way through a presidency. You can't cheat and fudge and fake running the world, for one good reason:

You don't own the course.

16

THE STAIN

Remember, Ricky, golf is a gentleman's sport.
—Jack Reilly

WHEN JAPAN SURRENDERED AT the end of World War II, my Army lieutenant dad was assigned to duty in Tokyo. He'd heard that Emperor Hirohito played golf. So he went to the Imperial Palace and knocked on the guard house door. When they asked what he wanted, he said, "Well, I wondered if the emperor might like to play golf with me this afternoon."

That's how it's always been in my family. Golf solves everything. Our very bones are made of balata. The whole family golfs—nieces, nephews, uncles, aunts, nearly every single one of us. I can remember, when I was six years old, my mom, dad, and brother being on the pages of the sports section because they all were playing in the same tournament. I have an aunt who still wins her flight and she's 91. We have a giant nine-hole family tournament every year—The Reilly Roundup—and everybody wears a yellow shirt, just like the one we buried my dad in.

So when a man like President Donald Trump pees all over the game I love, lies about it, cheats at it, and literally drives tire tracks all over it, it digs a divot in my soul and makes me want to march into the Oval Office, grab him by that long red tie, and yell, "Stop it!"

You can think Trump has made America great again. You can think Trump has made America hate again. But there's one thing I know: He's made golf terrible again.

We were just getting past the stereotype of golf being a game for fat, blowhard, rich white guys playing on fenced-off courses while people of color push lawnmowers behind them—and along comes Trump.

We were just getting people out of their stupid golf carts and back to walking, the way golf is best—when along comes Trump, a man who believes exercise only leads to death, who *never* walks when he plays, even in defiance of his walk-only rules at Turnberry and Aberdeen.

We were just getting millennials to think golf was cool again with stylish, athletic players like Tiger and Jordan Spieth and Lexi Thompson—when along comes Trump in his 1990 Dockers ready to bust at the seam playing overwatered, gold-doorknob golf courses with all his cronies, making golf about as cool as Depends and leaving a big orange stain on the game we may never get out.

Trump treats golf like it's some sort of reward for being rich. In fact, that's *exactly* what he thinks. "I'd like to see golf be an aspirational game," he has said more than once, "where you aspire to join a club someday, you want to play, you go out and become successful. That's the way I feel."

Enjoy bowling, poor people! Sucks to be you.

He said it to a *Golf Digest* reporter once, and the reporter was flabbergasted. He replied, "So you'd like [golf] to be an elitist activity?"

Trump: "It was always meant to be, and people get there through success."

No, that's *never* what it was meant to be. It was a game invented in Scotland by shepherds. In Scotland, it's still a game of the people. It's available and affordable to everybody from the blue bloods who live in the stately mansions to the rough hands who laid the bricks. At most golf clubs in Scotland, you finish your round, tip your caddy, then drink with him at the bar afterward. He's a member.

Golf in America isn't the least bit Trumpy, either. The average price of four hours of fresh-air fun in America is $35, according to the National Golf Foundation. It's too wonderful a game to confine to any one set of people. Ninety percent of golfers play primarily at public courses. Golf is for everybody of any age, race, or bank account. So what's wrong with that? Okay, they'll never have white Rolls-Royces or solid-gold telescopes, but why can't they have golf?

"Any golf, any place, any time is going to do a soul good," Ben Crenshaw once told me. "It's not just for the rich. Golf is for everybody. Golf makes a difference in people's lives. It doesn't matter who you are, young and old, rich or poor, it's a game that you can stay with the rest of your life. There aren't many games like that."

Golf should be aspirational? That's not what Arnold Palmer thought. The son of a club pro, Arnie brought golf to the plumbers and the typists.

Golf is a reward for making money? That's not what Tiger Woods thinks, either. The son of a Vietnam vet, the first black winner of the Masters, he's opened up the game to hundreds of millions of people.

Golf is a reward for success? That's not what The First Tee thinks. It gives low-income kids a chance to learn golf's gifts of skill, manners, and friendship, for free. Ask Tom Watson. You go to his house and his trophy cases are mostly empty. They're on loan to The First Tee.

If golf was only for country club kids, the world would've never known Sam Snead, Ben Hogan, Byron Nelson, Arnie, Seve Ballesteros, Tiger Woods, Michelle Wie, and 100 other great players.

But here's where Trump is killing my game: Only 8.5% of Americans play golf, which means 91.5% don't really know what it's about. They don't get the jubilation of watching a little ball that was just *sitting there* a few seconds ago rocket off against a bright blue sky to a target 300 yards away no wider than a broomstick. They don't get that 18 briskly walked holes carrying your bag is a joyous way to work out. They've never known the feeling of laughing with three friends all afternoon so hard that you just *gotta* go an emergency 9. How many of that 91.5% won't even try the game now because of Trump? How many more will listen to his blowhard golf bragging and hear about his shameless cheating and avoid golf like bed bugs?

Most people want to grow the game. Double Down wants to shrink it. "It shouldn't be a game for all strata of society," he once said. "It should be aspirational. By getting away from it, it actually hurt golf."

No, what's hurting golf is Trump.

You might be thinking, "What does golf have to do with being president? What does it matter that he cheats at it? What's it got to do with leading the country?"

Everything.

If you'll cheat to win at golf, is it that much further to cheat to win an election? To turn a Congressional vote? To stop an investigation?

If you'll lie about every aspect of the game, is it that much further to lie about your taxes, your relationship with Russians, your groping of women?

If you're adamant that that the poor don't deserve golf, is it that much further to think they don't deserve health care, clean air, safe schools?

I'm glad my dad didn't live to see a Commander in Cheat like Trump. It would've turned his stomach. Somebody who wins club championships from the next state is not a gentleman. Somebody who makes his caddies cheat for him to earn their tip is not a gentleman. Somebody who bullies and manipulates and yells that his courses are the best in the world when that world absolutely knows otherwise is not a gentleman.

I feel sorry for Donald Trump. I feel sorry for someone who has to juggle that many spinning lies, who has to fight that many endless feuds, who has to cheat and lie and insult so many good people just to stand on a rickety first-place podium that never stops needing rebuilding. How exhausting must that be?

The truth is, the person in golf Donald Trump cheats the most is himself. He's cheating himself of the joy, the endless challenge, golf brings. Every golfer who loves the game loves it for the battle it brings within himself—*Can I rise up to be as good as I want to be today?* In life, we're defined by the obstacles we overcome. That's the stuff we hang on our inner wall. But if you cheat to get around those obstacles, you never know the thrill of actually beating them.

It's like buying a trophy in a pawn shop. You can shine it up and show it off and pretend you won it, but when you get close to it, it only reflects the face of a loser.

Acknowledgments

I'm deeply grateful to Mauro DiPreta, who believed in this from the get-go and took it 93% of the way, through no fault of his own. *Non posso aspettare i tesori tu trovare prossimo, amico.*

Thanks, also, to my terrific researcher and tiny-shoulder-to-lean-on, Marianne (Moose) Moore, who was always there for me, no matter what giant cyclops she was having to slay at the same time. You are the strongest little person I've ever met.

A large debt of gratitude goes to some terrific friends and reporters in the golf-writing dodge, most especially John Huggan, Jeff Babineau, Michael Bamberger, Jaime Diaz, Alan Shipnuck, Stephanie Wei, Geoff Shackleford, Eamon Lynch, et al. If you'd ever stop working and come to the bar, I owe you each a cold beer.

Thanks to Gwenda Blair, Trump's biographer, who kept

taking my endless calls with kindness. If you were grinding your teeth, I never heard it.

Thanks very much to my fabulous pit-bull agent and life-long friend, Janet Pawson. (Good luck to us!) And thanks to the whole squadron of terrific and smart people who pushed this thing over the finish line: Sarah Falter, David Lamb (sorry about my damn laptop), Michael Barrs, and Odette Fleming.

Mostly, though, thanks and all my love to TLC, The Lovely Cynthia, who put up with a book that consumed me like a raging wildfire. She kept bringing me coffee and killer homemade pizza to fuel that fire. You are the double eagle of wives.

Lastly, thank you to every reporter out there who keeps pursuing the truth head-first into the worst hurricane of lies, insults, and constitution-trampling I've seen in my 40 years in this business. You inspire me.

In a time of universal deceit, telling the truth is a revolutionary act.

—Unknown

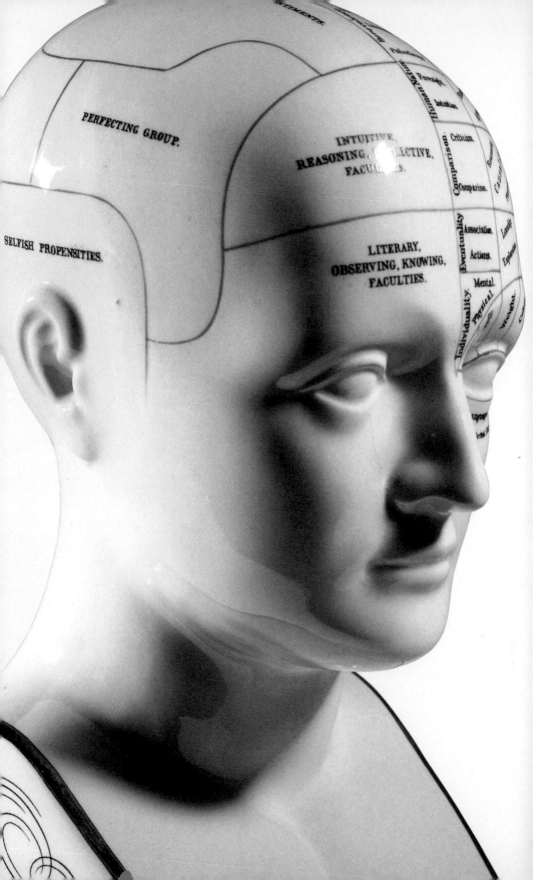

KILL
OR CURE

AN ILLUSTRATED
HISTORY OF MEDICINE

STEVE PARKER

LONDON, NEW YORK, MUNICH,
MELBOURNE, DELHI

Senior Editor	Angela Wilkes
Senior Art Editor	Michael Duffy
Editors	Andy Szudek
	Hugo Wilkinson
	Georgina Palffy
	Victoria Pyke
	Anna Fischel
Editorial Consultant	Martyn Page
Designers	Mark Lloyd
	Jane Ewart
Picture Research	Luped Media Research
Jacket Designer	Laura Brim
Jacket Editor	Manisha Majithia
Jacket Design Manager	Sophia M.T.T.
Producer, Pre-production	Lucy Sims
Production Controller	Mandy Inness
Managing Editor	Stephanie Farrow
Senior Managing Art Editor	Lee Griffiths
Publisher	Andrew Macintyre
Art Director	Phil Ormerod
Associate Publishing Director	Liz Wheeler
Publishing Director	Jonathan Metcalf

First published in Great Britain in 2013
by Dorling Kindersley Limited
80 Strand, London WC2R 0RL

Penguin Group (UK)
2 4 6 8 10 9 7 5 3 1
001–192575–Nov/13

Copyright © 2013
Dorling Kindersley Limited

A CIP catalogue record for this book is
available from the British Library.

ISBN 978-1-4093-3272-5

Printed and bound by
South China Printing Company, China.

Discover more at
www.dk.com

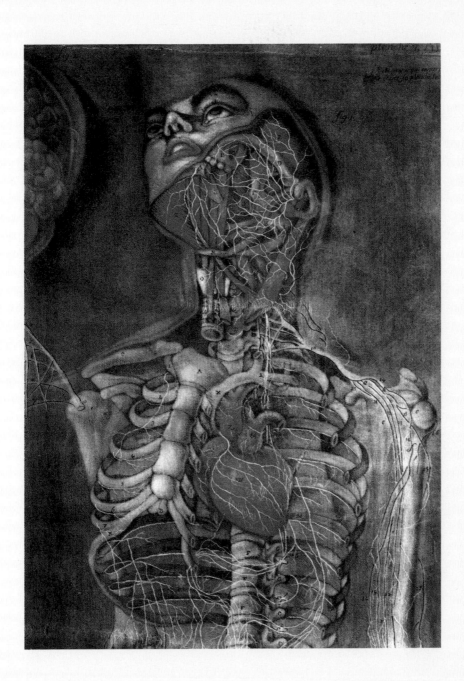

Contents

Introduction

What is a doctor? In ancient Egypt, healing was the perogative of sorcerers, while in early Greece doctors were considered itinerant curiosities more likely to harm than help. By the 16th century, innovative doctors were practising an eclectic mix of medicine, alchemy, astrology, herbalism, mineralogy, psychotherapy, and faith-healing, while in the modern world medicine has evolved to make it possible for doctors to operate on patients remotely from another continent.

Today, there is a complex array of scanning and imaging options with which to view the inside of the body, but in ancient Egypt such information would have been deemed utterly irrelevant: examining the patient was unheard of at a time when illness was considered to be the work of the gods. Hippocrates, who practised in ancient Greece and was considered by many to be the father of modern medicine, found himself imprisoned for many years when he rejected the idea that illness was the whim of deities. Yet by the time he died, he had revolutionized the practice of medicine and established the basic foundations of the role of the physician.

Many others contributed, of course – Imhotep of Egypt, Chakara in India, Galen in Rome, and Zhang Zhongjing of China in ancient times. Islam's medieval Golden Age boasted al-Rhazi and Ibn Sina (Avicenna), and the Renaissance had anatomist Andreas Vesalius and the groundbreaking Paracelsus, who founded many of the principles of modern medicine. All these figures contributed to medicine, often in ways that challenged the conventional views of the time.

Of course, there were many wildly inaccurate theories, and some – to our eyes – outlandish remedies, from boiled newborn puppies to the ashes of a burnt swallow (used to "cure" hirsuitism). So popular was bloodletting by leech that at one point doctors were actually known as "leeches". And so established were Galen's theories on human anatomy that for centuries, no one questioned the fact that his findings had been gathered by dissecting the bodies of dogs and monkeys, rather than humans. Alongside the more spectacular "medicines", however, were herbs and minerals that to this day form the basis of tried-and-tested drug cures, and in amongst the quacks and charlatans were many diligent and painstaking innovators.

Rigorous observation and detailed detective work have played a huge part in the development of medicine. Before English physician William Harvey published his momentous book on the heart and circulation in 1628, for example, he spent over 20 years dissecting and experimenting on the pulsing hearts of thousands of animals from more than 60 species. Building on concepts and evidence dating back to ancient times, Harvey also wove theory and practice into a scientifically sound, evidence-based

ENGRAVING OF MALE MUSCULATURE
Andreas Vesalius's great work *De Humani Corporis Fabrica*, 1543, established a new standard of clarity and accuracy in the study of human anatomy.

description of the circulatory system. Armed with this knowledge, physicians were able to make major improvements in the way they diagnosed and treated disease. There are, of course, famous instances where chance has also played an important role. Had the weather not been unseasonably cold when Scottish medical researcher Alexander Fleming left his messy laboratory to go on holiday, for example, he might not have discovered penicillin, which has since prevented immeasurable suffering and saved countless lives. It took the stimulus of World War II, however, to fully realise the potential of this, the first antibiotic.

War and conflict have given impetus to many branches of medicine, acting as a catalyst for innovation and learning. One of the earliest medical documents, the 3,600-year-old Smith Papyrus of ancient Egypt, describes treatment of wounds probably sustained on the battlefield; in ancient Rome, gladiators' injuries provided valuable medical insight at a time when human dissection was forbidden. In the 16th century, French army surgeon Ambroise Paré used innovative procedures, such as poultices and ligatures, that then filtered from the battlefield through to general surgery. Another French surgeon, Baron Dominique Jean Larrey, pioneered the use of ambulances and triage in the 19th century. During World War I, doctors noted that mustard gas affected fast-multiplying cells in the body, which ultimately led to the development of anti-cancer chemotherapy drugs. Medicine even benefited from the most deadly weapon of all, the atomic bomb: its effects indirectly led to bone marrow transplants and one of medicine's newest areas of research – stem cell therapy.

The journey made by the science of medicine is an astonishing one. Nowadays we take for granted our modern operating theatres with their rigorously germ-free environments and sterilized equipment, but it is worth remembering that the notion of germs as transmittors of infection has only existed since the 19th century. It is also hard to imagine that there was a surprising amount of surgery already taking place millennia ago: holes were being drilled in patients' heads from prehistoric times through to the 18th century, for example. And while in ancient Greece it was rare for the skin to be deliberately broken, surgeons in ancient Rome developed tools, equipment, and procedures not dissimilar to those in use today. However, modern surgery is also making use of robots, lasers, and mind-boggling technology. Just as we struggle to imagine prehistoric brain surgery, it is equally hard to imagine just how much has been achieved by modern medicine. It has waged war on age-old killers such as cholera, smallpox, and tuberculosis, decoded our DNA, mapped the human genome, and created the potential for nanotechnology and tissue-engineering. The future ambition for medicine is phenomenal, but the challenges are not to be underestimated.

Better nutrition, improved public health and hygiene, safety awareness, and health education have accompanied medicine in bringing immense strides in life quality and longevity over the past century. Prominent medical advances have included vaccinations, antibiotics, new drugs and medicines, safer surgery, improved care during pregnancy and childbirth, and recognition of health hazards such as carcinogens, pollutants, occupational issues, and risk factors for heart disease, stroke, and other major killers. However, medicine is now big business, with economics preventing equality from keeping pace with technology, so that millions of people still have little, if any, access to healthcare.

The episodes in this book have been selected to illustrate how medicine has changed from the inspired, dedicated, but often isolated individuals of the past to today's specialist teams equipped with the latest technology. Anecdotal rather than encyclopedic, the book aims to give non-technical insights into the intrinsically fascinating, occasionally horrifying, and always captivating subject of medicine.

Beliefs and Traditions

TO 900

Medicine is as old as humankind. More than 50,000 years ago, stone-age, cave-dwelling humans first crushed and infused herbs for their curative properties. Traditional forms of medicine – sadly, few of which are known to written history – evolved on all continents, from the deserts and jungles of Africa to North American plains, South American rainforests, and balmy Pacific islands.

Earliest records in West Asia, the Middle East, North Africa, China, and India document myriad diseases, healing plants, and surgical procedures. Ancient Egyptians had complex, hierarchical methods of medicine integrated into their religious beliefs. Gods and spirits were in charge of mortal disease, and priest-physicians – Imhotep is one of the first great names in medical history – mediated with the supernatural realm to ease human suffering.

The civilizations of Greece and Rome had their respective medical giants in Hippocrates and Galen. Hippocrates set standards for patient care and the physician's attitudes and philosophy that persist today. Galen wrote so extensively and authoritatively that his theories and practices attained quasi-religious status and effectively stalled medical progress in Europe for 1,400 years. After the Roman Empire ended, the murky arts of alchemy, sorcery, exorcism, and miracle cures flourished in Western Europe.

Ancient India and China also developed sophisticated medical systems with outstanding contributors. In India, in the centuries before and after Hippocrates, Susruta and Chakara produced encyclopaedic founding works of Ayurvedic medicine. Chinese physician Zhang Zhongjing, a contemporary of Galen, also compiled works that described hundreds of diseases and prescribed thousands of remedies.

Prehistoric Medicine

TIME: 30,000 YEARS AGO, approaching the depths of the last great ice age. Place: a clearing next to a rock cavern, in the Iberian Peninsula, Western Europe. As dusk falls, a band of stocky, thick-set humans, draped in rough, furry cloaks, gathers around a bed of ferns, heathers, and moss. On the bed lies the oldest of the group – a male aged about 40 years. His eyes are closed as if he is asleep, his skin is pale, and his breathing is weak. The onlookers murmur and chant with guttural sounds, occasionally raising their heads to gesture at the setting sun. In the flickering firelight, one of the younger females raises her voice to a passionate howl, leaps up, and comes forward to press a bitter-smelling paste into the old man's mouth. He stirs slowly, opens his eyes – and smiles.

The scene, of course, is fictional. But something like this may have happened at El Sidron, a well-studied archaeological site in northwest Spain. Here, hundreds of fossilized bones and teeth were found that once belonged to some 13 Neanderthals (*Homo neanderthalensis*) – our "sister" species of human, which died out 30,000–25,000 years ago. In 2012, scientists analysed teeth from five of the Neanderthals, using an advanced technique known as pyrolysis gas-chromatography mass spectrometry. Trapped in the hardened plaque layer (called "calculus") on each tooth were microfossils and other remains of plants that their owners had eaten. Evidence of wood smoke and starchy cooked plants was found, and one individual had eaten bitter-tasting plants, including yarrow and chamomile. These herbs have no real nutritional value, and their bitter taste must have been off-putting. So why were they eaten? One possibility is that the plants were used as natural medications. Yarrow has long been known as a traditional tonic and astringent, and chamomile as a relaxant and anti-inflammatory.

The evidence at El Sidron points to some of the earliest known human medicine – the prevention, identification, treatment, and curing of illness and disease. Our understanding of prehistoric times depends on the study of preserved human remains, artefacts such as tools and adornments, and natural objects like plant seeds and animal fossils. Cave paintings and rock art also help. Several prehistoric images show human forms with the heart included, but there seems to be little other graphic evidence of anatomical

THE FIRST TASTE OF MEDICINE
The fossilized teeth of Neanderthals who lived up to 30,000 years ago have been found to contain traces of various herbs, including chamomile and yarrow. Such herbs are thought to have been the very first medicines.

SOOTHING HERB
The plant species *Nepeta cataria* – commonly
known as catnip – was used in prehistoric
treatments for settling the stomach.

awareness. Vital insights into prehistoric
medicine also come from modern
anthropology – gathering information
from native cultures, especially in the
Americas, Africa, Asia, and Australasia.
Studies of these cultures suggest that
prehistoric peoples had a mix of religious
and spiritual beliefs about the causes of
disease – typically attributing them to
possession by evil spirits, or revenge for
sinful behaviour. To effect healing, they
combined mystical and supernatural actions, such as making
offerings to the spirits, sacrifices to the gods, and pleas to lift a curse,
with practical treatments such as poultices, ointments, and
concoctions made from herbs, minerals, and animal body parts such
as blood and powdered bones. In hunter-gatherer times, before
the advent of agriculture and settlement, long-distance organized
trade was very limited, so all forms of medication came from the
local environment.

Anthropologists have also suggested that one member of a group
would have held a special position in medical matters – a man
variously referred to as a healer, shaman, or medicine-man (see
pp.88–89), whose duties included being a priest, a soothsayer, an
oracle, an advisor, or even a ruler. This shaman was believed to hold
special powers, such as the ability to communicate with the gods and
spirits, and was also proficient at preparing herbal potions and
administering hands-on treatments such as massage.

Working back from modern anthropological knowledge, and using
preserved evidence such as bones and artefacts, the following
treatments are thought to date back to prehistoric times: fractured or
broken bones were put back in their natural positions to heal; clay or
mud was plastered onto broken limbs and left to dry hard, as a
prehistoric version of a plaster-cast; splints, made of wood, bone, or
horn secured with plant vines and fibrous bark, were bound to broken

limbs; wounds were dressed with poultices of healing herbs and covered with rudimentary bandage strips cut from animal hides; stomach and digestive problems were eased by chewing orchid bulbs or drinking their extracts; certain types of willow bark – the original source of acetylsalicylic acid, better known as aspirin – were chewed to relieve pain and reduce swelling; witch hazel and saps from various trees and plants were used to soothe burns and scalds; and some types of clay or soil were eaten (in a practice known as "geophagy") to neutralize harmful substances in contaminated foods and provide minerals lacking in the diet.

Dentistry was also practised. Among the tens of thousands of objects found at the prehistoric site of Mehrgarh, near Sibi in west-central Pakistan, were 11 human teeth – all molars, and probably from nine individuals – that had apparently been drilled using a device tipped with a sharp-pointed flint. Researchers have reconstructed the device – essentially an arrow with a bow-saw used to rotate it (see p.20) – and estimated that the holes were made in less than a minute. The condition of the teeth and the subsequent wear marks in the holes show that they were drilled while the owners were still alive – although, oddly, only four of them show signs of decay.

Drills were also used for trepanning (see pp.20–21) – a radical form of surgery that involved breaching the skull to expose the layers of tissue covering the brain (meninges), and sometimes even the brain tissue itself. The earliest known trepanning procedures were performed using the cracked edges of flints, which were used as chippers or scrapers to remove the bone, either fragment by fragment, or to gouge a channel around a central area of bone that could then be lifted clear. More sophisticated techniques involved using bow-saw rotary drills – larger ones than those employed at Mehrgarh. As for the purpose of

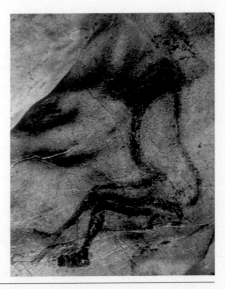

PREHISTORIC DEER DOCTOR
This 20,0000-year-old cave painting in Ariège, France, shows a figure believed to be a healing priest. Dressed in a deer skin and antlers, he may be dancing to drive away evil spirits.

trepanning, the oldest explanations centre on the notion of releasing evil spirits from the patient, who would then keep the removed piece of bone as a talisman to prevent the spirits returning. Modern interpretations suggest that these prehistoric patients may have been incapacitated by the unbearable pain of migraine, or the involuntary seizures of epilepsy. Other possibilities include intense depression and severe bipolar disorder, or internal bleeding causing intracranial pressure, compressing the brain tissue and causing life-threatening damage. As indicated by Hippocrates (see pp.30–39), trepanning was also useful as a drastic first-aid measure in the case of head wounds – again, to help relieve intracranial pressure by releasing the blood from a haemorrhage beneath the skull.

In 1991, a naturally preserved, mummified, and frozen male human body was found in the European Alps, near the border between Austria and Italy. He became known as Ötzi the Iceman, and is now one of the most studied of all human bodies. Ötzi was about 45 years old when he died 5,300 years ago. He had sophisticated leather garments and shoes under a woven-grass cloak, and carried a knife, axe, bow, arrows, bark containers, and what might have been a simple prehistoric medical kit. Two of Ötzi's possessions were thumb-sized lumps of a fungus or mould known as *Piptoporus betulinus* (birch polypore, razor strop, or birch bracket fungus). Each lump was holed to thread onto a leather strip so that it could be secured, probably to clothing. The medicinal properties of this fungus feature in many folklore traditions and have been supported by scientific analysis. It is a laxative, and eating it can bring on diarrhoea. It also shows antibiotic action, and contains substances that are poisonous to intestinal parasites such as whipworm, *Trichuris trichura*. It so happens that Ötzi had whipworm, as revealed by detailed medical examination of his remains that showed worm eggs in his large intestine.

Perhaps even more intriguing were Ötzi's tattoos. There were more than 50 of these scattered over his body – on the left wrist, left calf, right knee, both ankles, right foot, and on both sides of his

LIFE EXPECTANCY IN PREHISTORIC TIMES

25–40 YEARS

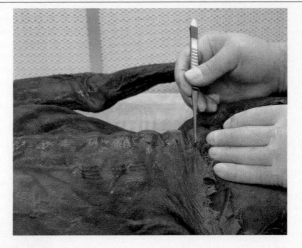

ICE AGE TATTOOS
A pathologist examines the remains of Ötzi the Iceman, whose tattoos may have been part of a prehistoric treatment similar to acupuncture or acupressure.

lower backbone – all arranged in groups of parallel lines. They were probably made by rubbing charcoal into incisions made in his skin, and being so widespread, and mostly hidden by clothes and shoes, it is unlikely that they were for decoration.

X-rays and CT scans show Ötzi's skeleton suffered from degenerative bone and joint conditions of the back, knees, and ankles. Some tattoos were positioned over these possibly painful areas. Perhaps they were some kind of symbolic therapy for relief. Another idea is that they were related to a form of acupuncture or acupressure therapy; many of the lines correspond to the acupuncture lines known as channels or meridians in Chinese medicine (see pp.64–73). Ötzi's full medical mystery is yet to be solved, but he does support the growing evidence that prehistoric medicine was more sophisticated than many modern experts have assumed.

Trepanning

As long ago as 10,000 BCE, in places ranging from France and western Asia to South America, surgeons practised trepanning – cutting or drilling holes in patients' skulls using flint tools. This treatment is the oldest known surgical procedure, and it may have been intended to relieve the pressure caused by depressed skull fractures, to treat seizures or mental health disorders, or to release evil spirits from the patient's head.

Prehistoric trepanning

Many of the earliest trepanning operations were carried out using a wooden bow drill. To spin the drill, the surgeon wound the leather thong around the drill shaft and moved the bow with a sawing motion.

TREPANNED PREHISTORIC SKULLS HAVE BEEN FOUND WITH HOLES DRILLED IN VARIOUS LOCATIONS ON THE HEAD

Parietal bone of the skull

BRONZE AGE SKULL
ISRAEL, 2200–2000 BCE
Excavated at Jericho (now in the West Bank, western Asia), this skull has a cluster of holes made by trepanning. The holes are circular, showing that the surgeon used a drill – incisions made by a knife are usually square or irregular in shape.

Flint drill tip

Shark's tooth drill tip

Bow

REPLICA NEOLITHIC TREPANNING BOW DRILL
BRITISH, 1930–70
British researcher Dr T.W. Parry used this bow drill and other tools in experiments to investigate ancient trepanning techniques.

At the edges of the holes, the bone is beginning to grow back, showing that this patient survived the risky operation – many did not

Frontal bone of the skull

Later tools

Trepanning was still common in the 18th century, and surgeons used sharp metal trepanning tools to treat head wounds and conditions such as epilepsy. However, high mortality rates, especially when the surgeon pierced the tissue beneath the bone, meant that the practice declined during the 19th century.

TREPANNING DRILL
BRITISH, 18TH CENTURY

The typical trepanning drill was shaped like a carpenter's brace and bit. The surgeon held the wooden top piece firmly and rotated the drill by turning the bulbous handle in the middle of the metal crank.

DRILL BITS
BRITISH, 18TH CENTURY

The drill came with metal bits of different sizes. Each has a central spike to help the surgeon position it precisely, and serrations designed to cut into bone.

The Priest-Physicians of Egypt

A S PREHISTORY SHADED INTO HISTORY, medicine developed into a more sophisticated art. Glimpses of this development can be seen in the early civilizations of West Asia's "Fertile Crescent", or Mesopotamia – the land of the Tigris–Euphrates river system, now mainly Iraq plus adjoining parts of Turkey, Syria, and Iran. From some 5,300 years ago, the wedge-like cuneiform writing of Sumeria and the following Akkadian, Assyrian, and Babylonian cultures provide tantalizing snapshots of physicians and their craft. Some medical practitioners of the time, known as ashipus, decreed that ailments were caused by spirits and could be cured by sorcery. They would divine which particular evil sprite was responsible for the problem, and then try to drive it away by means of chants, spells, and curses. Another class of practitioners, the asus, were more involved in practical treatments, such as preparing herbal potions, washing, massage, and bandaging balms onto affected parts of the body. Ashipus and asus often worked together, one helping the other, although they kept their trades distinct and carefully guarded their most precious secrets.

Hammurabi (meaning Kinsman Healer) was ruler of Babylon from around 3,800 to 3,760 years ago. His famous Law Code, written in cuneiform script on a pillar of diorite stone, included several pronouncements on medical care. These held physicians responsible both for success and failure. Rewards and punishments depended partly on the standing of the patient. Saving the life of a noble "with a bronze lancet" was worth ten shekels (more than a year's pay for the average tradesperson),

KINSMAN HEALER
Babylonian king Hammurabi (left) receives his royal insignia from the sun god Shamash.

while saving a slave was worth two shekels. However, if a wealthy patient died under the surgeon's knife, that surgeon could lose a hand – and a lost slave would have to be replaced. Frustratingly, the Code gives few descriptions of the type of surgery practised at the time, and no mention is made of the use of herbs or mineral potions for medical treatment – perhaps because the illnesses treated in this way were believed to be caused by evil spirits or sins, and so were not the physician's responsibility.

Gula, or Ninkarrak, was the Babylonian goddess of healing and the patron goddess of physicians. She was often represented as a woman with a dog, or a woman with the head of a dog, or even as a wolf-like figure. Patients dedicated dog statues and even live dog sacrifices to her, hoping to recover from disease. She came to prominence around 3,600 years ago, during the time of the Kassites – an ancient Babylonian civilization – and her main temples were at Isin (modern-day Ishan al-Bahriyat, Iraq) and Nippur (Nuffar in-Afak, also in Iraq). Herbal and other plant remedies were numerous in those times. Recipes for healing poultices included dregs of wine, prunes, and pine sap, all of which have antibacterial properties – although the addition of lizard excrement is less easy to justify.

Ancient Egypt's gods and spirits were deeply woven into the daily routine and working lives of tradespeople and professionals, so it is difficult, from our modern perspective, to disentangle the truly medical parts of the Egyptian physician's job from his religious and spiritual activities. This task becomes even more difficult when the physician in question is Imhotep (also known as Imuthes), who lived in Heliopolis 4,650–4,600 years ago.

Imhotep ("He who comes in peace") lived during the early phase of Egypt's Old Kingdom, and his fame rapidly spread far and wide. Even during his earthly life, he attained demi-god status, which was unique for an ordinary citizen or commoner in Egyptian society, where such honours were reserved for persons of royal descent. By the late New Kingdom, 3,000 years ago, he was regarded as a full

"Eat, drink, and be merry, for tomorrow we shall die"

IMHOTEP

deity and the son of Ptah, the creator-god or fashioner of the universe and the benefactor of craftspeople. Ptah's partner was Sekhmet (Sachmes), the lion-headed goddess of warfare and healing – and held to be the mother of Imhotep. Some historical sources describe Imhotep as a hands-on healer who was skilled at preparing soothing potions to treat conditions such as arthritis and gout. Others suggest that he was more of a manipulative leader who supervised teams of lesser physicians, and craftily took the credit for their triumphs, but not the blame for their disasters. Imhotep's standing as a cult medical practitioner persisted in Ancient Greece, where he was twinned or even merged with Asclepios (see p.32), the Greek god of healing.

Another great physician of Imhotep's day was Hesy-Ra, who served Pharaoh Djoser as Chief Dentist and Physician. He was venerated for his tooth-pulling and other oral skills, and he seems to have recognized what we now call diabetes mellitus by noticing that some patients urinated frequently and copiously.

Much is known about Ancient Egypt from preserved papyri – documents made from a grass-like sedge plant of the Nile known as the papyrus. Only a few papyri deal with medical matters. One is the Smith Papyrus, named after American Egyptologist and collector Edwin Smith, who purchased it in Luxor in 1862. The Smith Papyrus is incomplete, ends in mid-sentence, and dates to some 3,600 years ago, but the hieroglyphic style and phraseology suggest that it was copied from a much older document – possibly written or dictated by Imhotep himself. Dealing mainly with wounds, injuries, general trauma management, and surgery, the Smith Papyrus has little in the way of supernatural or magical content compared to other papyri of the time. There is only one chant or incantation pleading to the gods for assistance and blessing. Instead, the content is organized

DIVINE IMHOTEP
The Egyptian physician Imhotep was deified after his death, becoming the god of medicine and the son of the creator-god Ptah.

GODDESS OF HEALING
The lion-headed and cobra-crowned Sekhmet was a warrior goddess as well as a goddess of healing. She was said to be the mother of Imhotep.

in a rational progression from the head to the lower back, and the text demonstrates sound scientific knowledge in its treatment of muscles, bones, joints, and the blood supply. The papyrus discusses 48 case histories, each of which is laid out in a familiar, modern style, including a description of the problem all the way from examination and diagnosis to outlook and treatment. The practice of examining the patient to make a diagnosis is taken for granted today, but in Ancient Egypt, where gods ruled while moving in mysterious ways, interfering in this way was unheard of.

Among the Smith Papyrus cases are the earliest known descriptions of the cranial sutures (the joints between skull bones), the meninges (the layers surrounding the brain), and the cerebrospinal fluid (the liquid that surrounds and cushions the brain). Injuries at particular sites, including the brain and the cervical spine (neck vertebrae), are linked to loss of sensation and paralysis in various parts of the body, and to incontinence and quadriplegia. The Smith Papyrus treatments also include some of the first mentions of closing wounds with sutures (stitches), using raw meat to stem bleeding, and applying honey to prevent or treat infection. For example, Case Three states: "A man having a gaping head wound... penetrating to the bone... perforating his skull... After thou has stitched it, thou should lay fresh meat upon his wound the first day. Thou should not bind it... Thou should treat it afterward with grease, honey, and lint every day, until he recovers..." With its emphasis on trauma, the Smith Papyrus could be considered a manual for treating soldiers wounded in battle, or workers maimed on major construction projects, such as the pyramids – and the authors knew the limits of their craft. Of the 48 Smith Papyrus cases, 14 are classed as "Outcome Unfavourable: An ailment not to be treated… A case which the surgeon cannot cure and which he is led to discuss by his scientific interest alone".

Another valuable document of the time is the Ebers Papyrus, which, like the Smith Papyrus, physically dates from around 3,500 years ago, but was probably copied from much older documents, possibly originating in Imhotep's time. In 1872, it was bought by the German writer and Egyptologist Georg Ebers, who specialized in penning historical novels set in Ancient Egypt, Greece, and Rome. It has about 110 pages, is more than 20m (66 ½ft) long, is 30cm (12in) tall, and currently resides at the University of Leipzig, Germany, where Ebers was professor of Egyptian studies. In contrast to the Smith Papyrus, the Ebers Papyrus details hundreds of spells, chants, and incantations designed to expel evil and disease from the sufferer, as well as many herbal and mineral remedies. Also, the contents are less systematically organized. They begin with magic spells to ward off bad spirits, then describe an extensive array of parasitic gut infestations, bowel diseases, skin problems, ulcers, anal problems, heart conditions, head-based disorders, urinary difficulties, wounds, and gynaecological issues.

Even older is the Kahun Gynaecological Papyrus. Dating from about 3,800 years ago, it is one of the first medical documents known, and is now in the care of University College, London. It is concerned mostly with the female reproductive system, and discusses aids to fertility, conception, pregnancy testing, and contraception. For period pains, it prescribes: "Treatment for a woman who loves bed, she does not rise, and does not shake off… her gripings or spasms of the womb… Let her drink two henu [about one litre] of khaui, and let

DIVINE PROTECTION
Amulets such as this faience (glazed ceramic) brooch were worn by Ancient Egyptians to ward off evil and to protect against disease.

her spue it out immediately". There is also a recipe for a contraceptive preparation made from honey, sour milk, and crocodile dung, to be inserted into the vagina.

Slightly later than Smith and Ebers came the Hearst, Brugsch, and London Medical Papyri. Together with evidence from tomb carvings and other artefacts, including the equipment used for mummification, these provide a good account of history's first comprehensive system of medicine. Mummy preparation (see p.29) gave Egyptian physicians a patchy knowledge of the body's insides, and practice in the use of instruments such as saws, hooks, drills, and forceps. However, treatment by surgery – apart from traumatic injuries – was rare.

The Ancient Egyptians attached great importance to diet and hygiene. False eyes, false teeth, and similar prostheses were also being developed. Yet the spiritual and magical side of healing remained central. Neck, upper-arm, wrist, calf, and ankle amulets were worn to repel visits from demons or vengeful spectres that might bring disease and suffering. And if the demons did make it into the body, then the first recourses were spells and invocations, rather than rational examination and treatment.

Surgery in Ancient Egypt

The priest-physicians of Ancient Egypt were held in great esteem. They conducted surgery mainly for the treatment of traumatic injuries: doctors stitched wounds, performed simple operations to mend broken bones, and amputated limbs, using willow-leaf bandages for their antiseptic properties. They also cut out and cauterized tumours, and may even have performed delicate procedures such as tracheotomy (opening the airway), using a wide range of tools, including scalpels and knives made of flint or the glass-like rock obsidian, which they could hone to a razor-sharp edge.

Ancient prostheses

Archaeologists have found artificial toes from Ancient Egypt – one made of wood and leather, another from plaster, glue, and linen. These are the oldest known prosthetic devices. They would have been invaluable to people who had lost a toe through injury, or as a result of gangrene caused by a condition such as diabetes, helping them to balance and walk more easily when wearing traditional Egyptian sandals.

PROSTHETIC BIG TOE OF WOOD AND LEATHER, 15TH CENTURY BCE

Saw blade

Scoop probe

Flask

Tooth forceps

Cupping vessels

Shears

RELIEF SHOWING SURGICAL TOOLS
EGYPT, 2ND CENTURY CE
This Roman-period carved relief from the temple of the crocodile-god Sobek, at Kom Ombo, illustrates a range of surgical tools, together with items used in diagnosis and in the preparation of medicines.

Catheter

Knife

Bowl

Weighing scales

Scalpel

Sponge

Mummification

When important Egyptians died, their bodies were preserved by mummification. The process involved removing the internal organs and treating the body with preservatives – the Egyptians did not place a taboo on the handling of corpses, as some later cultures did. However, embalmers made only small incisions in the corpse, so their work did not give them a detailed knowledge of anatomy.

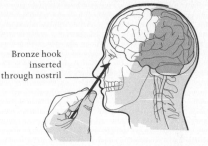

Bronze hook inserted through nostril

EXTRACTING THE BRAIN AND ORGANS
A long hook was used to pull the brain out through the nose, while the intestines, liver, stomach and lungs were removed through a cut in the left side of the body, before they could decompose. The heart – centre of emotion and intelligence – was left in for the afterlife, but all the other organs were dessicated.

ORGAN CONTAINERS
The embalmer either returned the dehydrated organs of the deceased to the body or placed them in containers called canopic jars. These jars, shaped to resemble miniature coffins and bearing the heads of guardian deities, were put in the tomb alongside the mummified body.

Hippocrates and
Greek Medicine

SOME 2,700 YEARS AGO, the original Olympic Games were being
established, and Greek civilization and influence were spreading
throughout much of Europe. Within 200 years or so, Greece had entered
its Classical phase, which saw glorious achievements in politics, art,
philosophy, and literature. In this centre of the ancient world,
Hippocrates of Cos (c.460–c.370 BCE) – perhaps the most important
figure in the history of medicine – was born.

Greek medicine borrowed much from preceding Egyptian beliefs
and practices (see pp.22–29), but it shifted away from the previous view
of disease as some kind of punishment from the gods. Greek physicians
moved towards the idea that illness was a natural phenomenon of the
body, caused by imbalances in what were known as the four "humours"
(see pp.106–107) – an idea that remained central to medicine for 2,000
years. Humorism, as it is called, may have reached Greece from
Egypt or Mesopotamia, or it may have come from the Greek idea of
the four elements – earth, air, fire, and water – as crystallized by the
philosopher Empedocles a few decades before Hippocrates. Whatever
its origin, humorism held that the body contained, or was even made
of, four fluids: blood, yellow bile, black bile, and phlegm. In a
healthy body, these humours were calm and well balanced, but if
something happened to disturb their equilibrium, illness ensued.
The type of humoral imbalance, and the particular humours
involved, defined the disease. This was because each humour had
its own special qualities, linked not only to one of the classical
elements, but also to a particular part of the body, and even to a
season of the year. Blood was associated with air, the liver, spring,
warmth, and moisture; yellow bile was related to fire, the spleen,
summer, warmth, and dryness; black bile was linked to earth, the
gall bladder, autumn, cold, and dryness; while phlegm was
related to water, the lungs, the brain, winter, cold, and dampness. So,
for example, if blood as a humour became "excessive", the illness was
likely to be warm and moist in character, with symptoms such as
redness, swelling, rapid pulse and breathing, perspiration, uneasy
sleep, and even delirium – the typical profile of a fever due to infection.

THE FATHER OF WESTERN MEDICINE
Hippocrates, here depicted treating a sick woman,
established medicine as a discipline distinct from
magic and religion.

The treatment would therefore be bleeding to reduce the quantity of
blood and its corresponding sanguine humour. Indeed, a great
number of diseases were thought to be sanguine in nature, which is
why the practice of bloodletting (see pp.132–33) became so common
in Europe. Other ways in which to restore balance to the humours
included taking herbs and foods associated with the particular
humour in question, either to increase or reduce its quantity and
influence, and the use of emetics and purges.

Hippocrates wrote a great deal about the humours in the collection
of works known as the Hippocratic Corpus, which consists of some 60
written documents, ranging from scattered notes and jottings to long,
well-argued theses and sets of case histories. The modern view is that
Hippocrates himself did not write all of these works – which vary not
only in style but in opinion – but that they were added to by students,
disciples, and later followers up to four or five centuries later. Certainly
this explains the vast scope of the Corpus, which ranges from
philosophical excursions into the nature of knowledge and the
standing of medicine within the sciences, to diagnoses of fevers and
epidemic infections, problems associated with fractured bones and
displaced joints, female infertility, veins, teeth, hygiene, dreams,
haemorrhoids, and epilepsy. This last condition was known as the
sacred disease by many Greeks, who saw it as a result of demonic

possession. The Hippocratic view rejected this idea, considering epilepsy to be a problem based entirely on the body: "Men believe only that it is a divine disease because of their ignorance and amazement".

Details of Hippocrates' life are somewhat limited, but he was a contemporary of Socrates and was referred to by various prominent Greeks, including Plato, who was about 35 years younger, and Aristotle, who was a teenager when Hippocrates died. His father may well have been a physician, and the young Hippocrates probably trained at the asclepeion on the isle of Cos, where he was born. The asclepeion was a temple dedicated to Asclepios, the Greek god of healing and medicine, and a place where the sick were treated. Asclepios himself was perhaps a derivation of one of the healing gods of Egypt, maybe the physician-turned-deity Imhotep. His trademark, known as the Rod of Asclepios, was a stick with a snake coiled around it – perhaps because potentially fatal snake venom was used in tiny doses as a therapy, or because the reptile's regular skin-shedding represented the casting off of old problems and illnesses and entering a new phase of life. Whatever its origins, the staff-and-serpent duo has been used as a symbol of medicine and the healing arts throughout the ages. Two of Asclepios's daughters also live on in medical terminology; Hygieia, linked to our word "hygiene", and Panacea, noted as the goddess of the universal cure-all.

Throughout his life, Hippocrates seems to have wandered the shores of the Aegean and inland, both in Greece and what are today Bulgaria and Turkey. He practised as a physician, wrote, lectured, tutored students, and argued about his medical ideas and practices. He was also said to be more than proficient at music, poetry, mathematics, and even athletics. At one stage he was apparently imprisoned for up to 20 years because he rejected the

GOD OF HEALING
Shown here with his snake-entwined staff, Asclepios was the Greek god of physicians, healing, and rejuvenation.

idea that deities and spirits were the causes of illness. He was sentenced by dignitaries who believed that their role was to mediate between humanity and the gods, and who saw that their power was being eroded by Hippocrates' new teachings. Sadly, Hippocrates' whereabouts in later life, and his place of death, are unclear – the latter perhaps being Larissa, northwest Greece.

Many aspects of the Hippocratic approach to medicine are still with us today. We distinguish between illnesses that are described as acute (sudden and short-lived) or chronic (long-term and persistent), and diseases that are endemic (occur frequently in a particular region or population) and epidemic (break out suddenly, then spread rapidly and affect a large proportion of the population). The Hippocratic School of Medicine also pioneered methods of clinical observation, examination, recording, and analysis of patient consultations – procedures we now take for granted in medical practice. Observation was already important at the time, but Hippocrates formalized it into a systematic process. It should be carried out at least once a day, in order to follow the diagnosis and natural history of the disease, which would then enable a doctor to give a prognosis or a prediction: "I believe that it is an excellent thing for a physician to practise forecasting. He will carry out the treatment best if he knows beforehand from the present symptoms what will take place later". Documentation included regular notes of signs and symptoms, such as pulse, breathing, temperature, skin complexion, appearance of the eyes and mouth, palpation of the inner organs, and excretions.

Hippocrates was keen on urine and faeces, since he believed that they offered much guidance on how the body was functioning: "In proportion to what a person eats, he should evacuate bowels two or three times daily... more copiously in the morning." Also: "It is better that flatulence should be passed than that it should be retained". Investigating the lower bowel involved an anal or

"Wherever the art of medicine
is loved, there is also a love
of humanity"

HIPPOCRATES OF COS

REFUSING GIFTS FROM THE ENEMY
According to legend, Hippocrates refused lavish gifts from Artaxerxes, king of the Persians, whose troops were being ravaged by plague. Hippocrates' refusal to help the enemy raised patriotism above the physician's duty to serve all men.

rectal speculum – a tongs-like device that opened the orifice to allow inspection of the interior. This was one of the earliest forms of endoscopy – peering into the body's innards through a natural opening or purpose-made incision. For troublesome haemorrhoids, the treatments ranged from ointments or salves to ligation (tying off).

Hippocrates advised that all records should be written in a clear, objective, and uncluttered fashion, so that the physicians involved could look back and draw from their experiences when dealing with new patients. Crucially, other doctors could also access the records and thereby learn from the information. This was the beginning of the vast health and medical databases that have become so important in the 21st century.

With so much attention paid to ascertaining the patient's condition, it may seem surprising that the Hippocratic attitude towards treatment was restrained, cautious, and even humble. The best remedies were peace, clean conditions, comfortable rest, good nutrition, and continued observation – allowing the body's natural powers of self-healing to do the work. Bandaging, massage, and soothing balms might be required now and then, but powerful medicines and invasive techniques were a last resort. A major edict for the physician was: "First, do no harm". Invasive techniques were rare, since at this time in Greece, as later in Ancient Rome (see pp.40–47), there were bans on most forms of human dissection for anatomical learning or treatment. Surgery was limited to patching up wounds and similar trauma. The skin was rarely broken deliberately, so the human body's insides were mostly a mystery.

Hippocrates had a trusted list of gentle, tried-and-tested remedies, which included olive oil, honey, and a range of more than 200 vegetables and herbs – either to be eaten whole or taken as extracts – from figs, garlic, and onion to parsley, poppy, hibiscus, chamomile, cumin, and saffron. Believing that some long-term conditions resulted from excessive or unwise dietary consumption, he espoused: "Let food be your medicine and medicine be your food".

Another aspect of Hippocratic thought is the notion of the crisis – the observation that a sickness develops, worsens, and reaches a kind of tipping point, at which either the body starts to fight back and the patient's recovery begins, or a downward spiral ensues,

GREEK SURGICAL TOOLS
This marble relief shows a case of knives, lancets, and bone levers flanked by a pair of vessels used for bloodletting.

from which the body can still rally into remission – or fade again, or relapse. These ideas of remission and relapse originate from Hippocrates' time, and probably come from Hippocrates himself.

Many diseases and conditions were first described by Hippocrates and his followers. One is the clubbing of the nails and fingers – a condition sometimes known as "Hippocratic fingers". This can be an important indication of pulmonary problems such as abscesses on the lungs or lung cancer, of heart diseases such as endocarditis, and of various congenital conditions.

The sheer scale of Hippocrates' influence tends to overshadow the achievements of other Greek physicians. One such doctor was Herophilus (c.335–280 BCE), who worked in Alexandria, where he was allowed to found a tradition of dissecting human corpses. He studied the heart, blood vessels, brain, eye, and the nervous system, and is regarded as one of the first true anatomists. Slightly later, Erasistratus (304–250 BCE) was also at Alexandria for a time, where he helped to establish the medical school and had influential ideas on the function of the heart and the blood system (see p.135).

Gradually, the Hippocratic movement changed the public's view of the physician as an itinerant curiosity who had little social standing (and who was likely to cause more problems than he solved) to that of an upstanding member of society. Vital to this transformation was another great Hippocratic health-care instigation – a code of conduct. We know its details under the general umbrella term of the Hippocratic Oath, and its requirements have resonated with patients and the general public through the ages. After all, who wants a doctor who is slovenly, unhygienic, shabby, immoral, unethical, a careless blabbermouth, and not up to speed with the latest advances?

The Hippocratic Corpus' *On the Physician*, and the texts derived from it through history, prescribe what the ideal doctor should be like. He should be upright, honest, stable, and beyond reproach or corruption, and must attend the patient with courtesy and consideration, take

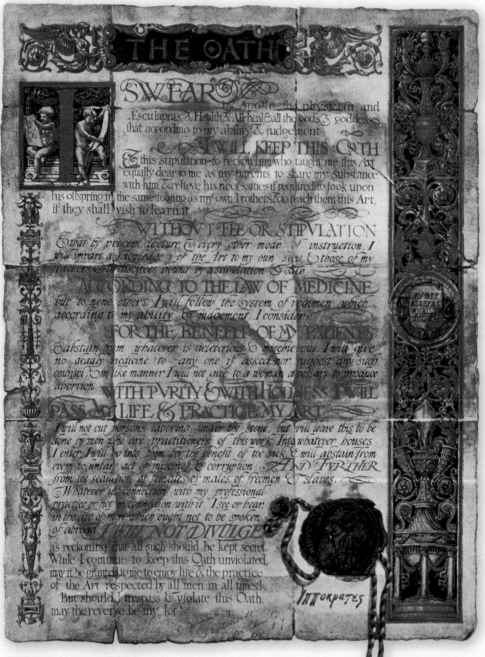

WITNESS ALL THE GODS
The Hippocratic Oath – shown here in a later
version, in English – requires a physician to
swear that he or she will abide by various ethical
principles, including that of confidentiality.

care of the patient's position, and note his symptoms diligently. The doctor's surgery should also inspire confidence by being clean, tidy, well lit, and organized, with each piece of equipment laid out methodically. Another Hippocratic idea was that information about the patient's ailment should remain confidential – and that if other people are involved in the consultation, then they too must respect this privacy. The instructions even go so far as to recommend what the physician should wear and how he should stand and move. This Hippocratic vision of the ideal doctor, so comforting to potential patients, has endured through evolving adaptations of the Hippocratic Oath. Extracts from various translations run approximately:

"I swear by Apollo the healer, Asclepios, Hygieia, and Panacea... Witness all the gods, all the goddesses, to keep according to my ability and my judgment, the following oath... I will prescribe regimens for the good of my patients, in accordance with my ability and my judgement... I will never do harm to anyone... I will give no deadly medicine if asked... I will preserve the purity of my life and my arts... In every house I will enter only for the good of my patients, keeping myself away from all intentional ill-doing and all seduction and especially from the pleasures of love with women or men, be they free or slaves... All that may come to my knowledge in the exercise of my profession or in daily commerce... I will keep to myself, holding such things shameful to be spoken about, and will never reveal..."

Medical students around the world can choose to swear upon their medical authority's version of the Hippocratic Oath. Although rarely used in its original form, the modern adaptations embody the spirit of the upstanding, ethical, moral, careful, clean, and compassionate physician.

Galen and the Rule of Rome

IF THERE WERE AN AWARD FOR the deepest and most enduring influence over Western medicine, then Galen of Pergamon, perhaps with Hippocrates of Cos (see pp.30–39), would head the shortlist. After travelling the eastern Mediterranean during his thirties, Galen settled in Rome – the imperial centre of civilization, with its empire stretching from the Atlantic Ocean east to the Red, Black, and Caspian seas. In Rome, Galen built up a massive body of work and a towering reputation that presided over human anatomy, physiology, and medicine for more than 1,400 years, and in some respects for a few centuries longer.

Claudius Galen (129–c.216 CE) was raised and educated in a well-to-do family in Pergamon – the modern-day city of Bergama, in western Turkey. One of the chief hubs of trade and learning in both Greek and Roman times, Pergamon had a library of approximately 200,000 works, which drew philosophers and other intellectuals from around the Mediterranean and West Asia. Young Galen's father apparently had a dream in which his son was commanded to study medicine by Asclepios (see p.32), the Greek god of healing. This Galen did, from the age of 16, before setting off at the age of 20 on travels that took him around mainland Greece and Turkey, to islands such as Crete and Cyprus, and to the hallowed city of Alexandria, Egypt – home of the ancient world's largest library and foremost medical school. Galen soaked up knowledge and experiences in all areas of medicine as well as philosophy, and returned to Pergamon in about 157 CE. Here he took the prestigious position of physician-surgeon to the gladiators who fought

GALEN OF PERGAMON
Perhaps the greatest physician of antiquity, Claudius Galen made numerous contributions to medicine, particularly in the fields of anatomy and pharmacology.

in front of thousands of baying spectators. His skills with knife, saw, and other surgical tools were soon famous throughout the region – and Galen himself recorded how he was able to treat gladiators' terrible wounds with far greater success than any of his rivals or predecessors. He also noted how gladiatorial injuries, particularly deep gashes and sliced innards, were like windows into the body. This fascination with dissection and anatomy would stay with him for life.

Pergamon soon became too small for a man of Galen's ability and ambition, and in 162 CE he decamped to Rome. He stayed in the Eternal City for the rest of his years, apart from a return to Pergamon between about 166 CE and 168 CE. In Rome, Galen worked his way into the upper echelons of medicine and into the favour of imperial appointees. However, the city's regular medical hierarchy felt threatened by this regional upstart, and their muttered intimidation forced Galen to make his brief return to Pergamon. He was commanded back by Emperor Marcus Aurelius, who wished him to serve as imperial physician, as did the emperor's successors, Commodus and Septimius Severus.

Rome was regularly hit by plagues during this period, most of which were epidemics of smallpox. The epidemic from about 165 CE to 180 CE, known as the Antonine Plague (from the emperor's full name, Marcus Aurelius Antoninus), has also been called the "Plague of Galen". This is because, while other commentators noted how the disease was jeopardizing Rome's military power, the imperial physician wrote extensively about its terrible human cost. Historians point to some five million dead across the Roman world during the Antonine Plague, thought to include co-emperors Lucius Verus in the first surge of 169 CE, and Marcus Aurelius during a later outbreak in 180 CE. Even the start of Rome's decline has been blamed on the plague, since it weakened armies and forced commanders to withdraw from politically unstable territories.

Galen completed most of his immense written work in Rome, during the rule of Commodus. Estimates of his total output range from five to ten million words, with some three million surviving. His language of choice was his native Greek. He dictated at speed to a small army of scribes, and his manuscripts were stored in various stately rooms and temples around the city, particularly the Temple of Peace. Much of the immense Galenic Corpus – the body of work attributed to him and his close helpers – has been copied and handed down relatively unscathed. Other works, however, were lost to much of

BLOOD SPORTS
This Roman mosaic shows gladiators fighting to the
death – a sport that gave Galen, as a physician, plenty
of first-hand experience of human anatomy.

Europe as the western half of the Roman Empire collapsed, although
they survived in the east as the Roman territories there were absorbed
by the Byzantine Empire. Several centuries later, Galen's works were
taken up by Islamic scholars, who translated them into languages
such as Arabic and Syriac (see pp.100–105). From here, many works
made their way back to Europe, especially during the early Renaissance,
where they were translated into Latin, and eventually into regional
European languages such as English, German, French, and Spanish.

Galen's works were so vast (both in scope and volume) that many
have been misinterpreted, poorly translated, and "corrected" along the
way according to the beliefs of later times. Writings that were actually
his have been appropriated by later authors, while scripts from other
writers have been wrongfully attributed to Galen. Today, experts still

disagree over whether Galen even wrote certain pieces, and, if so, how close our versions of them are to his originals. The basis of Galen's medical philosophy was Greek (see pp.30–39). He followed Hippocratic doctrines, such as the idea that the body is made of four humours – namely blood, yellow bile, black bile, and phlegm (see pp.106–107). He explicitly linked these to the four elements – air (gas), water (liquid), earth (solid), and fire (combustion and change) – blood corresponding to air, yellow bile to fire, black bile to earth, and phlegm to water. He also held that there were primary and secondary features of these elements that related to temperature and humidity – air being wet first and hot second; fire being hot and dry; earth being dry and cold; and water being cold and wet. According to Galen, imbalances or improper mixing between these features led to ill health.

Galen also grafted onto the humours and elements a series of behavioural types or personality traits that had been earlier postulated by Aristotle. Galen suggested that an excess of a certain humour in the body produced a particular temperament or disposition in that person. Thus a sanguine (blood) character is typically active, creative, and sociable, if perhaps impatient; a choleric (yellow bile) character is usually driven, passionate, and domineering, if aggressive; a melancholic (black bile) character is generally quiet, pensive, and self-contained, if prone to sadness; while a phlegmatic (phlegm) character is commonly calm, composed, kind, and lethargic.

Some of Galen's writings cover philosophy and philology. He devoured Greek texts and made extensive comments on works by Hippocrates, Herophilus, Erasistratus, and others (see p.37). He was keen on the details of language in medicine, and, concerned that many Greek works had become corrupted, he tried to recover their true medical meanings. To these, he added his own ideas on a huge range of health and medical topics, from diet, hygiene, and staying

"Every animal is sad after coitus, except the human female and the rooster"

CLAUDIUS GALEN

fit, to the causes of disease, examination of the patient, respiration, humours, elements, temperaments, herbal remedies, purging, bloodletting, and, of course, surgery and anatomy.

The practice of human dissection for teaching and demonstration purposes was forbidden by law in Ancient Rome (although surgical treatments were advanced for the time), so Galen resorted instead to opening up animals – from fish and reptiles to dogs, goats, pigs, and allegedly one of the emperor's deceased tame elephants. In particular, he valued "apes" as subjects – although his Barbary ape victims were actually a type of macaque monkey. From these species he confidently and authoritatively (and often erroneously) compiled a map of human anatomy.

Aside from the achievements of Galen, the rule of Rome brought progress in many areas of health and medicine. These included the encouragement of bathing and general hygiene, the provision of clean drinking water, improved sanitation, and advances both in surgery and in herbal and mineral-based remedies. The Roman surgeon's "tool kit" (see pp.46–47) boasted a varied array of scalpels and other blades, drills, and saws for bone removal and amputation, hooks and simple retractors to hold nerves and vessels aside or to close gaping wounds, and urinary catheters to relieve bladder and urethra blockages. Opium, alcohol, and herbs such as henbane provided relief from pain, while alcohol, hot oils, and vinegar were used to clean wounds and incisions. Around this time, general surgery expanded into specialisms such as chest, abdomen, limbs, neck, eyes, ears, and teeth. Dental crowns and false teeth were fashioned from gold, silver, ivory, bone, or wood, depending on the status of the patient.

ROMAN PHARMACIST
This tombstone of Armenian king Mithridates VI depicts a Roman pharmacist and his assistant preparing medicines.

Many plants were used for medicines, as much for religious reasons – being favourites of particular gods or priests – as for any therapeutic effect. These were listed by Greek physician, plant

PHYSICIAN'S JARS
Dating from the 1st century CE, these glass
containers held various ointments and
unguents designed for medicinal use.

expert, and herbalist Pedanius
Dioscorides (c.40–90 CE) in his
*De Materia Medica (On Medical
Substances)*. This massive work in
five-volumes was the first to
establish the idea of the pharmacopoeia
– an encyclopaedia of pharmaceutical preparations, healing herbs,
minerals, and other drugs and medications, explaining how they are
produced, what they are prescribed for, and their intended effects.

Another physician from Greece, who preceded Galen, was Soranus
of Ephesus (c.98–140 CE). Among his major works was *Gynaikeia
(Gynaecology)*, which covered not only gynaecology, but also obstetrics,
midwifery, perinatal care, and paediatrics (care of the infant), with
sections on abortion and birth control. Much of the description is given
in graphic, practical detail. For instance, Soranus spends time detailing
the characteristics he expects of the ideal midwife – including
discretion, literacy, mental ability, good memory, respectability,
soundness of limb, robustness... and long, slim fingers with short nails.

For all its other achievements, however, the medicine of Ancient
Rome will always be dominated by Galen. It was some eleven centuries
later that new trends for dissection were led by Mondino de Liuzzi at
Bologna (see p.117). With the ban on human cadaver dissection then
circumventable, Liuzzi reintroduced the process into his medical
courses. In 1316, he wrote *Anathomia Corporis Humani (Anatomy of the Human
Body)* as a manual for his students. A groundbreaking work, it
nevertheless upheld some of of Galen's anatomical errors. This was
followed by the pioneering work of Renaissance anatomists such as
Andreas Vesalius (see pp.116–25), which contradicted many of Galen's
declarations on anatomy. In the following century, Galen's complex
ideas on the physiology of heart and blood were superseded when
William Harvey clarified the process of blood circulation (see pp.134–43).
Such refutations of Galen may hardly seem surprising, given the
immense scope of his work and the strictures under which he worked.
Yet such was his gigantic sway, that even in the 19th century some
medical schools were still reliant on parts of his teaching.

Roman Surgical Tools

One of the most remarkable discoveries made by archaeologists in the Roman city of Pompeii, destroyed by a volcanic eruption in 79 CE, was a collection of surgical instruments in the building called the House of the Surgeon. Made of bronze or iron, these beautifully preserved 1st-century CE tools were typical of those used since the 5th century BCE. The design of such tools changed little until the 19th century.

CUPPING VESSEL
Heated and placed on the skin to draw out the blood, vessels like this were used for bloodletting (see pp.132–33).

SCALPELS
Like modern surgeons, Roman physicians used scalpels in a wide range of shapes and sizes. As well as large-bladed scalpels, they had instruments with smaller blades for making fine incisions or reaching parts of the body to which access was restricted.

SURGICAL SCISSORS
Shears were sometimes used in surgery, but achieving a sharp edge to them was hard. They were most often used to cut hair, which was believed to benefit health.

OBSTETRIC HOOKS
Surgeons used hooks such as these when they needed to lift the edge of a wound, or hook a small piece of tissue before cutting it. They also used hooks to grip or manipulate blood vessels or pieces of tissue during surgery.

VAGINAL SPECULUM
Used during the examination and treatment of vaginal and uterine disorders, this device opens using a lever mechanism with a screw thread. Similar instruments were still in use during the 18th century.

CLYSTER
This syringe-like instrument came in two parts: a vessel with tube, and a piston. It was used to administer enemas, or drain excessive fluids from the patient's body.

BONE LEVERS
Levers such as these were designed to ease a bone into its correct position when setting a fracture. The ends of the levers are curved and ridged so that they grip the surface of the bone well.

The Dark Ages
in Europe

IN THE YEAR 476 CE, A COALITION of Germanic and other tribes, led by warlord Flavius Odoacer, marched through Italy seizing lands and power. In Ravenna, the Roman emperor Romulus Augustus was deposed and exiled. This event commonly marks the end of the western Roman Empire, which had been fading for three centuries. It also signifies the drift of Europe into nearly a thousand years of confused, obscure history called the Middle Ages, which ended with the flowering of the Renaissance in the 14th century. During the earlier phase of the Middle Ages, up until about the year 1000, European societies and cultures fragmented. The rule of law weakened in the face of warring tribes, and much of the progress made by Ancient Greece (see pp.30–39) and Rome (see pp.40–45) was lost or even reversed. Historical records were scant, living conditions declined for many under feudal systems, and fear, poverty, and persecution were widespread. The popular term for this era is the Dark Ages.

It was a dark time for medicine too. Practitioners were often untrained and unlicensed, partly because there were few professional bodies or systems in place to oversee their activities and to rein in their excesses. Diagnoses were spurious, and driven by reward and the promise of influence. Some treatments helped, but others were damaging and even cruel. During these centuries, European medicine still relied on concepts from Ancient Greece and Rome – especially the theory of the four humours (see pp.106–107). Medical care now became the realm of the Church, which was primarily Catholic, and summarily organized courts and self-serving guilds. The lessons of Hippocrates, which had shown that sickness was a natural process within the body, and not the result of divine punishment or demonic possession, were largely discarded. As a result, quackery and charlatanism flourished. If a physician or healer treated a patient who then recovered, then all credit to the practitioner, who could claim a special link to the Almighty. If the outcome was a worsening of the condition, or even death – well, that too was God's will. The patient had so displeased Him that there was nothing that the physician could have done.

TRADITIONAL REMEDIES
A medieval apothecary and his assistant
prepare herbal remedies — treatments
that were often dismissed as witchcraft.

The most recent advances in medieval
medicine were the preserve of the
nobility, the rich, and the Church.
Some religious authorities even
shunned age-old cures, such as the
use of healing herbs, as "witchcraft".
The only way to a true cure, they
said, was total dedication and
obedience to God, who would
dispense reward by banishing the illness. The phenomenon of the
"miracle cure" also came to the fore, with some alleged physicians
claiming saintly powers. However, most peasants in the countryside
were far removed from such matters, and continued to use herbal
recipes and other treatments from ancient times.

From about the 12th century, early versions of hospitals began to
appear. Most of them were attached to monasteries, convents, and
similar religious institutions. Generally clean, with reasonable food
and compassionate staff, they provided much-needed care and
comfort to all manner of sufferers from most levels of society. They
were also stopping places for travellers, retreats for students, and
havens for the destitute, disabled, elderly, "feeble-minded", and
others who were disadvantaged. Worship was incorporated into a
highly organized daily routine, partly to encourage recovery and
partly as an institutionalizing force, and physicians visited regularly.
Nevertheless, a typical consultation with a physician — especially
during the Early Middle Ages — could be a dicey affair. In fact, it might
not even be with a physician, but with a herbalist, a midwife, an
occultist, or even a part-time witch. The practitioner might begin by
studying the skin, taking the pulse (which indicated heart "spasms",
since blood circulation had not been discovered), and noting the
breathing patterns. Perhaps he or she would make a few incisions in a
vein to assess the quality of the blood — runny or sticky, bright or
dark? — and then sniff, prod, decant, and generally scrutinize the
liquid and solid excrement. Tasting blood, urine, and even faeces
might be necessary, as well as swirling them around with various

chemical reagents. All of these observations helped to establish the balance of the humours and whether phlegm, yellow bile, or another humour was at fault. The patient's own account of the problem might also provide clues. For instance, he or she – being mindful of God's ability to punish – might admit to some recent transgression or immorality. If the local physician was not with the patient, all the results were communicated to him, and he would then diagnose remotely and convey the prescription back to the patient and carers.

The great cure-all treatment of the age was undoubtedly bleeding or bloodletting (see pp.132–33). This dated back to Hippocrates and Galen, the latter believing that among the four humors, blood was dominant. Many illnesses involved an excess of blood, a condition known as a plethora, and so removing some reduced the surplus and purged the body. Having no knowledge of the circulatory system, people thought that blood was made in the liver and consumed in the tissues (see pp.134–43). If this turnover became unbalanced, blood might accumulate and stagnate in the extremities. Again, bloodletting was the obvious answer.

Galen and his followers had devised sophisticated sets of instructions for bleeding. The manner of the procedure depended on the symptoms and their severity, details about the patient (such as age and pre-existing conditions), the time of day, week, and year, and even the prevailing weather. There were guidelines on whether to open either an artery or a vein, and where on the body to do so. Venesection (phlebotomy) involved releasing blood from a sizeable superficial vein, especially in the forearm; the blood oozed slowly, was easy to control, and clotted readily. Opening an artery (arteriotomy) was much riskier as the blood spurted out under pressure, was difficult to quantify, and took longer to congeal. The question of which vessel to approach was also highly complex. Theory linked certain internal organs, such as the liver and the lungs, with particular veins, although these were not always easy to access. This led to the practices of "derivation" and "revulsion". In derivation, blood was drawn from near the affected area; revulsion involved bleeding from a site far away. So neck pain might be treated in the revulsion manner by letting blood from the ankle, while a disorder of the spleen might require opening a vein in the left wrist. Medieval physicians added more detail to the bloodletting procedure, including what kind of knife or leech to use, and what the patient should do while

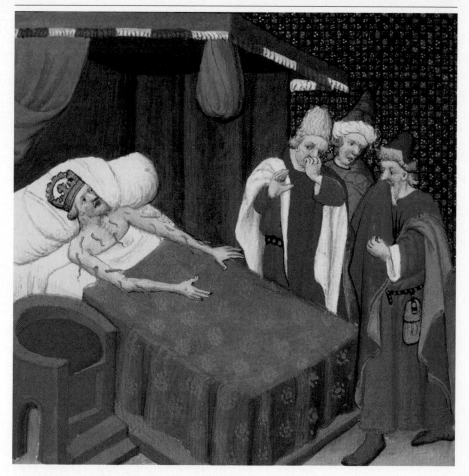

BLEEDING THE EMPEROR WITH LEECHES
This illustration from Boccaccio's *Decameron* shows the Roman
emperor Galerius being bled by leeches. According to the text,
his symptoms included putrefaction and an abominable stench.

the blood flowed – pray, recite poetry, even play a musical instrument.
Some conditions required only an eggcup of the red liquid. Others
stipulated that the patient be bled until they swooned or collapsed – a
positive sign that bad spirits had been expunged and that the humours
were back in equilibrium.

A handy medical reference text for physicians was the "leechbook",
perhaps so-called because physicians were nicknamed "leeches",
from the habit of using these worm-like creatures to drain blood for
almost any ailment. Most leechbooks contained remedies of the time
gathered indiscriminately from a vast array of sources. A well-known
surviving example dating back to the 10th century, perhaps derived

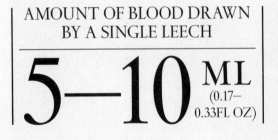

AMOUNT OF BLOOD DRAWN
BY A SINGLE LEECH

5—10 ML
(0.17–0.33FL OZ)

from a 9th-century version, is *Medicinale Anglicum*, commonly known as *Bald's Leechbook*. Its first part covers almost 90 external and infectious problems affecting the ear, face, teeth, and so on, down to the feet; the second part deals with internal disorders such as vomiting, stomach pains, and diarrhoea. Woven into the lists are dog bites, rash from bug stings, hair loss, headache, backache, liver pains, worries about evil spirits, men who lack virility, and women who talk too much.

Bald's Leechbook even has a surgical remedy (very rare for the time) for harelip: "Mash mastic very small, add egg white, mingle as thou dost vermilion, cut with a knife the false lip edges, sew tight with silk, smear all over with the salve, ere the silk rot". A more gentle treatment (if not for the bird involved) is given for excessive hair: "If hair be too thick, take a swallow, burn it to ashes under a tile and have the ashes shed on [the site]". A leechbook was an eclectic compendium covering practical advice, herbs and minerals, rituals, poems, incantations, religious pleas, and philosophical musings, some of which can be traced back to ancient Roman and Arabic teachings.

Without a leechbook, a physician might be inclined to experiment. One such experimenter was Johannes de Mirfield, a respected physician of St Bartholomew's Hospital, London, who recommended the following medicinal bath: "Take blind [newborn] puppies, gut them, and cut off the feet; then boil in water, and in this water let the patient bathe. Let him stay in the bath for four hours after he has eaten, and while in the bath, he should keep his head covered, and his chest completely swathed with the skin of a goat, so he does not catch a sudden chill".

One area of particular ignorance in Medieval Europe was anatomy. The Catholic Church, in particular, was against incisions and invasions of the body, unless it was for life-threatening wounds, and then only for the nobility and members of the ruling class. Those brave doctors who did try to open up patients were hampered on many fronts. Basic anatomical knowledge was scanty, so few doctors had any idea which organs were where and what they did. If the patient was conscious, anaesthesia and pain relief could only be provided by administering alcohol, opium, or something similar in terrifyingly hit-and-miss doses – and with no knowledge of germs or antisepsis, dirt and pus in the innards would almost certainly lead to infection and death.

One of the chief afflictions of the time was leprosy, more recently referred to as Hansen's Disease. Recorded since antiquity, especially on the Indian subcontinent, leprosy generated great fear, not only because it gradually attacked parts of the body until they rotted and fell away, but also because it was reputedly so easy to catch. Consequently, leprosy victims suffered intense social stigmatization, and many were quarantined or confined to leper colonies (otherwise known as leprosaria or lazar houses). Some of the colonies allowed the lepers no rights whatsoever, since Catholic doctrine decreed that people with leprosy had already died and were effectively the "living dead". At the other extreme, some saw leprosy as a pre-death visitation from God – a kind of purgatory and cleansing of sins in preparation for the ascent to Heaven – which gave lepers special sanctified status.

Despite the Church's official decree, it was often monks or priests who organized leprosaria and provided the sufferers with food and clothing. If lepers were allowed out, they had to carry and ring a bell, both to warn others of their coming and as a plea for charity. Few physicians or other healthy people ventured near. For reasons that are not entirely clear, leprosy became much less common during the 14th and 15th centuries in Europe – probably helped by the Black Death (see pp.54–55), which claimed the lives of so many who were already weakened by other forms of disease.

AIDING THE LIVING DEAD
An Augustinian monk brings food to a leper at a leprosarium. At the time, the Church's official doctrine was that lepers were people who had already died.

The Bubonic Plague

A scourge that swept Europe and Asia for centuries, the bubonic plague struck populations swiftly and brutally, killing millions and changing the world map irrevocably. Caused by the bacterium *Yersinia pestis*, carried by rat fleas, its main symptoms are swollen lymph nodes, seizures, and gangrene. It is often fatal, killing two-thirds of its victims within days, and spreads rapidly: pandemics occurred in the 6th–8th, 14th–18th, and 19th–20th centuries. There was no reliable treatment before antibiotics in the 20th century.

18TH-CENTURY PLAGUE DOCTOR WEARING HERB-INFUSED MASK

C.1650S–70S
So many people die in such a short space of time across Europe that they have to be buried pell-mell in brick-built **plague pits.**

C.1400 Europe's population is reduced by tens of millions, as the plague **spreads uncontrollably**, exacerbated by poor living conditions and ineffective treatments.

541–42 The plague arrives in **Constantinople**, triggering an outbreak that spreads from Persia across the Roman Empire to Ireland.

1348 The authorities in Venice and Florence enforce strict **sanitary laws**, removing plague victims from the streets.

1377 Ragusa (Dubrovnik) imposes a **30-day quarantine** on travellers to the city.

1647 The **Great Plague of Seville** kills around 150,000 people in Seville and some 350,000 in other parts of Spain.

1346 The outbreak known as the **Black Death** begins, probably in the Russian Steppes; it reaches the Crimea later in the year.

1351 The plague reaches most of Europe and the Middle East, killing **millions of people**.

1439 English Parliament states that **"noble physicians"** advise avoiding contact with plague victims.

1665–66 The Great Plague of London leads to the death of about **100,000** people; many more flee the city.

ESTIMATED
PERCENTAGE OF
THE WORLD'S
POPULATION
KILLED BY THE
BLACK DEATH
DURING THE
14TH CENTURY

20%

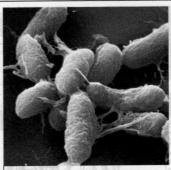

1898 French physician Paul-Louis Simond shows that *Xenopsylla cheopis* fleas (oriental rat fleas) **transmit** the plague.

1894 Hong Kong-based scientists Kitasato Shibasaburo and Alexandre Yersin isolate the **plague bacillus** and name it *Yersinia pestis.*

1896 The plague **pandemic** reaches India and Pakistan.

1710–11 Half the population of Riga, Latvia, is **wiped out** by the plague.

1720 The Great Plague of Marseilles is the **last major outbreak** of plague in Europe.

1899 Ships carry the plague to **new territories** such as Egypt and Hawaii.

1707 A *cordon sanitaire* is set up around Prussia, with all visitors **quarantined**.

1855 The **third plague pandemic** begins in Yunnan Province, China.

1945 Scientists carry out the first clinical trials of the antibiotic **streptomycin** against the plague.

1679 The Plague of Vienna is part of a larger outbreak in **Austria, Germany, and Bohemia** (now part of the Czech Republic).

The Alchemists

ALCHEMY CAN BE DIFFICULT TO PIN DOWN. It has long and varied traditions across Asia and Europe and was prominent in medieval times, but its roots go back thousands of years. It combines philosophies and beliefs dealing with magic, spirits, and the supernatural, with intensely practical analytical and laboratory techniques involving elements, minerals, and other substances that would be familiar in chemistry research centres today. Alchemists' aims have varied through time and from place to place. Some of their best-known quests have included: changing "base" metals (common, ordinary, or inexpensive ones) such as lead, into precious metals, especially gold, using an object or formulation known as the Philosopher's Stone; creating a substance that can dissolve any other substance – the Universal Solvent or Alkahest; inventing a potion that confers eternal youth on those who drink it – the Elixir of Life; producing a substance that can cure every disease and ailment – the Panacea or Universal Remedy. These laudable aims have had useful, practical results – but there are many more layers to the curious realm of alchemy. It is essentially concerned with transmuting matter from one form to another, or remodelling one being into another. Physically, this means creating the most valuable substance in existence or achieving immortality. On a spiritual level, it involves the pursuit of fulfilment, completion, or perfection.

Practical or functional alchemy developed from chemical processes such as fermenting beer, tanning leather, smelting ores to extract valuable metals and minerals, preparing medicinal potions and balms, and distilling extracts from plants and the earth. These procedures involved processing and refining commonplace base substances to gain a pure, desired final product. For example, in metallurgy, ordinary rocks were smelted and treated, eventually to yield valuable metals such as glistening gold or the amazing silvery liquid metal mercury (or quicksilver). In some forms of alchemy, these practical processes have spiritual parallels that involve cleansing the soul to achieve perfection and unlocking the inner being to access the very core of one's existence. Indeed, for alchemical medicines to work against disease, it was thought, physical effects such as relief from symptoms can only occur if accompanied by such psychic transformations.

HOPING FOR A CURE
An alchemist fires up a stove to heat one of his
concoctions. Hopeful customers sample his potions
in the background.

The spiritual, mystical, and symbolic aspects of alchemy can be
regarded as "esoteric" – that is, restricted to one or a few individuals
who possess special awareness and privilege. This links alchemy to
the tradition of Hermeticism, which is based on the pronouncements
of Hermes Trismegistus, a semi-mythical figure of Ancient Egypt.
According to legend, he received divine knowledge and insight that
was then passed down through the ages – knowledge that could
enable spiritual or magical forces to affect the physical, material
world. The *Tabula Smaragdina* (*Emerald Tablet*) attributed to Hermes
Trismegistus would have lasting influence on alchemists for centuries.
During the Late Middle Ages and the Renaissance, the Hermetic

"That which is above is from that which is below"

THE EMERALD TABLET

tradition included alchemy as one of its three major components, along with numerology and the "magic of letters" – cryptography. The useful, practical aspects of alchemy, on the other hand, can be seen not as esoteric but as "exoteric", or widely accessible to anyone. From a modern standpoint, the idea of chasing such miraculously unrealistic objectives as the Elixir of Life or the Universal Remedy seems doomed from the start, yet by doing so, alchemists have made immense contributions to the development of mainstream sciences, especially chemistry, materials science, and medicine.

Alchemy and its applications to medicine have long and illustrious histories in Asia, especially China and India. In Europe, it can be traced back to the times of Ancient Egypt, Greece, and Rome. One of its earliest texts was written or compiled by Zosimos of Panopolis, who was probably an Egyptian living in Alexandria at the time of Roman control, some 1,700 years ago. Zosimos expounded at length on the philosophical and mystical aspects of alchemy, saying, for instance, that the transmutation of metals can occur only with a similar spiritual transformation of the soul and its ascent into the divine realm.

With the demise of the Roman Empire, alchemy – like mainstream medicine of the time – faded from historical view in Western Europe. But in common with other scholarly and academic pursuits, the spread of Islam in Eastern Europe, North Africa, and West Asia brought exciting developments. One of these was greater reliance on tests and experiments using an early form of scientific methodology. Jabir ibn Hayyan (c.721–c.815), known in Europe as Geber, was based in Kufa, near Baghdad (in what is now Iraq). The writings attributed to him were extensive and eclectic, ranging from philosophy and astrology to "the behaviour of matter when subjected to forced change". These accounts recorded experiments and analyses using substances varying from mild acetic acid (vinegar) to extremely corrosive sulphuric acid, as well as sulphur and mercury. Jabir's practical work involved distillation, crystallization, precipitation, and other procedures widely used today, employing flasks, burners, filters, condensers, and other familiar laboratory apparatus. Physicians, herbalists, healers, and apothecaries adopted these methods to prepare a new generation of medicines. Jabir also revised the classical "elements" of antiquity. He proposed three categories of elements – "spirits" such as mercury or sulphur, which would vaporise when heated; metals, such as gold or silver; and non-malleable substances such as stones, which could be ground into powders. These systems of elements would persist in alchemy for several centuries, as would the medicinal use of compounds containing mercury and sulphur.

Mercury has a long and double-edged medical history. During Jabir's time, mercury-containing balms and ointments, usually prepared from the metal's main ore, cinnabar (mercury sulphide), were in common use for skin problems. Later, calomel (mercurous chloride) was prescribed as a laxative, purgative, diuretic, and as a treatment for syphilis. Sulphur compounds were also common on the alchemist's workbench and in the apothecary's jars. Sulphur-rich waters were said to ease skin conditions, joint problems, and parasitic infestations. Sulphurous mixtures acted as disinfectants and fumigants. Before the penicillin class of antibiotics, sulphonamides or "sulfa drugs" were widely prescribed for bacterial infections.

During the time of the Crusades, in the late 11th and 12th centuries, Arabic works on alchemy were brought back to Europe and translated into Latin, the language of scholars. Pivotal was Jabir's *Kitab al-Kimya* (*Book of Composition of Alchemy*), translated and made available in 1144 by Robert of Chester. In addition to early Egyptian mysticism and the philosophy of Aristotle, Arab practitioners

MASTER ALCHEMIST
Arab chemist, physician, and engineer Jabir ibn Hayyan wrote numerous pioneering alchemical and metallurgical works.

TOAD, SERPENT, EAGLE
In alchemical symbolism, the toad and serpent represent fixity and volatility, while the eagle stands for sublimation.

Serpens et Bufo gradiens sup terrā, Aquila volans, est nostrū Magisteriū.

such as Jabir added great amounts of practical information about preparing medicines according to alchemical methods. In turn, Europeans wove Christian beliefs such as religious purification, confessions to cleanse the soul, and ascent into heavenly afterlife into the new translations. European alchemy grew in stature and many prominent religious dignitaries, from humble monks to the highest clergy, began to practise it.

Among such practitioners were Albertus Magnus and Roger Bacon. Albertus Magnus (c.1193–1280) was a German cleric who had vast knowledge of the natural world in the tradition of Aristotle. He was also a practical experimenter, and in around 1250 may have isolated the chemical element arsenic. Like mercury and sulphur, arsenic became a mainstay of alchemy, its mineral- or plant-extracted compounds being stimulants in very small amounts, but disabling or deadly in fractionally higher doses. Accounts, which were probably written and embroidered after Albertus' death, describe how he discovered the Philosopher's Stone and passed its formulation to his pupil, Thomas Aquinas – who then destroyed it, fearing it had come from Satan.

Roger Bacon (c.1214–94) was also a cleric – in his case a Franciscan friar. As a student and teacher, he followed his Order's approach to investigation and experimentation: "Of the three ways in which men think they acquire knowledge of things: authority, reasoning, and experience; only the last is effective and able to bring peace to the intellect". Bacon attempted both to transmute base metals to gold and to divine the elixir for everlasting life. He saw these as related endeavours: "That medicine which will remove all impurities and corruptibility from the lesser metals will also, in the opinion of the wise, take off so much of the corruptibility of the body that human life may be prolonged for many centuries". Bacon's many texts rejected magic spells and incantations, but reinforced the influence of the Church and the authority of the Bible. His works were widely circulated, and inspired many to explore alchemy further, especially as applied to medicine. Bacon also studied optics, engineering, astronomy, and astrology, and – most importantly to him – mathematics. In 1267, he produced his 840-page *Opus Majus* (*Greater Work*), one of the foremost encyclopaedic works of the age.

European alchemy continued to flourish during the Renaissance. A famous proponent of the early 1500s was Paracelsus (see pp.110–15). His contemporary and fellow wanderer around Europe was Heinrich Cornelius Agrippa von Nettesheim, usually known as Cornelius Agrippa. German-born, he wrote widely on matters of magic, religion, the occult, and medicine, including alchemy. His major work was the *De Occulta Philosophia Libri Tres* (*Three Books Concerning Occult Philosophy*). In his medical opinions and prescriptions, Agrippa often mixed remarkable common sense with magic and superstition. He recommended the herb creeping cinquefoil (*Potentilla reptans*) to ease fever, but he attributed this ability to the number five, in line with the doctrine of numerology – cinquefoil meaning "five leaves". He wrote: "It resists poysons by vertue of the number of five; also drives away divells…" Later in the century, German physician Andreas Libavius produced a chemistry-based manual, *Alchemia* (1597). Like Paracelsus and Agrippa, he was keen on the use of minerals and extracts as drugs, but less enthusiastic about the mysticism and Hermetic traditions of alchemy. In this respect, Libavius was moving closer to a more practical, evidence-based use of alchemical remedies.

By the 1700s, alchemy in Europe was fading in the face of its rising successor, chemistry. The latter adopted a much stricter, more rigorous, no-nonsense approach that shunned notions such as divine intervention, ancient mystical traditions, and esoteric soul-cleansing. But in relation to medicine, chemistry continued one of alchemy's practical functions – to provide raw materials, elements, compounds, and ingredients from which physicians, apothecaries, pharmacists, druggists, and dispensers could concoct medicines that would heal and cure.

THE DAWN OF CHEMISTRY
By the 19th century, alchemy had given way to
chemistry, a subject based on purely empirical
principles. The quests for immortality and the
universal cure-all gave way to the microscopic
study of the flesh in all its forms.

Traditional Eastern Medicine

TRADITIONAL CHINESE MEDICINE HAS A RECORD as long and distinguished as anything in the West. As Hippocrates lectured in Ancient Greece (see pp.30–39), Chinese physicians were compiling medical texts that would likewise persist for millennia, in the form of works such as the *Huang-di Nei'Jing* (*The Yellow Emperor's Inner Canon*). And as Claudius Galen held sway in Rome (see pp.40–45), foremost Chinese physician Zhang Zhongjing was founding medical institutions that would endure for centuries, in some cases to the present day. Like the Hippocratic Corpus and Galen's multitudinous writings, the *Huang-di Nei'Jing* has been revised and translated many times, making its authenticity and original content difficult to pin down. In general, it recounts discussions between the Yellow (or Golden) Emperor, Huang-di, and his associates and advisors, including First Minister Ch'i Po. The semi-mythical figure of Huang-di is credited with establishing China as a great civilization more than 4,500 years ago. In the text of the *Huang-di Nei'Jing*, produced some 2,000 years ago, the proponents ask and answer questions, and in the process set out an encyclopaedic store of Chinese medical knowledge and practices of the time. The work deals extensively

with fundamentals such as feeling the pulse, examining bowel products, observing the tongue, acupuncture, moxibustion, and concepts such as the flow of qi (energy), yin-yang, zang-fu, and the five phases.

Feeling the pulse was central to diagnosis and formulating treatment. It sometimes took more than an hour, and was best done soon after waking. The focus was on the wrists, which had six

YIN-YANG DUALITY
The tension between opposites (yin and yang) is central to Chinese philosophy. Yin and yang are here represented by a snake and a dragon respectively.

pulse sites each. The nature or quality of the pulse had many aspects, described in the *Huang-di Nei'Jing* in poetic terms: "like water dripping through a roof", "smooth as a flowing stream", or, more worryingly, "dead as a rock". Urine and bowel motions were studied intensively, not only by physicians, but also by relatives, soothsayers, fortune-tellers, political colleagues, and even financial advisers. Frequency, volume, density, colour, consistency, smell, undigested contents, and other features were analysed to discover the cause of an illness and how it might be relieved. The tongue was another important indicator of health and diagnosis: the size, shape, colour, coating, and flexibility were all regarded as pointers to the body's well-being. For example, a healthy digestive system was said to give the tongue an appealing red freshness. This was especially true for the middle of the tongue, which was intimately linked to the stomach, intestines, and spleen. The tongue's tip related to the heart, lungs, and chest area, while the back of the tongue was associated with the kidneys and the urinary bladder.

The concept of yin-yang, pervasive in Chinese philosophy and culture for thousands of years, represents the complementary duality inherent in all aspects of the universe. Derived from "shady place" and "sunny place" (referring to a hill), one cannot exist without the other. Yin tends to be dark, watery, cool, passive, and feminine, while yang is bright, dry, hot, active, and masculine. The allied distinction of zang-fu characterizes the lungs, heart, liver, spleen, and kidneys as zang, or yin, and the stomach, intestines, gall bladder, and urinary bladder as fu, or yang. In turn, yin-yang and zang-fu were incorporated into the concept of the five phases, or wu-xing – namely earth, water, fire, wood, and metal. These phases were so-called because they were energy states, rather than elements, and were in a constant state of flux. As the *Huang-di Nei'Jing* states: "The five elemental energies... encompass all the myriad phenomena of nature. It is a pattern that applies equally to humans". So, the liver was characterized as a yin, zang, and wood organ, while the stomach was yang, fu, and earth, and so on.

Additionally, the five phases concept embraces four main ways or cycles in which these energies interact. In the sheng (generating) cycle, each phase is in effect a "mother" that nurtures the development of the following "child" phase. So the fire phase supplies a generating force, or foundation, for the earth phase, which spawns and develops the metal phase, and so on. The ke (controlling) cycle holds that each phase affects and is affected by another – for instance, water controls fire, but is itself kept in check by earth to maintain equilibrium. The cheng (overactive) cycle involves one phase becoming too dynamic and having too much control over its associated subordinate phases, leading to imbalance and illness. In the wu (contradictory) cycle, a reversal of forces involves a subordinate phase taking control of the phase that would normally dominate it. For instance, water, instead of smothering fire in the balanced way, would control and burn fire. Again, this imbalance leads to disease.

The *Suwen* — the first part of the *Huang-di Nei'Jing* — takes account of all these aspects and their effects on the body's health and wellbeing, explaining their role in qi energy disturbances that underlie illness. For example, the pulse should be felt at daybreak: "The yang qi has not yet stirred, the yin qi has not been dispersed". The *Ling Shu* — the second part of the *Huang-di Nei'Jing* — contains some of the earliest descriptions of acupuncture. This therapeutic system probably evolved as far back as 4,000 years ago, and even perhaps has its origins or parallels in ancient Europe (see p.19).

Acupuncture aims to correct problems in the flow of qi energy around the body. The term "qi" has various literal interpretations, such as gas, vapour, or flowing breath. The four or five forms of qi are likened to "life energy" or "vital force" and move along channels known as meridians around and within the body, numbering some 20 main ones with subsidiary branches. The healthy, harmonious flow of qi can be disrupted by malfunctioning organs — or vice versa, with yin or zang organs having different effects to yang or fu organs. To address imbalance, the acupuncturists of Ancient China consulted patients and carried out examinations, looking especially at the pulse and tongue, as mentioned above. Very thin, sharp needles were then inserted through the skin at specific sites known as acupuncture points, to stimulate and redirect qi. Most acupoints were located on meridians and chosen for their energy links to body organs. The *Huang-di Nei'Jing* identifies or implies the presence of nearly 300 acupuncture points. (Some modern acupuncturists recognize more than double this number.) The needles might be left in position for a set time, or rotated, vibrated, or otherwise manipulated.

POWER LINES OF THE BODY
Traditional Chinese medicine sees disease as a disturbance of the flow of qi (energy) in the body. This energy moves along channels that can be stimulated by acupunture.

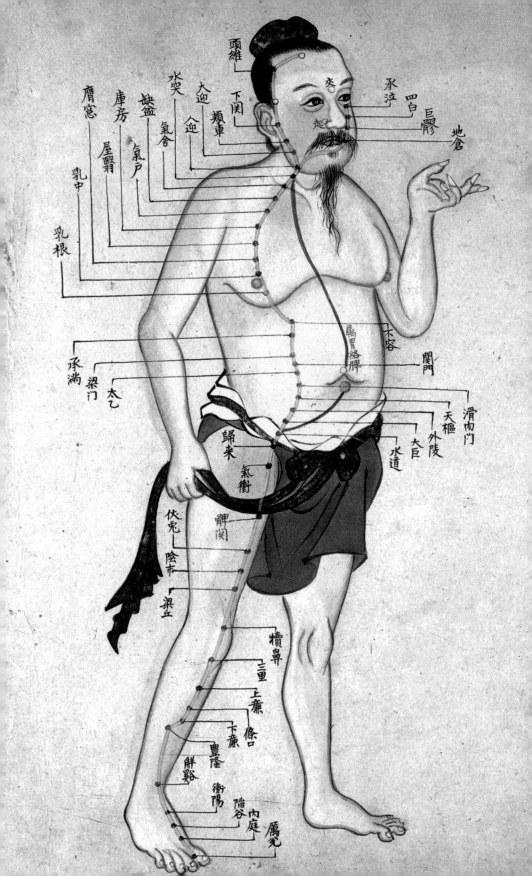

"The superior doctor prevents sickness; the mediocre doctor attends to impending sickness; the inferior doctor treats actual sickness"

CHINESE PROVERB

Traditional Ancient Chinese medicine also incorporated many other ways to promote health and prevent illness. They included extensive use of herbs, special diets, bathing, massage, meditation, and physical exercise ranging from the simple moves and postures of calisthenics to strenuous martial arts.

For four centuries, until the year 220 CE, the Han Dynasty ruled Ancient China. Its foremost physician was Zhang Zhongjing (c.150–c.219 CE), by whose time medicine had moved on from the *Huang-di Nei'Jing*, though it still relied on central concepts such as zang-fu and the five phases. Zhang practised at the end of Han rule, when conflict between rebel armies and the Han overlords was causing poverty and chaos. The desperate situation led to malnutrition and epidemic infections, giving Zhang and his contemporaries plenty of patients. Zhang produced works that introduced many pharmaceuticals to the body of Chinese traditional medicine. The general name for this work is *Shanghan Han Za Bing Lun*, often translated as *Treatise on Febrile Diseases Caused by Cold and Miscellaneous Causes*. As usual, the original knowledge has been revised and muddied by later editors. The first section, "Shang Han Lun" (On Cold-Induced Damage), covers infectious diseases common at the time, which caused symptoms such as the fevers of yang, and the chills and shivering of yin. It describes more than 100 herb-based remedies. For instance, certain fevers could be reduced with preparations containing mahuang (ephedra), guizhi (cinnamon wood), zhigancao (liquorice root), and xingren (bitter apricot stone). The second section, "Jin-Kui Yao Lue", is known in English as Synopsis of the Golden Chamber or Vital Prescriptions of the Golden Coffer. Zhang states that there are thousands of diseases, but people

THE AGONY OF MOXIBUSTION
This 19th-century statuette shows a patient
in agony during moxibustion therapy.
A burn mark is visible on his shin.

die from three main causes: external causes,
meaning outside forces (spirits or disease
"nuclei") that enter through the skin and
invade the body's interior; internal causes,
meaning harmful forces or particles that
spread along the qi meridians to the zang
and fu body parts; or neither of the above
– a diverse category that encompasses
insect stings, animal bites, wounds from
weapons, and sexual abuse.

Jin-Kui Yao Lue concentrates mainly on the internal conditions
and lists more than 250 recipes and preparations predominantly
using plants. Kidney yang deficiency could bring on back pain and
leg cramps, so the advised remedy was jingui shen qi'wan, the kidney
qi remedy – containing, among other herbs, fu zi (aconite root),
mudan pi (peony root), fu ling (China root), and sheng di-huang
(rehmannia or Chinese foxglove).

Animal products were also used in traditional Chinese medicine.
These included snake flesh for eye problems, pulverized seahorse for
goitre (swollen thyroid), and syrup of elephant skin for skin ulcers
and sores. Information on surgery in Ancient China is scant. One of
the few surgeons mentioned by name was Hua T'o (c.143–208 CE),
who was also proficient in acupuncture and other healing arts.
Apparently, he invented an all-purpose anaesthetic, known as
mafeisan, based on wine with added secret ingredients – extracts of
cannabis, opium poppies, datura (a type of nightshade), mandrake,
and even mixtures of these.

The herb mugwort (wormwood) of the genus *Artemisia* was – and,
like many ancient Eastern practices, continues to be – the chief plant
used in a therapy called moxibustion. This was often employed
in conjunction with acupuncture. There are several species of mugwort
with various names, such as yomoge and gaiyou in Japan, ssuk in Korea,
and mogusa, ai-ye, and huang hua'ai in China. Dried mugwort might be
heaped onto a skin acupoint and left to smoulder there, being removed
before it burned the surface – or, if the practitioner advised, left to singe

MOXIBUSTION
This 10th-century illustration shows a Chinese country doctor applying burning mugwort to a patient's back. This painful treatment, called moxibustion, stimulates acupuncture points to enhance the flow of qi (energy) in the body.

(which could cause blisters and scarring). This was the direct form of moxibustion. In the indirect method, the processed herb was pressed into a moxa stick, lit, and held near the skin to subject the site to heat and vapours. Alternatively, the moxa substance was piled around or on top of an inserted acupuncture needle and ignited, and left until the physician deemed it had taken effect. Moxibustion was mainly used for illnesses characterized by damp, cold, sluggishness, and stagnation. It aimed to banish cold, to warm the meridians, and to stimulate qi energy to flow again. Muscle pains, joint stiffness, headaches, stomach and intestinal complaints, painful or irregular periods, and even infertility were all treated in this way.

In ancient times, moxibustion made its way from China to nearby regions, including Korea, where it became associated with the legendary ruler Tangun (Dangun), who founded Korea more than 4,000 years ago. The legend describes how Tangun's mother, Ungnyeo, was initially a bear who wished to become a human. She was challenged to stay out of sunlight in a cave for 100 days, eating nothing but garlic and mugwort. Ungnyeo persisted, her wish was granted, and she later gave birth to Tangun – and the herbs mugwort and garlic have enjoyed importance in traditional Korean medicine ever since.

Korean medical traditions inherited many theories and practices from China. However, the former tended to place more emphasis on the inner causes of disease, including eating habits, lifestyle, personality, and behavioural traits. The concepts of yin-yang and the five phases were followed, and also yuk-gi, the six atmospheric natural influences: han (cold), yeol (heat), hwa (fire), pung (wind), jo (dryness), and seup (moisture). When these influences become unbalanced, people fall ill. In about 1614, during Korea's Joseon Dynasty, the eminent royal physician Heo Jun (c.1540–1616) produced *Dongui Bogam* (*Mirror of Eastern Medicine*). Its five main sections cover "internal" disorders, especially those of the heart, lungs, liver, spleen, and kidneys; "external" disorders, such as those of the bones, muscles, blood, and skin; varied conditions ranging from excessive worry to jaundice and gynaecological problems; herbal remedies; and acupuncture. This work established Korean medicine as distinct and independent from its Chinese-influenced background.

As far back as the 5th century CE, the classical medicine of China also greatly influenced developing medical practices in Japan – much of the knowledge arriving by way of Korea. Japanese practitioners incorporated elements of Chinese medicine into their own therapeutic system, which is known as kampo medicine. Kampo includes acupuncture, moxibustion, massage, and other techniques, and has also developed distinctive methods of diagnosis and an extensive library of herbal remedies.

One of the earliest written works on Japanese medicine was the 100-volume *Dido Rui Ju Ho*, compiled by the year 808 at the request of Emperor Kanmu. Its vast contents cover medical knowledge of the time, as well as folk remedies and those based on religion and worship. In 984, the *Ishimpo* (*Essence of Medicine and Therapeutic Methods*) was published, written by Japanese physician Yasuyori Tamba. Again, this is based on ancient Chinese texts with Japanese input. In the 15th century, Japan's medical traditions, still fundamentally adopted from China, were "Japanized" by Dosan Manase (c.1507–94). Raised as a Zen Buddhist in Kyoto, he studied medicine at the Ashikaga School, one of Japan's earliest institutes of learning, in Ashikaga, north of present-day Tokyo. It was a time of great communication between Japan and the Ming Dynasty of China, and both cultures benefited from the exchange of medical ideas and practices. Dosan accumulated huge amounts of information, both traditional Chinese methods, and from local and academic knowledge in Japan. This fairly amorphous mass was synthesized into his great work, *Keiteki Shu* (*Textbook of Internal Medicine*). It emphasized the logic of treating particular symptoms with specific herbs and became central to the further development and autonomy of Japanese medicine.

Kampo medicine emphasizes herbal treatments and is controlled and regulated as part of the national health care system in Japan. Like many of East Asia's classical medical systems, it has endured to the present day, adapting to the modern world.

KOREAN MASTER OF MEDICINE
Eminent physician Heo Jun wrote the defining text of traditional Korean medicine, *Dongui Bogam*.

Ayurveda

MOST MAJOR CIVILIZATIONS around the world have a so-called "Father of Medicine" – a real-life or perhaps mythical individual, who laid the foundations of an enduring system of medicine and healing – and who, ancient societies being what they were, was usually male. In India, this position is held by Charaka. Some 2,300 years ago, he compiled, wrote, and refined one of the classic texts that established India's primary form of traditional medicine – Ayurveda. This was the *Charaka Samhita*.

Samhitas are collections or compendia, usually written in the form of verses, hymns, or mantras. The term initially referred to India's most ancient religious texts or scriptures, the four *Vedas*, which date back at least 3,000 years, and were based on even more ancient texts. The Vedic traditions gave rise to Ayurveda (from "ayur", meaning life, and "veda", meaning knowledge) – a medical system that has parallels with other traditional systems, including those of Ancient Greece (see pp.30–39) and Ancient Rome (see pp.40–47). Central to the concept of Ayurveda are the five elements – namely jala or ap (water), tejas or agni (fire), privthi or bhumi (earth), pavana or vayu (air), and akasha (ether or space). These elements combine or compete in various proportions, and contribute to the three main doshas – which roughly correspond to the fluid-like bodily constituents that the Europeans called humours (see pp.106–107). The three Indian doshas are vata (wind), pitta (bile), and kapha (phlegm). As with the four humours theory, a serene balance of the doshas leads to health, whereas an imblance causes illness. Each dosha

BRAHMA, GOD OF CREATION
According to tradition, Ayurveda was given to humankind by Brahma, the Hindu god of creation, as a way of reducing our suffering.

has qualities linked to a particular type of illness. If vata, named after the Hindu god of wind, becomes excessive, it can cause digestive problems such as abdominal cramps, constipation, and flatulence. Kapha, which is linked to phlegm and mucus, is slow, oily, and has protective qualities — as do the mucous membranes lining the body's inner passageways such as the airways and digestive tract. Since kapha controls these moist tissues, an imbalance can lead to colds, coughs, and asthma. The doshas move and flow around the body along channels, or through pores called srotas. In some forms of Ayurveda, the srotas also carry nutrients and waste, and even knowledge or information.

The *Charaka Samhita* described 13 of these srotas. Three are interfaces between the body and the environment, forming conduits for incoming air, food, and water. Seven are associated with the seven bodily tissues, or dhatus (see below), and the final three carry away waste. Other classical Ayurvedic writers added three more srotas — the flow of thoughts in the mind, the flows of blood in menstruation, and of milk during lactation. These 16 srotas are largely accepted in Ayurveda today.

Two further concepts central to Ayurveda are the dhatus and agni. The dhatus are structural components, analogous to tissues. The seven dhatus are blood, lymph, muscles, bones, bone marrow, fat, and reproductive products (semen and eggs), and each dhatu has corresponding dosha channels. So the mamsa or muscle dhatu is accompanied by mamsavaha srotas carrying muscle nutrients and waste; while the majja or bone marrow dhatu corresponds with the majjavaha srotas supplying the bone marrow nutrients – plus, in this case, the nutrients for the nerves and nervous tissues, including the brain. Agni, which roughly means "digestive fire", is the final principle in Ayurveda. Agni is the Hindu god of fire, and in this context refers to the body's ability to assimilate and process many aspects of life, from food to the general mass of biochemical reactions known as metabolism, even to experiences and memories, while igniting or burning waste for removal.

Little is known about Charaka himself. He was probably born between 300 and 200 BCE and may have been a court physician. According to one legend, knowledge was handed by Lord Brahma (the Hindu god of creation), who wished to ease human suffering, to another deity,

Dhanvantari. He then transmitted it to humans, passing it from a series of teachers to their pupils, including Atreya and Agnivesa, and eventually to Charaka, who turned it into the seminal *Charaka Samhita*. His text has been revised and re-collated over the centuries. This encyclopaedic work is written in a poetic style and has eight main sections, more than 120 chapters, and some 8,400 verses (a mode of expression that helps students to memorize the content). It deals mainly with the area of Ayurvedic medicine called kaya-chikitsa — "body treatment", or internal medicine. Like the teachings of Hippocrates, the *Charaka Samhita* describes the qualities needed by a physician, and instructs how he should go about examining a patient to find the root cause of a disease, and how to make a prognosis and prescribe treatments. These treatments are minimally invasive, and involve specific diets and exercises, and more than 2,000 plant-based remedies. The emphasis throughout the *Charaka Samhita* is on preventing illness by maintaining good hygiene and a healthy diet.

The other great founding work of Ayurveda, the *Susruta Samhita*, was probably compiled a few centuries earlier than the *Charaka Samhita*. It deals chiefly with the field of Ayurvedic surgery, shalya-chikitsa, and is credited to Susruta, who, like Charaka, was a somewhat shadowy figure, and who dates to around 2,500 years ago. This text was also revised and expanded over the centuries, and given the content relating to traumatic injuries, parts of the book were probably written during times of conflict and warfare.

The *Susruta Samhita* is massive in scope and describes many surgical techniques that are sophisticated and daring, both in theory and practice, along with equipment and medications. Details vary among the later editions, but the procedures include extracting teeth, draining fluids using trocars (a kind of syringe), repairing hernias and broken bones, venesection (see p.132), eye surgery (including cataract excision), widening tubes such as the oesophagus or urethra with strictures, cauterizing haemorrhoids with powerful acids, alkalis, or hot irons, and caesarian section. Surgical training is described, including knifework practice on dead animals and vegetables, and there is advice

AYURVEDIC PHARMACY
This 19th-century painting shows an Indian pharmacist
preparing Ayurvedic remedies. The principles of Ayurveda
were laid down between 500 and 300 BCE and are still
relevant in the 21st century.

on how to deal with complications such as sudden bleeding, diarrhoea, vomiting, cough, impotence, and infertility. More than 1,000 medical conditions and 800 remedies, mostly herbal, are described altogether. The *Susruta Samhita* departs from mainstream Ayurveda's three doshas by suggesting a fourth – rakta, or blood – which is a dhatu or tissue in the standard system. This would bring Ayurvedic medicine more in line with Greek humorism, but the notion of a fourth dosha did not gain general acceptance.

After the *Susruta Samhita* and *Charaka Samhita*, and probably written between the 4th and 6th centuries, came the *Ashtanga Hridayam* and the *Ashtanga Sangraha*. These were probably the work of Vagbhata, a Buddhist healer and medical authority who may have lived in what is now Pakistan. Vagbhata organizes the *Ashtanga Hridayam* content into eight (ashta) sections: internal medicine; gynaecology and paediatrics; problems of the mind and spirit (what we might call psychiatry); head, eye, ear, and nose conditions; general surgery; toxicology (such as treating swallowed poisons and snake venom); rejuvenation; and sexual medicine, including aphrodisiac therapy. The author quotes or draws material from the two earlier works, but focuses more on the body's anatomy and physiology, and adds updated knowledge of surgery and drugs.

A fourth revered source for Ayurveda is the Bower Manuscript, named after the British military intelligence officer Sir Hamilton Bower, who obtained it while working in northwestern China in 1890. Dating from the 6th century, or even the 4th – roughly the same era as the *Ashtanga Hridayam* – the manuscript contains a great deal of information about medicine, particularly Ayurvedic medicine, and includes many recipes for remedies. One of the herbs cited at length at the start of the Bower Manuscript is garlic, *Allium sativum* (known as lahsun in Hindi, or lasuna in Sanskrit). This most revered of plants originally came from Central Asia, probably the Hindu Kush in the

"The person whose vata is unimpeded… lives for 100 years without sickness"

CHARAKA SAMHITA

western Himalayas. Its recorded medicinal uses go back at least 5,000 years, and it remains one of Ayurveda's most commonly advised plant remedies. Another founding treatise of Ayurvedic medicine, *Kashyap Samhita*, explains: "The taste of its seed is pungent, its stem salty and bitter, its leaves astringent and its vipaka [Ayurvedic term for post-digestive effects] is sweet". Vagbhata suggested that garlic is helpful for rejuvenation, for "smoothing" the digestion, and as a general stimulant, although it is also recommended as a decongestant and expectorant for coughs and colds, and (due to what we would now call its antimicrobial

INDIAN SAGE
Susruta, the author of the Ayurvedic classic the *Susruta Samhita*, lived in Varanasi, India, in the 6th century BCE.

properties) for alleviating skin problems. These range from plague sores, scrofula (a form of tuberculosis) ulcers, smallpox eruptions, and leprosy lesions to rabid dog bites, and oral and vaginal thrush.

Two popular spices in Ayurvedic medicine are cinnamon and cardamom. Cinnamon bark, from *Cinnamomum verum* and related trees, is reputed to have powerful effects on the kapha (phlegm) dosha, which makes it good for respiratory disorders such as colds, coughs, blocked nose, sore throat, and chest infections, as well as digestive complaints such as heartburn, indigestion, abdominal pains, and diarrhoea. Cardamom, from *Elletaria* and *Amomum* herbs, is regarded as "warm", and balances the vata and kapha doshas. Again, it is commonly used for problems with the stomach and intestines, such as nausea, stomach cramps, and flatulence, and problems in the lungs and airways, including allergies such as rhinitis. It is also reputed to stimulate the appetite and the general constitution.

Like many traditional medicines, the various forms of Ayurveda are still widely practised in its home region. It has also spread to other lands in recent times, taking its place as a contemporary form of complementary medicine (see pp.320–27).

PULSE DIAGNOSIS
According to Ayurveda, disease results from an imbalance in a person's doshas. For this reason, an Ayurvedic doctor spends considerable time feeling a patient's pulse – a practice that leads to diagnosis and treatment.

Native American Medicine

WHEN EUROPEANS FIRST EXPLORED the Americas, from the 1490s, they found a huge variety of native peoples with distinctive cultures, languages, customs, clothing, ceremonies – and systems of medicine. The number of main tribes in North America certainly exceeded 500, and with smaller groupings probably totalled over 1,000. Each followed its own beliefs and ways of dealing with disease and healing the sick, but they all had much in common. Many native North Americans viewed health as a balance between mind, body, and spirit, and healing involved addressing imbalances in a person's life, either by making offerings to the spirits, repairing personal thoughts and emotions, or receiving practical care such as a massage or herbal remedy. The key figures in this process, variously known as tribal healers, medicine men and women, or shamans (see pp.88–89) were regarded as mediators between the human world and the unseen realm of spirits and gods. Most medicine people underwent exhaustive training, including being apprenticed to a senior. They gained knowledge and experience to assess not just the symptoms of health problems but also the intricacies of the people who suffered them. These practitioners learned to select and prepare herbs, carry out ceremonies, employ tokens, charms, and offerings, make intimate contact with nature, and read signs and symbols from the spirits. Much of this was kept secret, since discussing matters with others might anger the spirits.

Many medicine people had bundles or bags containing treasured items and tokens known as medicine tools. These were often natural objects such as bones, feathers, crystals, and furs. One item usually included in the medicine bundle was a medicine pipe. Smoking herbs and other natural substances was a central part of healing ceremonies. The most sacred plant was tobacco. Exhaling its smoke made visible the body's breath, which was considered the most vital component of

RUNS MEDICINE
This picture, dating from around 1899, shows Runs Medicine, an Arapaho medicine man, in traditional dress.

SHAMAN'S DRUM
Shamans all over the world use a variety of instruments – such as this Native American drum – to summon spirits to effect healing.

life. Tobacco was also a gift that was offered to the spirits when they were being petitioned for help. During treatment, the medicine person might blow tobacco smoke at the patient to drive away evil – and the smoke then rose to carry messages to the spirits above. Drumming and chanting were also important for summoning spirits to ask them what was needed. Medicine people were rarely paid for their help, but they accepted gifts – tobacco was especially valued. Each patient was unique, so a medicine person's actions and treatments had to be carefully tailored. However, there was no automatic right for a sick person to demand help. The medicine man or woman could choose whom to treat, how, and when.

North American peoples used a multitude of herbs and other plants for medicine, some of which have been taken up by modern doctors. The bark or leaves of willow trees were chewed, or perhaps boiled to make teas, for all manner of aches and pains, from headaches to stiff joints. Willow bark contains acetylsalicylic acid (ASA) or salicylate – the pain-relieving, anti-inflammatory, fever-reducing active ingredient in one of the world's most widespread and useful drugs today, aspirin. Willow was especially effective in relieving the pain of dental caries and abscesses, earning it the nickname of the "toothache tree".

The most widespread and revered medicinal herb for many Native Americans was sage. Regarded as a powerful cleansing agent for body and soul, it was believed to transport prayers to the spirits and purify the air. Its traditional medical uses were legion – as a remedy for internal problems of the stomach, bowel, lungs, and liver, as an antiseptic salve for wounds, burns, and rashes, and as a soothing relaxant either inhaled as smoke or drunk as a tea. Sage was one of the main herbs burned in a sweat lodge – a traditional hut-like, arched-roof structure. The design and building materials of a sweat lodge varied greatly, but it was often fashioned from flexible saplings and covered by animal skins. It created a small, dark, calm space in which water poured onto hot rocks created steam that mixed with smoke from smouldering herbs. Rocks were usually heated by a fire near the lodge, passed inside (using deer antlers as carriers), and arranged in a pit within. The medicine person might waft or blow smoke at recipients as part of the healing ritual.

Hundreds of herbs and other plants were used by Native American healers: the boiled leaves of the creosote bush made a tea that was used for easing respiratory problems such as bronchitis, pneumonia, and tuberculosis; an infusion of broom snakeweed was prescribed to help women during childbirth; pleurisy root was given for many kinds of breathing problems and was especially good as an expectorant; the boiled, cooled extract from the inner bark of dogwood was employed to aid colonic irrigation; horsemint (bergamot, bee balm) was used variously as a cold or warm infusion for back and head pains, as an ointment to ward off infection, and as a mouthwash for toothache and painful gums; the boiled, reduced extract of the flowers of yellow-spined thistle was applied to the skin for burns, scalds, sores, and other lesions; the buds and leaves of the cedar tree were boiled and sipped to ease sore throats and coughs.

From the 14th century, the Aztecs rose to power in what is now central-southern Mexico. They too commanded a huge herbal medicine chest, and believed that many forms of ill health were handed down from gods and spirits. Other origins for disease included natural disasters such as plagues, earthquakes, floods, and erupting volcanoes. Aztec priests also believed that illnesses were sometimes visited on humans purely for the gods' fun or amusement, rather than as a punishment for forgetting to worship

HEALING SAGE
Sage is the most powerful herb in Native American medicine, providing relief from numerous ills and serving as a means for communicating with spirits.

or for some other sin. To appease the gods and have the sickness taken away, the patient might be rebuked by whipping or by having thorns and spines jabbed through their flesh, possibly accompanied by animal or even human sacrifices. One of the commonest Aztec "medications" was pulque or octli, a form of alcoholic beer fermented from a species of agave known as maguey (American aloe). It was usually drunk by rulers or priests, but could be offered to any sick person, especially when spiced up with other herbs, tree bark, and roots to help dull pain and reduce the symptoms of all manner of ailments. Another Aztec speciality was the black, glassy, volcanic rock obsidian, which was ground by healers into a powder and rubbed into the skin to treat ulcers, rashes, and injuries. Far more specialized was a mixture of squash plant, ayonel-huatl flesh, and eagle dung, which was used to bring on labour in heavily pregnant women.

During the first millennium, in the Yucatan Peninsula and northern Central America, before the glory days of the Aztec Empire, the Mayan people developed a sophisticated civilization with a complex medical system. They too regarded body, mind, and spirit as equally responsible for illness. In particular, they thought disease was due to misbehaviour or wrongdoing on the part of the sufferer. Cure demanded a mix of ritual, ceremony, worship of idols, and offerings of tokens to the angered gods, to pacify them and resolve the sin. The Mayans' written language recorded parts of their history and practices. Their treatments were extensive: herbal emetics (vomit-inducers) and purgatives (bowel-emptiers) to clean out the body's interior; massage; and sauna sessions in sweat baths akin to the North American sweat lodges. Also, like North American cultures, the Mayans had specialist healers or medicine men, known as ah'men – the equivalent of a modern-day doctor, herbalist, psychotherapist, and counsellor. An Ah'man spent time with the patient, asking details about his or her life, habits, and behaviour, and would gradually home in on worries and problems, such as an unhappy relationship, depression, or self-

"Before eating, always take time to thank the food"

ARAPAHO SAYING

MAYAN HERB JAR
This ceramic jar, dating from around 700,
was used by a Mayan ah'man to store
medicinal herbs, including tobacco.

doubt, which might contribute to the illness.
Ah'men used plants such as turbina, cacti-like
peyotes, and mushrooms – all with known
hallucinogenic properties – to induce trance-
like states that brought them closer to the
gods. One of their main plants was a bush-like
species of mimosa known as tepezcohuite,
jurema preta, or vinho de jurema (*Mimosa
tenuiflora*). The leaves, seeds, and especially
the root bark were infused, boiled, roasted, or
fermented to make treatments for a wide range of problems, from skin
rashes to coughs and backache. Plant extracts were often mixed with
animal body parts (especially from reptiles), birds' eggs, and guano.

The rainforests of South America's Amazon region are globally
acclaimed as a treasure store of medicinal plants. Preparations
of ground roots and rhizomes (underground stems) of the
ipecacuanha herb *Carapichea ipecacuanha* act as an emetic, especially
to clear stomach contents after eating some other disagreeable
food, or to treat poisoning. To kill animals for food, native Amazonian
hunters fired blow darts and arrows tipped with curare or ampi – the
extract of plants such as the trailing vine *Chondrodendron tomentosum*. The
active ingredient, an alkaloid called D-tubocurarine, works as a
muscle relaxant, which can still help as an addition to anaesthesia
during surgery. Native South Americans also made extensive use of
coca bushes (*Erythroxylum coca* or *E. novogranatense*). They chewed the
leaves of these as a pick-me-up to ward off fatigue, thirst, and
hunger. Its active substance, cocaine, a powerful stimulant, made
its way into Western medicine chiefly as a local anaesthetic, before
being replaced by safer and more effective compounds. However,
illegal use of cocaine as a highly addictive stimulant – "coke" and
its freebase form "crack-cocaine" – continue to cause massive
problems worldwide.

Shamanism

The shaman, or "medicine man", is a combination of priest, healer, and teacher found in many traditional or tribal societies. Shamans are believed to be in contact with the spirit world, and use rituals and amulets that are said to heal the sick and prevent disease.

MASK (1497)
Iroquois shamans wore a mask with a broken nose, representing a legendary healer named Hado'ih. Hado'ih had injured his nose on a mountain during a display of spiritual power between himself and the creator deity.

MEDICINE JAR (c.100–1550)
This Mexican ceramic jar bearing the image of a deity probably belonged to a shaman and may have contained hallucinogenic drugs used in healing rituals.

SHAMAN'S CROWN (19TH CENTURY)
This crown was worn by a shaman of the Tsimshian people of Alaska. Made of mountain goat horns, it indicates the shaman's belief that he could transform himself into the spirit of this powerful animal.

NECKLACE (1801–1900)
The human teeth and glass beads threaded onto this Apache medicine man's necklace were believed to protect the wearer from evil or illness.

HEALER'S CIRCLET (1880–1920)
Worn by a west African healer, this circlet is decorated with cowrie shells and red and blue beads. Used in Africa as money, cowrie shells were not only valuable but also had spiritual significance.

SOULCATCHER (c.19TH CENTURY)
Shamans believed that a person's soul could be drawn from their body, leading to disease. Amulets such as this were used to restore souls, and to draw out and trap evil spirits.

RATTLE (1884)
Shamans from the Haida people of British Columbia sang songs accompanied by rattles like these. Knowledge of songs and stories is a crucial part of a shaman's place in a tribe.

DIVINATION BONES (1880–1930)
One of the shaman's tasks was to make spiritual journeys to find the answers to important questions. An African shaman used tools such as animal vertebrae, pebbles, and similar objects in these divination rituals.

HAND DRUM (c.19TH CENTURY)
Shamans use percussion instruments, especially drums, to beat out a rhythm. The effect of the continuous drum beats helps the shaman to enter an altered state of consciousness, in which he or she can contact the spirit world.

African and West Asian Traditions

TRADITIONAL MEDICAL SYSTEMS in Africa have certain similarities with those of native America (see pp.82–89). In general, the root causes of ill health are viewed primarily as spiritual or supernatural, emanating from gods and the spirit world, rather than having natural origins within the body or the immediate environment. The usual reason for visiting disease on a person is some kind of misdemeanour or sin against the gods, the memories of ancestors or the local community, or perhaps disturbing harmony in the natural world's plants, animals, soil, rocks, and water. To effect healing, the spirits are appeased by offerings, chanting, ceremonies, and sacrifices, while the patient tries to feel remorse and repent. The spirits may also advise on practical remedies, often herb-based, but perhaps also massage, special diets, fasting, purging, and other treatments. They do so through traditional medical practitioners with special knowledge and powers who act as intermediaries between the human world and the dominion of the spirits. These individuals are known variously as healers, curers, witch doctors, diviners, shamans (see pp.88–89), and hundreds of local names.

Many traditional African practitioners do not identify an illness in the way that modern science-based medicine does – that is, by selecting the most likely condition from a range of related options, such as differentiating between pleurisy, bronchitis, and pneumonia. Rather, the traditional healer seeks the ultimate cause – the original reason for angering the spirits or displeasing the gods.

READING GOD'S WILL
Cleromancy is a form of divination in which stones or shells are cast onto the ground to form patterns. These reveal information about a person's past, present, and future.

Finding the cause then determines the spiritual aspects of the treatment, such as which incantations and offerings to employ. At the same time, practical remedies such as herbs are advised, and these can be selected as much for the symbolism attached to each remedy as for its known effects on symptoms.

Some patients may need the skills of a diviner. Common across Africa, divination takes many forms, and seeks to explain the past as well as predict the future. Divination by fire (pyromancy) may involve reading signs in flames or sparks, or throwing objects into the blaze to see how they burn. In water-based divining (hydromancy), the diviner studies ripples, splashes, or reflections in water, or watches the behaviour of objects such as floating twigs or leaves. This provides clues to the cause of an illness and how it can be addressed. The casting of lots (cleromancy) attaches mystical powers to special objects, which are thrown or cast onto the ground. A medical opinion is then divined from the arrangement or pattern in which they fall. Objects read in this way range from stones, seeds, and twigs to animal parts, such as bones, teeth, shells, skin, dried eyeballs, and fresh entrails. Each diviner has his or her own sacred groups of objects and chooses those that are relevant to each situation. Geomancy is a related technique, in which objects are cast onto patterns drawn on the ground.

For medical purposes, some diviners work in silence – others recite incantations, verses, or spells. They may talk to the patient and ask probing questions, which help to determine a course of action. Some diviners use no physical objects, but enter a trance and receive awareness of the spirit world intuitively, from within themselves. Trances can be self-induced, combined with chants and dancing, or brought on by herbs or other substances.

Among the Lobi people of Burkina Faso and the Côte d'Ivoire, diviners, known as buor, use idols or statues called batebas on which patterns are engraved that link them to the spiritual world. A medical diviner sits in front of the appropriate statue and holds the patient's hand. As the diviner questions the spirits, he also feels the way the patient's hand moves, perhaps tightening or loosening its grip. These changes indicate the basis of the sickness and offer ideas for treatment.

To heal the sick, traditional African medicine usually treats both the spiritual or religious realm and the physical body of the patient. Some healing focuses on restoring harmony between the patient and the gods. This can involve spells and ritual offerings such as money,

LOBI STATUETTE
The Lobi people of Burkino Faso
and the Côte d'Ivoire use statuettes
to call on the gods for spiritual aid.

food, drink, clothing, or jewellery. Through the healer, a god can demand an animal sacrifice – perhaps a wild creature like a monkey or a snake, or domestic beasts such as chickens, goats, or even cattle. This might be preceded by bleeding the animal and perhaps drinking its blood.

Many African practitioners are expert herbalists and have an encyclopedic knowledge of the plants, mushrooms, toadstools, and other fungi of their region. The violet tree *Securidaca longepedunculata* is known by local names such as uwar maganigunar, ezeogwu, mpesu, chipvufana, mufufu, umfufu, and maba. The main medicinal parts are the roots and bark, which are – like numerous medicinal substances – harmful in high quantities. In smaller amounts, usually taken orally as an infusion or soup, these serve as remedies for a huge array of ailments, ranging from headaches and toothache to coughs and chest infections, sexually transmitted diseases, and constipation. Boiled root or leaf infusions of the violet tree can also be applied topically (to the body's surface), such as by rubbing on the scalp (for headaches), bandaged onto swollen joints (for arthritis), or as a cleansing wash (for skin sores, insect stings, snake bites, and ulcers). The Venda people of South Africa make a drink of the powdered root with sorghum and maize to treat men who are "deficient below".

African pumpkin or balsam pear *Momordica balsamina* (mohodu, nkaka, intshungu) is another widespread plant remedy. The bark, leaves, fruits, and seeds have all been utilized. In the Okavango region of southwest Africa, watery or plant-oil infusions of its fruits are incorporated into poultices, balms, and liniments for skin sores, cuts, boils, bruises, burns, and blisters – and also for haemorrhoids.

Another widely used traditional plant is the African stinkwood tree *Prunus africana*. It too has many local names, such as entasesa in Uganda, tikuur-inchet in Ethiopia, m'konde-konde in Tanzania, muu'iri in Kenya, and inja'zangoma-ilimn'ama in southern Africa.

Traditional healers advise using its bark in preparations for stomach pains and bowel complaints, fevers, cuts, and abrasions, low fertility in men, and urinary difficulties.

With regard to urinary problems, the rainforests of West and Central Africa are busy with modern bioprospectors looking for native medicines to convert into the latest "wonder drugs". The bark extract from the stinkwood *Prunus africana* is processed in commercial quantities as the remedy pygeum. It is marketed worldwide for urinary problems in men with an enlarged prostate (benign prostatic hyperplasia). Harvesting the bark has made wild trees rare in many areas, so to make harvesting more sustainable, plantations are being established.

Traditional forms of medicine in North and East Africa have long cross-pollinated with those from the eastern Mediterranean and West Asia. Camel caravans and seagoing vessels transported herbal products for trade as well as the plants themselves. One example is the frankincense tree *Boswellia sacra*, producer of the legendary fragrance for perfumes, aromatherapy (see p.324), and herbal medicine. This small tree grows in dry, rocky regions of north-west Africa and Arabia. Its gum or sap is tapped and harvested to make frankincense. Its aroma was said to purify the "stale air" historically blamed for causing infections such as malaria and the dreaded Black Death (see pp.54–55). As a medicine, frankincense has been used across North Africa and Asia for several sets of conditions. Taken by mouth, it is said to ease digestive complaints, from stomach pains to ulcerative colitis. Local healers advise breathing it as a vapour or steamy inhalation for chest infections and tight, wheezy respiration. To help skin conditions such as rashes, eczema, and cuts, it is incorporated into salves and creams.

Frankincense has been known since antiquity. In the Bible it was offered to the infant Jesus by the Three Wise Men. It was mentioned by Hippocrates of Greece (see pp.30–39) and Galen of Rome (see pp.40–45), and the eminent Islamic

FRANKINCENSE GRAINS
Made from the gum or sap extruded from *Boswellia* trees, frankincense has long been used in treatments for chest infections, stomach complaints, and skin conditions.

AFRICAN MEDICINE MAN
A group of Bonda women stand with their
medicine man and his assistant in Freetown,
Sierra Leone, in 1900. A mask helps to
depersonalize the medicine man during
healing rituals in which he invokes the gods.

"The way a man dies is determined by his occupation"

AFRICAN PROVERB

physician of the Middle Ages, Ibn Sina (see pp.100–105) valued it for controlling fevers, vomiting, and diarrhoea: "If you give a drink of white flowers in wine, it helps [recovery] from dysentery... If you make a drug patch made from fresh flowers... it prevents conception".

Another tree product famous for thousands of years and still around today is mastic or arabic gum, from the mastic tree *Pistacia lentiscus*. It was chewed as a medication for halitosis (bad breath), toothache, inflamed gums, and mouth ulcers, and swallowed to combat digestive disorders such as gastric ulcers or an irritable bowel. Mixed with plant oils such as olive oil, it could be soaked into a pad of moss and tied onto snake bites and insect stings.

Not to be confused with arabic gum is gum arabic (meskar, awerwar, or chaar-gund) which comes from certain types of acacia trees, especially *Acacia senegal*. Aside from its many industrial uses as a binding and gumming agent in products ranging from confectionery to paints, gum arabic has a long history in traditional African and Asian medicine. Its soothing physical properties are believed to ease irritation, reduce inflammation, and promote the healing of body membranes and surfaces. Topically, it is advocated for swollen, painful areas and for sore nipples.

Yet another sap or gum highly prized by traditional Asian healers is asafoetida, obtained from species of the giant fennel *Ferula*. Native to Iran and Afghanistan, it is named from its foul or "foetid" smell and bitter taste. Its medicinal preparations come mostly from the underground stems or main roots. Popular through the ages in the Arab world, it is given for digestive upsets, to relieve pain, for colds and coughs, and – depending on mood – as a relaxant and aphrodisiac. It also embodies the popular global belief that if a medicine smells and tastes bad, it must be good.

Asafoetida was exploited in another way in both African and West Asian classic medicine – as an aid to exorcism. Combined with garlic for extra kick, it was worn around the neck during rituals to drive evil spirits from a sufferer's body and mind. More than 3,000 years ago, in Babylonia, royal physician Esagil-kin-apli compiled what has

READING THE FLAMES
Pyromancy is the ancient art of reading flames for signs
that shed light on the past and the future. A doctor
may use it to understand a patient's condition.

become known as *The Manual of the Exorcist*. It instructs training and
practice for exorcisms, with details on rituals, spells, omens, and
tokens. Esagil-kin-apli also produced *Sakikku* (usually translated as
Diagnostic Handbook). It was a huge compendium of symptoms and their
underlying conditions, and included many methods for divining the
deity responsible for each disease.

The Rise of Scientific Medicine

900–1820

While Europe was in its Dark Ages, Islam expanded in West Asia and enjoyed a golden age. Its most famous physicians included al-Rhazi and the polymath Ibn Sina, who wrote more than 40 works on health, medicine, and well-being. Taking leads from Greece and Rome, Islamic scholars kept both the art and science of medicine alive and moving forward.

Early in the Renaissance, Western medicine emerged from stagnation and became more formalized. Universities opened medical schools and set up recognized qualifications, soon creating a medical elite. There was still room for a rebel. In the Italian city of Padua in 1543, against the trends of the time, Andreas Vesalius produced *De Humani Corporis Fabrica* (*On the Structure of the Human Body*). This magnificent book helped to break Galen's spell and usher in a new age when doctors trusted their own eyes, ears, and hands, and examined and talked to their patients. Another unorthodox figure was Ambroise Paré, a French "barber-surgeon", whose harrowing battlefield experiences led him to raise surgery from a menial trade to a respected profession.

The roles of the heart and blood had been subjects of speculation since ancient times. In 1628, English doctor William Harvey grafted his own research on to earlier ideas to explain the workings of the cardiovascular system. Similarly, in 1798, another English physician, Edward Jenner, built on pioneering work with his own experiments to establish smallpox vaccination. The light microscope, invented around 1590, took a couple of centuries to permeate medicine but, in the 19th century, the ground-breaking work by German physician Rudolf Virchow became the foundation of that essential branch of modern medicine, cellular pathology.

Al-Rhazi, Ibn Sina, and the Arab Revival

DURING THE 5TH CENTURY CE, the Western Roman Empire was in decay. Roman military dominance, social order, public health, and medical services fragmented in the face of Visigoths, Vandals, and a host of other invaders. Societies became more varied and disorganized, and written works, including historical records, became scarcer and more sporadic. Europe was drifting into the so-called "Dark Ages". In contrast, from about the 8th century in the Middle East and western Asia, the spread of Islam ushered in a golden age. Centred on Baghdad, in what is now Iraq, pursuits such as philosophy, literature, art, architecture, and science flourished in an age of intellectual progress. Knowledge was gathered, recorded, expanded upon, and disseminated. Dominating the fields of health and medicine through the following centuries were two great figures whose works would hold sway for 500 years and more: al-Rhazi (or Rhazes) and Ibn Sina (or Avicenna).

Al-Rhazi (c.866–925) came from the Persian (now Iranian) historic city of Rey (Rayy), now subsumed into Tehran. He was educated, became a physician, and held senior positions at hospitals both in Rey and in Baghdad. Like many great minds of those times, al-Rhazi was widely versed and active not only in medicine, alchemy, and chemistry, but also in philosophy, Islam and allied faiths, and other intellectual pursuits. He wrote widely and prolifically, producing more than 50 major works and more than 200 articles and smaller publications. In the area of medicine, he took his lead from many noted works of classical history, including those by Hippocrates of Greece (see pp.30–39) and Galen of Rome (see pp.40–45), the traditions of his own Persia, the Indian

MUHUMMAD AL-RHAZI
One of the greatest figures of the Arab revival, al-Rhazi made contributions to numerous fields of medicine, particularly pediatrics and ophthalmology.

Ayurvedic approach (see pp.74–81), and Chinese concepts such as yin-yang and qi (see pp.64–73). He drew upon these works and synthesized them, modernized them with the latest knowledge of his time, and added his own experiences from in-depth observation and sympathetic treatment as a practising physician.

Al-Rhazi championed a strict ethical code and a humane approach to patients that echoed those of Hippocrates. He recognized that some diseases were incurable, that physicians should not be blamed for such cases, and that they should not subject sufferers to supposed "cures" that were likely to worsen their quality of life. Physicians also had a duty to research and assimilate the latest medical knowledge and practices, and to treat each and every patient with equal courtesy and attention. Al-Rhazi was an acknowledged expert on ophthalmology, one of the great specialisms of the time, although he himself suffered cataracts and gradually lost his eyesight.

Clinically, al-Rhazi was probably the first physician to record the distinction between the terrible scourge of smallpox and the less deadly but still debilitating measles. He espoused a "fermentation theory" of disease, whereby the blood bubbles and boils in the manner of a fermenting alcoholic drink, giving off morbid vapours through the skin – manifested by the blisters and sores of the pox and measles. His work *al-Judari wa al-Hasbah* (*Concerning Smallpox and Measles*) advises: "Restlessness, nausea and anxiety occur more frequently with measles... pain in the back is more apparent with smallpox".

Therapeutically, al-Rhazi described many medicinal herbs and minerals, and introduced several drugs that contained mercury. He also improved medical equipment. Based on his work in alchemy and chemistry, he introduced new versions of utensils and tools that would persist for centuries, including the pestle and mortar for grinding, flasks for mixing, and phials for storage. He was also an early proponent of animal gut for sutures and a material similar to plaster of Paris for casts to immobilize and protect the patient.

Al-Rhazi's numerous writings include two massive encyclopedic works encompassing medical theory and practice, medical philosophy, and life in general. *Kitab al-Mansouri fi al-Tibb* (*The Book on Medicine Dedicated to al-Mansur*), known as *Liber almansoris* in Latin, was named in honour of Mansur ibn Ishaq ibn Ahmad ibn Asad, the governor of his home city of Rey. Its ten chapters cover diet, hygiene, anatomy, physiology, pathology theory, and aspects of medical practice such as diagnosis, therapy, and surgery. The second work was *Kitab al-Hawi fi al-tibb* (*The Comprehensive Book on Medicine*), Latinized to *Continens Liber* (and morphed to *Virtuous Life* in English), which comprises a multi-volume compendium of al-Rhazi's clinical observations, notes, and records, and views on previous medical works going back to Ancient Greece, Rome, and India. Parts of this volume were his own work, and others were assembled after his death.

Both books were soon established throughout the Islamic world. They were translated into other languages (including Latin for Europe), and became recommended reading for physicians and their students for several centuries. Al-Rhazi also produced numerous smaller books, articles, and commentaries, ranging from *Misconceptions of the Abilities of the Physician* to *Fruits Before and After Lunch*.

A century after al-Rhazi, Ibn Sina (c.980–1037) gained fame in western Europe under the Latin version of his name, Avicenna. His interests were even more extensive than those of al-Rhazi, and his written output greater. He was born near the historic Silk Road city of Bukhara (now in Uzbekistan), and apparently qualified as a physician by the age of 18, after which he set off on extensive travels around the Persian lands of West Asia. During these, he assimilated vast amounts of knowledge, treated patients, lectured on a variety of topics, penned over 40 works on physical and spiritual well-being, and managed to gain the patronage of rulers. These included Abu Ja-far Ala Adduala, the ruler of Hamedan (in northeastern Iran), with whom he spent his last decade as a physician and scholarly companion. His two most celebrated works are *Kitab al-Shifa* (*The Book of Healing*) and *Al-Qanun fi al-Tibb* (*The Canon of Medicine*), the latter being his masterpiece. Published in about 1025, *Al-Qanun* rapidly gained prominence throughout the Islamic world, and was translated from Arabic into Persian, Latin, most major European languages, and even Chinese. It influenced

"That whose existence is necessary must necessarily be one essence"

IBN SINA

TREATING SMALLPOX
A miniature from a Turkish edition of Ibn Sina's
Al-Qanun shows a remedy being prepared for a
smallpox victim.

physicians and medical students for the next five centuries, in Europe
and beyond, and is still regarded as one of the greatest works in the
history of medicine.

Among the attractions of *Al-Qanun* were its methodical and orderly
organization, and its vast scope as a self-contained work of reference
for both trainee and practising physicians. It selected, summarized,
and extended the medical knowledge of the ancients, and interwove
progressive contemporary ideas about diagnosis and treatments,
especially regarding transmissible diseases and drug therapies.

To modern eyes, some of the content of *Al-Qanun* is difficult to
appreciate. In first part of the work, Ibn Sina discusses the aims and
methods of medicine as "a science from which one learns the
conditions and states of the human body with regard to health and
the absence of health… the aim being to guard health when it exists
and restore it when it is lost". Following the medical philosophies of
his age, he invokes and describes many causes of illness – elements,
humours, temperaments, formal and efficient and accidental causes,
vital force, vital faculties and abilities, and much more that is

أراك قَدْ أبرزْتَ لى رأسِكَ قَبْل أنْ تُبرزَ قرطاسَك وولْتنى قذ الَّك وَلَم تقلّذ الَك ولشَّ
مِنْ بيع نقدًا بدين ولا يطلب أثرًا بعد عينٍ فانْ أنتَ رضختَ بالعينِ جمتَ فى

PUBLIC VENESECTION
Surrounded by spectators, an Arab physician draws blood from a patient. The procedure was believed to bring balance to the patient's humours.

unfamiliar today. Some of these concepts derive from earlier ages, such as the four humours and four temperaments as described by Hippocrates, some are adapted from the ideas of al-Rhazi and others, while some were added by Ibn Sina himself.

Al-Qanun has five main parts. The first section covers the origins of health and illness, and various aspects of the body's structure and function. Ibn Sina regards the body as amenable to observation and dissection — however, the cause of disease and methods of treatment should be arrived at by reason and deduction. There are detailed descriptions of the brain and eyes, general therapeutic procedures, and the best ways to maintain health, namely through attention to exercise, food, and sleep. The second part of the book is a *materia medica* — lists and assembled information for more than 700 mineral preparations, herbal extracts, compound remedies, and other drugs and medicines. The third part concerns the diagnosis and treatment of diseases specific to certain parts of the body, following a pathway from the brain and nerves, eyes, and ears, down to the feet and toes, and including swellings and joint pains. Next come conditions that affect the whole body, such as fevers, poison bites, various fractures, broken bones, and even obesity. The fifth part lists compound remedies and their uses.

Scattered throughout *Al-Qanun* are Ibn Sina's personal experiences, anecdotes, advice, and pronouncements. He muses on the contagious or transmissible nature of phthisis or consumption (pulmonary tuberculosis); on how some diseases seem to be spread by water or in soil; and on sexual activities such as masturbation in men and women: "Women [with hysteria] should not resort to rubbing... this is suitable only for husbands and doctors".

Al-Rhazi and Ibn Sina kept alive and advanced much medical knowledge that had largely vanished from Europe — knowledge that had originated in Ancient Greece and Rome, and then spread through Constantinople and Gundeshapur to Baghdad and Bukhara, where it was combined with learnings from India and China, and was eventually translated back into European languages to form a basis for the flowering of the Renaissance. This reawakening of Classical thought inaugurated the age of the university, when medical schools were established throughout Europe, the Middle East, and beyond.

The Four Humours

The Ancient Greeks believed that the body contained four fluids, called humours — blood, yellow bile, black bile, and phlegm. To be healthy, they had to be kept in balance; their proportions could be changed by diet, activity, the season, or a person's age. Physicians from the time of Galen in the 1st century CE (see pp.40–45) to the 19th century believed that bloodletting (see pp.132–33) removed excess humours from the body and restored its natural balance.

ZODIAC LUNAR SCHEME FOR BLOODLETTING
ENGLAND, 1486
This device, from the guild of barber surgeons of York, England, calculated times for bloodletting. It had two movable discs: the "index of the sun" pointed to the day of treatment; the "index of the moon" (now missing) pointed to the cycle of the moon and a corresponding zodiac sign. Each sign related to one of the four elements, and to one of the humours — bloodletting of the relevant body part (see below) was to be avoided in that lunar phase.

The four elements

One of the oldest theories of matter, going back to Ancient Greece but also influencing Christian physicians in the Middle Ages, stated that everything in the world is made up of four elements — air, fire, earth, and water. Each of these elements was associated with one of the humours: air with blood, fire with yellow bile, earth with black bile, and phlegm with water. Ancient writers also linked parts of the body with the elements, for example, the lungs with air and the digestive system with fire.

15TH-CENTURY ILLUSTRATION SHOWING CHRIST BINDING THE FOUR ELEMENTS

Signs of the zodiac, each linked to one of the four elements

Each sign occupied thirty degrees

John the Baptist, one of the patron saints of the guild.

Days of the week

Months of the year

The "index of the sun" movable disc was set to the day of treatment

Numbers indicating the cycles of the moon

Saint Cosmas, the physician saint, opposite his twin brother, Saint Damian (right)

John the Evangelist, the
guild's other patron saint

The four temperaments

According to the theory of humorism,
physicians believed that the humours
influenced a person's character,
emotions, appearance, and mental
health. Galen named four personality
types, each corresponding to, and
influenced by, a specific humour.

SANGUINE
Men and women with a
sanguine (blood-influenced)
temperament were said to be
impulsive, sociable, and good
with people. Other character
traits associated with this type
included courage, optimism,
and pleasure-seeking.

CHOLERIC
People believed that
yellow bile made choleric
individuals ambitious and
disposed them to be good
leaders. The downside was
that they were inclined to
lose their temper easily.

PHLEGMATIC
Phlegmatic people were
generally relaxed, made
loyal friends, and were able
to keep calm in a crisis.
However, they also tended
to be rather unemotional.

MELANCHOLIC
Those with a
melancholic disposition,
influenced by black bile,
were thought to be
pessimistic and often
suffered from insomnia.
They were also said to be
thoughtful, inventive,
and artistic.

Schools of Medicine
and Life

MOST BIG TOWNS AND CITIES have medical schools and teaching hospitals. Indeed, where people's lives are at stake, it seems vital to have highly trained professionals gaining qualifications from officially recognized organizations. In the early Middle Ages in Europe, however, this was far from the case. Almost anyone could set up as a medical practitioner, and almost anyone did. Religion and medicine were intricately entwined, and many diseases were viewed as punishments for sins in this life or a previous one. Priests, monks, and nuns practised their cures in infirmaries and sick-houses attached to churches and monasteries, and wandering healers preached the wonders of their magical potions to anyone who cared to listen and pay. All this began to change towards the end of the First Millennium, as the achievements of Islam's golden age gradually spread through Europe.

The first generally recognized European school of medicine was the Schola Medica Salernitana in Salerno, southwest Italy. Here, great medical works by Arabic practitioners and communicators such as al-Rhazi (see pp.100–102) and Ibn Sina (see pp.102–105), carrying knowledge from Ancient Greece and Rome and augmented by their own advances, were translated into Latin, the language of Europe's scholars. Many of these works came from the library at Monte Cassino – the great Benedictine centre of religion and learning that stood 120km (75 miles) northwest of Salerno on the road to Rome.

One of the Schola Medica's inspirations was Alfanus I, who was Archbishop of Salerno for almost 30 years from 1057. A multilingual physician, he worked to establish the school and translated many of the Arabic texts, then used his position as Archbishop to increase the school's funding and powers. Another major figure of this time was Constantine the African, who first arrived in Salerno in around 1065. A scholar and trader from Tunisia, Constantine had travelled widely through Islamic regions and gathered a marvellous collection of books. Able to translate between Arabic and Latin, he also had knowledge of West Asian and Indian medicine. Alfanus welcomed Constantine and encouraged him, after several visits, to settle in

Salerno and to continue his studies. As a result, Constantine produced many lengthy translations that became staples in medical libraries around Europe for the next five centuries. He also lectured and demonstrated at the Schola Medica, before becoming a Christian convert in his final years at Monte Cassino.

During the late 11th and 12th centuries, the reputation of the Schola Medica spread and Salerno became known as Hippocratica Civitas (the Town of Hippocrates). Aspiring physicians, healers, surgeons, and apothecaries arrived to learn their craft and to gain certificates. The sick and ill also flocked in with the hope of a cure, or at the least of redemption. Arabic and also Jewish medical influences continued to spread across the Mediterranean, and Greek and Roman learning was integrated into the literature. Salerno became a gateway for medical knowledge entering Europe.

Training courses were highly organized at Salerno, with students passing from one level to the next only upon achieving the required passes. There could be three years of initial study, then four years of medical training, including practice with specialist physicians, surgeons, medical herbalists, and others. High standards were upheld in all fields, from hygiene to ethics, and (almost unheard of at the time) women were admitted and given licenses, not just for gynaecology, obstetrics, midwifery, and pre- and postnatal care, but also for general practice on both women and men. The physician's behaviour and bearing were also taught. *The Coming of a Physician to His Patient* advises the doctor on bedside manner: "When the doctor enters the dwelling of his patient, he should not appear haughty nor covetous, but should greet

CONSTANTINE THE AFRICAN
Benedictine monk Constantine the African lectures on uroscopy – the art of studying urine for signs of disease.

CAUTERIZING WOUNDS
A miniature from the 14th-century manuscript *The Surgery of Master Rogerius* shows a physician at Salerno's medical school cauterizing a wound.

with kindly, modest demeanour those who are present... Put the patient at his ease before the examination begins and the pulse should be felt deliberately and carefully... The friends standing round will be all the more impressed because of the delay and the physician's words will be received with just that much more attention".

Salerno became the model for other medical schools wishing to attract the most able physicians, papal approval, and royal patronage. One of these was the medical school at Montpellier, on France's Mediterranean coast. Another school was founded at the university of Bologna in northern Italy, around 1200, and it was here that the controversial practice of dissection appeared on the curriculum, from where it spread to other universities. As Bologna University matured, however, its promise of freedom to learn became compromised, and many students moved to Padua, where a university had been founded around 1200. Padua's medical faculty remained a progressive institution, and appointed a series of free thinkers to professorships such as anatomy and surgery, most famously the Flemish anatomist Andreas Vesalius (see pp.116–25).

Gradually, during the 14th and 15th centuries, more and more organized medical schools were established around Europe, each insisting on high levels of scholarship, unblemished morality, and wide-ranging studies, from Hippocrates and Galen to the Islamic golden age advances. This was fine and good for the well-connected and the wealthy. But for peasants in the countryside, healthcare remained entrenched in the Dark Ages, rooted in superstition and religion.

Philippus Aureolus Theophrastus Bombastus von Hohenheim was not quite from peasant stock. Born in Switzerland, his father was a minor-league physician who encouraged Philippus Aureolus to study theology and medicine, first at Basel in Switzerland, then Vienna,

Austria, and then at Ferrara, Italy. But no mere college could hold the youngster for long. Driven by wanderlust, and the desire both to make a name for himself and to help humanity, Philippus Aureolus decided to call himself Paracelsus – meaning "Better than (or beyond) Celsus", in barbed honour of Aulus Cornelius Celsus of Ancient Rome, who compiled massive encyclopedic works, including *De Medicina*. Being "better than" Celsus was, of course, a manifesto – a statement that the Ancients should not be trusted, and that the best teachers might not be found at universities, but rather in nature herself.

Paracelsus spent most of his time on long journeys, not only around Europe, but north to Scandinavia and Russia, south to North Africa, and east to the Holy Land and Asia Minor – perhaps even as far as India and Tibet. All the time, he learned and lectured, treated the sick, devised new operations and drug-based cures, and argued with anyone who cared to offer a contrary view. Details of his life are sketchy, but it seems that he was opinionated and awkward, spiky of temperament, probably emotionally unstable, perhaps an alcoholic, forever keen to tilt at the establishment and rebel against tradition. However, he also possessed a sharp intellect, an enormous amount of knowledge, and an obsessive need to write about and publish his discoveries – his fields included alchemy, religion, astrology, the occult, philosophy, and numerous other disciplines.

At one juncture, in 1527, Paracelsus found himself back in Basel as town physician and medical professor at his old university, where his unconventional views and rejection of the old authorities (such as Hippocrates and Galen) soon created controversy. He advocated, for example, that a wound should be allowed to drain itself freely of pus and fluids, rather than be bound tightly or cauterized. There were also arguments over his finances and his appointment of like-minded insubordinate junior physicians without the knowledge of the city council or the university congress – but

"Medicine rests upon four pillars – philosophy, astronomy, alchemy, and ethics"

PARACELSUS

A LESSON IN LIFE
Physicians at the Montpellier medical school give students a lesson in human anatomy. Founded in the late 11th century, the school attracted numerous surgeons and teachers – and patients hoping for a cure.

real trouble came on Midsummer's Day, when, in a public demonstration of his contempt for tradition, he made a bonfire out of the revered works of Galen, Ibn Sina, and others – an act that outraged the city's establishment. In a now-familiar pattern, Paracelsus had settled down with high hopes, stirred up a hornet's nest, and within the year had moved on again.

The doctrines of Paracelsus seem mystifying to us today. He adhered to the time-honoured idea of the four humours (see pp.106–107), and to this he added a "holy trinity" of three minerals: salt, sulphur, and mercury. He claimed that these substances contributed certain qualities to objects and beings, from mountains to humans, in line with each mineral's chemical properties. Salt, for example, signified stability and solidity; mercury (or quicksilver) brought change and transformation; while sulphur mediated between the two, leading to a balance between change and permanence.

Paracelsus's overall view of medicine was based on four central pillars: philosophy, astronomy, and alchemy, coordinated by the fourth, the virtue of the physician. Later, he also described disease as emanating from the interaction of five entities – namely, the body's own constitution, astrological influences, toxins, spirits good and evil, and God. Another of Paracelsus's many guiding ideas was that the human body is a microcosm – a distillation and focused reflection of the whole of nature, which is the universe or macrocosm. He wrote: "Man is a microcosm, or miniature world, being an extract from all the stars and planets of the whole firmament, from the earth and the elements; and thereby he is their quintessence". Health followed when the microcosmic body was in balance and harmony with the macrocosmic universe. Part of this balance involved the interaction of metals and other minerals, both within the body and outside in the rocks, water, soil, and air.

PARACELSUS
German-Swiss physician Paracelsus is often called the "father of toxicology" for his work on the effects of poisons on the human body.

THE GOOD PHYSICIAN
A woodcut from Paracelsus's *The Great Surgery Book* shows a sick man being attended to by a serving woman and a physician. The book encourages doctors to observe and experiment with nature, rather than simply to rely on textbooks.

Such ideas indicate that minerals were among Paracelsus's abiding passions – and herein lies one of his main contributions to medicine. He is often cited as the founder of toxicology – the study of the harmful effects of certain substances (i.e. "toxins" or poisons) on living things, and especially the damage they cause in the human body, and how these injuries can be treated. Paracelsus gained expert chemical, alchemical, and mineralogical skills from his extensive travels. He gathered knowledge from all manner of sources, including gypsies, outlaws, "old wives", and farm workers. He extracted a vast range of substances, mainly from plants, but also from soil, rocks, and occasionally animal bodies. He believed that any material could be both poisonous and therapeutic, depending on the amount, or dose, absorbed by the body. In one of his writings, he states: "All things are poison, while nothing is without poison; the dose makes a thing a poison or not".

This approach led to Paracelsus recommending mercuric minerals to treat syphilis. He also championed improved ways to deal with wounds, devised several new surgical procedures, and wrote copiously, not only on mineral-based medications and their uses, but on a wide range of topics from magic to the stars and planets. Probably his major book, earning him fame and financial security, was *Die Grosse Wundarzney* (*The Great Surgery Book*) of 1536. But even during his final years in Salzberg he remained cussedly independent. As he claimed: "No man should belong to another, but answer only to himself".

Vesalius and the Anatomists

IT SEEMS SENSIBLE that the best way to understand the human body is to open one up – preferably a newly dead body, and a healthy one that has died by accident or execution, so that its innards are not distorted by disease. Sensible indeed, since anatomy (the study of the body's "fabric" or structure) is a cornerstone of medicine. In the early 16th century, however, an obstacle stood in the way of this idea – indeed, it had stood there for 13 centuries – in the person of Claudius Galen (see pp.40–45). Such was the status of this legendary Roman physician that his pronouncements on anatomy, physiology, and disease were not questioned by the academic medics of medieval Europe – even though his works had been handed down in various forms of Latin and cod-Latinized texts, had been translated into Arabic and back again, had been added to by all manner of do-gooders, and were full of illustrations that had been copied and re-copied with varying degrees of quality and accuracy. And if a physician opened a body and dared to see things that Galen had not described, then either his eyes were at fault, or the body was malformed, or someone had introduced an error into Galen's text – or indeed the human body had changed since Galen's time. On no account, however, could it be said that Galen was wrong.

Luckily for medical progress, Andreas Vesalius (1514–64) had never really fallen under Galen's spell. Often credited as the founder of modern scientific anatomy, Vesalius came from a family of eminent medical men based in what was then the Hapsburg Netherlands. His father, Anders van Wesel, was apothecary

ANDREAS VESALIUS
Flemish physician Andreas Vesalius overturned centuries of medical dogma through his pioneering anatomical work.

(pharmacist) to Archduchess Margaret of Austria, and to Holy Roman Emperor Maximilian I and his successor Charles V. His grandfather was the royal physician to Maximilian I, and his great-grandfather had been a physician and instructor at the University of Leuven (Louvain), in present-day Belgium. At the age of 15, despite his medical background, Vesalius began studying art at the University of Leuven, and developed a talent for illustration. Five years later, however, he switched to studying medicine in Paris, where he read and re-read the works of Galen and other ancients, which had recently become widely available due to advances in printing technology. It was here, under the eyes of tutors Johann Winter von Andernach and Jacobus Sylvius (Jacques Dubois), that he learned the science of anatomy – Sylvius particularly impressed him by allowing his students to see inside corpses. These lessons showed Vesalius that the wisdom of the ancients – and that of the 14th-century Bolognese professor Mondino de Liuzzi – might not agree with what he was uncovering on the autopsy slab himself.

In 1536, when war broke out between France and the Holy Roman Empire, Vesalius returned to Leuven. He obtained basic medical qualifications, quarrelled with his superiors, and spirited away the corpse of a criminal from the scaffold to further his dissecting skills. He then moved on via Venice to the famed University of Padua, Italy, where his talents were quickly recognized. In 1537, apparently the day after his graduation, Vesalius was offered the post of Professor of Anatomy and Surgery, which he accepted.

Vesalius's Paduan superiors knew little of his rebellious streak, but this soon became apparent when he began teaching. Extending Sylvius's lead, he wielded the knife and opened up the dissection bodies himself, allowing his students to peer inside. The standard practice of the day was to allow an assistant or lowly barber-surgeon (see pp.126–33) to do such work, and even then, this physical side of the lesson was usually just a supplement to the reading of the sacred works of Galen, de Liuzzi, and the rest. Another of Vesalius's innovations was to record what he saw with his own eyes in the form of detailed illustrations that were faithful to the specimens before him, rather than relying on older renderings. Using his drawing skills, and taking advice from professional artists, Vesalius built up a collection of accurate and skilfully executed illustrations. News soon spread of Vesalius and his fresh approach, and in 1538 this led him to publish six of his early works as *Tabulae Anatomicae Sex* (*Six Anatomical Plates*), the illustrations of which were possibly prepared from his originals by Jan van Calcar, a pupil of the painter Titian. Vesalius's work was soon "pirated", which rapidly spread his name and fame around Europe, but left him concerned about unauthorized replications of his work.

By 1540, Vesalius had edited one of Galen's works, *Institutiones Anatomicae*, and published "revisions" of some of the details. He also had an encounter during a public dissection at Bologna with one of Italy's top professors, Matteo Corti, about details of the liver and muscles. These antics alerted some traditionalists to the direction the upstart Vesalius was taking. Meanwhile, a local judge in Padua, fascinated by medicine, and by Vesalius's approach in particular, permitted him to use the corpses of executed criminals for autopsies. As a result, Vesalius soon had numerous corpses in various stages of dissection taking up space in his university rooms – including his personal quarters.

As part of his academic duties, Vesalius visited Pisa, Bologna, Venice, and other universities to lecture and lead teaching sessions. One such trip to Bologna in 1541 reminded him forcefully that much of Galen's anatomical work – especially dissection – had not been carried out on humans. Such work had been forbidden in Ancient Rome, so Galen had therefore opened and described the anatomy of animals (ranging from pigs to macaque monkeys) instead and assumed that their insides were similar to ours. Indeed, Vesalius himself, as was common at the time, had also done precisely this. He now came to realize that this was the origin of the "discrepancies" in Galen's work, and that, for the good of medical knowledge (and for patients), they had to be corrected.

ABDOMINAL CAVITY
This illustration from *De Humani* shows a man's abdominal cavity – minus its intestines.

"I am not accustomed to saying anything with certainty after only one or two observations"

VESALIUS

An emboldened Vesalius, equipped with fresh human corpses and a new slant on Galen, decided to produce his own great work on anatomy. Two years later, the immense seven-volume *De Humani Corporis Fabrica (On the Fabric of the Human Body)* was published, and was a great success. By the year's end, despite its immense size and breathtaking price, the book had sold out. Not only were *De Humani*'s originally woodcut images (probably prepared in Venice on pear wood) hugely detailed and beautifully executed, they were also accurately taken from life. They showed bodies in lifelike poses and familiar contexts, with many set against the Italian countryside. An illustrated aside showed a dog with one paw as a human foot, perhaps a reference to the fact that Galen's animal subjects included many dogs.

Aged just 30, Vesalius had masterminded the project himself, but others had almost certainly produced the illustrations. Some experts again suggest Jan van Calcar, who was an acknowledged expert copyist and mimic (and occasional forger) of great works. Other authorities consider the *De Humani* pictures to be by general studio artists familiar with the style of Titian. Nevertheless, Vesalius had attended to every detail of *De Humani*, and chose the renowned printer Joannis Oporini of Basel to produce it – which he did using the intaglio method, in which engraved copper plates are taken from woodcuts. The resulting detail and clarity astonished Vesalius's readers.

The 663 pages of *De Humani* were divided into seven "books", more akin to what we might today call chapters, that summarized Vesalius's extensive findings. The sheer size of the pages – 42cm (16½in) by 28cm (11in) – was daunting, as were the 400-plus individual images that they contained, which featured textures and contours in three dimensions, quite different from the "flat" style of the times. Then, of course, there were Vesalius's observations, which were born of his recognition that form reflects function. He understood that the positions, shapes, sizes, and connections between the body's organs, muscles, tubes, ducts, and other parts gave clues to what they did. His discoveries included that men and women have the same number of ribs; that the lower jaw, or mandible, is a single bone, not two (an error derived from dog anatomy); that the breastbone, or sternum, has three parts, not seven (an error derived from monkey anatomy); that nerves are solid, not hollow, and that they are involved in muscle control and sensation; that nerves either originate or end in the brain, and do not run between other organs, such as the heart, as had been believed since Aristotle's time; that the liver has two lobes and not five; that the heart rather than the liver is central to the vascular system; that there are no traces of connecting holes or pores in the septum between the heart's left and right sides, as had long been imagined – which had great implications for later investigators such as William Harvey (see pp.134–43). He also gave detailed descriptions of several complex abdominal parts, such as the omentum (a fold of tissue lining the abdomen), and suggested that the kidneys filter blood to produce urine, which travels along ureters to the bladder (previously it had been thought that the kidneys filter urine). By far the mainstay of the book, however, are the hundreds of pictures of muscles, showing the tendons and ligaments that connect them to the skeleton, and the manner in which they move.

As well as being an ingenious anatomist, Vesalius clearly had a flair for furthering his own career, which he surely did when he dedicated the first edition of De Humani to Holy Roman Emperor Charles V, whom his father had served. A special silk-bound, vellum-paged, hand-coloured copy was presented to the emperor – and indeed, Charles duly responded by appointing Vesalius court physician in 1545. Vesalius accepted the post and literally burned his bridges to medical academia, by burning many of his learned works and notes, including volume after volume of Galen. Then off he went, accompanying the emperor and his entourage to their various palaces and homes, and on forays to visit allies around much of Europe. In the early 1550s, Vesalius also established a lucrative practice as a private physician in Brussels,

COLOURED FRONTISPIECE OF *DE HUMANI*
The frontispiece of *De Humani* shows the author conducting a dissection at the School of Medicine, Brussels. A single-coloured edition was produced for Holy Roman Emperor Charles V.

a job that came with a magnificent house, stables, and an orchard. In 1556, Charles abdicated as emperor, but Vesalius had perhaps knowingly covered this eventuality as well when he dedicated an abridged "digest" version of De Humani (published in 1543, less than three months after the original) to Charles' son, Philip. Usually known as Epitome (from De Humani Corporis Fabrica Librorum Epitome), this version of De Humani had more images and a shorter, simpler version of the text. In 1556, this same Philip, now Philip II of Spain, invited Vesalius to be his royal physician, which of course Vesalius accepted – along with the awards, titles, and wealth that also came his way.

During this time, there was a backlash against Vesalius, his methods, his disregard for long-held beliefs and ancient teachings, and the more radical elements of De Humani and his other works – particularly those contradicting Galen. Some critics were outraged at the immoral sacrilege of organized dissections, which desecrated "God's handiwork". Vesalius was also taunted as a "mere barber" by eminent court physicians, academic professors, and others of nobility and title – barber-surgeons being the main practitioners of the time, though they were generally regarded as uneducated inferiors by medicine's upper strata (see pp.126–31). Vesalius himself rarely responded, although criticism did lead to errors being recognized in a second edition of De Humani, which appeared in 1555. In this edition, he covered greater ground, removed more animal material and added a good deal more about female anatomy, including pregnancy.

In 1564, Vesalius arranged a pilgrimage and medicinal plant-hunting expedition to the Holy Land, perhaps to escape the confines of Philip's court and the pressures of the infamous Spanish Inquisition. His itinerary included Jerusalem and Jericho, where he wished to collect and study therapeutic herbs. However, the trip was allegedly curtailed when a message arrived in Jerusalem requesting that Vesalius return to take up his former professorship at Padua following the death of Gabriele Falloppio. Vesalius duly sailed back, but adverse weather shipwrecked him on the Ionian island of Zante (Zakynthos), where, far from the courts of Europe, he is said to have died in confused and lonely circumstances, perhaps of plague. His burial site is unknown.

The momentous De Humani echoed the spirit of the age. As in other areas of Renaissance science, literature, and art, it hastened a break with ancient traditions and long-established but unverified information. Through it, Vesalius pioneered the approach of relying on personal observations and investigations. He also set new scientific benchmarks and ethical standards that gradually permeated the whole of medical practice. In establishing the modern science of anatomy, Vesalius corrected long-held misbeliefs, introduced new discoveries, and inspired a fresh breed of anatomists, physicians, and surgeons.

Among Vesalius's pupils and contemporaries were Gabriele Falloppio and Bartolomeo Eustachi, both of whom contributed a deeper understanding of anatomy. Falloppio advanced anatomical studies of the head, especially the ear, describing the tiny organs of hearing such as the eardrum and cochlea that lie deep within the temporal bone of the skull. He also studied the reproductive organs, and his name lives on in this area. In the female body, ripe eggs released from the ovary travel to the womb along the oviduct – the fallopian tube.

Eustachi also furthered knowledge of the ear. The small air tube that equalizes pressure between the middle ear and the back of the throat (and thence to the general outside atmosphere) is called the eustachian tube. Nine years after Vesalius and *De Humani*, Eustachi completed his own epic anatomy work, *Tabulae Anatomicae* (*Anatomical Engravings*), but he forbade its publication in case he was prosecuted or excommunicated by the Catholic Church. To avoid confusion with Vesalius' earlier *Tabulae Anatomicae Sex*, this later work is sometimes known as *Tabulae Anatomicae Bartholomaei Eustachi*. It did not become generally available until 160 years later, in 1714.

A poignant reminder of Vesalius resides at the University of Basel, the city of *De Humani*'s launch. The "Basel Skeleton", as it is known, originally belonged to a notorious local villain by the name of Jakob Karrer von Gebweiler. While overseeing *De Humani*'s publication in 1543, Vesalius happened to visit Basel when von Gebweiler was being publicly beheaded. Since he was known for his great skill with the knife, Vesalius was invited to carry out an autopsy on von Gebweiler – also in public. After the autopsy, the bones were reassembled into a preparation or specimen that Vesalius presented to the city. The Basel Skeleton still resides at the University's Museum of Anatomy. For a man who gave the medical world such an epochal publication, and a springboard to a new era of progress, the skeleton remains the only known well-preserved specimen prepared by Vesalius himself.

VESALIUS IN PADUA
Vesalius conducts an anatomy lesson in the world's first dedicated anatomical theatre, at the University of Padua. It was here that it became normal to study anatomy by dissecting human corpses, rather than by studying ancient texts.

Paré and the Barber-Surgeons

THE BARBER-SURGEONS of medieval Europe practised a curious mix of trades: haircutting and shaving, with lice and flea removal often thrown in for free; also removal of warts and similar skin blemishes; perhaps a few tooth-pullings; the always-popular bloodletting by leech (see p.132–33); and cauterizing open wounds by pouring on boiling oil – plus emergency limb amputation, usually in hellish battlefield conditions. Ambroise Paré was schooled in all of these procedures, but he was also a pioneer who led a revolution in surgery – one that greatly eased pain and suffering, promoted healing, and vastly improved prospects for the seriously wounded.

Paré was brought up in an unremarkable artisan family in Laval, northwest France. From 1532, he trained at the Hôtel Dieu, Paris's leading hospital and seat of medical learning. As in much of Europe, its approach was rooted in the teachings of Ancient Rome's Claudius Galen (see pp.40–47), whose colossal reputation meant that even 13 centuries later, physicians almost blindly followed his doctrines. They refused to accept the evidence of their eyes and acknowledge Galen's mistakes in human anatomy, even when confronted time and again with dissected corpses whose body parts were not where Galen said they should be (see p.116). These physicians were highly educated, principled men, usually from privileged, well-connected backgrounds. They haughtily held court to diagnose patients' ills, recommend treatments, and perhaps even administer an occasional tincture or potion, but they rarely got their hands dirty. Practical treatment was left to barber-surgeons, who were generally from middle-class or perhaps peasant stock, less educated, or even

AMBROISE PARÉ
French barber-surgeon Ambroise Paré is one of the fathers of modern surgery. His revolutionary techniques were tested on wounded soldiers.

illiterate, aware of their status, but with hands-on skills, and tolerant of pus, blood, urine, excreta, and gangrenous flesh. Indeed, by the time Paré attended the Hôtel Dieu, the reputation of barber-surgeons was growing. The Hôtel Dieu was affiliated to the Faculty of Medicine at the University of Paris, so trainees could attend university lectures on surgery and anatomy.

A fast learner, Paré progressed rapidly through his barber-surgeon apprenticeship, and was appointed army regimental surgeon in 1536. At the time, France was embroiled in several military campaigns, so Paré was kept busy treating war wounded in extremely primitive field hospitals; a common duty was running hopelessly mutilated soldiers through with a sword, or cutting their throats, to end their suffering.

The traditional treatment for open wounds was to cauterize and seal them with boiling oil (elder oil was favoured) or red-hot irons. This reduced complications such as gangrene, but it also brought further agony and prolonged suffering. Such treatments were especially favoured for the relatively new phenomenon of gunshot or firearm wounds. Gunpowder itself, and the burns and penetrating damage its projectiles caused, were considered poisonous to flesh and so required detoxifying with scalding oil.

Intense pain and dreadful suffering were common at the time. Indeed, they were viewed as essential components of surgical treatment and recovery. Pain relief was limited, with no anaesthetics as we know them available, only roughly prepared potions containing worryingly approximate amounts of potentially deadly opium, henbane, mandrake, or alcohol. This was also the pre-antibiotic era, and an agonizing but swift treatment such as boiling oil or red-hot iron reduced the risk of infection, and improved chances of eventual survival, albeit with the legacy of disfiguring scars, missing limbs, and long-term discomfort.

Paré was appalled at such barbarous procedures and vowed to do better – and his chance came in 1536, when King François I declared war on the Duke of Savoy, leading to a siege of Turin. In the ensuing bloodbath, the fighting was so destructive of the army ranks that Paré ran out of boiling oil. Freed from the stricture of his army orders to use the treatment, he jumped at the opportunity to try an alternative. This was a soothing balm made from turpentine, egg yolk, and oil of roses. Paré had confiscated supplies to mix the balm, which he developed from a combination of folk remedies. The following day, Paré checked and compared his patients. Those who suffered boiling oil or hot irons were in great pain, feverish, even delirious, with wounds and surrounding tissues swollen, red, and raw. Those who had been treated with the balm had less pain and were healing faster. In 1545, Paré publicized this new approach in his *Method of Treating Wounds*. Following his convictions, and eager for his fellow barber-surgeons to benefit from his discoveries, he wrote this not in the Latin used by qualified physicians and learned scholars, but in vernacular French.

Paré trialed a further innovation at the Turin campaign in 1537, and went on to develop this as a reliable procedure. It concerned sucking chest wounds leading to collapsed lung – or pneumothorax, in modern terminology. Penetrating sword or lance wounds to the chest could allow air into the interface between the outer covering of the lung and the inner lining of the chest. Normally there is no air here and the lung adheres to the chest lining, so that as the ribs and chest expand on breathing in, the elastic lung tissues are stretched with it and increase in volume, sucking in air down through the windpipe. With a penetrating chest wound, air can take an easier route. On breathing in, air is sucked in through the wound and creates an air gap around the unstretched lung, which comes away from the chest lining and collapses. Breathing out pushes the air in the reverse direction, leaving the lung still collapsed. Fighting for breath, but with no air exchange inside the lung itself to provide oxygen for the blood, the patient in effect suffocates. The conventional emergency procedure was to suture (stitch) the wound closed, but this rarely helped, as most battlefield surgeons understood. As dreadfully injured victims lay dying all around, a surgeon would often pass by a soldier with a sucking chest wound to look for someone whose injuries were easier to treat successfully. Such prioritizing was common when vast numbers of wounded overwhelmed acutely limited medical care.

Paré described how he attended a soldier at Turin with a deep wound under the left breast. The wound had been sutured by another medic, trapping air and blood from internal bleeding around the lung. For the soldier, the end was near. Paré removed the stitching to reopen the gash, then he positioned the soldier with his legs elevated, and his head and chest low over the side of the bed. He advised the soldier to breathe in slowly to maximum, close his nose and mouth, and try to compress his chest as if breathing out hard. His hunch was that this should force out material from around the lung. Paré reported that this caused a fluid filled with congealed lumps of blood "to jet through the wound… I put my finger deep in the wound to break up the coagulated blood, and seven to eight ounces of fetid and corrupt blood drained". Paré then irrigated the wound with barley water containing rose oil, honey, and sugar candy, while placing the soldier at various angles and positions to encourage maximum drainage. "To conclude, this injury was so well handled that beyond my expectation, the patient recovered".

Following wound balms and sucking chests, Paré introduced another revolutionary technique. Many soldiers with gruesomely extensive limb damage underwent rapid amputation, but then

THE SURGEON AT WORK
A barber-surgeon removes a stone from a man's head at a public fair. Other such stones hang in the background as proof of the surgeon's skill.

bled profusely and died from medical shock brought on by blood loss. This could occur even after attempts to sear and seal the amputation wound using a red-hot iron. Acutely observant, Paré saw that most of the blood gushed from one or two severed arteries at the stump, rather than from general tissues such as muscle. He reasoned that if these arteries could somehow be compressed slightly nearer the heart, haemorrhaging would be reduced. So he tried tying ligatures or tight cords adjacent to the proposed amputation site. It worked: upon amputation, the restricted artery no longer spurted high-pressure blood from the stump. Survival rates climbed, and Paré used his anatomical knowledge to find the best ligature sites for various levels of amputation.

News of Paré's handiwork spread through the army ranks and other barber-surgeons took up his idea. He gained fame and promotion within the military, but few in the medical establishment, especially back at the Faculty of Medicine in Paris, were receptive to his ideas. However, despite such academic snubs, in 1552 he was appointed to a royal position, in the service of Henry II of France. It was the first of many royal appointments, which saw him employed for almost 40 years under four monarchs – Henry II, Francis II, Charles IX, and Henry III – holding the office of chief surgeon to the last two.

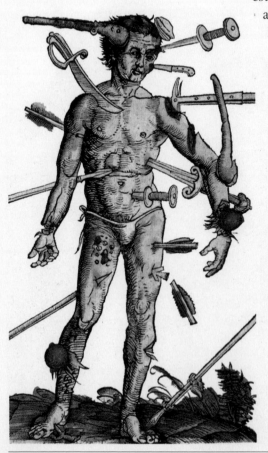

Rather than enjoying the luxuries of the royal court, Paré continued his pioneering

"WOUND MAN"
This 15th-century illustration from a barber-surgeon's manual indicates the various wounds a soldier could receive in battle.

"The art of medicine is to cure sometimes, to relieve often, to comfort always"

AMBROISE PARÉ

work on amputation. He designed and made a series of limb prostheses – artificial arms, legs, hands, and feet – as well as trusses, artificial eyes, and tooth implants.

Experimentation and rational deduction also continued to fascinate Paré. He had long been suspicious of so-called "bezoar stones" – masses of material extracted from the stomach or digestive tract of humans and animals. According to legend, the stones had medicinal properties, and were in particular an antidote to all manner of poisons. In 1567, an opportunity arose to test this notion. A thief at the royal court was sentenced to death by hanging, but he agreed to take poison instead, provided he could then take a bezoar preparation. If he survived, he would be freed. Paré recorded the proceedings and noted that the thief died from taking the poison after several hours of excruciating pain, thereby showing that a bezoar was ineffective in this case.

For all his achievements on the battlefield and elsewhere, perhaps Paré could be excused his occasional lapses. His book *On Monsters and Marvels* was an illustrated compendium of human and animal birth defects, fanciful beasts from hearsay and legend, and other weirdly wonderful phenomena. His causes of birth defects in human babies included "Wrath of God", "Corrupt seed", and "Indecent posture by the expectant mother". A two-headed child, for instance, resulted from "Too much seed". Nevertheless, despite initial scepticism and even rebuttal from the medical establishment, Paré's reputation grew over the centuries, and he is now regarded as a major innovator in battlefield surgery, and a humane and caring barber-surgeon. Devoutly religious throughout his long life and distinguished career, he retained the motto: "I treated him; God healed him".

Bloodletting

First-century Roman physican Galen believed that blood, as the strongest of the four humours (see pp.106–107), had a powerful influence on health. He theorized that blood was created by the heart and liver and consumed by other organs, and that it could stagnate in the extremities of the body, causing disease. Based on this idea, surgeons bled patients to remove stagnant blood, and to restore the balance of the humours. This practice, common since the time of the Ancient Greeks to treat a range of diseases, was such a popular procedure that it continued long after the 17th-century discovery of blood circulation.

LEECH JAR AND LANCETS
ENGLAND, c.18TH–19TH CENTURY
A popular method of bloodletting was to place medicinal leeches – bloodsucking freshwater worms – on a patient's skin. Leeches have triple jaws that pierce the skin so they can suck out blood. Surgeons stored them in special jars.

A cure for all

Bloodletting was recommended for all kinds of diseases, from headaches and indigestion to pneumonia and strokes. The treatment was often carried out by surgeons and barber-surgeons, who combined shaving and hair-cutting with basic surgical work (see pp.126–31). Surgeons also bled healthy people as a preventive measure. The most common method was venesection – applying a tourniquet to the patient's arm so that a vein would swell, cutting open the vein, and draining off the blood.

Bleeding bowl for collecting the patient's blood when a lancet – a needle or small double-edged scalpel – was used for the procedure

17TH-CENTURY ILLUSTRATION OF A MAN WEARING A
TOURNIQUETBLEEDING INTO A BOWL

Ventilation holes in
the lid allowed the
leeches to breathe

The jar held
water, in which
the leeches lived

A metal box holds
two sharp lancets for
opening a vein

The medicinal leech
(*Hirudo medicinalis*) secretes
an anticoagulant, to make
the blood flow

Tools of the trade

The use of leeches was widespread in the 19th century — so much so that the high demand almost made the species extinct. This was one of the reasons surgeons resorted to other methods of bloodletting, including cupping and the use of mechanical devices to remove patients' blood.

BRONZE BLOOD CUP
This blood cup from Sicily dates back to between 400 and 100 BCE. Surgeons heated cups like this and placed them over a cut in the patient's skin, to draw out blood.

SCARIFICATOR
In the 18th and 19th centuries, instruments called scarificators, consisting of several blades mounted on a handle, were used to make multiple incisions in the skin, piercing numerous superficial blood vessels. Designed to be less painful and more efficient than a single lancet, scarificators were usually used in conjunction with cupping.

MECHANICAL LEECH
This syringe-like suction device enabled surgeons to control the amount of blood removed. It did not fall off the skin and reattach itself somewhere else as real leeches tended to do, and could be used on parts of the body on which it was not practical to use a live creature.

Harvey and Blood Circulation

SINCE ANCIENT TIMES, blood has been regarded as the very stuff of human existence – a red liquid that, as it leaked away, took life with it. Likewise, the heart has always been at the centre of our ideas about character – today, to "have a heart" means to be generous and forgiving. Perhaps no other parts of the body have been subject to so much myth and superstition, nor had their workings guessed at so many times – the simple fact that the heart pumps blood around the body took until the 17th century to be discovered. The breakthrough came in the 1620s, when English physician William Harvey performed experiments that overturned centuries of guesswork about veins, arteries, and the workings of the human heart.

About 2,000 years ago, the immense Chinese work *Huang-di Nei' Jing* (*The Yellow Emperor's Canon of Medicine* – see p.64–69) referred to a form of "circulation" by which blood, mixed with qi (life energy), was distributed around the body. In Ancient Greece, Hippocrates (see pp.30–39) also suggested that there might be a form of circulation in the body. The trouble was that in most dissected corpses the arteries seemed to be empty, while the veins were always engorged with blood. This led Hippocrates to think that arteries contained air, while only veins contained blood – the truth being that arteries (which move blood *away*

WILLIAM HARVEY
English physician William Harvey demonstrates the circulation of blood in a stag. His was the first complete account of the mechanics of the heart and the blood system.

from the heart) have thick, muscular walls, which contract after death, shifting along any contents, whereas veins (which *return* blood to the heart) have thin walls and tend to retain their contents. Another Greek physician, Erasistratus, studied the heart, blood vessels, and lungs, and suggested that a life-force called "pneuma" was breathed into the lungs (from the air) and passed into the heart, where it was converted into a form of "animal spirit" that spread like a vapour around the body – via the apparently empty, hollow arteries. For Erasistratus, then, veins were still the principal vessels of the blood system, and the fluid within them ebbed and flowed, to and fro, into the heart and out, with each heartbeat.

In Ancient Rome, Claudius Galen (see pp.40–47) had given vent to copious opinions on the heart and the blood, and cleverly combined several existing beliefs into a complex theory that would, like many of his pronouncements, last for centuries. One advance he did make, based on experiments with live animals, was that arteries contained blood, rather than air, and that this blood was bright red and actively spurted – unlike venous blood, which was dark and slow. So Galen appreciated that there were two sets of blood vessels – arteries and veins – but he regarded them as distinct systems. With no microscope, he had no knowledge of the capillaries in the tissues that linked the two, but he did suggest another set of tiny connections – in the heart itself. He contended that digested food went from the gut to the liver, where it transformed into blood, and from here the sluggish venous blood ebbed and flowed to and from all the major parts of the body, distributing nutrition and also a variant of pneuma known as "natural spirit". The heart's job was to mix blood that came into its right side from the liver, with air from the lungs, which arrived along what we now call the pulmonary arteries. Blood impurities were removed in the heart and returned to the lungs, where they were breathed out, while the cleaned blood returned to the liver. On the issue of the connection between veins and arteries, Galen proposed that some of the blood in the heart's right side managed to seep through tiny pores in the dividing wall (known as the septum) into the left side. There was no visible evidence of these septal pores, but Galen was convinced that they existed. In the heart's left side, the formerly dull, oozing blood was energized by a version of pneuma called "vital spirit", from air conveyed along the vessels that we call the pulmonary veins. Now vivid and pulsing with "vital spirit", this blood then spread around the body and was consumed, especially in the brain.

The Galenic view of the heart and blood persisted through medieval times, with only minor modifications here and there. One such modification came in the 13th century, when Arab physician Ibn al-Nafis commented on the works of Ibn Sina (see pp.100–07), and challenged the latter's belief in Galen's septal pores. Instead, al-Nafis contended that blood flowed from the heart's right side to the lungs, where it mixed with air and then returned to the left side. He also conjectured on minute pores or networks between the arteries and veins in the lungs – which, four centuries later, were identified as capillaries. Al-Nafis' account thus describes the pulmonary part of the blood's circulation as we know it today.

It was during the Renaissance that Galen's view was finally overthrown. In the early 1500s, Leonardo da Vinci drew the heart's outer and inner structure with accuracy and elegance, distinguishing four chambers, as opposed to Galen's three (which came from his study of the three-chambered hearts of reptiles). Based upon his knowledge of mechanics, da Vinci also guessed at the function of valves as flow controllers – but he failed to make the leap to the idea of continuous circulation. Instead, he stuck with the ebb-and-flow model, and even illustrated Galen's tiny "pores" in the septum, though he never saw them.

In the 1540s, Amato Lusitano, a Portuguese-born physician and anatomist working in Italy, experimented with the membraneous, flap-like, one-way valves in the main veins. By blowing through the veins, he showed that air, and so presumably blood, could not stream past them away from the heart, according to the age-old conviction. In the 1550s, the celebrated Renaissance anatomist Andreas Vesalius (see pp.116–25) declared that he had failed to find Galen's septal pores – and in 1559, one of Vesalius's successors, Matteo Realdo Colombo, proposed that blood flowed between the lungs and the heart along the pulmonary vein. Colombo came to this conclusion by observing living animals, in which the pulmonary vein from the lungs to the heart always contained blood, not air. He also demonstrated that the blood vessels pulsated in time with those of the heart. Thus, he

DA VINCI SKETCHES
Leonardo da Vinci produced many accurate drawings of the heart and the blood system. He proved both that the heart is a muscle and that it does not warm the blood.

proposed that with each beat, the heart's muscle forcefully contracted to push blood out into the vessels – the phase of the heartbeat we know as "systole". This idea turned on its head the old view that the heart actively enlarged to suck in blood. In fact, that phase, known as "diastole", allows blood to flow in from the veins as the heart passively relaxes. Another Italian to pen ideas about the heart, and who used the concept of blood "circulation", was botanist-cum-doctor Andrea Cesalpino, who at one stage declared: "The movement of blood... is constant from the vena cava [great vein] through the lungs and through the heart to the aorta".

Such was the state of cardiovascular science at the turn of the 15th century. Strands of evidence had accumulated about the structures and workings of the heart and blood vessels, and there had been several accounts that used the concept of "circulation". But no one had yet fashioned them into an overall proposal and fully understood the idea of a circulatory system.

Enter English physician William Harvey. In 1599, after graduating from Cambridge, Harvey arrived at the University of Padua, Italy, where he studied under Hieronymus Fabricius, follower of famed anatomist Gabriele Falloppio (see p.123), himself successor to Realdo Colombo. The young Harvey read Colombo's works on the heart and blood, and also those of Fabricius, who had provided the first accurate descriptions of valves in major veins. Returning to England, Harvey worked his way through London's medical establishment to become Chief Physician at St Bartholomew's Hospital, a celebrated lecturer on anatomy, and eventually a physician to the rich and powerful, including King James I and his heir Charles I.

An enthusiastic demonstrator and experimentalist, Harvey reputedly dissected the bodies of both his father and his sister. After travelling around Europe in the 1630s, he accompanied Charles I to

"All we know is still infinitely less than all that remains unknown"

WILLIAM HARVEY

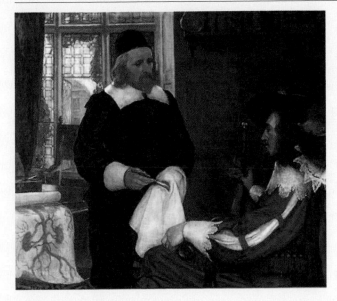

ROYAL PHYSICIAN
William Harvey gives
Charles I of England
a lesson in blood
circulation. During the
English Civil War, Harvey
treated many of the
wounded, and looked
after the king's children.

Oxford during the troubles of the English Civil War, settled there for
a time, and spent his later years in retirement back in London. His
historic publication – *Exercitatio Anatomica de Motu Cordis et Sanguinis in
Animalibus* (*An Anatomical Exercise on the Motion of the Heart and Blood in Living
Beings*), usually known as *On the Motion of the Heart and Blood*, or *De Motu
Cordis* – appeared in 1628. A slim 72 pages, it was the result of more than
20 years of deliberate, detailed, step-by-step, occasionally obsessive
dissections, observations, and experiments on over 60 different species
of dead and living animal – ranging from tiny freshwater shrimps,
snails, crabs, and fish to toads, frogs, birds, dogs, pigs, and, in particular,
snakes. Cold-blooded creatures like frogs and reptiles were useful to
Harvey because the motions of their hearts and pulsating vessels were
generally slower and easier to follow than those of warm-blooded birds
or mammals – and their bodies stayed fresh longer when they were
opened up and subjected to various procedures. Harvey peered intently
and recorded diligently as he prodded, twisted, nicked, sliced, injected
with fluids, emptied by needle aspiration, tied off, and removed their
hearts and vessels for detailed inner examination.

De Motu Cordis was the first well-rounded, scientific, evidence-
supported description of the circulatory system and its function –
how the heart pumped blood round and round the body. As we know
today, there are in fact two "sub-circulations". One, as uncovered by
several of Harvey's predecessors, is from the heart's right side along
the pulmonary arteries to the lungs, where the dark, "stale" blood

picks up fresh supplies of oxygen – and then returns, refreshed and bright red, along the pulmonary veins to the heart's left side. This is termed the pulmonary or lesser circulation. From the heart's larger, more muscular left side, blood surges with each pulsing contraction of a heartbeat, out along the major arteries. Like the bronchi in the lungs, these arteries divide and narrow repeatedly to supply all of the body's organs and tissues with blood. Gradually, the blood's pressure, speed of flow, and oxygen content fall – and then the blood returns along tiny veins that merge into wider ones, all the way to the great veins, and finally flows again into the right side of the heart. This is the greater or systemic circulation. Along the main veins and in the heart itself, one-way valves ensure a one-way current – there is therefore no "ebb and flow".

In all of this, the heart is a muscular pump – an amazingly tireless, highly adjustable, self-maintaining one, but chiefly a pump, requiring no such thing as a "pneuma", "animal spirit", or "vital force" to keep it going. Like Vesalius (see pp.116–25), Harvey knew that he would come under fire for contradicting Galenism – especially the idea that blood is manufactured in the liver, and that it ebbs and flows, to and fro, in two separate sets of vessels. But he was ready with mountains of evidence from his work with animals. In fact, he had already tested the main conclusions of *De Motu Cordis* 12 years earlier, in 1616, during a London lecture designed to "test the water" – and he had indeed received criticism then, which only strengthened his resolve.

One of Harvey's key pieces of evidence was a series of simple calculations involving the quantity of blood. He estimated how much blood was ejected by a heartbeat, and multiplied this by the beat rate. Since the blood could not return to the heart because of the valve system, it must be freshly and continuously made. Harvey's measurements were not particularly accurate, but they suggested that more than 240kg (540lb) of blood were pumped by the heart each hour – which is about three times the entire body's weight. He concluded that far more blood comes out of the heart than could be supplied by digested food. Simple observation supported this reasoning. For instance, if a single artery is cut, blood soon drains from the whole body, and is not replenished. Harvey summarized: "…The blood is driven into a round by a circular motion… it moves perpetually". Vein valves were another key to Harvey's arguments. In a famous illustrated sequence in *De Motu Cordis*, a ligature (tight band) is tied around the upper arm. The arteries and veins are compressed, and, without a supply of fresh, warm, oxygenated blood, the lower arm becomes cooler and pallid. Next, the ligature is slackened slightly. This allows blood to flow to the lower arm through the arteries, which are cushioned in muscles deep below the skin, but prevents it from returning along the veins near the surface. The lower arm now becomes engorged and florid. Blood can be seen queuing in the veins below the ligature, and the valves appear as little lumps here and there. Massaging the blood in these veins towards the hand has little effect, since the one-way valves prevent its motion. But stroking it the other way helps the blood to head back up the arm to the heart.

Why did blood circulate? Harvey suggested that it might be to distribute heat and nourishment, which is correct, but he went little further. Another vital feature of the circulation eluded him: how did blood travel from the tiniest arteries into the minute veins, as part of its complete circulation? If Harvey had used a microscope, rather than the simple magnifier lens he relied on, he might have discovered the capillary network. Early microscopes (see pp.150–51) were available at the time, but they were rarely used by physicians. The discovery of capillaries was left to Marcello Malpighi (see pp.145–46) in about 1661, 33 years after *De Motu Cordis*, and four years after Harvey's death.

Acceptance of Harvey's ideas was far from immediate. Galen's supporters were numerous and vociferous, especially in continental Europe. Harvey's findings also went against the theory, practice, and popularity of blood-letting (see pp.132–33). As a sign of those times, Harvey's medical practice in London suffered considerably after publication of *De Motu Cordis*. But gradually, sense prevailed. Physicians and surgeons accepted Harvey's findings well within his lifetime. Medicine would never be the same again, and patients would be eternally grateful.

CURE FOR SCURVY
Harvey prepared Aqua Cochlear, or "scurvy grass water", for his patients at St Bartholemew's Hospital. It was based on the vitamin C-rich herb, cochlear, also known as scurvy grass.

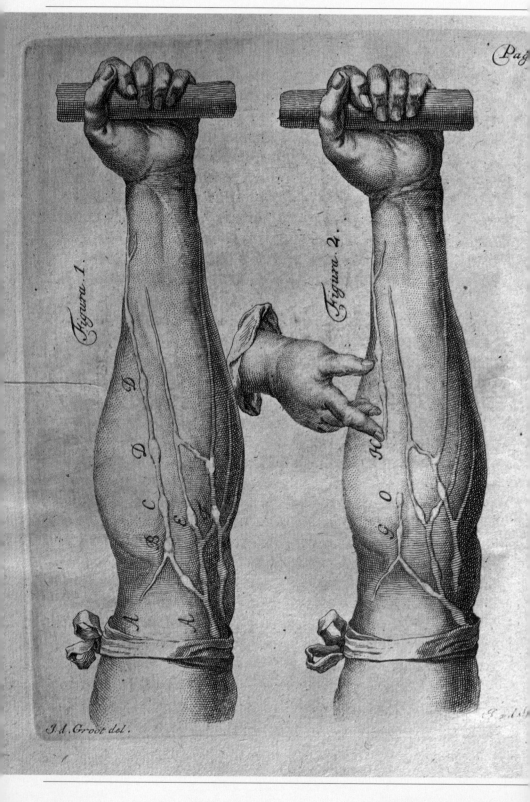

J.d.Groot del.

DE MOTU CORDIS
These illustrations from Harvey's *De Motu Cordis* show how the blood in the veins flows towards the heart (left), rather than away from it, and that the direction of flow is maintained by valves, which appear as bumps under the skin (right).

The Microscope Revolution

GERMS (SUCH AS BACTERIA AND VIRUSES), germ cells (including eggs and sperm), tiny parasites (such as malaria's plasmodium), and the smallest blood vessels known as capillaries – all these are invisible to the naked eye, and were unknown before the invention of the light microscope in the late 16th century. This simple device revealed the world of the very small, enabling medical researchers and doctors to explore afresh the human body's anatomy, both in health and disease. It was developed around 1590–1610, probably first in the Netherlands, and thought to be by either father-and-son lens experts Hans and Zacharias Janssen, or by Hans Lippershey. Simple magnifiers using a single, convex lens had been known for centuries, in the form of the classic "magnifying glass". The new microscope, however, was compound, using two or more lenses carefully shaped and distanced to make small things look much bigger. An early and enthusiastic user was astronomer Galileo Galilei, who built his own improved versions and demonstrated them to eminent academics and royalty.

One of the earliest works celebrating the microscope and illustrating its potential was the impressive *Micrographia* (1665), by English scientist, inventor, naturalist, philosopher, and architect Robert Hooke. His work portrayed all manner of fascinating tiny objects, from insect bodies, eyes, and legs to bits of blossom, seeds, and other plant specimens. *Micrographia* was one of the first bestselling books on science, and in it Hooke first used the word "cells" to describe tiny, box-like

ROBERT HOOKE'S MICROSCOPE
This illustration of the compound microscope used by Robert Hooke shows the oil lamp he employed to shed light on the specimens he examined.

ANTONI VAN LEEUWENHOEK
Dutch merchant and naturalist Antoni
van Leeuwenhoek was the first scientist
to observe single-celled organisms.

compartments in plant specimens of
cork. He likened them to the rows of
similar-shaped spartan chambers
or rooms occupied by monks.
His term soon passed into
general usage for the smallest
living components of plant
and animal bodies.

Perhaps the greatest pioneer microscopist, however, was Dutch
draper and businessman Antoni van Leeuwenhoek of Delft. Familiar
with the magnifiers used to count the threads in woven textiles, he
became fascinated with the design and construction of lenses, and
devised a secret way of producing tiny glass globules that could
magnify dozens of times, and eventually over 200 times. These were
in effect very powerful single-lens magnifiers, rather than compound
microscopes. Van Leeuwenhoek continually experimented, improved
his specimen preparation and lighting, and produced more than 500
lenses for use in a variety of holders. From the 1670s, his observations
and illustrations were published by The Royal Society of London, and
he kept contributing to its journals right up until his death.

Van Leeuwenhoek gathered specimens widely and observed
astutely. In water from ponds he saw what he termed "animalcules" –
in modern terminology, single-celled microorganisms. Looking at the
human body, he found what we now call bacteria in the fluid taken
from his mouth: "In the said matter there were many very little living
animalcules, very prettily moving. The biggest... had a very strong
and swift motion, and shot through the water (or spittle) like a pike
through water. The second sort... spun round like a
top". He also described blood cells, sperm cells in seminal fluid
from dogs and men, and the banded effect in striated (striped)
skeletal muscle cells.

A contemporary of van Leeuwenhoek was Italian scientist,
physician, and anatomist Marcello Malpighi. Working mainly at Pisa
and Bologna, he too employed the microscope to study the natural

MAGNIFICATION OF ANTONI VAN LEEUWENHOEK'S MICROSCOPES	MAGNIFICATION OF MODERN MICROSCOPES
275x	2000x

world and the human body. In the 1660s, he distinguished capillaries from surrounding tissues and saw tiny blobs moving through them, which he suggested were globules of fat. Capillaries were the "missing link" between small arteries and veins, whose existence had so perplexed William Harvey in his account of blood circulation (see pp.134–43). In the 1680s, with improved microscopes and better conditions for observation, Malpighi refined these ideas and described the beads as "red blood cells". His name lives on in several areas of microanatomy, such as the Malpighian layer at the base of the skin's outer layer (the epidermis), the Malpighian bodies (filtering units) in the kidney, and the Malpighian corpuscles (nodules of white blood cells) in the spleen.

Another pioneer microscopist, also Dutch like van Leeuwenhoek, was Jan Swammerdam. Reluctant to bend to his father's wishes and pursue a career in medicine, he became a leading entomologist (an expert on insects). His well-organized, systematic studies greatly advanced the understanding of the anatomy and life cycles of insects, especially how they change, or metamorphose (e.g. from caterpillar to chrysalis to butterfly). Swammerdam conceived many improved ways to preserve, prepare, and observe specimens under the microscope, which scientists would benefit from for two centuries.

In 1653, Italian philosopher-scientist Petrus Borellus published what may have been the first work on using microscopes for medical matters. Among some 100 procedures and observations, he described how to find and treat the tiniest of ingrowing eyelashes that produced otherwise puzzling inflammation and pain. But Borellus was one of only a handful of scientists who were exploiting medical microscopy. This was largely because physicians were conservative, and were worried about what the microscope might reveal. For instance, in

1761, Giovanni Morgagni, the foremost Italian anatomist of the day, published *De Sedibus et Causis Morborum per Anatomen Indagatis* (*The Seats and Causes of Diseases as Investigated by Anatomy*), in which he established the disciplines of pathology and morbid anatomy – the study of the body's structure and fabric as affected by disease. This was a century after Hooke and van Leeuwenhoek, yet this landmark work took little notice of microscopic anatomy.

Some 80 years later, Morgagni's opus was read in detail by German trainee physician and natural historian Rudolf Virchow, who was learning microscopy, among other things, at the Charité Teaching Hospital, Berlin. Virchow formed the opinion that the effects of disease should be visible not only to the naked eye, but also under the microscope. This was part of his great fascination with the cell as the basic building block of living tissues. He began to note the differences between cells in healthy and diseased specimens, such as the appearance of abnormal-looking white blood cells in various forms of leukaemia. For example, there could be an odd-shaped nucleus (control centre) in the cell, or suspicious granules, vacuoles, and other strange contents in the cytoplasm (the general bulk "jelly" of the cell), or a spiky, hairy, or crinkly cell membrane (outer skin). Such deformed cells might also react differently, compared with normal ones, to the stains or colouring substances used to highlight their different parts.

Virchow also read the works of French anatomist and surgeon Marie-François-Xavier Bichat, who first championed the concept of "living tissues" – layers, sheets, or membranes from which major body organs and parts were built. Today, a living tissue is regarded as a group of similar cells, such as bone cells, nerve cells, and so on. Bichat had little time for the latest compound microscopes and was wary of the concept of the cell. He trusted only his own eyes – aided by a simple magnifying lens, yet he managed to differentiate 21 different kinds of tissue, including muscle, skin, nerve and connective tissues, and grouped them into three main classes: fibrous, mucous, and serous (fluids). Bichat also turned to detailed autopsy as the route to discover the causes and consequences of disease. He carried out hundreds of autopsies, noting and describing the physical alterations in different tissues affected by morbid conditions. He used similar techniques to examine the effects of treatments such as drugs and surgery. Bichat came to the conclusion that abnormal changes in tissues, rather than changes in larger parts or whole organs, were the basis of disease.

Virchow appreciated Morgagni's contributions and the thrust of Bichat's approach. He then took Bichat's tissue-based ideas and applied them to the cellular level. Today, Virchow is famed as the author of *Die Cellularpathologie in Ihrer Begründung auf Physiologische und Pathologische Gewebelehre*, usually known in English as *Cellular Pathology*, and is viewed as the founder of this most essential and fundamental branch of medicine. Microscopic examination of tissues and cells, known as histology and cytology respectively, can reveal whether they are healthy or abnormal, and are invaluable tools that are widely used in modern medicine in the diagnosis of many diseases – for example, in the diagnosis of cancer, by identifying pre-cancerous changes in cells.

Virchow regarded cellular changes as the basis of many, if not most, diseases. Indeed, he went much further, decreeing in 1858 that cells, besides being the fundamental units of life, were the only way that life maintained itself. His celebrated pronouncement "*Omnis cellula e cellula*" is roughly translated from Latin as "All cells come from other cells". This statement was the third basic tenet of the cell theory that underpins all of the modern life sciences, including medicine. Previously, German biological researcher and embryologist Theodor Schwann, in correspondence with plant expert Matthias Schleiden, had formulated the first and second parts of classical cell theory: all living things are composed of one or more cells, and the cell is the basic unit of life in all living things. Even lifeless body parts such as hair and fingernails derive from once-living cells in the form of the tough protein they produce, called keratin.

However, Schwann and Schleiden's theories perpetuated the ancient idea of "spontaneous generation", whereby living cells or organisms can arise anew from non-living ingredients. In about 1855, spontaneous generation was denied by Polish-German physiologist Robert Remak, who declared that cells can only arise from the division of other cells – around the same time that Virchow first published a similar idea. Three years later, Virchow restated this view, and he is sometimes accused of taking credit for it without sufficiently acknowledging Remak's contribution. Later investigations by Louis Pasteur (see pp.196–203) and others consigned the idea of spontaneous generation as a medical phenomenon to history (conversely, modern evolutionary theory suggests that at some stage, probably more than three billion years ago here on Earth, life did indeed begin from a complex mix of non-living ingredients).

Through the groundbreaking work of early microbiologists, and the endeavours of Virchow and others, the light microscope is now an essential tool in medicine. However, light rays are too big or "wavy" to enlarge the view more than about 2,000 times clearly – to achieve greater magnification than this with clarity, an electron microscope is needed. Developed in the 1930s, the electron microscope has extended magnifying power to up to two million times, and enables the user to peer inside cells, to see the structure of their nuclei, membranes, "power-house" mitochondria, and other tiny parts known as organelles. Research into this realm of "ultrastructure" has yielded many breakthroughs in biological and medical knowledge, from how nerve signals travel and how drugs get into cells, to visualizing the changes in genetic material that signal inherited conditions, and how the most dangerous viruses multiply and wreak their destruction.

RUDOLF VIRCHOW OBSERVES
Pathologist and anthropologist Rudolf Virchow (centre, in black, seated) observes a cerebral operation in the Sorbonne, Paris, in 1900. Virchow himself never performed an operation.

Early Microscopes

The first microscopes were made in the early 17th century, in the Netherlands. Some were simple microscopes with a single lens, while more complex models with several lenses were known as compound microscopes. As lens-making techniques, precise focusing mechanisms, and clear illumination developed, scientists were able to use microscopes to see single-celled organisms for the first time, and to understand complex organic structures such as plant cells.

CAMPANI MICROSCOPE (c.1670–90)
Italian optical craftsman Giuseppe Campani was probably the first person to make a compound microscope with a screw-thread for more precise focusing.

LEEUWENHOEK MICROSCOPE (1670)
Dutch scientist Antoni van Leeuwenhoek (see p.14) made simple microscopes with a tiny lens between brass plates, and a pin to hold the specimen. Some of his lenses achieved a huge magnification of x275.

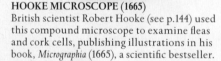

HOOKE MICROSCOPE (1665)
British scientist Robert Hooke (see p.144) used this compound microscope to examine fleas and cork cells, publishing illustrations in his book, *Micrographia* (1665), a scientific bestseller.

CUNO HAND MICROSCOPE (c.1700)
This microscope, by Cuno of Augsburg, has two metal plates – one holding the lens, the other the specimen. A screw controls focus by adjusting the distance between the plates.

CULPEPER COMPOUND MODEL (1738)
British instrument-maker Edward Culpeper's
microscope used a concave mirror to
illuminate samples. With interchangeable
lenses, it could magnify up to x200.

NACHET COMPOUND MODEL (c.1860)
French scientist Louis Pasteur (see pp.196–
203) used this microscope to investigate the
diseases of silkworms. It has precision metal
construction, for perfect focusing.

Conquering the Dreaded Pox

THE BODY'S IMMUNE SYSTEM provides self-defence against diseases of many kinds. Chief among these are infestations and infections of tiny invaders such as minuscule worms and flukes, fungi and yeasts, single-celled protozoal parasites, even smaller bacteria, and tiniest of all, viruses. The details of how immunity works are fiendishly complex and still being unravelled. Yet well before this complexity was even guessed at, medical workers found ways of encouraging the body to build immunity against infections without actually suffering from them. Along with antibiotics and antiseptic surgery, the practise of vaccination is high on the list of medicine's all-time life-savers and is often quoted as the most effective.

In 1798, English country doctor Edward Jenner privately published *An Enquiry Into the Causes and Effects of the Variolae Vaccinae, a Disease Discovered in some of the Western Counties of England, Particularly Gloucestershire, and Known by the Name of the Cow Pox*. It described his treatment of 23 patients with the aim of protecting them against one of the greatest global infectious diseases, smallpox – then known by several names, including "variola" (from the Latin word for "pimples"), which is now the scientific name for the virus germ that causes the disease.

Jenner's slim volume established scientific evidence for what we now call vaccination: introducing a substance into the body that causes or increases immunity against a disease. Our term "vaccine" was first used somewhat later, by Louis Pasteur (see pp.196–203). It comes from the Latin word *vacca*, meaning "cow", and honours Jenner's use of the

EARLY VACCINATOR
The first vaccinators were simple devices, such as this wood-and-ivory model. The spike was dipped into the vaccine and then pressed into the arm of the patient.

infection known as cowpox to
protect humans against smallpox –
cowpox being similar to smallpox,
though rarely disfiguring, let alone
fatal, in humans.

Today, the term "vaccine" applies to
almost any substance that initiates or
bolsters immunity. The often-misused
term "inoculation" refers to administering,
implanting, introducing, or grafting a substance that will spread,
grow, multiply, or be similarly active in the body. Inoculating a
vaccine is called vaccination. Depending on the particular vaccine, it
may be inoculated by injection, by mouth (orally), jabbed through
the skin, or introduced by some other route. The whole process of
introducing a substance into the body to stimulate or boost the body's
immune system is known as immunization.

In his youth, Jenner had himself been inoculated against
smallpox. This process, then called "variolation", was well known,
having been brought to Britain from Constantinople (now Istanbul)
in the 1720s by Lady Mary Wortley Montagu, the wife of the British
Ambassador to the Ottoman Empire. She had suffered and been
scarred by smallpox a few years earlier, and her brother had previously
died from the infection. In Constantinople, she saw fluid being taken
from the blisters (or pus from the sores) of a person with a mild
case of smallpox, and then slipped into an incision or punctured
into the skin of the recipient. Another method was to jab or blow
dried, powdered smallpox blister scabs into the nose. Thereafter, the
recipient had a hugely improved chance of resisting the full force of
the smallpox infection. Overall, depending on the methods and
circumstances, variolation was estimated to reduce the death rate
from smallpox from as high as one-in-three, to one in 20 or below.

Variolation techniques had been known for many centuries, and
probably originated farther east, in India and China. Various claims
of an Indian origin go back more than 3,000 years to the Vedas

EARLY CHINESE INOCULATION
It is thought that by 1000, Chinese physicians were
inoculating against smallpox by scratching matter
from the sores of smallpox sufferers (above) and
inserting it into the arms of healthy people.

(ancient Indian texts), while Ayurvedic records describe the healer
Madhav and other wandering "variolators" during the 7th and 8th
centuries (see p.80). More concrete evidence comes from 16th-century
China, where the procedure became something of a traditional ritual,
with ornate pipes for puffing the material up into the nose. Further
versions of variolation were practised in the Middle East and Africa
during the 17th century. Some involved inoculating dried scab
material from smallpox sufferers, others pus and fluid from their
blisters and sores. The inoculation route into the recipient was
generally through cuts or scrapes in the skin of the arm. These
methods spread as far west and north as Turkey.

In 1701, Venetian doctor Giacomo (Jacob) Pylarini described
variolation in Constantinople in an article for the Royal Society. In
the 1710s, also in Constantinople, Greek physician Emmanuel Timoni
was seconded to the British Embassy. A member of the Royal Society,
he too became interested in the process of variolation and wrote a
treatise on the topic, which was published by the Royal Society in
1714. It set in train a series of reports by other widely travelled doctors.

It was a few years later, in around 1716–18, that Lady Montagu
observed variolation, again in Constantinople, during her husband's
time as ambassador there. She appreciated its effects and had it
applied to her own son before returning to London. In 1721,
another smallpox epidemic threatened England, and Lady Mary
persuaded her husband (Lord Montagu), the Princess of Wales, and

royal doctor Hans Sloane to support the idea of variolation. She also agreed to her daughter being treated. At the same time, variolation was tested on six London prisoners who had received the death penalty, and according to some accounts, on some orphan children too. When these people were later exposed to smallpox, none of them caught the disease. The prisoners were granted their freedom, and variolation caught on. Royalty took it up, and it spread through the fashionable English populace and gradually to continental Europe.

Variolation was also tried in Boston, America, which had a smallpox epidemic in 1721–22. Puritan minister and activist Cotton Mather had heard about the procedure from an African slave named Onesimus. He may also have read Timoni's article on variolation. To try and save residents from death and suffering – and to avoid the ensuing disruption to business and trade – he petitioned local physicians to carry out variolation. Doctor Zabdiel Boylston responded by testing the technique on his own son and two slaves, who survived. He then inoculated nearly 250 more people. Records show about six or seven of these succumbed to smallpox – a death rate of 2–3 per cent. In the general Boston population, nearly 6,000 people contracted the infection, of which some 850 died – a death rate of almost 15 per cent.

Such statistics reflected the positive results of variolation, but it was still a risky procedure. The recipient could die from the procedure itself, or not receive protection and die after encountering smallpox. Also, the variolated patient carried "live" smallpox germs and so was a source of infection, and was best kept away from others for two weeks. In 1783, faith in variolation was shaken when King George III's four-year-old son Octavius died after undergoing the process.

Despite such concerns, however, variolation was considered a great success. Jenner himself had survived the process when he was young, although it had made him very ill. Intrigued by the procedure, he also mused on the traditional country conviction that milkmaids who contracted a much milder form of the disease, called cowpox, rarely caught smallpox. Cowpox produced sores on a cow's udders and also on the milkmaid's skin, but it had no lasting effects. Jenner resolved to investigate further by embarking on a series of carefully calculated medical experiments that combined variolation and smallpox with cowpox.

Jenner was not the first to have such thoughts. More than 20 years previously, in 1774, Benjamin Jesty, a farmer from Dorset, had carried out what Jenner was now planning to do. Jesty saw how his milkmaids who had contracted cowpox were able to care for smallpox victims without themselves being affected. When a cowpox outbreak came to his area, Jesty attended infected cows in secret with his wife and sons, whom he inoculated with material from the cowpox sores, using a darning needle. The sons showed little reaction, but when his wife fell ill, the story became public knowledge. Even though Mrs Jesty recovered, Mr Jesty was ridiculed. Not only had the farmer deliberately tried to make his family ill, it was said, the cowpox material could have wreaked havoc on their bodies – and even given them horns.

The Jesty family eventually moved away and settled in Worth Matravers, Dorset. But after Jenner's success, Jesty's story prompted support and a campaign for his official recognition from the authority of the time, The Original Vaccine Pock Institute. In 1805, the Institute partially agreed. However, Jesty's lack of medical or other standing could not threaten Jenner, who was by now a lauded celebrity. Jesty's gravestone at Worth Matravers states: "... Particularly noted for having been the first Person (known) that Introduced the Cow Pox by Inoculation..."

In the two decades before Jenner's work, others besides Jesty had reported on the ability of cowpox infection to protect against smallpox. These included Doctor John Fewster and Doctor Rolph, both from Gloucestershire. Fewster's 1765 article "Cow Pox and its Ability to Prevent Smallpox" was presented to the Medical Society of London, but was thereafter sidelined. Also espousing the procedure around Europe were government official Jobst Bose of Göttingen, Germany, in 1769; a Frau Sevel in Germany, in 1772; Peter Plett, a teacher in Denmark, in 1791; and Herr Jensen, a farmer from Holstein, Germany, also in 1791. But none of these individuals had Jenner's authority, his number of case histories, or his profile in the scientific community.

The most celebrated of the 23 case histories described by Jenner in his 1798 *Enquiry* had occurred two years earlier. Of Case Number 17, he wrote: "The more accurately to observe the progress of the infection, I selected a healthy boy, about eight years old, for the purpose of inoculation for the Cow Pox. The matter was taken from a sore on the hand of a dairymaid, who was infected by her master's cows, and it was inserted, on the 14th of May, 1796, into the arm of the boy by means of two superficial incisions, barely penetrating the cutis [outer skin layer], each about half an inch long". The boy's name was James Phipps, and he was the son of Jenner's gardener; the milkmaid was Sarah Nelmes, herself the subject of Jenner's Case Number 16. Like the previous cases, Sarah had caught cowpox naturally, and not suffered from smallpox. James, however, had not caught the disease naturally. Jenner had given it to him on purpose – and the inoculation

SAVING LIVES
Edward Jenner vaccinates a child – one of the
millions who would be saved by his work. Thanks to
his pioneering vaccine, the science of immunology
was born.

material was not from a cow, but from a human who had recovered from cowpox. About a week later, James suffered some minor swelling, fever, and chills, but then recovered. Six weeks after that, Jenner gave James a deliberate dose of smallpox, inserting the material fresh from a sufferer's pustule into several incisions on the boy's arms. With relief, Jenner recorded: "No disease followed".

As usual, there was initial opposition to Jenner's conclusions, especially from quarters of the generally conservative medical profession. Echoing Benjamin Jesty 25 years earlier, but on a national scale, popular mockery led to newspaper cartoons of vaccinated people mooing in Jenner's defence and morphing into cows (or, perhaps worse, humble milkmaids). But after the hit-and-miss history of variolation, the efficacy of the new procedure was soon recognized. Within three years, Jenner's work progressed into mainstream medicine and soon became government public health policy. With official organizations set up, researchers applied the idea of vaccination to other infections.

By 1840, the original variolation method using live smallpox material from human sufferers had been prohibited in England. Yet no one, including Jenner, his supporters, and his immediate successors, had any real idea how the whole thing worked. The variola virus was only discovered and characterized in the late 19th and early 20th centuries. More recently, some researchers have suggested that the vaccine material developed from Jenner's pioneering techniques may not have involved cowpox at all, but a related virus more similar to the smallpox one. It could be that vaccinators infected cows not with cowpox, but with human smallpox, leading to a variant virus that was similar to both but actually neither. Even horses and another variant, horsepox, have been implicated. Sadly no 19th-century vaccine samples survive for analysis.

Was Jenner justified in his work? Carrying out hopeful experiments on human subjects, without what we today would regard as official permission, risk analysis, and proper safeguards would now be regarded as unethical and unprofessional. Especially controversial was the use of James Phipps, a child. However, given the standards of the age, Jenner had already done a great deal of background work and completed similar trials on adults. He was confident of success, and saw the immense benefits to mankind. Giving James cowpox was not a great risk since it was a mild disease, although admittedly, Phipps may never have caught it naturally. Inoculating him with live smallpox material involved more serious hazards. Yet this was basically the procedure of variolation, which many people accepted because it provided an increased chance of

YEAR OF THE LAST KNOWN CASE OF SMALLPOX

1978

surviving smallpox when, rather than if, they were exposed to the disease. Also, from Jenner's accumulating evidence of previous case histories, the odds were that Phipps would have only a small reaction to the deliberately introduced smallpox, and then be resistant – immune – for many years after. In the event, Phipps had a possible minor reaction one week later, described by Jenner: "He complained of uneasiness in the axilla [armpit]... He became a little chilly, lost his appetite, and had a slight headache... He spent the night with some degree of restlessness, but on the day following he was perfectly well". Years later, as a thank-you for his involvement, Jenner provided the adult, newlywed Phipps with a house in their local village of Berkeley.

The move from variolation to vaccination was not only a great leap forward in the long, complex battle against smallpox, it was the start of research into vaccines against many other infections, which have since saved millions of lives (see pp.286–95). Jenner's legacy continued to grow after his death, and it came to fruition in 1980, when the World Health Organization announced the global eradication of "the smallpox".

Eradicating Smallpox

Smallpox was a deadly virus that ravaged populations throughout the world – it is also the only human disease to have been eradicated. Caused by the *Variola* virus, it attacked the small blood vessels of the skin, mouth, and throat, giving victims widespread blisters filled with fluid. Around a third of sufferers died; survivors were left with scars and sometimes went blind. Inoculation (see pp.292–93) could create immunity, but also risked causing full infection. Vaccination using the related disease cowpox was safer, and eventually led to the eradication of smallpox.

THE CHINESE GOD OF SMALLPOX

1718 Lady Mary Wortley Montagu, living in Turkey, has her son **inoculated** against smallpox.

1796 British doctor Edward Jenner uses pus from the **cowpox blisters** of a dairymaid for his first successful smallpox vaccination on a boy called James Phipps.

1721 Physician Zabdiel Boylston brings inoculation to North America during a smallpox **epidemic** in Boston.

1803 The **Spanish colonies** in the New World receive vaccine from Spain.

1520 Spanish **conquistadors** bring smallpox to the Americas.

1800 Harvard professor Benjamin Waterhouse carries out the **first vaccinations** in the US.

1661 Chinese physicians practise **variolation** by blowing powdered smallpox scabs up patients' noses.

1721 Lady Montagu brings inoculation to the UK and campaigns for it to be **widely adopted**.

1768 Physician Thomas Dimsdale successfully inoculates **Catherine the Great** of Russia.

1802 Massachusetts becomes the **first US state** to endorse smallpox vaccination.

TOTAL ESTIMATED NUMBER OF DEATHS WORLDWIDE FROM SMALLPOX BY THE LATE 20TH CENTURY

300 MILLION

1967 The entire population of Costa Rica is inoculated against **smallpox, measles, and polio** in a campaign carried out by the government and US medical volunteers.

C.1900 Material from vaccinated calves is used for human vaccination, reducing the chance of **accidentally transmitting** other diseases.

1820 Deaths from smallpox in London plummet to **fewer than half** the rate in the years before vaccination.

1918 The development of **freeze-dried vaccine** helps to control smallpox in tropical countries.

1949 The **last cases** of smallpox in the US are recorded, including one fatality.

1980 The World Health Assembly declares the world **free of smallpox** and in 1986 ceases vaccination.

1853 In the UK, vaccination becomes **mandatory** in the first three months of a child's life.

1864 French doctors experiment with material from vaccinated **livestock**.

1967 The **World Health Organization** launches its Intensified Smallpox Eradication Programme.

Medicine in the Industrial Age

1820–1920

Medicine gained momentum during the 19th century. The Industrial Revolution gathered pace in grimy cities, where overcrowding, malnutrition, and poor sanitation encouraged contagious diseases. English doctor John Snow's work on cholera in the 1850s was a landmark for epidemiology, although it was recognized at the time only with reluctance.

Other scientific disciplines fed into medicine. Taking cues from chemistry, US physicians in the 1840s investigated substances to make patients insensible to pain during operations. Two decades later in Scotland, surgeon Joseph Lister conducted research into chemicals for their infection-preventing powers. Within 40 years, these two operative advances, anaesthesia and antisepsis, had made surgery immeasurably safer. Meanwhile, in France, Louis Pasteur harnessed microbiology to medicine in a string of successes, including pasteurization of milk and wine, and vaccines for several animal diseases as well as for rabies in humans. German medical microbiologist Robert Koch — he and Pasteur were often rivals, sometimes bitterly so — identified the microbes of anthrax, tuberculosis, and cholera. At last, the coffins of the obsolete ideas miasmas and spontaneous generation were nailed firmly shut and replaced by the germ theory of disease.

The 19th century saw other welcome areas of progress. Elizabeth Blackwell in the US and Elizabeth Garrett Anderson in the UK campaigned successfully for women to receive equality in medical training and qualifications. They both set up medical schools for women. Although English nurse Florence Nightingale's feats in the Crimea in the 1850s have recently been debated, her subsequent founding of the modern nursing profession has not. And as the 19th century ended, Austrian neurologist Sigmund Freud's psychiatric approaches stimulated debates that continue today.

Women in Medicine

WOMEN HAVE ALWAYS PLAYED A VITAL ROLE in providing medical care – particularly as nurses (see pp.188–93), midwives (see pp.214–21), and herbalists – but throughout history, men have dominated the medical profession. In Renaissance Europe, women were effectively prevented from becoming doctors when a university qualification became a requirement – something women couldn't receive since they were already barred from universities. It was only in the 1900s that women won the right to study and practise medicine, and only later in the 20th century that they began to be treated on equal terms with men.

One of the first female physicians mentioned by name was Merit-Ptah, some 4,700 years ago, around the time of Ancient Egypt's physician-deity Imhotep (see pp.22–27). There are few clues to her abilities, save that her High Priest son placed the inscription "Chief Physician" on her tomb near Saqqara. During Ancient Egypt's lengthy history – it lasted longer than the millennia from its demise to today – the authority of women in medicine waxed and waned. Women mostly undertook caring roles, although 3,500 years ago, female students could attend medical school at Heliopolis. In Ancient Greece, more than 2,600 years ago, Homer's *Iliad* mentions Agamede, daughter of Augeas, King of the Epeians: "Fair-haired Agamede who knew of all the medicines that are grown in the broad earth". As in Egypt, a woman's place in medicine varied with time and place, since cities independently made their own rules through the centuries. Metrodora's *On the Diseases and Cures of Women*, written around 2,300 years ago, is one of the first medical books written by a woman. Metrodora covered gynaecology with a combination of personal experience and Hippocratic knowledge (see pp.30–39). Greek female physicians were generally limited to treating female conditions – a practice that Agnodice tried to avoid by assuming a male disguise (see p.214). This ruse has cropped up now and again throughout history. As late as 1865, the autopsy of British Army surgeon Dr James Barry showed that "he" – a medical graduate from Edinburgh, who had served in India, South Africa, the Mediterranean, and the Caribbean, become Inspector General of military hospitals, and enjoyed more than 40 years promoting diet, hygiene, and public health – was in fact a woman.

In the Islamic world, female healers are cited treating female conditions as early as the 8th century, and by the 15th century, female surgeons are depicted in the surgical manual *Cerrahiyyetu'l-Haniyye* (*Imperial Surgery*), produced by Sabuncuoglu Serefeddin. In the Germanic regions, the 12th-century abbess, poet, composer, and naturalist Hildegard of Bingen was one of the great physicians of her day. Her work *Liber Simplicis Medicinae* (*Book of Simple Medicine*), later called *Physica*, extols the medicinal values of hundreds of herbs, trees, animal parts, and minerals. Her *Liber Compositae Medicinae* (*Book of Composite Medicines*), which became *Causae et Curae* (*Causes and Cures*), also compiled in the 1150s, discusses the symptoms and treatments of physical and mental diseases holistically – as an interplay of body and soul. During a fever of humoral imbalance (see pp.106–107), for instance: "... the soul lies depressed in the body and waits... So it continues until the seventh day because it cannot yet free itself from its foul humours... However, if it notices that the intensity of these humours, through the grace of God, is beginning to recede somewhat... It gathers its forces again and by sweating it drives these foul humours out of its body".

Another great name of the time is Trotula di Ruggiero of Salerno, who lived during the latter half of the 11th century, although her personal life is shadowy and opinions vary on whether she was real or mythical. Salerno in southwest Italy boasted Europe's first generally recognized school of medicine (see pp.108–15), and one of its many innovations was allowing women to qualify as physicians – at the time, women were generally prohibited not just from formal medical training, but from most higher education. Trotula's name became attached to many publications that were a mainstay of medicine for several centuries; collectively known

HILDEGARDE OF BINGEN
Twelfth-century composer, philosopher, and Benedictine abbess Hildegarde of Bingen was one of the great physicians of her day.

as "The Trotula", these included *Diseases of Women*, *Treatments for Women*, and *Women's Cosmetics*. The style of the texts is direct and practical, and few references are made to the occult. The texts recommend diagnosing ailments by asking the patient questions and noting pulse rate, breathing, skin appearance, and urine analysis – all of which was unusual for the time. Remedies of herbs and animal parts are offered, and advice is given on rest, stress, cleanliness, exercise, diet – and how to disguise freckles. If Trotula was real, then she was a pioneer in gynaecology, obstetrics, and women's health. The texts cover feminine hygiene, menstruation, fertility, conception, pregnancy, and childbirth. Among her more radical ideas was that failure to conceive could be the fault of the man. She also advocated pain relief for childbirth – against the prevailing Christian view that women should endure the pain because of Eve's sinful behaviour in the Garden of Eden.

SALERNO MEDICAL SCHOOL
Duke Robert II of Normandy is received by a female
doctor at the Salerno Medical School in the 11th century.

Sadly, Salerno's inclusive tradition did not persist, and a trend for barring women swept across Europe. In 1220, the bar was enforced at Paris University, and in 1390, women were effectively excluded from medical schools in London. There were a few exceptions – in 1390, Dorotea Bocchi succeeded her father to begin a 40-year stint as Professor of

RUSSIA HAD MORE WOMEN DOCTORS IN 1914 THAN ALL OF WESTERN EUROPE COMBINED:

1,600

Medicine and Philosophy at the University of Bologna – but by the 16th century, the bar was in place at most European universities. In 1732, Laura Bassi, the daughter of a well-connected lawyer, became Professor of Anatomy aged just 21 years, again at Bologna – and in 1755, Anna Manzolini succeeded her husband in the same position.

Bassi's achievement made a great impression on one Dorothea Erxleben of Quedlinburg, Prussia. When she was young, Erxleben decided to follow her father's profession and study medicine. Her father, who had a reputation for rebelliousness, even petitioned Frederick the Great to allow her to pursue her studies, and the Prussian king conceded. Erxleben wrote *Inquiry into the Causes Preventing the Female Sex from Studying*, and in 1754, graduated in medicine from the University of Halle as Prussia's first qualified female physician. Again, this was an isolated case; it was not until 1901 that another woman qualifed as a doctor at Halle.

In 1847, Elizabeth Blackwell was accepted as a student at Geneva Medical College, New York State, USA, having applied to many other medical schools to no avail. The college authorities were said to have shied away from making a decision about her request and offered it to a vote by the students – who thought it was a hoax, and gave a unanimous "yes".

Born in Bristol, England, Blackwell emigrated with her family to New York in 1830 and moved to Cincinnati eight years later. The family's sugar business involved a great deal of slave labour, but young Blackwell's instincts were for social reform, the abolition of slavery, and education for the poor and disadvantaged – especially women. A medical career would suit such ambitions, so Blackwell worked as a teacher to raise funds while studying medicine in her spare time.

At Geneva, Blackwell graduated in 1849 with a medical degree – the first awarded to a woman in the USA. However, hospital employment was hard to find, so she went to London, and then to Paris, where she found work in a maternity hospital. Her obstetric skills received great praise, and she moved to St Bartholomew's Hospital, London. However, the British attitude towards women doctors was even more intransigent, and by 1851, Blackwell was back in New York, where she set up a medical practice, and then a dispensary that provided free medications and treatments for poor women and children. In 1857, with her supportive sister Emily and like-minded reformer and Cleveland Medical College graduate Maria Zakrzewska, she opened the New York Infirmary for Indigent Women and Children. This was so successful that in a year it needed bigger premises, eventually becoming what is now the New York University Downtown Hospital.

The movement started by Blackwell gathered pace, and soon medical schools for women were opening in Boston, Philadelphia, and New York. Then, in 1869, Blackwell left the US to return to England, where she was instrumental in founding the London School of Medicine for Women in 1874, along with Sophia Jex-Blake and Elizabeth Garrett Anderson. Jex-Blake was one the first women doctors in Britain, and she went on to establish the Edinburgh School of Medicine for Women in 1886. Elizabeth Garrett Anderson had met Blackwell in 1859, and been immediately inspired to pursue a career in medicine. She started as a nurse at London's Middlesex Hospital in 1860, and with her family's financial and moral backing, she had private lessons in related fields such as anatomy, physiology, and materia medica (medicines), and attended chemistry lectures. The following year, she graduated in materia medica and chemistry, and in 1862, she enrolled with the Society of Apothecaries, again engaging private tuition. Three years later, the Society approved her licence for medical practice – the first for a British woman – although it too then changed its rules and banned the admission of women.

ELIZABETH BLACKWELL
The first woman to receive a medical degree in the USA, Elizabeth Blackwell founded the New York Infirmary for Indigent Women and Children.

ELIZABETH GARRETT ANDERSON
English feminist Elizabeth Garrett Anderson passes
her examination to obtain an MD from the University
of Paris in 1870.

Women were still being treated unequally in hospitals, so like Blackwell, Garrett Anderson opened a private practice, and in 1866 founded the St Mary's Dispensary for Women and Children. In 1872, the dispensary gained in-patient beds and became the New Hospital for Women – renamed the Elizabeth Garrett Anderson Hospital in 1918. Garrett then co-founded the London School of Medicine for Women, and became the first female member of the British Medical Association in 1873. From 1883 to her retirement in 1902, she was the first female dean of the London School of Medicine for Women, and for many years she strenuously campaigned for the suffragette movement.

In 1876, British Parliament at last approved a bill allowing women to enter the medical profession fully. Other nations did the same. In 1875, Madeleine Brès became the first woman to receive a French medical licence, and in 1900, Japanese physician and women's rights campaigner Yoshioka Yayoi founded Tokyo Women's Medical University. Two years later, the Hackett Medical College for Women opened in Guangzhou, China. Finally, women had opportunities – but it was well into the 20th century before anything like equality between the sexes was established.

NURSES AND MIDWIVES
A group of trainee nurses and midwives pose for
the camera at a training college in London in 1908.
In Britain, women were finally allowed into the
medical profession in 1876, following the tireless
campaigns of Elizabeth Blackwell and others.

Anaesthesia

TODAY, NO PERSON OF SOUND MIND would choose to be operated on in filthy, germ-ridden conditions, and without pain relief. But before the mid-19th century, which heralded the monumental advances of anaesthesia and germ-killing antiseptics (see pp.206–13), this was the reality faced by patients. General anaesthesia renders the body temporarily unconscious and unresponsive to stimuli, even great pain; it allows the surgeon to work on the quietened body without the patient screaming and writhing in agony. The first successful public medical demonstration of anaesthesia, in which dentist William Morton used the gas ether, occurred on 16 October 1846. This date marks the era of modern anaesthesia, and is celebrated each year as World Anaesthesia Day. But, like most other medical practices, anaesthesia has a long and colourful history.

The first anaesthetic of sorts was stumbled upon 6,000 years ago by winemakers of Eastern Europe and West Asia. Doubtless enjoying the fruits of their labours, they found that overindulgence resulted in blunted sensibilities, and that alcohol masked stimuli such as pain. Another ancient option was opium, prepared from the sap of the opium poppy. Its mind-altering, sleep-inducing properties were mentioned on tablets from Ancient Sumer, and opium became a part of life in many Asian cultures. From the 16th century, opium became popular in Europe, too. Luminaries such as Paracelsus (see pp.110–15) and, in the 17th century, Thomas Sydenham, combined opium, alcohol, and other ingredients to produce laudanum. Patent medicines based on laudanum achieved a degree of analgesia (pain relief) and anaesthesia, along with other consequences – notably, addiction.

Other plants long used for their narcotic qualities – having a stupefying effect, reducing pain, and causing loss of consciousness – include cannabis, henbane and other nightshades, mandrake, bryony, hemlock, metel, thorn-apple, saw-wort, and wild or opium lettuce. In the Americas, coca plants were exploited for analgesia and other properties (see pp.82–87). Ancient Egyptian pain-relief practices were described in *Incantations of Analgesia* from the Ebers Papyrus (see pp.26–27), and Greek physician Dioscorides listed the properties of mandrake extracts. In 2nd-century China, physician-surgeon Hua Tuo performed operations using a mysterious substance

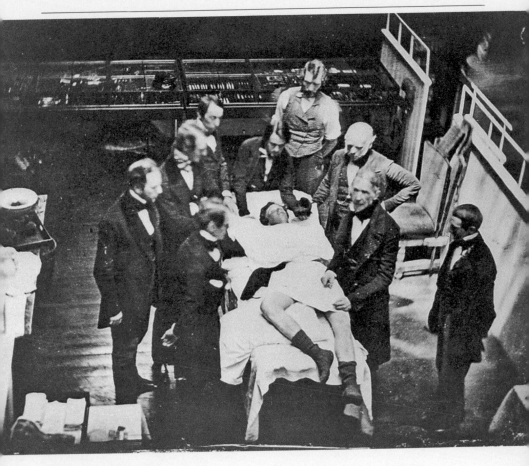

FIRST USE OF ETHER
Dentist William Morton's demonstrations of anaesthesia took
place here in the surgical amphitheatre at the Massachusetts
General Hospital. The amphitheatre is now known as the
Ether Dome and is a designated US historical landmark.

known as mafeisan. Much later, in the early 1800s, Japanese
physician-surgeon Hanaoka Seishu revisited the idea of mafeisan to
create tsusensan, using nightshade extracts. Hanaoka's patients
reportedly drank the tsusensan, sinking from consciousness before
the surgeon got to work.

In the Middle Ages, sense-nullifying potions multiplied unchecked.
Methods of administering included the "soporific sponge", where
preparations were soaked into rags or sponges and held over the
patient's nose and mouth. This way, if things went wrong, the sponge
could be rapidly removed. Arab physician Ibn Sina mentioned the
sponge in his epic *Al-Qanun fi al-Tibb* (see pp.100–105). The major flaw

in using such potions was the unpredictable quantity and quality of active compounds. With no way of securing a standard dose, the effects veered from virtually nothing to helpful anaesthesia or even sudden death. As a result, non-chemical methods of anaesthesia were attempted. These ranged from packing the body in ice or giving a knockout blow to the head to strangling the patient to the point of collapse. Taking a rather less violent approach, hypnotic anaesthesia and analgesia rose to prominence in Europe during the 19th century, thanks to Franz Anton Mesmer. Physicians reported some success with "mesmerism", but the procedures were far from reliable.

All these methods were overshadowed by the events of the 1840s, which changed the course of anaesthesia for good. A number of discoveries, beginning in 16th-century Europe, led up to this moment. In about 1540, German scientist Valerius Cordus discovered how to make ether from ethanol and sulphuric acid, and consequently, this volatile liquid became more available. Wandering physician Paracelsus, who had earlier created laudanum, noted that adding sweet oil of vitriol (ether) to food "… quiets all suffering without any harm and relieves all pain, and quenches all fevers, and prevents complications in all disease". But he made these observations in chickens. By the late 18th century, ether vapour was being inhaled for pain relief – and, later, at "ether frolics". At these gatherings, participants inhaled the gas and entertained the audience with their giddy, confused antics. Nitrous oxide was another fashionable inhaled drug of the time. This gaseous compound was first produced by English chemist-theologian Joseph Priestley in 1772, who was also an early pioneer of isolating oxygen. In 1800, another eminent English scientist, Humphry Davy, reported that inhaling nitrous oxide not only caused uncontrollable laughter – he dubbed it "laughing gas" – but also helped to deaden pain such as toothache. One day, he mused, might this gas be used to alleviate pain during surgical procedures?

In the US, ether frolics and laughing-gas parties became popular in the early 19th century, especially with students of chemistry and medicine. Some students noticed that painful injuries sustained during frolics seemed not to trouble the participants. Going on to qualify in medicine and dentistry, and remembering the apparently analgesic effects of the two gases, they reasoned that a larger dose could work as an anaesthetic during surgery. In January 1842, in

LAUGHING PARTY
Nitrous oxide was used as a recreational drug in the
19th century. Guests inhaled "laughing gas" at parties
and revelled in its euphoric, pain-numbing effects.

Burlington, Vermont, William Clarke allowed a dental patient to
inhale ether from a towel during a tooth extraction. Two months later,
in Jefferson, Georgia, another physician, Crawford Long, administered
ether by inhalation while removing a tumour from patient's neck. But
neither Clarke nor Long reported their actions at the time.

In December 1844, dentist Horace Wells watched a nitrous oxide
stage demonstration in Hartford, Connecticut. He was intrigued to
see that one of the participants was injured, yet seemed not to notice.
The next day, Wells asked another dentist, John Riggs, to remove
Wells's painful wisdom tooth, while the show's organizer, Gardner
Quincy Colton, put Wells "out" with nitrous oxide. The experiment
worked, and Wells started to use nitrous oxide on his patients. Keen
to prove his success, he arranged a public demonstration of his new
technique at Boston's Massachusetts General Hospital in January
1845. Sadly, the plan backfired, and the patient moved and groaned
during the operation. Wells was distraught: "The gas bag was by
mistake withdrawn much too soon... Several expressed their opinion
that it was a humbug affair". His reputation plummeted. Despite his
continued efforts to champion the method, he failed to regain his
credibility, and committed suicide three years later.

The following year, in September 1846, Wells's former partner and
fellow dentist William Morton – who had helped to arrange Wells's
failed demonstration – began using ether to anaesthetize his patients.

Encouraged by early successes, he too set up a staged demonstration at Massachusetts General Hospital. On 16 October, Morton administered ether to patient Edward Abbott while leading surgeon John Collins Warren partly removed a lower-jaw tumour. The ether worked – Abbott did not cry out or react to the surgery. Warren noted that the patient "… sank into a state of insensibility… did not experience any pain at the time, although aware that the operation was proceeding…" Medical observers were impressed, and news spread rapidly: the era of controlled general anaesthesia had begun.

Meanwhile, across the Atlantic, Europeans reacted to the news by creating their own anaesthetic. Their gas of choice was chloroform. In March 1847, French physiologist Marie-Jean-Pierre Flourens showed that animals that inhaled chloroform experienced a temporary state of insensibility. Eight months later, Scottish physician James Young Simpson introduced chloroform anaesthesia for humans, using it on women in childbirth. Simpson had first tried it himself with friends – a risky business that he was lucky to survive. Pioneer epidemiologist and anaesthetist John Snow (see pp.180–87) helped to determine safe amounts of chloroform, and later, ether, for varying levels of pain relief and unconsciousness. In 1853, under Snow's supervision, Queen Victoria of England took chloroform for the birth of her son Leopold, and, four years later, for her daughter Beatrice. She wrote: "Dr Snow gave that blessed chloroform and the effect was soothing, quieting, and delightful beyond measure". Encouraged by this royal endorsement, the general public rapidly took to the idea of anaesthesia.

Back in the US, ether anaesthesia faded as chloroform became the favoured drug. But chloroform had dangerous – sometimes fatal – side effects, so by the early 20th century, it was replaced. Intense research has since brought safer, more effective general anaesthetics, including ethyl chloride (1903), ethylene (in the 1920s), halothane

CLOVER AND CHLOROFORM
Joseph Thomas Clover invented an apparatus for administering quantities of chloroform through a face mask.

(1950s), methoxyflurane and enflurane (1960s), isoflurane (1970s), desflurane (1987), and sevoflurane (1990s). As the gases used for anaesthesia improved, so too did ways of administering them. In the wake of hit-and-miss sponges and towels came inhaler

APPROXIMATE DEATH RATE AFTER OPERATIONS BEFORE THE 19TH CENTURY

80%

designs with flasks, tubes, and pumps. In the late 18th century, English doctor Thomas Beddoes devised several innovative designs, aided by steam-engine expert James Watt and Humphry Davy, of laughing gas fame. In the 1860s, wire face masks were developed, onto which an anaesthetic liquid was dripped, which then vapourized. Joseph Thomas Clover, an English physician, added regulators and bags to face masks. In 1917, Henry Boyle, at St Bartholomew's Hospital, London, introduced an "anaesthesia machine" – a wheeled trolley with gas supplies, pumps, reservoirs, valves, flow and pressure meters, masks, and other equipment needed to administer a continuous flow of anaesthetic gases and monitor the patient's condition. By this time, gas tubes were being placed into the trachea (windpipe), enabling more accurate control, and in the 1930s, the barbiturate sodium thiopental became the first general anaesthesic to be given intravenously (directly into the blood circulation).

As well as "knock-out" general anaesthesia, other types were developed. In the 1870s, the first local anaesthetic – one that removes sensation from a small area – was cocaine. This had been purified from coca plants in 1860 by Albert Niemann at the University of Göttingen, Germany. The subsequent discovery of cocaine's toxicity led to the introduction of safer "locals", such as procaine in 1905 and lidocaine in the 1940s. Regional anaesthesia numbs a larger or deeper part of the body, such as the abdomen. In the 1890s, German surgeon August Bier introduced spinal anaesthesia to remove sensation from the body below the injection site; and in the 1940s, an improved method, the epidural, entered mainstream practice (see pp.214–21).

Our expectations of medicine have been shaped by the advances of anaesthesia. Imagine a major operation – or even a visit to the dentist – without it. The quest for safer, more effective anaesthesia continues. Estimates vary widely, but with the latest care, the risk of death directly linked to general anaesthesia ranges from one in 7,000 to one in 200,000.

Early Anaesthetics

In the 1840s, the use of anaesthetics – substances that cause temporary loss of sensation or consciousness – developed rapidly. Patients inhaled substances such as chloroform, ether, or nitrous oxide in the form of a vapour, to render them insensible to pain. As the use of anaesthetics during surgery became more commonplace, both physicians and manufacturers devised improved equipment so that chemicals could be administered more safely.

SKINNER'S IMPROVED MASK FOR ANAESTHESIA (1862–1901)
Gynaecologist Thomas Skinner designed this mask to be portable and easy to use. Liquid chloroform or ether was dropped onto a flannel covering, which the patient held or clipped onto the nose before inhaling the anaesthetic.

MURPHY-TYPE CHLOROFORM INHALER (1850–1900)
This inhaler, which contained a sponge soaked in chloroform, was widely used as an anaesthesic for women in childbirth during the second half of the 19th century.

SNOW'S CHLOROFORM INHALER (c.1848)
James Simpson discovered chloroform was an anaesthetic in 1847 (see p.176). John Snow, Britain's first specialist anaesthetist, then devised this inhaler. The top of the tube was attached to a lead mask worn by the patient.

NITROUS OXIDE CYLINDER (1840–68)
In 1868, a way was found to turn nitrous oxide (also known as "laughing gas") into liquid form, so that it could be stored in cylinders. When it was sold in this form, the gas became popular as an anaesthetic, especially in dentistry.

MORGAN-TYPE ETHER INHALER (1881–90)
British surgeon John H. Morgan developed this inhaler. A sponge soaked with ether was placed in the narrow end of the cone and the patient inhaled through the wide end.

HYPODERMIC SYRINGE (1885–1900)
Hypodermic syringes such as this American model became increasingly popular in the 19th century, especially for dental anaesthesia.

HYPODERMIC SYRINGE SET (1885–1910)
Packed in a compact aluminium case, this syringe has two needles and a supply of anaesthetic tablets. The surgeon crushed these and diluted them before injection.

ETHER (1891–1930)
Using ether as an anaesthetic caught on quickly after it was demonstrated in public in the US in the 1840s. It was used in a wide range of procedures, from tooth extraction to removing tumours.

TRICHLOROETHYLENE (1940–60)
Marketed as Trilene, this volatile liquid chemical was inhaled through a mouthpiece to provide pain relief during labour. Although popular for decades, it was later replaced by nitrous oxide.

"ESO" CHLOROFORM APPARATUS (1945)
Designed to deliver chloroform vapour through a mouthpiece, this device was developed during World War II and made robust enough to withstand parachute drops and use on the battlefield.

John Snow and Epidemiology

EPIDEMIOLOGY IS THE STUDY of the patterns, causes, and effects of disease (and health) in populations. It investigates and analyses the patterns of diseases, and looks for ways of controlling them and preventing their return. However, identifying diseases with any accuracy has only been possible since the discovery of bacteria in the late 19th century (see pp.222–27). Before that, it was widely thought that epidemics were caused by "noxious air", or "miasma" (see p.196–97), which was believed to emanate, among other things, from rotting organic matter. One of the first people to challenge this idea was English physician John Snow, who, during an outbreak of cholera in London, England, in 1854, suggested that there was a link between the disease and the water supply. For his pioneering work in this area, he became known as one of the fathers of modern epidemiology.

Cholera's long history is often confused by the fact that there are many conditions that have similar symptoms. Such symptoms are described in the *Susruta Samhita* of Ancient India (see pp.77–79), the Hippocratic Corpus (see pp.30–39) – in which *chole*, bile, is one of the four humours (see pp.106–107) – and the works of the 11th-century Arab physician Ibn Sina (see pp.100–105). Today, we know that cholera is caused by a bacterium called *Vibrio cholerae*, which affects the intestines, causing copious, watery vomiting and diarrhoea. This can so disturb the body's balance of fluids and salts that dehydration and even death may follow.

One group of cholera deaths in London in 1854 occurred in the west-central area of Soho. John Snow lived just a few streets away and knew the area well. He had also come across cholera during an epidemic in 1831–32, and recalled vividly the suffering it had caused in crowded, working-class mining areas. After his early upbringing in York, Snow had been apprenticed to Newcastle surgeon William Hardcastle. By 1930, Snow was in London, and in 1836 he set up a practice in Soho. The following year he went to Westminster Hospital, where he became a member of both the Royal College of Surgeons (in 1838) and the Royal College of Physicians (in 1850). In late 1846, Snow became interested in developments in anaesthesia taking place in the USA (see pp.172–79). He took up this new speciality, designed new equipment, and published *On the Inhalation of the Vapour of Ether* in 1847. By 1853, his reputation as an anaesthetist was so good that he was asked to administer chloroform to Queen Victoria during the birth of her son Leopold.

Snow maintained his interest in epidemic diseases, especially cholera, and deliberated on the patterns of outbreaks he had experienced in northeast England, London, and other regions, and on factors such as overcrowding, hygiene awareness, the quality of food and drink, and general living conditions. From Snow's point of view, the evidence pointed not to "miasmatic air", but to something in the water, partly because cholera's initial symptoms were in the gut, rather than in the lungs or the blood. In 1849, the same year of another cholera outbreak, Snow published *On the Mode of Communication of Cholera*, in which he argued that cholera "is contained in the evacuations, and communicates the disease by being swallowed", principally through drinking water – but his work was largely ignored by the medical establishment.

During the summer of 1854, cholera flared up around London. The Soho outbreak was sudden and vicious, starting on August 31. Three days later, more than 100 people were dead, and after two weeks, the toll had exceeded 500. Hoping to prove that contaminated water was the cause, Snow identified the dwellings where people had died, and investigated the local street pumps that raised water from the wells. Much of the mortality was clustered around Broad Street and on questioning local residents, with the help of the Reverend Henry Whitehead, Snow learned that the water from the Broad Street water pump had been cloudy and smelling odd for several days. To stop the spread of the disease, Snow proposed removing the pump handle to prevent people from using the water. This was done, and the cholera cases subsided immediately. Snow conceded that the number may already have been falling, if only because so many

JOHN SNOW
British physician John Snow correctly deduced that cholera was transmitted through fluids, including drinking water.

MICROCOSM dedicated to the London Water Companies

MONSTER SOUP commonly called THAMES WATER, being a correct representation of that precious stuff doled out to us

"MONSTER SOUP"
This satirical engraving of 1828 shows a lady viewing
disease-riddled river water, but it was years before
people were convinced of the direct link between
polluted water and diseases such as cholera.

people had fled the area or died, but he plotted the locations of those who had died on a map, visually demonstrating the link between the deaths and the water pump.

Investigations eventually showed that the Broad Street well, which was 9m (30ft) deep, was very close to an old cesspit, and that leakage of contaminated excrement from this had polluted the water from the well. It was also discovered that those who had survived the disease had used water from their own wells – and that a family that died some distance away had relied on water from the Broad Street well. Nevertheless, once the outbreak had faded, very little changed in Soho. The pump handle was replaced, and a Board of Health report recorded: "In the general use of one particular well... at Broad Street... having (it was imagined) its waters contaminated... After careful inquiry we see no reason to adopt this belief". There were no public health changes of note.

In 1855, Snow published a hugely expanded, revised edition of *On the Mode of Communication of Cholera*, in which he noted: "Within 250 yards of the spot... there were upwards of 500 fatal attacks of cholera in 10 days… I suspected some contamination of the water of the much-frequented street-pump in Broad Street". However, his ideas continued to be ignored, and cholera continued its deadly attacks. The miasma theory prevailed, and was only questioned after it was challenged by the experiments of Louis Pasteur in the 1860s (see pp.196–203). Unfortunately, Snow had already died by then, from a stroke at the age of 45, shortly before the publication of his book *On Chloroform and Other Anaesthetics and Their Action and Administration*.

Snow's work, then, did not overturn the standard view of his day – despite its proof of the contrary – nor did Snow "invent" epidemiology as such. Other pioneers included Dane Peter Anton Scleisner, who reduced the incidence of newborn babies in Iceland dying of tetanus by introducing hygiene measures, and Hungarian Ignaz Semmelweis, who also brought down infant mortality rates, this time in Vienna, by bringing in disinfection methods. Back in England, Snow was a founding member of the Epidemiological Society of London, the establishment of which was first mooted after an earlier epidemic. The society's aims included "rigid examination into the causes and conditions which influence the origin, propagation, mitigation, and prevention of epidemic diseases". It was founded in 1850 and was subsumed into the Royal Society of Medicine in 1907. One of its primary tools was the study of death certificates and similar civic records, the use of which, for medical purposes, was pioneered by amateur scientist John Graunt in the 17th century. Historically, each parish was responsible for its own birth, death, and marriage records, but England and Wales introduced a nationwide information bank in 1837, thus enabling scientists to track mortality rates and disease trends more effectively. In the 19th century, many other countries established similar systems

"As great a benefactor in my opinion to the human race as has appeared in the present century"
REVEREND HENRY WHITEHEAD, ON JOHN SNOW

to help with social surveys, public health needs, and economic planning. These changes were of enormous help when epidemiologists began studying international trends in the spread of diseases. When the International Epidemiological Association held its inaugural meeting in Noordwijk, the Netherlands, in 1957, 20 nations were represented; today, it has members in more than 100 countries. In 1983, the Association stated: "The ultimate aim and purpose of epidemiology [is] to promote, protect, and restore good health".

The chief job of the epidemiologist is to compare health-related data between given groups of people, using numerical expressions such as "XXXX per YYYY people" to express the rates of occurrence of certain health conditions. These "raw" figures might be refined by making adjustments for factors such as gender, age, season, occupation, lifestyle factors such as smoking, and so on. Two major phenomena measured by such comparisons are incidence – the number of new cases of a condition or symptom per group during a specified time period – and prevalence – the total number of cases at a specific time. So if two people in 100,000 develop a condition each year, its incidence is two per 100,000. If this condition lasts for one year, its prevalence is also two per 100,000, but if it lasts for ten years (and does not cause death in this period), its prevalence is eventually 20 per 100,000. Such data analysis led to one of the 20th century's greatest medical advances – revealing the links between smoking tobacco, lung cancer, and other serious diseases. In the 1920s, German clinicians noted the increase in the incidence of lung cancer and investigated factors such as industrial air pollution, road asphalting, exposure to fuel with the spread of motor vehicles,

MARLBORO MAN
The "Marlboro Man" image was used to advertise Marlboro cigarettes from 1954 to 1999. Three of the men who modelled the figure over the years later died of lung cancer.

the influenza pandemic of 1918, and even exposure to gas warfare in World War I. In 1929, German physician Fritz Lickint, who invented the term "passive smoking", published epidemiological evidence that lung cancer patients were especially likely to be smokers, and advocated anti-tobacco measures. In 1939, a German survey by Franz Müller reported: "the extraordinary rise in tobacco use was the single most important cause of the rising incidence of lung cancer". By 1950, despite the best diversionary attempts of the tobacco industry, more statistical evidence had accumulated, and a British team led by Richard Doll and Austin Bradford Hill published results showing that the common factor among lung cancer patients was the inhalation of tobacco smoke. Doll worked tirelessly to raise the status of epidemiology, turning it from one of medicine's backwaters to one of its most vital branches.

By 1955, a huge US epidemiological study of almost 200,000 men, led by E. Cuyler Hammond and Daniel Horn, concluded that cigarette smoking increased the death rate overall, the lung cancer rate by ten times, and the death rate from coronary artery disease by a similar factor. The risks of smoking were exposed, an achievement that has saved millions from suffering and premature death.

John Snow was passionate about hygiene, sanitation, and public health measures, which figure greatly in epidemiology. He paved the way for the work of bacteriologists such as Russian-born Waldemar Haffkine, who introduced cholera vaccinations to India. Today, Snow would be astounded by the ease with which data can be collected, the immense analytical powers of computing, instant global communications, and fields such as evidence-based medicine (see p.383–84). Soho's Broad Street, with which he will always be associated, was renamed Broadwick Street in 1936, and in 1992, a memorial pump was installed near the site of the original – the place where, it could be said, epidemiology was born.

ANTI-CHOLERA INOCULATION
Waldemar Mordecai Wolff Haffkine inoculates
a community against cholera in Calcutta, India,
in 1894. One of epidemiology's first case-study
infections was cholera, and Haffkine pioneered
vaccines against both cholera and bubonic plague.

Florence Nightingale

NURSING TODAY IS THE ULTIMATE caring profession, but until the 19th century, nurses required neither skill nor training. Instead, their motivation ranged from fashionable fancy or family obligation to feelings of guilt or a religious vocation. Nursing tasks — such as cleaning or feeding a patient — were seen as a servant's role and traditionally took place in the home. As hospital treatment became more common, the need for better sanitary conditions and higher levels of care and training became apparent. Florence Nightingale was instrumental in bringing about these reforms.

Ancient references to nursing abound. Egyptian papyri mention temple attendants who cleansed patients and implemented regimes of diet and exercise. Greeks and Romans used terms such as "assistants", "caretakers", and "helpers". The Greek god of healing was Asclepius, whose daughters Hygieia (meaning "health") and Panacea (meaning "all-healing") were worshipped for their caring attitudes to the sick (see p.32). Nursing and religion were closely intertwined, and the earliest hospitals were established by religious institutions. Towards the end of the 4th century, the noble Roman matron Fabiola converted to Christianity and used her family riches to establish a hospital for all-comers in Rome. There, she cared for patients, working alongside male physicians. Similarly, at the Hôtel Dieu (hospital) in Lyons, France, which was set up in around 542, both men and women tended to patients' daily needs. The Hôtel Dieu in Paris was founded about a century later, staffed by one of the first Christian orders created specifically to provide nursing care — the Augustinian Sisters. But it

NURSE FLORENCE
Florence Nightingale eschewed marriage and children to dedicate her life to nursing. She founded the first formal nursing training school.

was men, especially the Benedictine monks, who dominated nursing in the European Middle Ages. The Crusades saw the arrival of first aid and post-emergency nursing care for the battle-wounded (see pp.356–57).

Elsewhere in the world, nursing skills flourished. Dating from about 2,500 years ago, the Sanskrit text *Susruta Samhita* (see pp.77–78) recounts: "... The physician, the patient, the drugs and the nurse are four feet of... the medicine, upon which cure depends". In 7th-century Islamic hospitals, known as bimaristans, teams of staff included physicians, nurses, porters, and cleaners. Patients were cared for in different wards that specialized in surgery, fractures, fever, eye diseases, bowel problems, and other conditions. One of the first female nurses of this era was Rofaidah, the daughter of a physician, who was praised for her empathy, clinical skills, kindness, and her ability to organize and inspire others. Back in Europe, the Protestant Reformation of the 16th century saw many European nations break with the Roman Catholic Church. Through the ensuing conflicts, the Catholic caring orders went into decline. In England especially, conditions in hospitals – many attached to now-closed monasteries and convents – worsened. Standards of hygiene and sanitation declined, and nursing skills faded. Matters had degenerated further by the mid- to late 18th century, as the Industrial Revolution created overcrowding in already unsanitary cities.

Against this backdrop of industrial grime and disease, Florence Nightingale was born into a wealthy English family in 1820, and named after the Italian city of her birth. The Nightingales returned to England the following year. Blessed with money and connections, Florence grew into an independent, strongly religious young woman. She relished learning and was especially adept at mathematics; she was also a talented writer. In 1837, Nightingale had the first of several religious experiences that would guide her life and work. She began to show an interest in nursing, citing the example of the Catholic nuns who helped others in hospitals. Several years later, despite eligible suitors, she announced her decision not to marry and have children. Instead, she pursued her new interest, reading widely about hospitals, nursing, medicine, hygiene, and sanitation. She gained some practical experience in hospitals and convalescent homes, and even travelled to Egypt to spend time with the Sisters of Charity of St Vincent de Paul in Alexandria – an offshoot of the original Sisters of Charity community, which had been established in Paris in 1633. Rather than remain in convents, the sisters visited the sick in their homes. Nightingale was impressed by

LADY WITH THE LAMP
Florence Nightingale in the military hospital at Scutari, where she gained an almost saintly reputation for her efforts to improve care.

"... the very first requirement in a hospital [is] that it should do the sick no harm"

FLORENCE NIGHTINGALE

their nursing work and high standards of care, compared with their lax, ill-educated English counterparts. In 1851, she enrolled on a three-month nursing training course at a Protestant deaconry in Kaiserwerth, near Düsseldorf, Germany. Founded by Pastor Theodor Fliedner, the course was run by deaconesses, and followed the Catholic tradition of helping the sick, poor, and children, as well as prisoners and ex-prisoners. Deaconesses had been around for centuries; the Bible describes Phoebe, who offered care, food, and medicine as an early visiting nurse. As well as providing care, the deaconesses of Kaiserworth encouraged self-reliance and female emancipation through teaching and mentoring. Greatly struck by her experience in Germany, Nightingale returned to England, and in 1953, took her first post as the superintendent of the Establishment for Gentlewomen During Illness on Harley Street, London. By now, she was already becoming an acknowledged authority on hospitals and nursing.

As Nightingale settled into her new role, the Crimean War began. Russia threatened Turkey, and France and England sent armies to assist the Turks. The main battles took place on the Crimean Peninsula (now part of Ukraine). Reports of the war's progress arrived in record time via the relatively new telegraph; war photography was another recent feature that enabled the public to connect closely with the unfolding drama. Nightingale read about the horrific conditions in the hospitals for the war-wounded, and was eager to do something to help. Secretary of State at War and close friend Sidney Herbert asked her to prepare a group of nurses. In November 1854, Nightingale and her 38 female charges arrived at Scutari's Selimiye Barracks Hospital (today part of Istanbul) in Turkey. Conditions there were even more terrible than anticipated. Aside from patients, almost everything was in short supply: "There were no vessels for water or utensils of any kind; no soap, towels, or clothes, no hospital clothes; the men lying in their uniforms, stiff with gore and covered with filth to a degree and of a kind no one could write about; their persons covered with vermin..." Nightingale set about restructuring the facilities and improving food and water supplies. She reorganized the orderlies (assistants) and demanded more, and better, equipment. Using her contacts in England, she summoned the Sanitary Commission, who arrived the following spring to clear sewers and upgrade general hygiene. She also campaigned for better nutrition, recognizing the importance of a healthy diet. Death rates at Scutari dropped. By how much, how quickly, and why, has been much disputed since; Nightingale herself never claimed any special responsibility. Nevertheless, back in England, the public followed *The Times* reports of her tireless dedication: "When all the medical officers have retired for the night and silence and darkness have settled... she may be observed alone, with a little lamp in her hand, making her solitary rounds". She thus acquired her title of the "Lady with the Lamp".

When the Crimean War ended in 1856, Nightingale arrived home, and soon after petitioned Queen Victoria to prioritize military hospital reforms. Determined to prevent the return of such appalling conditions, she used her skills with statistics to convince the authorities of the importance of cleanliness in avoiding infection. She invented a mathematical chart, similar to a modern pie chart, to compare how soldiers had died – whether from wounds, preventable diseases, or other causes. Nightingale lived quietly and wrote prodigiously, and her accounts of the Crimea in *Notes on Matters affecting the Health, Efficiency and Hospital Administration of the British Army* (1858) were instrumental in bringing about better sanitation, updated nutrition, and overall improved care in military hospitals. Her talents were applied elsewhere, too: news of the Indian Mutiny drew her attention to conditions for the British troops there, and to the poverty and malnutrition suffered by local people. Nightingale was able to use her influence to convince the government of India to establish a sanitary department. In 1859, she published her famous work *Notes on Nursing*: "It is recognized as the knowledge which every one ought to have – distinct from medical knowledge, which only a profession can have". The following year, she founded the Nightingale Training School and Home For Nurses at St Thomas's Hospital, London. The school established nursing as a formal occupation, with proper training, accreditation, career progression, and payment. Teaching methods were theoretical and practical, records were kept of student progress, and the carefully selected students would reside in nurses' houses designed to "encourage discipline" and "form character".

Nightingale campaigned tirelessly, writing thousands of letters over the years despite being hampered by her own health. In 1855, on a visit to the Crimea, she had contracted a 12-day illness, known as Crimea fever, that was to cause periods of disability and bed rest throughout the rest of her life. But Nightingale was not alone in her efforts to improve levels of care and sanitation. Mary Seacole was a Crimean War contemporary, who went to the Crimea in 1855. There, she set up the British Hotel near Balaklava, offering care, food, and rooms to wounded European Allies soldiers, albeit on a commercial basis. Although she did not have the impact of Nightingale with regard to the formal nursing system, she gained a reputation for her nursing prowess and bravery in visiting battlefields, along with the nickname "Mother" Seacole.

In line with the medical establishment at the time, Nightingale's attitudes to medical progress were conservative. She was wary of the germ theory of disease (see pp.222–27), but even so, in Quain's Medical Dictionary of 1882, she advised: "Always have chlorinated soda for nurses to wash their hands, especially after dressing or handling a suspicious case. It may destroy germs at the expense of the cuticle, but if it takes off the cuticle, it must be bad for the germs".

Florence Nightingale's ceaseless work launched the nursing principles and practices of today. Her long career inspired many others to establish professional nursing schools, and she was the first woman to be awarded an Order of Merit, in 1907. Her name lives on in the form of many Nightingale nursing colleges and organizations, and in various awards. Each year, International Nurses' Day is celebrated on her birthday – 12 May. Yet in life, Nightingale was ever reluctant to seek recognition or appear in public, and her burial was a quiet family affair in Hampshire.

MARY SEACOLE
Half-Jamaican nurse Mary Seacole was also influential in improving conditions for wounded soldiers.

Measuring Blood Pressure

Blood pressure is the pressure that is exerted on the artery walls by circulating blood, and it is measured using instruments and the pulse to help diagnose a patient's health. High blood pressure (hypertension) results from a high volume of blood or narrowing of the arteries, and can be caused by lack of exercise, alcoholism, high salt intake, and other factors. It puts stress on the heart and arteries, and can increase the risk of strokes, heart attacks, kidney disorders, and other diseases. Low blood pressure (hypotension) can be caused by age, illness, or blood loss, and may result in dizzyness, fainting, and, in extreme cases, shock. Both conditions can also be hereditary. Blood pressure varies during each heartbeat, and so is measured as a range (see opposite).

Pulse and pressure in history

For thousands of years, physicians have used the pulse as a diagnostic tool. The Ancient Egyptians took simple pulse readings, and ancient cultures from China to Greece theorized about its strength, rhythm, and quality. Blood pressure was discovered in 1733 by clergyman Stephen Hales, who inserted tubes into animals' arteries and measured how far the blood rose. From the 19th century, measuring devices arrived that used a cuff and did not break the skin, such as the tonoscillograph and the sphygmomanometer (see opposite).

CHINESE PULSE
DIAGNOSIS CHART,
LATE 17TH CENTURY

The cuff fits around the patient's arm. It incorporates a valve, so that the physician can let out the air during use

TONOSCILLOGRAPH
BRITAIN, 1931–40

Hungarian scientist and doctor Janos Plesch, a friend and physician of Albert Einstein, developed the tonoscillograph, which was widely used during the 1930s. Featuring an inflatable cuff, it was a precursor of the instruments in use today. It was easy to use and produced a record in graph form.

How it works

Blood pressure is measured at its highest (systolic) and lowest (diastolic) points, today with a sphygmomanometer (blood pressure gauge). An inflatable cuff is fitted around the upper arm, and a listening device called a stethoscope (invented by René Laennec in 1816) is placed below the cuff. The inflated cuff closes the artery and stops blood flow. Listening through the stethoscope, the physician slowly deflates the cuff, noting the first sounds as the artery opens under systolic pressure, and when blood flows freely under diastolic pressure.

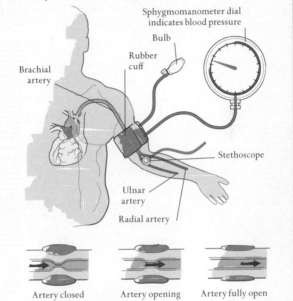

Sphygmomanometer dial indicates blood pressure

Bulb

Rubber cuff

Brachial artery

Stethoscope

Ulnar artery

Radial artery

Artery closed   Artery opening   Artery fully open

The patient's blood pressure is recorded on a removable graph, known as a tonoscillogram

The device contains a mechanism to measure pressure that works like a barometer: changes in pressure make a metal cell expand or contract, and levers transmit these movements to the dial

The bulb is used to inflate the cuff with air, to stop the blood flow temporarily in the patient's artery

Pasteur and Microbiology

GERMS ARE INVISIBLE ENEMIES. These miniature life forms can harm the human body and other living things, but they are so small that they can only be seen under a microscope. Not just any old micro-organisms or microbes, germs are pathogenic – they multiply in the body and cause infectious diseases or infections. In the 17th century, early light microscopes (see pp.150–51) revealed multiple microbes of countless kinds. But it wasn't until the 19th century that these miniscule invaders were shown to cause illness, leading to the germ theory of disease. French scientist Louis Pasteur's extraordinary achievements were pivotal to this development, as were those of German scientist Robert Koch (see pp.222–27).

For centuries, infectious diseases and other ill health were blamed on a variety of causes, which included revenge from angry gods or a sinful existence. Two major theories prevailed. The first, miasma, was a general notion that foul, poisoned air somehow spread diseases. The idea was not wholly ridiculous – nasty smells from soil or water polluted with decaying matter and excrement invariably accompanied cholera, dysentery, and similar diseases. In Ancient Greece, Hippocrates considered noxious air akin to pestilence. Similarly, Vitruvius, a Roman architect and engineer from the 1st century BCE, mused on the harmful effects of nostril-wrinkling air from sources such as swamps, stagnant water, and sewers. Two centuries later, Galen linked bad air and disease with his concept of humours (see p.43). Galen's popular theories persisted through the Middle Ages, and were adapted to explain pandemics such as those of smallpox and bubonic plague. The toxic gases that were thought to spread disease became known as miasms. Air was supposedly

LOUIS PASTEUR
Together with his long-term rival, German physician and scientist Robert Koch, Pasteur is considered a founding father of microbiology.

charged with an "epidemic influence", and when this encountered emissions of decay, it was believed to turn into malignant miasms that led to disease. Restless minds in Renaissance Europe began to probe the mystery. In the 1540s, Italian physician and scientist Girolamo Fracastoro suggested that minute particles – spores – might be responsible. A century later, the microscopes of Antoni van Leeuwenhoek and others revealed "animalcules" (see p.145). In 1700, French practitioner Nicolas Andry recorded his observations of tiny, wriggling "worms", which he thought might cause disease. Some of these worms were known parasites, such as tapeworms. Others, which Andry suspected might cause venereal disease, were actually sperm cells, or spermatozoa. A keen proponent of the miasma theory, he suggested that bad air might contain "seeds of worms".

The second theory was first recorded by Aristotle in Ancient Greece. He believed in spontaneous generation or abiogenesis, in which living matter could arise from non-living ingredients due to some manner of "life-force". It seemed a sensible explanation for mould that suddenly sprouted on old bread, maggots that seemingly appeared from nowhere on rotting meat, and infestations of lice and fleas where there had been none. As new microscope technology revealed more about microbes, existing theories were questioned by sceptical scientists seeking evidence. In 1668, Italian naturalist-physician Francesco Redi described his experiments with jars containing old meat. He left some jars open, covered some with close-mesh cloth, and stoppered others with cork. Redi noted that maggots appeared in the meat only if flies could actually land on it; therefore, maggots were not arising spontaneously from the dead meat. At the time, however, belief in spontaneous generation was so widespread that Redi's work made little headway. In the mid-18th century, English priest and biologist John Needham tried a different approach, first boiling chicken broth to destroy any life, then sealing it from air. The broth became cloudy, which Needham attributed to spontaneous generation of microbes. He claimed that "vital atoms" harboured the quality of life, permeated the natural world, and animated their surroundings to create life. In retrospect, it is likely that Needham's boiling time did not destroy all of the microbes in the broth, and that flies may have landed on the broth and contaminated it as it cooled in the open air. Another priest, Italian Lazzaro Spallanzani, took Needham's experiments further in the 1760s. He boiled the broth for longer, and ensured that it was then sealed quickly and securely in glass phials. The sealed broth samples remained intact and uncontaminated, whereas those open to air soon swarmed with small life. Clinging to the belief in spontaneous generation, opponents countered that such severe treatment destroyed Needham's "vital atoms", which needed contact with air for their gift of life.

A disease affecting silkworms (silk moth caterpillars) that spread through Europe in the early 19th century piqued the interest of Italian insect expert Agostino Bassi. He embarked on a laborious series of experiments, eventually concluding in 1835 that the disease was caused by some kind of contagion or transmissible particle – a microbial life form, spread as powdery spores by contact or close proximity. Ten years later, he postulated that microbes could act as disease agents in humans, too. Bassi's work provided early sound evidence of contagion as a cause of disease, and the fungus that attacked the silkworms was later named *Beauveria bassiana* in his honour. By now, he was far from alone. In Germany, rising star in anatomy and histology Friedrich Gustav Jacob Henle penned an article supporting the contagium vivum ("living germ") proposal: "The material of contagions is not only an organic but a living one... [it] is, in relation to the diseased body, a parasitic organism". Two other significant advances helped the contagion cause. In Vienna, obstetrician Ignaz Semmelweis reasoned in 1847 that "cadaverous particles" carried by doctors and medical students were the cause of an unusually high incidence of puerperal fever (see p.220). Seven years later, in London, John Snow carried out his celebrated removal of a water pump handle during a cholera outbreak, suspecting that contagions were at work (see pp.180–87). The contagion or germ theory of disease gained ground, but even so, the concept of miasma still held sway in 1860s Europe. Miasma appeared to explain, for example, why cholera was so prevalent in cities with crowded, deprived neighbourhoods, and poor hygiene and public health. According to this theory, the foul air, reeking of decay and human waste, was highly charged with miasms, so more people succumbed to the disease.

France was one of many countries across Europe and Asia that suffered regular cholera outbreaks; the disease raced through Paris in 1832 and again in 1849. Enter Louis Pasteur, future giant among microbiologists. Born in Dole, eastern France, in 1822, Pasteur gained his bachelor's

CLOUD OF CHOLERA
The belief in miasma – that diseases were spread by
"bad" air – was so strong in the 19th century that
germ theorists struggled to make themselves heard.

degree at the regional Royal College of Besançon. It was not until 1843,
however, when he was admitted to the prestigious École Normale
Supérieure in Paris, that Pasteur's aptitude for chemistry was
acknowledged as more than mediocre. He graduated and became a
chemistry assistant, then briefly taught physics in Dijon before
becoming professor of chemistry at the University of Strasbourg.
Having married Marie Laurent in 1849, Pasteur moved with his family
in 1854 to Lille, where he was appointed professor of chemistry and
dean of the science faculty. Two years later, he returned to his old
school in Paris, taking on the role of director of scientific studies. From
his base in the capital, Pasteur's reputation soared. He had high
standards and a hawk-like eye for detail, which he applied with great
success to diverse problems within the fields of livestock farming,
veterinary science, and human health and medicine, among others.

Pasteur's work evolved through several main phases, beginning
with research on how light passes through different shapes and
arrangements of crystals. By the mid-1850s, his interests had turned
to fermentation and why liquids go sour. During his time at Lille, he
was asked to investigate beer spoilage, with a view to saving the

"Never will the doctrine of spontaneous generation recover from the mortal blow struck by this simple experiment"

LOUIS PASTEUR

brewing industry huge losses. Working with wine and beer, Pasteur demonstrated that, contrary to popular belief, fermentation was not a purely chemical process, but involved microbial forms of life. He also noted that a particular sort of microbe – rounded yeasts – had to be present in normal fermented beer. Samples of sour beer contained the wrong sort of microbe. In 1859, recalling the work of Needham and Spallanzani, Pasteur carried out a decisive set of experiments, using boiled meaty broth and glass flasks that were variously sealed or open to air, like his predecessors. Some of Pasteur's flasks had extended, downward-curving necks, which allowed air to flow in and out, but kept out airborne dust and passing contagion particles. The broth in these flasks stayed uncontaminated for longest. In flasks with the neck bent up to allow potentially contaminating particles to enter, the broth developed moulds much sooner. These results, from such a respected scientist, dealt a huge blow to supporters of spontaneous generation, bolstered the case for germ theory, and furthered the argument that contaminating particles might cause human diseases. Pasteur went on to work with acclaimed French physiologist Claude Bernard in the early 1860s, and between them they devised an answer to the drink spoilage problem: heat to kill the contaminators without altering the product's flavour. This form of heat treatment is now known universally as pasteurization.

From about 1865 to 1871, Pasteur also researched silkworm diseases. In an echo of Bassi's earlier work, described above, Pasteur showed that the diseases were caused by microbes (one later established as fungal, the other viral), and thereby helped to revive the French silk industry. Emperor Napoleon III offered his grateful thanks to Pasteur for his contributions to the drink and silkworm industries, which enhanced Pasteur's escalating reputation still further.

By the 1870s, Pasteur had developed an interest in vaccination. This was already widely practised for smallpox (see pp.152–61), but Pasteur's ambition was to find vaccinations for other human and livestock diseases, especially cholera and anthrax. He assembled a team that included promising young physicians Emile Roux and Charles Chamberland, and carried out tests on fowl cholera – the form that affected chickens, turkeys, and similar birds. Roux went on to work on diphtheria, while Chamberland invented a filter to trap bacteria from a solution. Both later worked at the Institut Pasteur, which was founded by Pasteur in 1887. Pasteur and his team cultured – purified and grew in the laboratory – the germ that causes fowl cholera, a bacterium since named *Pasteurella multocida*. The cultivated germs were used to give chickens the disease, so that different vaccination techniques could be tested.

In 1879, partly as a result of Chamberland's forgetfulness, one batch of these microbes failed to thrive as normal. They produced only mild symptoms in the birds, which then, unusually, recovered. Puzzled by this, Pasteur inoculated these same chickens with a full-strength bacterial preparation. The birds did not develop fowl cholera. He suspected that the strange culture consisted of germs that had somehow become weakened or attenuated. Normally, the batches were not exposed to air, but the forgotten culture had been. Did this weaken them? To test his theory, Pasteur grew some new cholera microbe cultures. Some were exposed to air, while others were sealed in tubes, where the oxygen was rapidly used up. Pasteur then tested their virulence by inoculating chickens to see how many of them became ill and died. The results were conclusive: "Remarkably, the experiment shows that the virulence under these conditions [with no oxygen] is always the same as that which was used to inoculate the original closed tubes [the full-

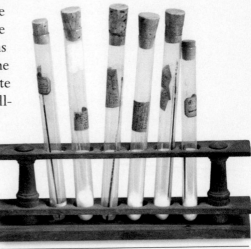

BLOOD BANK
These test tubes from the museum at the Institut Pasteur in Paris, France, contain samples of blood from hens that died as a result of being inoculated with fowl cholera.

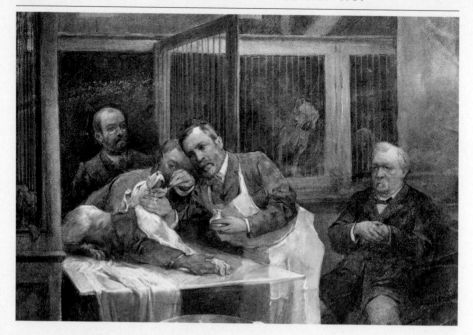

FOAMING AT THE MOUTH
Knowing that rabies is transmitted by saliva, Pasteur
investigated the disease further by taking samples of
foam from the mouth of a rabid dog.

strength microbes from the first set of experiments]. Meanwhile, the
cultures which have been exposed to air are either dead or possess a
very weak virulence… Our problem is therefore solved: it is the oxygen
which brings about the attenuation in virulence". Pasteur had
succeeded in producing an artificially weakened strain of an infectious
microbe that could be used for vaccination. This differed from the
smallpox vaccine, which was a naturally occurring version. Poultry
farmers were grateful, the discovery stimulated much research into
other diseases, and vaccines for human cholera arrived by 1900.

Around the same time, Pasteur was also investigating anthrax, a
serious disease of cattle, sheep, other livestock, and wild animals that
can also be deadly in humans. The causative *Bacillus anthracis* had already
been isolated and identified in the mid-1870s by Pasteur's rival Robert
Koch (see pp.222–27). Working from several farms, Pasteur adopted the
approach he had taken for chicken cholera, developing a weakened
strain to use in a vaccine against the full-strength version. In 1881, he
carried out a trial at a farm at Pouilly-le-Fort near Melun, southeast of
Paris. He used two groups of livestock, each containing 25 sheep, along
with a few cows and goats. Each animal in the first group was given

two inoculations of the new anthrax vaccine, 15 days apart. The animals in the other group received none. Fifteen days after the second inoculation, the animals from both groups received a dose of live anthrax bacteria. The results were startlingly clear. All of the vaccinated stock survived – they "frolicked and gave signs of perfect health". The rest of the animals died within two days. Doubters of vaccination were deflated, as were supporters of spontaneous generation and miasma. Farming quickly benefitted, although a human vaccine for anthrax did not become available until 1954.

The final main phase of Pasteur's vaccination work focused on the dreaded disease of rabies (see pp.204–05). Rabies is best known for afflicting dogs, but any warm-blooded animal can be infected and it can be passed on to humans if they are bitten. Pasteur studied writings on rabies by Girolamo Fracastoro, mentioned earlier, and by German scientist Georg Gottfried Zinke, who, in 1804, proved that rabies is transmitted by saliva. The rabies microbe – a type of virus – affects the nervous system, especially the central nervous system (the brain and spinal cord). Pasteur's colleague Roux developed a method of producing vaccine by infecting rabbits, and then dissecting out and drying the spinal cord to weaken and kill the microbes. By 1885, the vaccine was being tested on dogs. That same year, nine-year-old Joseph Meister was mauled by a rabid dog. Desperate for help, his mother took him to Pasteur. Rabies was so feared at the time that some people committed suicide after rabid dog bites rather than endure the agony. Pasteur considered the situation and consulted others: "The opinion of our wise colleague and of Dr Grancher was that by the intensity and the number of bites, Joseph Meister was almost inevitably to come down with rabies". Despite not being qualified to treat humans and risking the wrath of the authorities, Pasteur administered the vaccine. Joseph did not develop rabies, so the vaccine was assumed to be successful. Trials proceeded rapidly, and Pasteur's reputation ascended to new heights.

Joseph Meister later became caretaker at the Institut Pasteur in Paris. This world-renowned institution has led the way in medical research against infectious diseases and is a lasting tribute to the great man's achievements.

The Horror of Rabies

Rabies is a dangerous viral disease that inflames the brain, producing a hideous range of advanced symptoms, from thrashing out and biting to phobias and hallucinations. It is fatal if the patient is not swiftly vaccinated. Rabies can be passed between species, and humans often catch it from the bite of an infected dog; the disease was untreatable until the first human vaccine in the late 19th century. Vaccines are now also available to prevent the disease in animals, but 55,000 people die from rabies globally every year.

VIAL OF RABIES VACCINE

1548 Italian physician Girolamo Fracastoro attributes rabies **transmission** to a substance in the sufferer's saliva. Fracastoro also named the virus after the Latin word for "rage"; both human and animal victims slather at the mouth and act aggressively.

1885 Pasteur and Roux produce a rabies vaccine; several hundred patients are successfully **vaccinated** within the year.

1271 Thirty people are killed by an outbreak of rabies in Germany, after **infected wolves** invade a village.

1804 German scientist Georg Gottfried Zinke **injects animals** with rabies, proving that the disease is infectious.

1884 Pasteur and Roux describe how rabies is found in the **spinal cord** and brain.

1881 French scientists **Louis Pasteur** and Emile Roux begin research on rabies.

1793 Physician Samuel Argent Bardsley proposes a **quarantine** system in the UK for isolating animals and eradicating infection, but this idea is not implemented.

1881 French professor Pierre-Victor Galtier injects sheep with rabies-carrying saliva; this seems to make them **immune** from further infection.

1883 Emile Roux publishes a paper on his and Pasteur's **research**.

MORTALITY RATE FOR UNVACCINATED PATIENTS DIAGNOSED WITH RABIES

100%

1936 Leslie Webster and Anna Clow grow the rabies virus in the lab; it has a distinctive **bullet-like** shape.

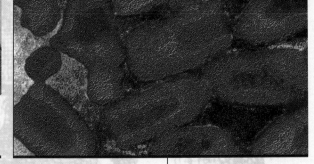

1970S–80S European authorities use **oral vaccination** via food left for foxes to control high numbers of rabid animals.

1902 The UK is declared **free of rabies**, although there have since been isolated cases.

1976 The HDCV vaccine is licensed in Europe; it requires a shorter course of **injections** than previous vaccines.

2008 Germany is declared **free of rabies** by the World Organization for Animal Health.

1932 Dr Russ Pfister discovers rabies in **vampire bats**.

1979 Scientists in the Philippines produce a **vaccine for dogs** that gets rid of rabies in parts of the country.

1955 Vaccinating dogs against rabies becomes a **legal requirement** in nearly all parts of the USA.

1967 The highly effective **human diploid cell** vaccine for rabies is developed.

2009 A total of **67 countries** report no cases of rabies within the previous 12 months.

1984 The **VR-G vaccine**, which can be given to animals orally, is developed at the Wistar Institute in the US.

Lister and Antiseptics

"OPERATION SUCCESSFUL, PATIENT DIED" was a common entry in 19th-century hospital records. The revolution in medical anaesthesia in the 1840s meant that surgeons no longer had to struggle with victims writhing in agony, or work in double-quick time to minimize the torment (see pp.172–77), and with their patients at rest and insensible, surgeons could explore new procedures using greater care and caution. Yet even in the best hospitals, many patients still died soon afterwards, usually from infection.

By the mid-1860s, the germ theory of disease had started to infiltrate medicine, thanks to the work of Louis Pasteur (see pp.196–203). John Snow's insight into the London cholera epidemic a decade earlier (see pp.180–87) contributed, as did the experience of Ignaz Semmelweis with puerperal fever in 1840s Vienna (see p.220). Even so, it took a long time for the idea to be widely accepted. Traditional theories had held sway for centuries: these included miasma, in which some kind of malignant chemical quality in foul air set off disease; and spontaneous generation, in which parasites and pestilence arose from inanimate matter (see pp.196–98). The medical establishment, notoriously suspicious of even slight change, took a cautious stance. Some surgeons still did not accept the advantages of anaesthesia, insisting that pain was integral to treatment and recovery. They argued that circumventing pain with anaesthesia, or even the anaesthetic agents themselves, could lead to problems such as post-surgical festering wounds, oozing pus, or the rotting flesh of hospital gangrene. Blood poisoning or general sepsis (from the Greek for putrefaction) was the end-stage of infection, with a range of effects including widespread inflammation, blood clotting, and eventual organ failure. With such a high mortality rate from post-surgical infection, something had to change.

JOSEPH LISTER
Lister worked hard to banish filth from operating theatres and destroy the germs responsible for high post-operative death rates.

British surgeon Joseph Lister revolutionized surgery and immeasurably improved patients' fortunes by demonstrating that infecting microbes could be tackled by germ-destroying substances called antiseptics.

Joseph Lister gained his early medical qualifications in 1852 at University Hospital, London, becoming a Fellow of the Royal College of Surgeons. In 1853, he moved to Edinburgh, and the following year began working with celebrated surgeon and medical reformer James Syme, whose daughter Lister later married. Guided by Syme's pioneering spirit, Lister was a keen researcher, studying and writing reports on muscle action, blood coagulation (clotting), and inflammation. He was appointed Regius Professor of Surgery at the University of Glasgow in 1860, and started to practise at the attached Glasgow Royal Infirmary. Today's onlookers would be horrified by a typical operating theatre of the time. Surgeons, nurses, and other staff took little or no notice of hygiene. Their hands, clothes – ordinary working ones – and instruments were rarely cleaned before, after, or between patients. In the recovery wards, seeping pus, the stench of gangrene, and the dreaded sepsis were commonplace. At the time, it was widely thought that oxygen in the air had a direct chemical effect on exposed flesh, triggering gangrene. The solution was to dress and bind the area tightly to keep air out. This reduced blood flow to and oxygen levels in the tissues – ironically, conditions that gangrene-causing microbes loved. Keen to make an impact on such a depressing situation, Lister tried a different approach. He began to keep himself clean in theatre, along with his attire and his instruments; he also used tourniquets to reduce blood loss and provide a clearer view of the operative area. Other surgeons smirked at Lister's efforts, and a few even openly ridiculed him, since blood and gore on their apparel was symbolic of their great status. Lister persevered; his measures began to yield results and his operating success rate crept up.

In the mid-1860s, a professor of chemistry at Glasgow University, Thomas Anderson, showed Pasteur's work to Lister, suggesting how microbes might be responsible for hospital gangrene and other infections. Lister also learned of Semmelweis's campaign for cleanliness to foil puerperal fever. He conjectured: "... Decomposition of the injured part might be avoided... by applying in a dressing some material capable of destroying the life of the floating particles". Pasteur had identified three measures against spoilage organisms: filters, heat, and chemicals. Lister, ever keen to help his patients and boost his own success rate, began looking round for an appropriate chemical substance to experiment with. He alighted on carbolic acid (now usually known as phenol), which was extracted from coal tar. First produced in the 1830s, carbolic acid had already found various uses as a preservative, and in neutralizing effluent in sewers. Its powerful and distinctive smell, sweet and tarry, was intended to destroy the foul disease-causing vapours known as miasms. Lister recalled: "In the course of the year 1864 I was much struck with an account of the remarkable effects produced by carbolic acid upon the sewage of the town of Carlisle [North-West England]... Not only preventing all odour from the lands irrigated with refuse material, but as is stated destroying the entozoa [worms and similar parasites] which usually infest cattle fed upon such pastures... I saw that such a powerful antiseptic was peculiarly adapted for experiments... The applicability of carbolic acid for the treatment of compound fracture [see below] naturally occurred to me". Lister researched carbolic acid's effects on human skin and flesh, obtained supplies from Anderson, and carried out preliminary trials. Encouraged by the results, he began to use carbolic acid liquid before, during, and after surgery, for cleaning his hands and instruments, and for soaking bandages.

An accident on 12 August 1865 brought 11-year-old James Greenlees into Glasgow Royal Infirmary. Injured by a cart, he had sustained a compound fracture of the left tibia (shin bone). In a compound or open fracture, not only is bone broken, but also skin, allowing in dirt, germs, and other contaminants. In Lister's time, such injuries usually progressed via sepsis to death, unless the limb was amputated – another risk-ridden procedure. Lister himself cleaned the break and wound, dressed it with lint soaked in carbolic acid solution, and splinted the leg. Every few days, he repeated the cleaning and dressing process. In six weeks, against all odds, James was infection-free, and able to walk on two good legs. Following this triumph, Lister decreed that all surgery under his supervision should follow the new procedures involving carbolic acid. Meanwhile, he

CHANCES OF SURVIVING SURGERY BEFORE ANTISEPTICS ARRIVED

50%

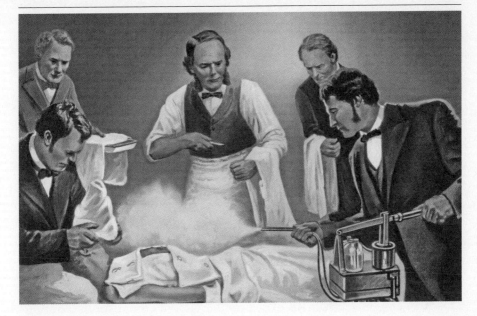

SPRAY CLEAN
Lister invented a machine for killing airborne germs
with a fine mist of carbolic acid. He would direct the
distribution of the spray before an operation.

continued to search for improvements. Neat, crude carbolic acid caused
problems such as skin irritation and sloughing, so he requested purer
forms, tested dilutions, and mixed them with other substances such as
linseed oil and carbonate of lime. Increasingly confident, he also began
to lecture and publish his results, summarizing his early methods in
Antiseptic Principle of the Practice of Surgery, which was published in
an edition of the *British Medical Journal* in 1867: "In conducting the
treatment, the first object must be the destruction of any septic germs
which may have been introduced into the wound... by introducing the
acid of full strength into all accessible recesses of the wound by means
of a piece of rag held in dressing-forceps and dipped in the liquid...
Limbs which otherwise would be unhesitatingly condemned to
amputation may be retained with confidence of the best results".
Mortalities from major surgery under Lister's supervision fell from
nearly 50 per cent to 15 per cent. Antiseptic methods were applied more
widely to contusions (bruising), lacerations, and abscesses.

In 1869, Lister returned to Edinburgh as Professor of Clinical
Surgery. Around this time, he devised a spray to kill floating
contaminants in the operating theatre – and cover everyone and
everything there with a fine mist of diluted carbolic acid.

FRENCH SPRAY MACHINE
Lister's techniques were promoted in France
by Just Marie Marcellin Lucas-Championnière,
who reinvented Lister's spray machine.

Lister's spray machines went through several incarnations: the first were laboriously hand- and foot-pumped – these were known as "donkey engines" – but, by 1871, they were steam-powered. These were later phased out when airborne contamination was found to be less of a risk than breathing in the carbolic spray. Some British surgeons remained unconvinced, even dismissive, and proposed other reasons for Lister's results – from better diet and nursing care to the local climate. They were reluctant to admit that their time-honoured practices could actually cause infection by transferring germs, or to alter their habits for little creatures they could not even see.

Antisepsis – the process of killing or inhibiting the growth of any germs present – was adopted faster and more enthusiastically in continental Europe, especially Germany, than England. As the germ theory of disease gradually became accepted, other antiseptics were tried in place of carbolic acid. Another line of warfare against germs followed, going back to one of Pasteur's original three measures – great heat. In 1879, Pasteur's assistant Charles Chamberland (see p.201) invented an oven-like device called the autoclave, which killed germs with high-pressure saturated steam. Seven years later, in Berlin, Latvian-born surgeon Ernst von Bergmann introduced steam sterilization for surgical instruments and dressings. He had previously adopted Lister's methods while a military surgeon, with great success. Von Bergmann's sterilization initiative marked a shift away from antisepsis to asepsis – in which there is a complete absence of germs. Along came the operating theatre's familiar white masks, gowns, and trays of sparkling, clean instruments.

Lister was not the first to use antiseptics – microbe-killers or inhibitors that can be applied to living tissues with relative safety. But he did formalize their use and demonstrate their efficacy in medicine. Disinfectants do much the same, but for inanimate objects such as instruments, beds, or floors. Since ancient times, some substances have filled both needs. Alcohol (ethanol) and vinegar were recorded in Ancient Greece, India, and China, while in Rome, Aulus Cornelius Celsus (see pp.111) used vinegar and thyme oil. For millennia, pitch or oils were poured on to open injuries or hurried amputations (see pp.126–31). Compounds of copper, silver, and mercury were also tried, although some of these proved rather toxic. Today, hand-sanitizers in many hospitals are based on alcohol or iodine. The latter, isolated in 1811, was incorporated into an iodine solution in 1829 by French physician Jean Guillaume Auguste Lugol. Lugol's iodine went on to become a widespread antiseptic, disinfectant, and cure-all for a great variety of health and hygiene problems.

The *British Medical Journal* finally acknowledged Lister's achievements in 1879: "… The man who has done the most to take the 'disgrace' out of surgery is Mr Lister". By this time, he was already Chair of Clinical Surgery at King's College, London, and Personal Surgeon in Ordinary to Queen Victoria. Royal approval was sealed when he had the privilege of lancing a large abscess in the queen's left armpit. She recorded: "… I bear pain so badly. I shall be given chloroform… The abscess, which was six inches in diameter, was very quickly cut… Mr Lister, whose great invention, a carbolic spray to destroy all organic germs, was used…" In 1883, Lister was made a baronet; in 1891, he co-founded and became chairman of the British Institute of Preventive Medicine (now called the Lister Institute of Preventive Medicine); and in 1897, he was the first surgeon to be made a baron for his medical achievements.

Lister may not have had exceptional surgical skills, nor did he have much of a sense of humour: medical students met with a muted response when they joked about his carbolic spray machine, saying before an operation, "Let us-s-pray". But however private and emotionally detached he may have been as a man, Lister's quest to rid the operating theatre of its septic legacy saved the lives of many patients, and secured his place in history.

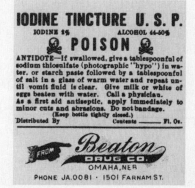

IODINE TINCTURE
Iodine, first incorporated into iodine solution in 1829, was one of the most widely used early antiseptics. It is still used in hospitals today.

SPOTLESS SURGERY
Despite initial scepticism, Lister's methods of using cleanliness to combat germs spread rapidly across Europe. This Austrian painting from about 1900 depicts the disinfection process in a hospital operating theatre of the time.

Mother and Baby Medicine

IN TODAY'S CONVENTIONAL MEDICINE, the central figures in the care of mothers and babies during the postnatal period are the obstetrician and the midwife. Obstetricians are qualified doctors who specialize in the medical care of pregnant women and new babies. Midwives are qualified professionals who provide care and advice that usually extends from mother and baby to partners and family, taking in emotional and social care in a more holistic and rounded way. In general, the midwife's role is to support and monitor women during a "normal" healthy pregnancy and birth; the obstetrician is there for women experiencing more difficult or complex problems, which may need more specialist intervention.

From the earliest times in Babylonia and Egypt, female birth attendants were depicted helping the new mother. Egyptian images from more than 2,500 years ago show mothers squatting or sitting to give birth, and midwives are described in the Ebers Papyrus (see pp.26–27). A prominent name in Ancient Greece, more than 2,300 years ago, was Agnodice (see p.164), although it is unclear whether she was mythical. At the time, women were allowed to treat other women during pregnancy and birth, but could do little else in medicine. It is said that Agnodice cut her hair and dressed as a man to qualify as a general physician. As recounted by Gaius Julius Hyginus three centuries later: "She heard a woman crying out in the throes of labour so she went to her assistance. The woman, thinking she

AGNODICE REVEALED
Agnodice shows herself to be a woman after years pretending to be a man in order to practice medicine.

was a man, refused her help; but Agnodice lifted up her clothes and revealed herself to be a woman and was thus able to treat her patient". Female patients learned to ask for "him" by name, which made doctors suspicious. Angered by accusations, Agnodice finally came clean by raising her robes in public. She was accused of deception and condemned to death, but patients' lobbying brought her pardon, and women were then allowed to practise medicine more widely.

In the 1st century CE, Greek physician Soranus of Ephesus wrote *Gynaikeia* (*Gynaecology*), which contained a great deal of detail on obstetrics and midwifery. He described the difficulties of breech presentation, in which the baby is positioned to exit the womb bottom- or feet- first, and showed how a baby can be "turned" by manipulating it inside the womb. He recommended that the midwife sat in front of the mother on her birthing chair, ready to receive the baby, with bandages, oils, and herbs at the ready. She would encourage the baby to breathe, cut the cord, and sprinkle the stump with healing substances, and then check and clean the infant so that it was ready to present to the mother – some of which are classic midwifery procedures still practised today. Parts of Soranus' *Gynaikeia* were adapted in the 6th century by an author named Muscio (Mustio), and were again recycled in the 16th century by Eucharius Rösslin (also known as Rhodion; see below).

One of the oldest known surgical procedures is Caesarean section – the delivery of a baby through an incision in the mother's abdominal wall and womb. In Greek mythology, the sun god Apollo removed Asclepius, the god of healing and medicine, in this way. The name is popularly believed to originate from the birth of Roman Emperor Julius Caesar by this method – however, in Roman times, the operation was usually performed to save the baby when the mother was dead or dying, yet Julius's mother, Aurelia, lived. It is more likely that the name comes from the Latin word *caedare*, meaning "to cut". In 1598, influential French royal surgeon Jacques Guillemeau published a work on midwifery in which he used the term Caesarean "section" rather than "operation", which then passed into common usage.

In East Asia, around 850, Chinese physician Zan Yin compiled the 52-chapter *Jing Xiao Chan Bao* (*Treasured Knowledge of Obstetrics*, or *Tested Prescriptions in Obstetrics*). The first major Chinese work on gynaecology and obstetrics, it incorporated many aspects of Chinese traditional medicine, such as the conditioning of qi energy (see pp.64–73), as well as more than 300 herbal formulas and prescriptions. Zan Yin covered

ANATOMICAL MODEL
This ivory model of a pregnant woman
with removable parts, of a type common in
17th-century Europe, was used by midwives
to educate women about giving birth.

miscarriage, excessive bleeding, hyperemesis
gravidarum (a severe form of morning sickness),
premature birth, and difficult presentations,
such as breech presentation. Texts from ancient
India indicate that Indian midwives were from well-
to-do families and had great expertise. The *Susruta
Samhita* (see pp.77–79) recounts how the expectant
mother should lie on her back with pillows for
support, thighs flexed, and be aided by four older,
experienced midwives with well-trimmed nails.

Midwifery as the formally organized speciality
we know today began to take shape in Europe
during the 16th century. Famed French battlefield surgeon Ambroise
Paré (see pp.126–31) was one of many eminent medical men who began
to take an interest in obstetrics. He used a method of "podalic version",
whereby a baby lying sideways in the womb could be repositioned for
an easier, feet-first birth. The recently invented movable-type printing
press, and the tendency of eminent medical men like Paré to write in
the language of the day rather than in scholarly Latin, opened the
study of medicine and health care to the public, giving budding male
physicians opportunities in pregnancy and childbirth. In Germany,
apothecary and physician Eucharius Rösslin was dismayed at the low
standards of midwifery, and published *Der Schwangeren Frauen und
Hebammen Rosengarten* (*The Rose Garden for Pregnant Women and Midwives*) in
an attempt to raise standards. In 17th-century France, Louyse
Bourgeois became the first woman to write a scholarly book on
obstetrics, *Observations diverses sur la stérilité, perte de fruits, fécondité,
accouchements et maladies des femmes et enfants nouveaux-nés* (*Various
Observations on the Sterility, Fruit loss, Fertility, Childbirth and Diseases of Women
and Newborn Infants*), published in 1609 – but the encroachment of men
into the traditionally female world of the midwife continued, giving
rise to the term "man-midwife", or *accoucheur*, in French. Historical
accounts from the Netherlands tell of how the local surgeons' guild
organized midwife training under its appointed *accoucheur*, whom the

midwife had to call for professional advice if birth complications arose. Midwives' status was eroded and numbers fell. The Dutch city of Leiden was typical in having only ten active midwives on its registers during the 17th century, a number that halved during the 18th century.

In the first half of the 1700s, obstetric forceps, which fitted around the baby's head to make delivery easier, became widely available, largely thanks to Scottish obstetrician William Smellie. Smellie trained in Glasgow, Paris, and London. He greatly improved knowledge of labour and showed how forceps could be used to deliver a baby safely, even if the mother's life was not threatened. This shifted the emphasis towards saving the lives of both mother and infant, rather than just the infant.

MAN-MIDWIFE
In the 18th century, cartoonists caricatured the
male midwife, or man-midwife, as a half-male,
half-female figure.

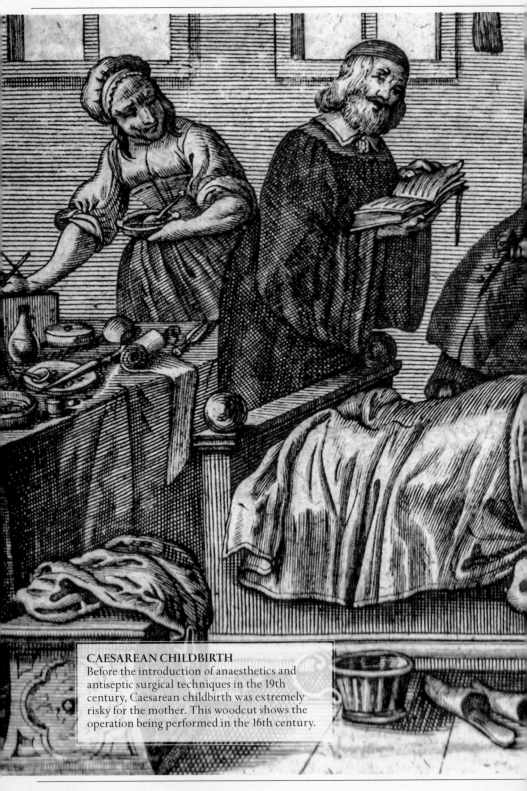

CAESAREAN CHILDBIRTH
Before the introduction of anaesthetics and
antiseptic surgical techniques in the 19th
century, Caesarean childbirth was extremely
risky for the mother. This woodcut shows the
operation being performed in the 16th century.

Jonas Arnold
Delineavit

He published widely, including *A Treatise on the Theory and Practice of Midwifery*, which appeared in the 1750s. The vaginal speculum, which had existed since at least Roman times (see pp.46–47), also came into greater use in the 18th century. It permits an interior view of the vagina, particularly during childbirth. Again, it was an instrument for the obstetrician rather than the midwife – one benefit being that the doctor had less need to touch a woman's genital area.

By now, queens and other aristocratic women were requesting the obstetric services of male doctors, exacerbating the trend away from midwives. The shift in birth patterns from home to hospital also played into the hands of obstetricians. Some members of the medical establishment even suggested that midwifery should be abolished. In 1842, the renowned British medical weekly *The Lancet* carried a letter stating: "It is notorious that the attendance of midwives… is in many respects positively injurious, and in numberless cases women would be much safer if intrusted entirely to nature". The same attitudes were spreading across several other European countries and North America.

Around this time, Hungarian doctor Ignaz Semmelweis was working in obstetrics at Vienna General Hospital. He puzzled over the pattern of cases for the common and dreaded "childbed fever" – puerperal fever, now known to be a bacterial infection. One clinic in particular had an unusually high incidence. In 1847, Semmelweis reasoned that "cadaverous matter" could be the cause, since those staffing the high-incidence clinic were medical students, who often came from autopsies, cadaver dissections, and other similar duties. Semmelweis recommended that students clean their hands with a chlorine-based handwash – and the effects were immediate. Within a year, cases of puerperal fever in the clinic plummeted, a fact that helped establish the germ theory of disease (see pp.222–27), and the use of antiseptics in hospitals (see pp.206–13). In 1860, Florence Nightingale founded the first modern-style school of nursing (see pp.188–93). Midwives received similar recognition in

"… midwives ought to be… sober, patient, and discreet, free from external deformity…"

WILLIAM SMELLIE

A MIDWIFE ON CALL
A female midwife transports an analgesic gas-air machine on the back of her bicycle in 1938. At the time, men still dominated both obstetrics and midwifery.

1881, when wealthy Russian-born philanthropist Louisa Hubbard set up the Midwives' Institute, which aimed to "raise the efficiency and improve the status of midwives and to petition parliament for their recognition". In 1902, the Midwives Act in England and Wales made midwifery an established profession, complete with systems of supervised training, certification, and registration. The profession was still dominated by men, but it was now illegal for anyone to practise as a midwife without qualification.

Internationally, midwifery progressed in different ways. In the Netherlands, it benefited from having training schools much earlier than elsewhere in Europe, so it avoided being marginalized; the first Dutch training school was established in 1861. French midwives gained considerable status, being allowed to diagnose and treat a wide range of conditions. The American College of Nurse-Midwifery was chartered in 1955. By the mid-20th century, the profession had a sound footing in most developed nations, ensuring the future well-being of mothers and babies alike.

The Germ Theory
of Disease

DISCOVERIES ABOUT BACTERIA and other disease-causing micro-organisms multiplied almost as fast as bacteria themselves in the late 19th century. Scientific researchers peering into microsocopes recorded all sorts of new bacteria, yeasts, protozoa (single-celled, animal-like organisms), micro-worms, and others. Microbes were grown or cultured, fixed, and preserved in new ways, and they could now be coloured or stained for easier study. These tiny life forms gained a new significance as their roles in fermentation, decomposition, disease, and the whole of the natural world became apparent. Along with Louis Pasteur (see pp.196–203), a key founder of bacteriology was hard-working German physician and microscopist Robert Koch. Although the two scientists had much in common, they soon took strenuously against each other. Mirroring the political rivalry of France and Germany at the time, their battles were conducted chiefly through the medical press. While Koch insulted Pasteur's "poor methods", Pasteur retaliated by accusing Koch of being "a debtor of French Science". But whatever Pasteur's opinion, there is no doubt that Koch made colossal leaps in the field of medical microbiology.

Born and raised in Clausthal, northwest Germany, Robert Koch studied medicine at the University of Göttingen and qualified with distinction in 1866. Koch's career would soon lead him away from treating people to his main passion – microbes. He was doubtless inspired by the professor of anatomy at Göttingen, Jacob Henle, who had conjectured in 1840 that certain diseases were caused by parasitic organisms (see p.198). After several hospital and general practice jobs, Koch volunteered for medical duties in the Franco-Prussian War. He moved to Wollstein

ROBERT KOCH
Koch was famous for his pioneering work on anthrax and cholera, and for identifying the germ that causes human tuberculosis.

(now Wolsztyn, Poland) in 1872, as District Medical Officer. Between his official duties, Koch worked on his research at home. His wife, Emmy, had given him a microscope as a present; the rest of his equipment he begged or improvised. It was here, in his cramped, home-made laboratory, that Koch made his first set of radical findings – on anthrax.

In 1850, French physicians Pierre Rayer and Casimir Davaine had observed microbes in the blood of diseased sheep; German doctor Aloys Pollender had seen "staff-shaped little bodies" a year earlier. No one really knew if these microbes were the cause of the disease, a side effect, or a result of it. More than a decade later, Davaine showed that transferring infected blood between animals also transferred the disease, anthrax. Anthrax was a real problem at the time, with regular outbreaks among livestock, and the occasional but serious human case. Even isolating animal herds did not work because the disease seemed to pop up at any time. Koch decided to investigate. Using improvised splinters of wood, he inoculated mice with samples from the spleens of healthy and diseased farm animals. Those inoculated with diseased samples developed anthrax, but those inoculated with healthy samples did not, confirming that the disease can be transmitted by blood. Koch then set about purifying the microbes and growing them away from host animals, in a laboratory culture created using the fluid from the inside of ox eyeballs. Over the course of his career, he would try a host of different nutrient substances for breeding bacteria, from potato slices to meat broth, eggs, bread, and seaweed extracts. Koch also pioneered photography through the microscope, testing the technique with the anthrax germs, and he invented ways to add pigmented substances – stains – to colour microbes, making them easier to identify.

Koch grew multiple generations of anthrax microbes, noting that when they were put into animals, they still caused anthrax. He also observed that in less favourable conditions, each microbe seemed to form inside itself a rounded object. This resisted adverse conditions such as heat, cold, dryness, and lack of oxygen; as conditions improved, the object – an endospore – gave rise to the bacterium again. This explained how anthrax could suddenly reappear in livestock that had had no contact with infected animals: the endospores survived in the soil. In 1876, Koch demonstrated his work to a number of eminent scientists, including botanist and microbiologist Ferdinand Cohn, who had already studied the anthrax

FIG. 5   FIG. 6   FIG. 7   FIG. 8

BOTTLED GERMS
These samples of
different bacteria were
recorded by Ferdinand
Hueppe, one of Koch's
co-workers. Figures 7
and 8 show the
tuberculosis culture.

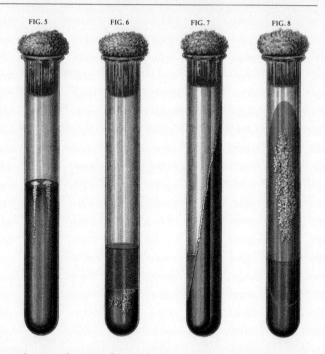

microbe *Bacillus anthracis*. The word *Bacillus* stems from the Latin for a
small staff, stick, or wand, indicating the bacterium's rod-like shape;
anthracis comes from the Latin for coal or anthracite, and refers to the
areas of dead, dark skin in some forms of the disease. Koch explained
his findings about the microbe's life cycle and transmission, and
control measures. Cohn was impressed and arranged publication, to
great acclaim. It was another great step for the germ theorists, while
the supporters of spontaneous generation and miasma (see p.196) had
been dealt a further crushing blow.

Koch moved to the Imperial Health Bureau in Berlin in 1880. Later
in the decade, he devised a set of conditions known as Koch's postulates
– a set of criteria used to establish that a microbe causes disease. Over
time, he would apply these to each new germ he discovered. Koch's
postulates can be summarized in four points: an infected organism
(plant, animal) or tissue contains the microbes in question in
abundance, while healthy ones do not; the microbes must be isolated
from infected organisms or tissues and grown as pure cultures; when
the cultured microbes are introduced into a healthy organism, that
organism develops the disease; and lastly, these "second generation"
microbes are extracted and isolated again, and shown to be identical
to the original microbes. With his postulates, Koch was trying to
ascertain whether the microbe and the disease were inseparable. But

medicine is never so clear-cut. For instance, some humans or animals are "carriers" of a disease — outwardly healthy with few or no symptoms, while their bodies are reservoirs of the germs to pass to others. So, rather than absolute rules, Koch's postulates became an ideal set of criteria, and remain as such today.

In Berlin, Koch finally had a proper laboratory, with assistants, and it marked the start of his second great phase of work, on tuberculosis. He and his team continued to develop new methods and techniques: a significant innovation in about 1881 was the growth of microbes on a jelly-like nutrient substance, gel agar, using agar-agar extracted from seaweed. The microbes grew visibly in small patches that could be conveniently accessed — far better than swishing around in nutrient broth or buried deep in test-tubes. This method was developed by one of Koch's assistants, Walther Hesse, whose wife Angelina had suggested including agar as a gelling agent after making jellies and jams. Another of Koch's assistants, Julius Richard Petri, gave his name to his invention — Petri dishes. The agar was spread on these shallow, circular glass plates with close-fitting lids, so the microbes within could be easily observed. Both agar and Petri dishes are still used in experiments worldwide.

By now, Koch was on the trail of the germ that caused one of the world's most common, long-term, and often deadly diseases — tuberculosis. This germ is smaller than its anthrax counterpart, and also reacts differently to coloured stains. The work was detailed and painstaking. On 24 March 1882, a triumphant Koch announced that he and his team had found and identified the germ, tubercle bacillus: "If the importance of a disease for mankind is measured by the number of fatalities it causes, then tuberculosis must be considered much more important than those most feared infectious diseases, plague, cholera, and the like". Koch went on to describe his new staining methods and other techniques, and explain how he used guinea pigs as experimental laboratory animals, as well as studying tissues from humans, apes, and

PROPORTION OF ALL DEATHS IN EUROPE IN THE 19TH CENTURY DUE TO TUBERCULOSIS

25%

farm animals. The germs were taken from one animal source, grown in culture, and put into other animals, each time causing tuberculosis. For added proof, Koch produced microscopes, glass slides with stained microbe cultures, jars with tissue samples, and other equipment, so that members of the audience could see for themselves. Within a month, the news had spread across Europe, followed by North America, Africa, and Asia. Initially known as Koch's bacillus, the microbe is now called *Mycobacterium tuberculosis*.

Next, Koch turned his attention to the cholera germ. In 1883, he was sent by the government as Leader of the German Cholera Commission to study an outbreak in Alexandria, Egypt. There, he identified a suspicious, comma-shaped bacterium. Another trip took him to India, where he continued his investigations. Eventually, he was able to pinpoint the causative germ. He described its spread – through contaminated drinking water and contaminated food (see pp.180–87) – and recommended prevention and control measures. These achievements earned Koch a huge reward of 100,000 Deutschmarks and further boosted his global reputation. The cholera microbe – since named *Vibrio cholerae* – had, in fact, been discovered almost 30 years earlier, in 1854, by Italian anatomist Filippo Pacini. But the germ theory of disease was so unfashionable then that Pacini's achievements went unrecognized.

After his epochal work with anthrax, tuberculosis, and cholera, Koch finally stumbled. In 1890, amid great fanfare, he introduced tuberculin – a remedy for tuberculosis. He refused to disclose its origins and said it had been tested on animals. Initial reports from human trials were positive, but tuberculin induced severe reactions in some – and death in others. This so-called cure was anything but; Koch admitted that tuberculin was a particular extract of the bacteria, but he was unable to describe its exact contents. Public opinion swung against him. Matters worsened when it became known that he was financially involved with the tuberculin producers, even though his research was government-paid. Having drifted apart from his wife, his new relationship with teenager Hedwig Freiberg did not help. Koch left the country and embarked on his travels once again. He visited Italy, Africa, India, and New Guinea, studying bubonic plague, leprosy, malaria, rabies, and exotic fevers in humans and livestock. In 1897, he presented a new version of tuberculin; this too failed, but it would in time make a useful diagnostic test for tuberculosis. An

MOTHER CARE, 1918
This poster was produced by the American Red
Cross to raise awareness of child mortality rates
from diseases such as tuberculosis.

effective vaccine against tuberculosis in humans was finally
developed in the 1920s – ironically at the Institut Pasteur, founded
by Koch's great rival Louis Pasteur.

Despite his later failures, Koch had inspired a new wave of medical
research into germs and infection. His students included Friedrich
Loeffler, who identified and cultivated the diphtheria germ in 1884;
Kitasato Shibasaburo, who was also involved with diphtheria, and
who, in 1894, was co-discoverer of the bubonic plague microbe; Emile
von Behring, who was awarded the first Nobel Prize in Physiology or
Medicine in 1901 for his work on diphtheria; August von Wassermann,
who formulated a diagnostic test for early syphilis infection in 1906;
and Paul Ehrlich, who discovered the anti-syphilitic drug
arsphenamine (Salvarsan) in 1909. In 1905, Robert Koch received the
Nobel Prize in Physiology or Medicine for "his investigations and
discoveries in relation to tuberculosis". It was a testament to his
groundbreaking discoveries, which were fuelled by his ceaseless work
ethic. A motto he had attached to a prize-winning essay at medical
school read *Nunquam Otiosus* – Never Idle.

Viruses in action

Viruses are tiny infectious particles – about a thousand times smaller than bacteria – which can only be seen with an electron microscope. Each particle contains a set of instructions on how to make thousands of identical copies of itself. There are millions of different viruses and they cause illnesses ranging in strength from the common cold and flu to deadly diseases such as AIDs, polio, and hepatitis.

Viruses lie in the environment, waiting to invade bacteria, plants, and animals. They can be spread in the air, in fluids, or via insects. Antibiotics have no effect on viruses, but vaccination (see pp.286–93) can help to provide immunity against some of them.

Dmitri Ivanovsky

In 1890, Russian biologist Dmitri Ivanovsky went to the Crimea to study a disease in tobacco plants. He crushed infected tobacco leaves and passed an extract through a filter with microscopic holes that would exclude bacteria. Yet he found that the source of the infection was still present: he had discovered something infectious that was even smaller than bacteria – a virus.

IVANOVSKY IS CONSIDERED ONE OF THE FATHERS OF VIROLOGY

HOW A VIRUS WORKS

A virus has no cells of its own, so in order to live and make more viruses, it has to invade a cell of a bacterium, plant, or animal and take over its replication mechanism. The virus usually kills the host cell in the process.

1 Attachment – the virus binds to the cell membrane of the host cell

Host cell

3 Replication – the virus's genetic material enters the nucleus of the host cell

2 Penetration – the virus enters the cell, and its casing breaks down to release the genetic material inside

Host nucleus

Virus shapes

In 1931, the electron microscope was invented in Germany, and by the end of the decade German physician Helmut Ruska was using it to examine viruses. Scientists soon established the basic structure of a virus. They found that viruses vary enormously in form and structure, to enable them to target and penetrate the right host cells, and resist attack from the host organism's immune system. Four main virus shapes have been identified.

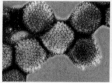

ICOSAHEDRAL
Many animal viruses take the form of a polyhedron.

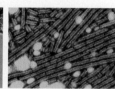

SPIRAL-HELICAL
Some viruses have a casing in the shape of a helix.

COMPLEX
Complex viruses show variations to the casing, such as a "tail".

ENVELOPED
Some viruses coat themselves in the host-cell membrane.

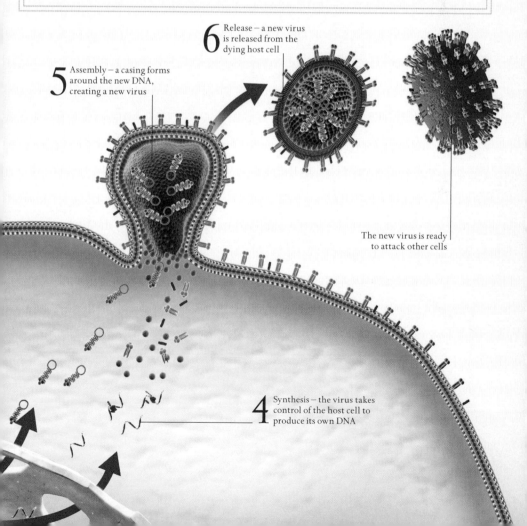

6 Release – a new virus is released from the dying host cell

5 Assembly – a casing forms around the new DNA, creating a new virus

The new virus is ready to attack other cells

4 Synthesis – the virus takes control of the host cell to produce its own DNA

Medicine and the Mind

THE NAMES OF CONDITIONS HAVE CHANGED, but mental illness has been with us throughout history, and may have been one of the reasons for the earliest form of Stone Age surgery – trepanning (see pp.20–21). In early civilizations, mental disorders were generally seen as punishments from the gods, and were sometimes linked to the phases of the Moon – hence the term "lunatic". The sufferer tended to be the family's responsibility, which often brought shame and stigmatization, and there was little in the way of treatment, other than a calming environment and some soothing herbs and minerals. At best, if the disorder was brief and episodic, the sufferer could be considered to be a conduit through which the gods could communicate their prophecies and decisions – at worst, he or she might be physically restrained or isolated. In Mesopotamia and Egypt, priest-physicians performed ritual incantations and sacrifices to rid the sufferer of demons, and in Babylon, patients were encouraged to sing, dance, and paint to purge themselves of evil. This supernatural view of mental illness held sway in many societies for millennia, and in some parts of the world it even persists today.

In Greece, 2,300 years ago, the physician Hippocrates (see pp.30–39) had other ideas. He suggested that mental problems were rooted entirely in the body, particularly in the balance of the four humours (see pp.106–107). Slight humoral disparities between people generated the normal range of human personalities, it was thought, but a marked imbalance in a single individual could result in mental disturbance. Hippocrates described several conditions that we recognize today, including paranoia, mania, and depression – the latter known as melancholia, since it was believed to be caused by an excess of the black bile humour, called melanchole. As ever, Hippocrates recommended gentle remedies for melancholia, such as calm, quiet surroundings and relaxing herbal potions. Galen of Ancient Rome (see pp.40–45), whose medicine endured throughout the Middle Ages, followed the Hippocratic trend, although he tended to focus on major symptoms rather than overall conditions. The traditional Ayurvedic medicine of India (see pp.74–81) has a version of humoral theory in which an imbalance in the fluid-like doshas can lead to mental problems. In Ancient China, texts such as the *Huang-di Nei'Jing* (see pp.64–68) advocated treatment by negating a

REMOVING THE STONE OF MADNESS
Trepanning – boring holes into the skull
– has been practised throughout history
as a way of surgically alleviating madness.

mental condition with opposing moods or emotions – so a person with depression might receive gifts and treats, while anxiety could respond to intense support and reassurance.

Societies that emphasized respect for the family and the honour of ancestry were extra-sensitive to the indignity and dishonour of mental disorders. Suspicions that such illnesses might be contagious or run in the family could lead to the isolation of a family within the community. In China, for instance, sufferers were quietly removed from public life, and often hidden, or even abandoned. These attitudes hardened in Europe during the Middle Ages as the stigmatization of the mentally ill increased. Despite Christianity urging goodwill to all people, sufferers who were too difficult to care for in the family risked being abused, beaten, and locked up. The lucky ones were taken in by monasteries and convents – others found their way into workhouses or general hospitals, survived on charity, or undertook the most lowly, menial tasks to earn a crust. All kinds of quacks and charlatans offered treatments, including protective charms and amulets that were worn to relieve, or prevent the onset of, various mental illnesses. Worn around the neck or forehead, these amulets bore biblical images or quotations, and were adorned with therapeutic herbs such as Saint John's wort. Their power relied on the wearer reciting prayers and chants, frequenting church, and making pilgrimages to saints' shrines.

Thoughtful, humane treatment of the mentally ill emerged during the Golden Age of Islam (see pp.100–105). As the Qur'an states: "Do not give to [those weak of understanding] their property that God has assigned you to manage: provide them and clothe them out of it, and speak to them honourable words". In the 8th century, soon after Baghdad was founded, a hospital ward was put aside for such patients, and similar facilities were set up in Fez, Cairo, Damascus, and Aleppo over the next few centuries. However, this more enlightened attitude spread only sporadically across Asia – it was unusual in cities, and even rarer in rural areas. In Europe, from the 15th century, events took a different

PROTECTION AGAINST EVIL
Amulets bearing biblical images were worn throughout Christendom to protect against all kinds of mental and physical illness.

LUNATICS' TOWER
Vienna's fortress-like Narrenturm (Lunatics'
Tower), built in 1874, had 139 cells in which
the mentally ill were incarcerated.

turn. Sufferers who were not cared for by a family, religious order, or
charity were gathered together into asylums. One of the first of these
was established in Valencia, Spain in around 1410. More asylums
followed in Spain and throughout Europe, notably La Maison de
Charenton in Paris, in the early 1640s, and the Narrenturm (Lunatics'
Tower) in Vienna, 1784. So began a notorious period in which the
mentally ill suffered all kinds of horror and degradation. Visitors told of
barbaric conditions, neglect, and cruelty. In crowded, cold, dark,
stinking rooms, which were often worse than prison cells, the sick were
manacled, or shackled, or put in stocks and left for days at a time.
Clothes, food, cleanliness, and sanitation were desperately inadequate.
Asylums also became dumping grounds for criminals (both sane and
insane), syphilis sufferers, and the rest of society's unwanted.

Treatments, if any, were harsher than ever before. Under the humoral
view of mental illness, ways to restore a sound body and mind included
purging with emetics and laxatives, cupping, blistering, and bloodletting
(see pp.132–33), the favoured treat-all. Bloodletting from the jugular
vein in the neck removed blood that came directly from the brain, which
was thought to contain the worst humoral imbalance. Drenching in

HUMANE TREATMENT OF THE SICK
Pioneering doctor Philippe Pinel releases the
mentally ill from their chains at the Hospice
de la Salpêtrière for women, Paris, in the 1790s.

scalding or icy water, subjection to deafening noises, whipping, hanging
by the arms or the feet, starving, burning with acids and other chemicals,
semi-suffocation, and semi-drowning – almost every form of torture
was tried in the name of therapy. Many of these "madhouses", as they
were known, were paid for and run by the state, but some, most
notoriously in Britain, were privately owned. Families paid to have their
mentally ill relatives incarcerated, and the owners grew rich as greed
produced ever-worsening conditions. One profitable sideline was
charging the public to view these "inmates" and their antics. Infamous
for this was London's "Bedlam", as the St Mary Bethlehem hospital, or
Bethlem, came to be known. French traveller and letter-writer César de
Saussure wrote of Bethlem in 1725: "On the second floor is a corridor...
reserved for dangerous maniacs, most of them being chained and
terrible to behold. On holidays numerous persons of both sexes, but
belonging generally to the lower classes, visit this hospital and amuse
themselves watching these unfortunate wretches, who often give them
cause for laughter". The hospital itself, now regarded as a pioneering
institution, moved premises several times, and continues today as the
Bethlem Royal Hospital near London.

Despite – or perhaps because of – such horrors, attitudes gradually changed. Public visiting at Bethlem ceased around 1770, and in 1793, French doctor Philippe Pinel took over L'Hôpital Bicêtre, an asylum for men in Paris, inaugurating an era in which the mentally ill began to be treated more humanely. According to Pinel, residents of asylums should be

SPECTATORS VISITING BETHLEM EACH WEEK BEFORE 1770

2,000

called patients, rather than inmates, and should be given normal food and clothing, as well as sunlight and fresh air, rather than dank darkness. In 1794, he read out his paper titled *Memoir on Madness* to the Paris Natural History Society, in which he explained his "psychologic treatment" and belief that mental illnesses could be cured. He urged physicians to spend time with their patients, to interview them, and to take notes and write case histories, which should include a record of any events that precipitated their patients' conditions. Of the severely mentally ill he noted: "I cannot here avoid giving my most decided sufferage in favour of the moral qualities of maniacs. I have no where met… fonder husbands, more affectionate parents… than in the lunatic asylum, during their intervals of calmness and reason". *Memoir on Madness* was one of the earliest works of what we now call psychiatry – the diagnosis, treatment, and prevention of mental illness.

In 1795, Pinel assumed the role of chief physician at the huge Hospice de la Salpêtrière for women, and continued to apply his philosophy. At Bicêtre, he had been greatly helped by the hospital's like-minded superintendent, Jean-Baptiste Pussin. In 1797, Pussin decreed that patients, except in extreme cases, should no longer be chained, and soon after that he joined Pinel at Salpêtrière. In 1804, Pinel was elected to the French Academy of Sciences and became a founding member of the Academy of Medicine in 1820. His work *Nosographie* concerned the medical field of nosology (the classification of diseases), while his *Traité Médico-Philosophique sur l'Aliénation Mentale* (*Medical-Philosophical Treatise on Mental Alienation*) furthered his "psychologic approach".

Advances were also made in other areas. In the mid-19th century, outstanding French physician Jean-Martin Charcot laid the foundations of neurology, the study of the nervous system, which had particular relevance to psychiatric disorders. In Italy, in the late 1780s, physician Vincenzo Chiarugi had instituted improved

"You never saw a very busy person who was unhappy"

DOROTHY DIX

conditions at Santa Dorotea Hospital and then at San Bonifacio Hospital, both in Florence. In 1796, in England, William Tuke, a Quaker and well-to-do merchant dealing in teas and coffees, had set up the York Retreat, a charitable organization that provided a humane environment for the mentally ill. Others joined the movement for reform, which became known as *traitement moral*, or moral management, since it emphasized moral virtue and religious duty in its treatments. After visiting England and experiencing these Quaker-inspired reforms, teacher and American campaigner Dorothea Dix returned to the US in 1840 and pushed long and hard for change, establishing a movement that became known as the "mental hygiene movement".

Back in the 1770s, hopes for a radical new way of treating mental disorders had risen with the "animal magnetism" movement of Franz Anton Mesmer, who believed that there was a "life energy" in each individual that could be passed to the sick through a Christian-style "laying on of hands". This idea gained popularity and spawned offshoots such as hypnosis, but it faded from the science-based medical community by the early 20th century. Phrenology came to the fore in the early 19th century with the work of German physician Franz Joseph Gall. This involved feeling and measuring the contours of the skull to determine the sizes and relative development of the brain regions or "organs" underneath. Each brain "organ" controlled a particular mental, intellectual, or moral faculty. Neurology has since shown that regions of the brain are indeed specialized, but not in the way phrenology proposed. Despite its phenomenal popularity, it had no scientific basis, and by about 1900 it too had drifted out of conventional medicine.

Another chapter opened in 1895, when Austrian physicians Josef Breuer and Sigmund Freud published *Studies in Hysteria*. They described a new form of therapy, called psychoanalysis, which Freud developed in detail over the coming decades. *Studies in Hysteria* investigated several women with a condition then called hysteria. Patient "Anna O" had symptoms including a nervous cough, disordered vision and hearing, partial right-side paralysis, and fainting. In conversation, Breuer and

Anna talked about all the possible causes of her condition, and she recalled events from her youth, some traumatic. One technique that Breuer used was "free association", in which the patient said anything that came to mind, and then – guided by the doctor – spoke about what it might mean or symbolize. It was treatment simply by talking.

Freud developed these and other techniques into his own brand of psychoanalysis, according to which the most important events of a patient's life happened in childhood and have since been repressed. Freud also proposed three basic components to the mind: the "id" was in effect the unconscious – the realm of the primal sexual and aggressive drives; the "superego", both conscious and unconscious, resisted the id and tried to exert a civilizing effect; the "ego" mediated between the two, balancing basic desires with social acceptance. Conflict between these elements of the mind, or psyche, could trigger mental problems, and delving into the unconscious to expose its deep-seated content was part of treatment. Techniques for access to the unconscious included analysing dreams, or working through fantasies, as described in *The Interpretation of Dreams* (1900), and *The Psychopathology of Everyday Life* (1901).

During this time, asylum conditions were improving and the number of asylums grew rapidly, especially in the West. In the USA, the number of people in asylums increased from some 40,000 in 1880 to more than 250,000 in 1900. This led to the increasing problem of institutionalization. New treatments for mental illness continued to surface, including insulin shock therapy, lobotomy, electroconvulsive ("electroshock") therapy, and the administration of chlorpromazine and other antipsychotic drugs. As for "talking cures", psychoanalysis had its supporters and detractors. Inspired or alarmed by Freud, others developed alternative systems, such as the individual psychology of Alfred Adler and the analytical psychiatry of Carl Jung. Their ideas still provoke debate, even as millions of people daily consult their "analysts" for help with mental health problems today.

SIGMUND FREUD
The founding father of psychoanalysis,
Freud believed that many mental
disorders were caused by the suppression
of childhood traumas.

"SCENE IN BEDLAM"
Satirist William Hogarth depicted Bedlam in his 1730s series *A Rake's Progress*, as the resting place of the disgraced hero. In the background, well-dressed visitors amuse themselves at the antics of the insane, as was customary at the time.

Modern
Medicine
1920–2000

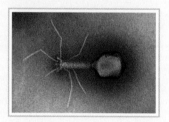

Medicine took giant strides through the 20th century. An early breakthrough was Karl Landsteiner's work on blood groups, which helped emergency treatment and surgery of all kinds. In 1921 and 1922, Frederick Banting and his team in Toronto started insulin treatment for diabetes and, a few years later, Alexander Fleming noticed mouldy growths contaminating his bacterial samples. The "culprit" was penicillin, but it took the pressures of World War II to ensure that this first antibiotic was mass-produced.

Just after this came the first major inroads of chemotherapy into cancers. The vaccine for polio put it on the growing list of preventable diseases that already included smallpox, diphtheria, tuberculosis, and influenza. Urgent vaccine research continues for diseases that threaten globally, from the old enemy malaria to serious infections that have recently emerged, especially HIV/AIDS. Elsewhere, immunosuppressant drugs led to greater success for transplanted organs – in 1967, South African surgeon Christiaan Barnard shook the world with the first heart transplant. Medical technology and biomechanics also made the headlines. John Charnley's work brought artificial hips to millions and, in 1969, the world reeled at more heart news, this time of a (temporary) artificial implant. From the 1970s, CT, MRI, and other computerized scanners created new generations of body images.

The work of pioneer geriatricians such as Marjory Warren, and Cicely Saunders' founding of the modern hospice movement, transformed the end of life for elderly and terminally ill patients. In 1978, there was a new approach to the start to life too, with Patrick Steptoe, Robert Edwards, and the first test-tube IVF babies.

Blood Groups and the Sugar Disease

MOST BLOOD LOOKS THE SAME – whether from humans or animals – so early physicians wondered whether it was possible to replace lost blood with blood from another living being, and in particular, whether blood from animals could be used as transfusions for humans. After William Harvey's discovery of blood circulation in 1628 (see pp.134–43), physicians started to experiment with blood transfusion. In 1665, English physician Richard Lower demonstrated that blood could be transferred between two dogs, and in 1667, French physician Jean-Baptiste Denys infused lamb's blood into a feverish teenage boy. Denys carried out several more animal-to-human transfusions, until he was charged with murder after the death of his fourth patient. Later that year, Lower and Edmund King attempted the first animal-to-human blood transfer in England, on "freakish" scholar Arthur Coga, observed by Samuel Pepys. Coga's brain "was sometimes a little too warm", according to King, and the aim of the experiment was to cool it with lamb's blood. Similar experiments were conducted in Italy. One problem was that as soon as blood was exposed to air, it clotted. With no way of preventing this, early transfers were made directly along a tube from one body to the other. That these

ANIMAL-TO-HUMAN BLOOD TRANSFUSION
In England and France, transfusion was attempted from both lambs and calves, as shown in this engraving based on a drawing of 1679.

early transfusions succeeded at all – without any knowledge of anticoagulants, blood groups, or modern procedures – was probably due to the small amounts of blood involved. But the frequency of deaths led to experimental transfusions being prohibited in France, England, and Italy, and they were abandoned for 150 years.

Experiments began again in around 1820, when London obstetrician James Blundell attempted transfusions to save new mothers from excessive bleeding during or after childbirth (puerperal or postpartum haemorrhage). Blundell rigged up human donors – often the husband standing by the bedside – whose blood was transfused along tubes to the patient. He also experimented with transferring blood using syringes or containers. The results were mixed: some patients died and others survived. This was sufficiently encouraging for physicians to try new methods of transferring blood, using hand-squeezed rubber bulbs, pumps, stopcocks, and adding ingenious valves to tubes. Others attempted to forestall clotting by diluting blood with saline solution (saltwater) or mixing it with other chemicals. However, results remained stubbornly inconsistent.

Then, in the mid-1870s, German physiologist Leonard Landois made a breakthrough regarding blood clotting. Using blood samples, laboratory reagents (substances that force a chemical reaction), and microscopes, he showed that mixing animal blood with human blood made the red blood cells clump together (agglutinate). In some cases, the red cells also ruptured, which may have led to a type of anaemia. A further advance was made by Austrian Karl Landsteiner, who first identified the existence of different blood groups. Landsteiner had qualified in medicine from Vienna University in 1891 and joined research staff at the Vienna Hygiene Institute, one of the university's pathology departments. He was particularly interested in immunity – the way in which a body defended itself against germs, cancerous cells, and "foreign" substances such as allergens – and how it made antibodies to counteract these (see pp.286–91). Immunity also involved the new field of serology – the study of blood serum, which is plasma (the liquid part of blood) with the clotting substances removed.

In around 1900, Landsteiner began experimenting with mixing human blood samples. He observed that red blood cells clumped together and ruptured only when samples from certain individuals were mixed together. He painstakingly tested each blood sample against a range of others in order to determine the effects of each combination. From the results, he deduced that each person had one of three different types or groups of blood – A, B, and C (which we now know as O). Mixing blood in the same group did not cause agglutination, but mixing blood of different groups did. This was because of the different antibodies that each blood group carried in the blood serum. In 1902, a fourth blood group, AB, was identified by Landsteiner's Viennese co-workers, researcher Adriano Sturli and kidney transplant pioneer Alfred von Decastello. Landsteiner refined this work through the 1900s, while another team of researchers, Ludwig Hirszfeld and Emil von Dungern at the Heidelberg Institute for Experimental Cancer Research, demonstrated that blood groups show a pattern of inheritance. Landsteiner had suspected this, and proposed that these patterns could be used to resolve cases of disputed paternity.

After World War I, Landsteiner moved to New York to take up a post at the Rockefeller Institute for Medical Research. His enthusiasm was undimmed as he continued to identify more blood groups – the MN group and P group, both discovered in 1927 in collaboration with Philip Levine. In 1940, along with Alexander Wiener, an innovator in forensic medicine, he helped to discover the rhesus (Rh) factor in blood. This has an indirect connection with the rhesus macaque monkey, a well-known laboratory animal. Rhesus monkey blood mixed with rabbit serum caused agglutination, as did human blood and rabbit serum. The Rh factor is involved in haemolytic disease in newborn babies, in which a baby suffers jaundice, anaemia, and other severe symptoms, due to incompatibility between the Rh factors in the baby's blood and that of its mother.

Landsteiner received the 1930 Nobel Prize in Physiology or Medicine for his 1901 "discovery of human blood groups". The lapse of 29 years reflected the time it had taken to turn his discoveries into practical, life-saving measures. Landsteiner's work paved the way for safer transfusions by matching the blood groups of the donor and the recipient, but two further grouping systems had confused the issue – Czech professor Jan Jansky's I, II, III, and IV groups (equivalent to O, A, B and AB) in 1907, and William Moss's in the US in 1910, which reversed Janksy's I and IV. This nomenclature problem was not resolved until the late 1930s, when the ABO system became standard.

As is often the case with medical advances, it took a massive conflict, in this case World War I, to boost the technology of transfusion. Surgeons discovered that blood could be chilled, and sodium citrate added as an anticoagulant to slow its natural tendency to clot. This overcame the need to have a live donor on the spot. From January 1916, recipients could receive stored blood, which gave medical staff sufficient time to make sure that the blood groups matched. By World War II, blood transfusion was routine, and civilians were called upon to donate blood to treat wounded soldiers.

As Landsteiner was discovering blood groups, another line of research was heading towards a breakthrough in our understanding of how energy is transferred from the blood (in the form of glucose) to the billions of cells around the body. It was discovered that the process was controlled by insulin, a hormone produced in the pancreas, and that disruption of this process led to diabetes – a fatal disease that had already been known to the Ancient Egyptians by 1500 BCE. The full name of the disease, "diabetes mellitus", meaning "to pass honey", was coined by the 2nd-century Greek physician Aretaeus because an early test of the illness was to taste a person's urine for sugar. This sugar, or blood glucose, is the body's main source of energy, and it is replenished by stores from the liver and elsewhere with the help of insulin. In type 1 diabetes, the pancreas is unable to make enough insulin because the body's immune system attacks the beta cells that produce it (as opposed to type 2 diabetes, in which the body becomes insulin-resistant). These beta cells are produced in

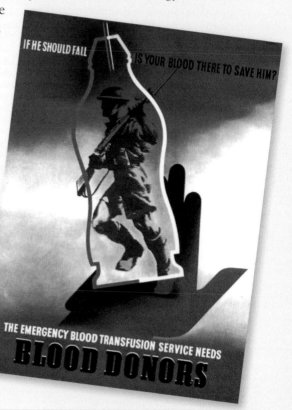

GIVE BLOOD!
During World War II, posters were used to call upon civilians to donate blood for soldiers to the blood transfusion service.

IF HE SHOULD FALL

IS YOUR BLOOD THERE TO SAVE HIM?

THE EMERGENCY BLOOD TRANSFUSION SERVICE NEEDS
BLOOD DONORS

a million or so tiny structures in the pancreas called the islets of Langerhans – named after Paul Langerhans, the German medical student who first described them in 1869. Lack of insulin results in cells being unable to take up glucose from the blood, and so ceasing to function properly. The unused glucose then builds up in the blood, a condition known as hyperglycaemia. To provide energy for the body, the liver breaks down fats instead, leading to a dangerous build-up of acidic substances called ketones in the blood (ketoacidosis). This in turn damages tissues and organs and can be severe enough to cause a "diabetic coma". The excess blood glucose is filtered out by the kidneys into the urine (glucose in the urine is called glycosuria) – hence the age-old urine taste test for diagnosing the "sugar disease".

In 1889–90, Lithuanian-born pathologist Oscar Minkowski and German physiologist Joseph von Mering at Strasbourg University first established the vital role that the pancreas plays in glucose regulation, by removing the pancreas from dogs. Over the next 35 years, dogs remained at the forefront of diabetes research. In 1891, American pathologist Eugene Lindsay Opie, who was based at Johns Hopkins University, Baltimore, US, observed that the islets of Langerhans seemed to degenerate in people who had diabetes. A series of experiments showed that if the tube carrying digestive enzymes from the pancreas into the intestine (the pancreatic duct) was ligated (tied), the parts of the pancreas (acini) that made these enzymes deteriorated. The islets of Langerhans, however, remained intact, and glucose did not pass into the urine. These findings focused researchers' attention on the islets themselves.

Today, the term "hormone" is familiar – it refers to chemical substances that circulate in the blood and control the various body processes. The name was originally used in 1905 by British physiologist Ernest Henry Starling, who, with William Maddock Bayliss, had discovered secretin, the first known hormone, in 1902. Another British physiologist, Edward Albert Sharpey-Schafer, had proposed in the 1890s that pancreatic islets might make a substance that affected blood glucose. The hormone concept fitted this idea well and, in 1913, Sharpey-Schafer proposed that the sugar-affecting substance could be called "insuline". In fact, the name "insuline" had been suggested in 1909 by Belgian physiologist Jean de Meyer.

Minkowski and other researchers were already trying to extract and purify the substance produced by the islets. When tested, some extracts did lower blood glucose, but they also had adverse side effects, causing

GLUCOMETER
Invented by Joseph Long, an instrument-maker in London, this early glucometer was used to check a patient's urine for signs of glucose.

abscesses and fever. In 1920, Canadian researcher Frederick Banting read about the link between islets and the conjectured hormone "insuline". Since the pancreas made digestive enzymes, he wondered if the enzymes might be digesting the hormone. Would the ligated ducts of dogs, in which the enzyme-manufacturing parts of the pancreas degenerated but the islets did not, yield a purer extract? He noted, with erratic spelling: "Diabetus. Ligate pancreatic ducts of dog. Keep dogs alive till acini degenerate leaving islets. Try to isolate the internal secretion of these to relieve glycosurea".

Banting took his idea to Toronto University's Head of Physiology, John J. R. Macleod, who was working on glucose and diabetes. Banting and Macleod did not get along well, but Macleod agreed to furnish Banting with laboratory facilities, dogs, and an assistant, Charles Best. In May 1921, Banting and Best set to work, overseen by Macleod. The pace was rapid – others were chasing the same goal. The duo tried chemical techniques to purify the hormone extracted from ligated dog pancreases, and tested it by injecting dogs that had been made diabetic by having their pancreases removed. Step by step, their results improved. One dog – known as Marjorie, or lab dog 33 – was kept alive by injections for ten weeks, but the results were inconsistent. Eventually, Banting and Best refined their methods to obtain greater yields of the active ingredient, to which they gave the working name "isletin". However, to their frustration, the research was delayed by Macleod asking for trials to be repeated – leading to tension and clashes with Banting. The team knew that dog pancreases would never yield enough hormone for human use, and devised techniques to extract it from the pancreases of cows instead.

At last, they felt ready for a human trial. On 11 January 1922, at Toronto General Hospital, the latest cow pancreas extract was injected into 14-year-old diabetic patient Leonard Thompson. The results were sadly disappointing: his blood glucose levels showed only slight improvement and he suffered some side effects. At this point, Canadian biochemist James Bertram Collip joined the team to lend expertise in the extraction process. A week after the first human trial, Collip found an improved way to purify the extract. He injected it into healthy rabbits, and it lowered their blood glucose levels.

A few days later, daily injections of the new extract were given to the same patient – this time with success. Leonard's blood glucose, ketoacidosis, and other features normalized; the side effects were greatly reduced; and his overall condition improved dramatically. Over the following weeks, more young patients at Toronto General Hospital were treated and recovered from diabetic coma, to the delight of staff, family, and friends. The early results were published in March 1922 in the *Canadian Medical Association Journal*: "These results taken together have been such as to leave no doubt that in these extracts we have a therapeutic measure of unquestionable value in the treatment of certain phases of the disease in man". As the project grew, the team produced a more detailed account, presented in May 1922 by Macleod to the Association of American Physicians. They named the active ingredient insulin, unaware that this name had already been suggested. However, there were still many obstacles to surmount: scaling up production, reducing contaminants, standardizing strengths, and working out suitable doses. Pharmaceutical companies came on board: Eli Lilly and Company solved many of the problems, especially how to prepare extracted insulin within a certain acidity range to boost yield and purity. By early 1923, Lilly's facilities were manufacturing enough insulin of sufficient quality to help hundreds, then thousands of people with diabetes. Within two years, type 1 diabetes had been transformed

NUMBER OF PEOPLE WITH DIABETES TODAY

37,000,000

MARJORIE, LAB DOG 33
Frederick Banting (right) and Charles Best
on the roof of the University of Toronto's
Medical Building, with Marjorie, the dog kept
alive for weeks with insulin injections.

from a potentially fatal condition into one in which insulin treatment allowed a normal life.

Sadly, running parallel to this life-saving work was a tale of resentment and jealousy. Banting and Macleod never got on and Collip was an uneasy participant. In 1923, the Nobel Prize in Physiology or Medicine was jointly awarded to Macleod and Banting "for the discovery of insulin treatment". Banting was enraged that Best had been excluded and shared his own prize money with him; Macleod did the same with Collip. Other scientists working with insulin also claimed recognition. In later years, the Nobel committee revisited the insulin episode, gave Best fuller credit, and also recognized the prior achievements of Romanian professor of physiology Nicolae Paulescu. He had discovered insulin (or "pancreatine") in cows in 1916, but had not found a way to use it in humans.

Progress in insulin treatment continued. In 1982, human insulin was the first major therapeutic agent produced by recombinant DNA technology, or "genetic engineering" (see pp.338–49), and, by 2000, more than 300 insulin analogues were available – including 70 derived from animals, 80 derived from humans, and 150 synthesised by DNA technology. These various types of insulin, and the sophisticated blood glucose meters now available, have made it possible for doctors to customize treatment and for diabetics to monitor and control their own blood glucose levels more successfully. These advances in diabetes care have greatly improved diabetics' quality of life and significantly increased their life expectancy.

Receiving Blood

Physicians first tried blood transfusions as a treatment in the 17th century, with little success. By the 19th century, scientists suspected that blood differed from one person to another, so before transfusion, they mixed blood from the donor and recipient to see if there was any clotting. By 1902, physician Karl Landsteiner and his team (see pp.243–44) had defined four different human blood groups: A, B, AB, and C (now called O). He realized that transfusion went wrong when antibodies in the recipient's blood – which neutralize foreign bodies – attacked the donated blood, causing a fatal allergic reaction. Today, transfusion is a common and safe procedure, with around 92 million blood donations collected every year.

The first transfusions

After William Harvey described blood circulation in 1628 (see pp.134–43), there were some early transfusions, often from animals. Many recipients died as a result. A few survived, either through luck or because only a tiny amount of blood was transfused, which limited the detrimental effects.

CONTEMPORARY ILLUSTRATION FROM AROUND THE 17TH CENTURY SHOWING A MAN RECEIVING A BLOOD TRANSFUSION DIRECTLY FROM AN ANIMAL

Tourniquets

Mounting plate

Interchangeable needles

Plunger handle

Central chamber

The plunger is inserted into the top of the central chamber

TRANSFUSION SYRINGE
FRENCH, c.1940
This transfusion apparatus is double-ended, meaning that blood could be transferred directly between donor and recipient. Before the use of "blood banking" and refrigeration in the early 20th century, all transfusions were done person to person.

Blood groups

The variation in blood groups is due to antibodies and antigens present in the blood. Antibodies – in the plasma – detect unusual or dangerous substances in the body and attack red blood cells that do not match their own. Antigens – found on the surface of the red blood cells – bind with antibodies of the right type. In modern transfusions, patients are given only red blood cells, rather than whole blood, which limits the chance of harmful immune responses.

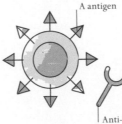

A antigen

Anti-B antibody

GROUP A
Blood in group A has A antigens and anti-B antibodies. It cannot be given to people with groups B or O.

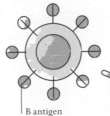

B antigen

Anti-A antibody

GROUP B
Blood in group B has B antigens and anti-A antibodies. It cannot be given to those with groups A or O.

B antigen

A antigen

GROUP AB
Blood in group AB has both A and B antigens, but no antibodies. It can be donated only to people with blood of the same group.

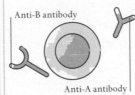

Anti-B antibody

Anti-A antibody

GROUP O
Group O has no antigens but both anti-A and anti-B antibodies. Group O blood can be donated to people of all groups.

The First Antibiotic

MOST MEDICAL DISCOVERIES ARE THE FRUITS of diligent and exhaustive research by teams of scientists and physicians. One of the most significant breakthroughs in medical history, however, came about by chance. In 1928, Scottish medical researcher Alexander Fleming returned to his unseasonably cold, messy laboratory from holiday and noticed the strange effects of a patch of mould. He had inadvertently stumbled upon penicillin, the very first antibiotic. The drug would go on to save millions of lives, as it still does today, but it did not come into widespread use until the 1940s. Why was there such a long gap?

The germ-killing properties of moulds have a long history. For centuries, medical experts regarded oozing pus and foul discharge as a sign that the body was expelling noxious material. For centuries too, folk remedies recommended the use of mouldy bread, cakes, or fruit to treat suppurating wounds. Many of these anecdotes could have been referring to the antibiotic effects of the *Penicillium* mould – tiny, unprepossessing fungal cells found in the soil and many other places. In established medicine, sporadic notes by John Tyndall, Louis Pasteur, Joseph Lister, and others had recorded that moulds prevented bacterial infection of laboratory samples and damaged the bacterial cultures they were trying to grow (see pp.201–203). In 1896–97, a young French physician, Ernest Duchesne, went so far as to find that injections of a *Penicillium* mould seemed to counteract the bacterial infection typhoid in laboratory animals. He could not establish a definite correlation, however, so the French medical establishment took no notice and Duchesne was subsequently whisked away on army duty.

The term "antibiotic", meaning "against life", dates only from 1942, when it was first used by US-based microbiologist Selman Waksman (see p.258). It is usually used to refer to agents that act against bacteria, but while plenty of substances, such as hot tar and strong acids, kill bacteria, the term antibiotic is generally reserved for a substance produced by another living thing, often another microbe. The similar term "antibacterial" is usually applied to substances not produced by living processes. These include the sulfonamide (sulfa) drugs, which opened a new era in medicine in the 1930s. They were not antibiotics as they were synthesized in the laboratory, but they were antimicrobials

– a category of substances that kill or inhibit microorganisms. The first sulfonamide on the market was Prontosil, quickly followed by many similar antibacterials before World War II. German bacteriologist Gerhard Domagk was awarded the Nobel Prize in Physiology or Medicine "for the discovery of the antibacterial effects of Prontosil" in 1939 – six years before Fleming and his team were awarded the same prize for pioneering penicillin.

Alexander Fleming grew up in a farming family in Ayrshire, Scotland, where he attended Kilmarnock Academy. At the age of 13, he moved to London to live with his older brother Tom. Alec, as he was known, worked for a shipping company until he inherited a small sum of money from an uncle four years later and decided to follow Tom into medicine. In 1906, he qualified with distinction as a doctor at St Mary's Hospital Medical School, West London. St Mary's was his working home for the rest of his peacetime career. During World War I, Fleming joined the Royal Army Medical Corps. Based at the military hospital in Boulogne, France, he was struck by how many soldiers died from infected wounds. Antiseptics had a limited effect because they could not penetrate deeply enough, and Fleming became convinced that they were in fact harmful to the blood corpuscles that destroyed bacteria.

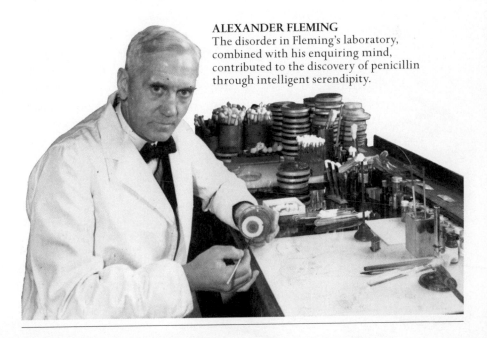

ALEXANDER FLEMING
The disorder in Fleming's laboratory, combined with his enquiring mind, contributed to the discovery of penicillin through intelligent serendipity.

At the end of the war, Fleming returned to to his research post at St Mary's. Encouraged by his mentor, eminent bacteriologist and immunologist Almroth Wright, he started to research bacteria-killers. In 1922–23, he identified a naturally occurring substance that he called lysozyme; this enzyme, found in saliva, tears, mucus, and egg white, had antibacterial effects. Its action, however, was limited and it proved difficult to purify and concentrate.

On Monday 3 September 1928, Fleming returned from a holiday with his family at their residence in Suffolk. Back at work, he set about tidying his laboratory – Fleming was not known for his neatness. He had been working with the bacterium *Staphylococcus*, whose harmful strains cause abscesses, boils, respiratory infections, and food poisoning. Test tubes, flasks, and Petri dishes were put aside in piles, ready for cleaning. Exact accounts of what happened next vary, but while he was chatting to colleague and former research assistant Mervyn Price, Fleming noticed something odd. On one of the dishes where colonies of bacteria were supposed to grow, there was also a colony of mould with a bacteria-free area around it. Something – apparently the mould – had stopped the bacteria from growing. How the mould had arrived on the dish was unclear. Microscopic fungal spores float almost everywhere, but the laboratory windows were fixed shut.

Intrigued, Fleming kept the dish, took samples, and grew them. This was the turning point. A colleague from the mycology unit, Charles La Touche, identified the fungus as a type of *Penicillium*, provisionally *P. rubrum*. In fact, La Touche was also growing moulds, including *Penicillium*, as part of an asthma research project, and the spores may have drifted up from his lab. Fleming embarked on a standard series of experiments to test his findings, refining extracts of the fungus into a broth, which

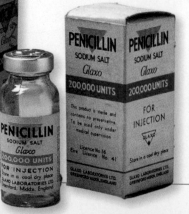

1950s PENICILLIN
By the 1950s, penicillin was being manufactured on a large scale. British drug companies such as Glaxo, producers of this penicillin, relied on US technology to improve their output.

"One sometimes finds what one is not looking for"

ALEXANDER FLEMING

he called first "mould juice", then penicillin. In 1929, he summarized some of his early results in the report "On the antibacterial action of cultures of a *Penicillium*, with special reference to their use in the isolation of *B. influenzae*", which was published in the *British Journal of Experimental Pathology*.

Penicillin killed or inhibited the growth of many bacteria, including *Staphylococcus* and *Streptococcus*, which were responsible for illnesses that ranged from sore throats to pneumonia. These bacteria were all Gram-positive – they reacted to a dye known as Gram's stain by turning dark blue or purple. Most bacteria harmful to humans are Gram-positive, but some are Gram-negative – they turn pink or red in reaction to Gram's stain. Penicillin seemed largely ineffective against Gram-negative bacteria. Later research demonstrated that penicillin works by damaging the way in which Gram-positive bacteria build their cell wall, so that as each bacterium grows and divides, its weakened cell wall disintegrates, spilling the contents. Gram-negative bacteria, on the other hand, have an additional layer around the cell wall that penicillin is unable to penetrate.

Fleming's early hopes that he had discovered a wonder cure faded. Further investigation showed that penicillin was toxic neither to animals nor humans, which was good. However, it did not remain in the body for long, as it was rapidly excreted in urine; it was hard to obtain and purify, and it tended to deteriorate in storage rather than remaining stable. Furthermore, the mould did not always yield the desired antibacterial substance. Unknown to Fleming, *Penicillium* only does this in adverse conditions, as a survival trick to neutralize bacteria that might compete for the same food source. It was only years later that Fleming's research assistant Ronald Hare demonstrated that a cold spell in August 1928 had stressed the *Penicillium* while Fleming was on holiday, producing the antibiotic effects that he observed. Although the results were not all that Fleming had hoped for, he still thought penicillin might be useful as an antiseptic and it was kept at St Mary's as a useful laboratory "tool" for several years. Because it inhibited some bacteria, but not others, it was helpful in purifying bacterial cultures for research and vaccines. Elsewhere, Cecil Paine, a former student of Fleming's, had some success in curing eye infections with penicillin at Sheffield Royal Infirmary in 1930, but never reported his results. Fleming, in the meantime, began to research other areas, including sulfonamides. As he later admitted in 1940, he "forgot about [penicillin] some years ago".

In 1939, the story shifted to Oxford University, where Howard Florey was Professor of Pathology at Lincoln College. Originally from Australia, Florey had moved to England in 1921, taking up his position at Oxford in 1935. Ernst Boris Chain was also working in pathology there. A chemistry graduate born of Jewish parents in Berlin, he had emigrated to England in 1933 after the Nazis' rise to power. In 1938, Chain took on a project to find out how antibacterial substances worked. With Florey, he read Fleming's work and selected penicillin as a subject. The third key member of the Oxford team was biochemist Norman Heatley, a research associate with an aptitude for laboratory equipment and techniques. Like Fleming, Chain and Florey found penicillin hard to extract and purify. Despite its promise, it yielded only tiny amounts. World War II had started and funding in Britain was scarce, so the research team appealed to the US Rockefeller Foundation for funds. With its support, they had produced enough penicillin by mid-1940 to test on mice; four injected with the antibiotic did not succumb to a lethal dose of *Streptococcus*, whereas four untreated mice died overnight. Work began to standardize dose strength, with all kinds of equipment – milk churns, bottles, rubber and glass tubing – commandeered to grow the moulds.

In February 1941, the first trial of penicillin on a human was carried out, on 43-year-old policeman Albert Alexander. An infected scratch had produced terrible abscesses affecting his face and lungs – the type of infection that is rarely seen today because of antibiotics. Injections of penicillin set him on the road to recovery, but the supply ran out before he was fully cured, and he died. However, out of the next five patients, four recovered. After these results were published in *The Lancet*, the Northern Regional Research Laboratory (NRRL) in Peoria, Illinois, part of the US Department of Agriculture, backed the research. Drug companies Merck, Squibb, Pfizer, Lilly, and Lederle also showed an interest. A search began for higher-yielding strains of *Penicillium*, with fruit and soil samples sent to Peoria from all over the world, especially by the US military. In 1943, a Peoria housewife contributed a mouldy cantaloupe with a huge *Penicillium* yield. Shining ultraviolet light on samples to cause genetic changes increased yields further. Improved ways of growing the mould were also found and companies in the US and the UK were soon producing penicillin on an industrial scale. More supplies and intense demand from the battlefield led to more clinical trials and, in 1944, supplies of penicillin to troops at the D-Day landings dramatically reduced the death toll from infected wounds. Wider use among the military and civilians followed. By the end of the war, enough penicillin was produced each month to treat hundreds of thousands of cases. Fleming, Florey, and Chain were jointly awarded the 1945 Nobel Prize in Physiology or Medicine for their research, and Fleming and Florey were both knighted. Ever modest, Fleming insisted: "I did not invent penicillin. Nature did that. I only discovered it by accident".

The story of antibiotics is not over, but nor is it an entirely happy ending. While penicillin and the drugs developed in its wake are still used all around the world, their effectiveness has been undermined by their inappropriate use for diseases that are viral rather than bacterial, and patients' failure to complete courses of treatment. There are now 150,000 deaths globally every year from multi-drug-resistant tuberculosis, and antibiotic-resistant bacterial illnesses such as the hospital-acquired infection MRSA pose major health issues.

WORLD WAR II POSTER
Treatment of infected war wounds stimulated research into penicillin in the 1940s. Use of the antibiotic reduced deaths from infection in the later stages of the war.

Antibiotics at Work

By the late 19th century, scientists understood that many diseases were caused by bacteria, and researchers tried to find ways of killing these microbes or impeding their growth. In 1928, Alexander Fleming (see pp.252–57) discovered that a *Penicillium* mould inhibited the growth of *Staphylococcus* bacteria. In the early 1940s, a team derived a stable form of the antibiotic penicillin suitable for mass production from the mould, and soon it was being used to treat many diseases, including pneumonia and syphilis. Further types of antibiotics were produced in the 1950s. Scientists classify antibiotics into groups, according to the ways in which they act on the cells of bacteria.

A flagellum acts like a tail to propel the bacterium

Bacterium DNA – the quinolone group of antibiotics stops DNA replicating, so bacteria cannot multiply

Ribosome – streptomycin restricts the bacterium's protein growth by binding to the ribosomes (where protein synthesis occurs). Without proteins, the bacterial cell rapidly dies

Selman Waksman

American microbiologist Selman Waksman came up with the term "antibiotic". In 1943, he and a colleague, Albert Schatz, were working on organisms that live in soil. This led to the production of streptomycin, an antibiotic that proved to be effective against tuberculosis. Waksman's laboratory at Rutgers University in New Jersey synthesized several other antibacterial drugs.

A US CITIZEN FROM 1910, WAKSMAN CAME FROM A PART OF THE RUSSIAN EMPIRE NOW IN UKRAINE

Plasma membrane – the drug polymixin binds to the membrane around bacterial cells, making it permeable: pressure drives water into the bacterium, which eventually kills it

Messenger RNA – rifamycin drugs block RNA, which conveys genetic information to synthesize proteins

Protein, essential for the bacterium to survive

Plasmid ring, a small DNA molecule

Peptoglycan sheet – a mesh-like layer that forms part of the bacterial cell walls; bacteria cannot grow without complete cell walls, so penicillin and several other widely used antibiotics work by preventing bacteria forming the peptoglycan sheet

Pilus (hairy projection) can connect to another bacterium

ANTIBIOTICS IN ACTION

This diagram shows the different actions of some types of antibiotics on a bacterium. These actions include inhibiting the cell's protein growth, interfering with the working of its DNA, preventing the cell wall from developing, and damaging its protective membrane.

How drugs work

Many drugs work by imitating a chemical that controls a particular biological process in the cell. Drugs that stimulate a process are called agonists, while those that supress a process are called antagonists. This was discovered in 1940 with experiments on sulphanilamide, a compound similar to a bacterial nutrient. When introduced to bacteria, it took the place of the nutrient; deprived of the actual nutrient, the bacteria died.

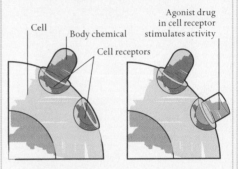

Cell

Body chemical

Cell receptors

Agonist drug in cell receptor stimulates activity

AGONIST DRUGS

Most cell activity is controlled by natural body chemicals that fit into receptors on a cell's surface. An agonist drug can mimic one of these chemicals, triggering the receptors, which in turn stimulate a process inside the cell.

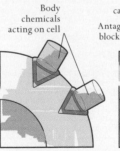

Body chemicals acting on cell

Body chemicals cannot enter receptor

Antagonist drug blocks receptors

ANTAGONIST DRUGS

Antagonist drugs, including antibiotics, also mimic natural body chemicals and fit into receptor sites in the cell. Unlike agonists, they do not trigger the cell's receptors, instead blocking them. As a result, the natural process controlled by the receptors is reduced or stops completely, damaging or killing the cell.

The Fight Against Cancer

ATTITUDES TO ILLNESS CHANGE OVER TIME. In the mid-20th century, cancer was a word to avoid. Public perception and stigma meant knowing glances and hushed whispers, as if the diagnosis were an automatic death sentence. This was far from true then, and even less so today. In the mid-1970s in the US, the five-year relative survival rate (relative to the rest of the population, taking into account that they might have died even without cancer) for adults for all forms of cancer was around 50 per cent. Thirty years later it was approaching 70 per cent. For children, these numbers were 60 per cent and 80 per cent respectively. Other developed nations saw similar improvements. The trend today is for five-year survival rates to increase in some regions by more than one per cent per year – although ageing populations may affect future figures.

Advances in the past half-century include hugely increased understanding of cancers, groundbreaking discoveries about their causes, the boon of earlier diagnosis, and a wider range of improved treatments. In 2012, the American Cancer Society stated: "Scientists have learned more about cancer in the last two decades than had been learned in all the centuries preceding."

There are more than 200 different types of cancer. Underlying them all are microscopic cells multiplying out of control to form tumours (growths) that are malignant – that is, they have the potential to spread to other parts of the body. In a healthy body, each type of cell continually divides to make more of its kind in a controlled, organized manner. In the small intestine lining, cell turnover is measured in days; in skin, about one month; in the pancreas, a year or two. When cells become cancerous, they ignore the usual restraints and multiply faster, which can create pressure on neighbouring cells, disrupting how they function. Cancerous cells may fail to carry out their own specialized tasks and start to look more like unspecialized stem cells (see pp.364–69). Unlike the cells of a benign (non-cancerous) tumour, cancer cells can invade adjacent tissues. They can break away from the primary site and travel, usually in the blood or lymph system, to other places where they lodge, continue to multiply, and set up secondary growths. This process, which is so characteristic of cancer, is known as metastasis.

One way of classifying cancers is by their primary site – bone, skin, liver, and so on. Another system is by the types of cell affected, since most organs are made from several kinds of cell and tissue. Lymphomas involve the white blood cells known as lymphocytes (see pp.286–91); carcinomas affect epithelial cells, which form the coverings and linings of body parts and organs; sarcomas affect the connective tissues, such as bone, cartilage, and muscle; and melanomas derive from pigment-making skin cells known as melanocytes. Such details about cancer were unknown until the invention of the microscope made it possible to study cells and tissues and then, in the mid-19th century, cellular pathology

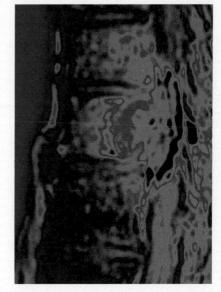

METASTASIS IN THE SPINE
This scan shows a malignant secondary tumour (coloured pink) on a disc between two thoracic (middle) vertebrae.

(see pp.144–49). Before that, there were only vague notions about what cancers were and how they arose. In ancient Greece and Rome, they were attributed, like most diseases, to an imbalance of the bodily "fluids" called the four humours (see pp.106–107). The term "cancer" (Latin for "crab") arose at this time, probably because Hippocrates and others likened the appearance of some tumours, which had a dense centre and radiating lines of blood vessels, to the shape of a crab's body and legs.

Most cancers occur more frequently with advancing age. In medieval and Renaissance times, people died younger, so cancers were less prominent than today. They were also less well documented. With no knowledge of cancers' common feature – uncontrolled cell proliferation – there were few reasons to link the different kinds of tumour. In the 18th century, indicators of the causes of cancer were first spotted. Italian physician Bernardino Ramazzini, who pioneered occupational medicine with his book *Diseases of Workers*, noted in around 1713 that breast cancer occurred more frequently in nuns than in other groups of women. He speculated that this was linked to lack of sexual activity. The causes of breast cancer are still unclear today, but factors that reduce its likelihood include having children, and having them sooner rather than later. In general, women who have children are about 30 per cent less likely to develop breast cancer than those who do not. In the 1770s, surgeon Percival Pott, at St Bartholomew's Hospital, London, described cancer of the scrotum (the skin bag containing the testes) in chimney sweeps – since classified as a form of skin cancer known as squamous cell carcinoma. It was the first conventional medical report of a carcinogen, a substance that causes or triggers cancer – in this case, soot.

Momentous 19th-century strides in surgery included anaesthesia and antisepsis/asepsis (see pp.206–213). Operations such as surgical removal of tumours grew longer and more complex. Surgeons found that cutting out only the growth could allow recurrence, but removing the surrounding tissues as well, especially lymph glands (channels and nodes), reduced the likelihood of this. Radical surgery developed – excision of the cancerous growth, plus the local blood and lymph supplies, and neighbouring tissues. Professor of Surgery William Stewart Halsted started performing radical mastectomy for breast cancer in the US in the 1880s at Johns Hopkins University, Baltimore (although a surgeon called Bernard Peyrilhe had undertaken the first such operation a century earlier in France). Around 1900, London surgeon Sampson Handley showed that lymph channels were the main route for breast cancer to spread.

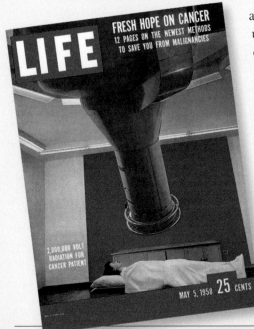

The radical approach for breast and other types of cancer continued until the mid-20th century. More conservative operations, removing the tumour alone, guided by sophisticated imaging techniques (see pp.302–311), and supported by drugs and radiotherapy, became the treatment of choice from the 1950s in Europe, and the 1970s in the US.

FRESH HOPE ON CANCER
The cover of *Life* magazine in 1958 heralds radiation therapy as a ray of hope in the search for cancer treatments.

Radiotherapy, in which cancerous tissues are exposed to X-rays, gamma rays, or similar forms of energy, is one of the main forms of cancer treatment today. This treatment dates back to Wilhelm Röntgen's discovery of X-rays in late 1895 (see pp.302–303). Within weeks, doctors noticed that X-raying patients to view their bones also seemed to shrink or obliterate some skin tumours, so they quickly adapted the new X-ray machines for cancer treatment. At first the radiation was given in one massive blast, but it had dire side effects, including skin burns, bleeding from the orifices, pain, inflammation, confusion, hair loss, and fatigue, collectively known as radiation sickness. Worse, new cancers sometimes appeared. The double-edged nature of X-rays became clear – they could kill as well as cure. The X-ray energy damages molecules within cells, including gene-containing DNA, which duplicates itself as each cell divides. Cancer cells generally divide faster than healthy cells, so they are more affected, but exposed normal cells are also damaged.

During the 1910s and 1920s, French physician and radiotherapy pioneer Claudius Regaud experimented with animal, and then human trials to show that a series of shorter, lower-dose X-ray bursts could be effective while reducing side effects. Another French physician, Henri Coutard, continued his work and, by the 1930s, had established the principles of fractionated radiotherapy – controlled low doses given at regular intervals – that are still in use today. Regaud also helped to develop therapies using the radioactive metal radium, discovered in 1898 by French physicist Marie Curie. Radium became all the rage, and not only to treat cancer. It found its way into all manner of products from bath salts and toothpaste to bracelets and belts. But mounting evidence showed that this "treatment" was, in most cases, at best ineffective and at worst deadly.

The infamous 1920s case of the Radium Girls involved women who added glow-in-the-dark paint containing radium to watch and clock dials at a factory in New Jersey, US. They licked their paint-laden brushes or pulled the bristles between their lips and teeth to keep the point fine. Many of these women went on to develop diseases and cancers of the lips, teeth, and mouth, and suffered general radiation sickness. By the 1930s, the damaging effects of radium and similar substances had become well known. Using radium for radiotherapy became more limited, specialized, and controlled. The same principle of radiation from a substance (rather than X-rays) is used today, most often with caesium-137, iridium-192, and iodine-125. Small seeds (containers) are implanted around the growth to control and shrink it. This is known as internal radiation therapy, or brachytherapy. Other methods include radiation-dosed tubes or wires and swallowed or injected liquids that contain radioactive substances that accumulate naturally in the target tissues.

Radiotherapy using X-rays improved throughout the mid-20th century, with more controlled doses targeted at cancerous tissues. As with cancer surgery, a new era of radiotherapy became possible in the 1970s, in the form of image-guided radiation therapy (IGRT), which used techniques such as computerized tomography (CT) and magnetic resonance imaging (MRI) to show the position, shape, and size of growths. This made it possible to analyse the cancerous area in three dimensions for conformal radiation therapy (CRT), in which radiation machines with devices called multi-leaf collimators "mould" several beams into the same shape as the tumour, thus avoiding the healthy surrounding tissue. More recently, intensity-modulated radiation therapy (IMRT) has been developed, in which radiation energy and aim are adjusted even more precisely, to spare nearby normal cells. As well as X-rays, other forms of radiotherapy include proton therapy. This uses beams of protons (positively charged atomic particles), but prohibitively expensive and complicated equipment is needed to generate the protons – a particle accelerator in effect – so the treatment is not widely available, even now.

The third mainstay of cancer treatment is chemotherapy (treatment with chemicals). Historically, the term was applied to drug treatment for a variety of diseases. In 1909, German scientist Paul Ehrlich developed the anti-syphilitic drug arsphenamine (sold under the name of Salvarsan) – the first modern chemotherapeutic drug. Today, the term chemotherapy applies to anti-cancer agents that are cytotoxic – meaning that they harm, disable, and even kill cells. Methods include disrupting the cells' DNA, latching on to their membranes (outer coverings), and tricking the cells into undergoing a process known as apoptosis (programmed cell death) – in effect, making them commit suicide. Chemotherapy has to tread a fine line between damaging rapidly dividing cancer cells and leaving normal cells as undamaged as possible. Cancer chemotherapy had a curious beginning. Over the course of two world wars is was noted that the devastating chemical warfare agent mustard gas reduced blood cell production in bone marrow – cells that otherwise multiplied at a rate of several million per second (see pp.364–73). By 1943, scientists were investigating mustard-gas-type compounds, both for use as chemical weapons and as defences against them, and had begun looking into their potential use against rapidly multiplying cancer cells. Work at Yale University in the US produced the substance nitrogen mustard (mustine or mechlorethamine). In 1943, it was tested by injecting it into a patient suffering from the white blood cell cancer Hodgkin's lymphoma, with promising results.

After World War II, medical research continued into nitrogen mustard compounds. These stop DNA from being able to copy itself for cell division. Studies have yielded several nitrogen mustard chemotherapies over the past 50 years, including bendamustine, busulphan, chlorambucil, cyclophosphamide, ifosfamide, and melphalan. Another group is the platinum derivatives, first studied in the 1960s. Platinum is more usually associated with vehicle exhaust catalytic convertors, but is used in cancer treatment to trigger cell death. Cisplatin was introduced in the 1970s and carboplatin, a widely used, second-generation platinum anti-cancer drug, in the 1980s.

At Harvard Medical School in the US, American paediatric pathologist Sidney Farber pursued another line of chemotherapy research. In 1947 and 1948, he was looking at treatments for acute lymphoblastic leukaemia – a cancer that affects white blood cells. Concentrates of the newly discovered folic acid (a B-group vitamin) had reduced mammary tumours in mice but Farber noticed that they accelerated the leukaemia process. A diet low in folic acid, on the other hand, seemed to reduce proliferation of cancer cells. So Farber tried aminopterin, a drug that interferes with the action of folic acid, then another, amethopterin, hoping that the drug might inhibit the multiplication of the abnormal leukaemia cells. The results were encouraging. Farber's reasoning led not

FATHER OF MODERN CHEMOTHERAPY
In 1947, pathologist Sidney Farber gave children the first drug – aminopterin – to prove effective against acute leukaemia, earning some temporary remissions.

only to a new line of chemotherapeutic drugs, but also to a logical way of looking for them. Modern chemotherapy was up and running. Amethopterin, now called methotrexate, remains a key drug against cancers and autoimmune disorders, among other diseases. In the second half of the 20th century, chemotherapy itself mushroomed into a vast business. Advances include targeting chemotherapy specifically at cancer cells, rather than indiscriminately destroying body tissues in general.

Biological (bio-) therapy uses substances produced naturally by the body, or similar synthetic varieties. Better targeting have led to it being used to sabotage cancer cells. One bio-therapy is immunotherapy – exploiting the tricks of the body's own immune system. Certain white blood cells make antibodies that adhere to and disrupt "foreign" substances called antigens, on germs for example (see pp.222–27). Some cancer cells have distinctive antigens not found in other body cells. Monoclonal antibodies, produced by cloned (genetically identical) cells all obtained from a single original white cell, can be manufactured to target these specific antigens. They were first made in the 1970s, using a white blood cell which was itself created from multiple myeloma, a cancer. Their role is to bind onto and destroy cancerous cells, or to mark them for attack by the immune system, while ignoring all the normal cells. In each tailor-made batch, all the monoclonal antibodies are the same, so they are very accurate in selecting their targets. As well as counteracting cancers, they are used against autoimmune disorders, both for diagnosis and in research.

Hormonal therapy for cancer is another expanding field. Tamoxifen, a compound first produced in the 1960s, has become a major treatment for breast cancers that need the hormone oestrogen in order to grow and multiply. Tamoxifen latches onto the oestrogen-receiving units on cell surfaces, which prevents oestrogen itself from attaching, so the cancer cells cannot grow.

As cancer specialists (oncologists) increase their research and knowledge, the list of carcinogens grows ever longer, from those in tobacco smoke to industrial pollutants.

TOBACCO USE CAUSES OVER

20%

OF ALL CANCER DEATHS
WORLDWIDE

EXPENSIVE BUT EFFECTIVE
The bio-pharmaceuticals industry is researching the growth of monoclonal antibodies – protein drugs – in algae to lower the cost of drug production.

Lifestyle, diet, obesity, and occupation are all now implicated in cancerous changes, as are genetics. Oncogenes – a term that dates from 1969 – are genes that are involved in causing or facilitating cancerous changes. Another set of genes, the tumour-suppressors, make substances that prevent cells from becoming cancerous, so if a tumour-suppressor gene in a cell is faulty or fails to work, the cell may mutate and become cancerous.

The first human oncovirus (a virus that causes cancer) discovered was the Epstein-Barr virus, which was identified in the 1960s in Burkitt's lymphoma. In the early to mid-1980s, German virus researcher Harald zur Hausen discovered the role of human papilloma virus (HPV) in cervical cancer and duly received the 2008 Nobel Prize in Physiology or Medicine. HPV is thought to cause perhaps three-quarters of cervical cancer cases and is now the target of a major vaccination campaign in the UK that began in 2008. The vaccine is also widely available in the US.

Tracking down the many causes of cancer, and the biological mechanisms in its development, in the hope that this will lead to better prevention, diagnosis, and treatment, is a major thrust of cancer research today. This is all the more important as people in developed countries live for longer. As age is one of the major risk factors, this is making cancer occur with increasing frequency.

Deadly Cells

Cancer is on the increase worldwide. It is the second largest cause of death after cardiovascular disease, and can begin anywhere in the body, caused by cells spreading out of control in tissues such as skin, bone, and muscle. Cancer cells may cluster together to cause tumours, which can be malignant – this occurs when a tumour invades surrounding tissue and replaces it with more cancer cells, as they replicate out of control.

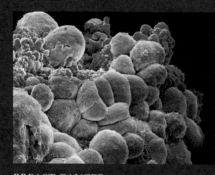

BREAST CANCER
Breast cancer often originates in the milk ducts, and is a carcinoma (cancer of lining tissues). It was one of the earliest forms of cancer to be studied, and is one of the more easily treatable cancers.

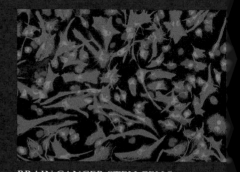

BRAIN CANCER STEM CELLS
Cancers have stem cells, just as ordinary tissues do (see pp.364–73). These trigger the growth of cancerous cells and can make cancers appear again after apparently successful therapy.

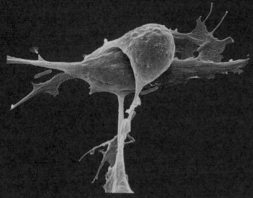

LYOMYOSARCOMA CELLS
A rare form of cancer, lyomyosarcoma affects smooth muscles – those that work involuntarily, such as the muscles found in the heart and blood vessels.

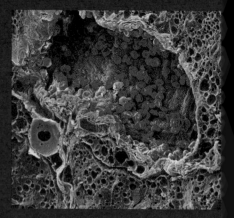

BLOOD VESSEL AND MELANOMA
Cancer cells send out messages encouraging blood vessels to grow into tumours. Seen in cross-section, here a blood vessel (centre, with red blood cells) has grown into a melanoma (a form of skin tumour).

SKIN CANCER CELL SPLIT OPEN

The structure of cancer cells is varied: this one is frozen and spilt open to display an enlarged nucleus. Cancer cells can also be irregularly shaped or folded. The nucleus holds the DNA, which dictates how the cell grows.

CANCER CELLS UNDER ATTACK

T-cells (above, red) are a type of white blood cell that attacks germs. They can also take on cancer cells (above, green), but struggle to identify them. Gene therapy (see pp.338–47) can improve their detection abilities.

PANCREATIC CANCER CELL

Cancers that grow deep in the body, such as those that occur in the pancreas, are hard to spot. As a result, they sometimes reach an advanced stage before detection and treatment.

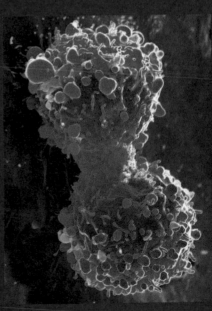

CERVICAL CANCER CELL DIVISION

HPV (human papilloma virus) is a relatively common virus. In a small proportion of women it may cause changes in cervical cells, which then ignore messages to stop multiplying and become cancerous.

New Parts for Old

R EPLACEMENT HIPS, ARTIFICIAL HEARTS, and other implants have come a long way from ancient Egyptian artificial hands and toes, Etruscan bone or ivory false teeth, Greek wooden and metal noses, and Roman iron hands, metal feet, and carved ears. Many a medieval warrior had a custom-made arm, hand, leg, or foot. Eminent 16th-century astronomer Tycho Brahe even had a selection of brass, copper, silver, and gold noses to wear after part of his own was sliced off in a duel. And in the 18th century, first US President George Washington commissioned several sets of dentures, some carved from hippopotamus ivory and incorporating human teeth.

These pre-20th-century artefacts were all early prostheses – substitutes to replace a missing part – that were worn externally. Today, a prosthetic hand could be an advanced robot, bristling with mechanics and electronics, able to detect the user's nerve signals and move its fingers separately with graduated force (see pp.350–55). Prostheses are not necessarily worn externally. For example, an artificial heart valve or plastic blood vessel can be implanted into the body, but not all implants are prosthetic (replacements). Non-prosthetic implants range from surgically imlanted cosmetic "eye jewels" to pacemakers and contraceptive or other hormone inserts. Each year, up to one million people around the world have their mobility and lives transformed by a new hip. Total hip arthroplasty (THA) or replacement is usually carried out for hip joints that have been degraded and roughened by osteoarthritis. The earliest attempts at hip-repair surgery date back to 1890s Germany, after anaesthesia came into use. First, surgeons

ARTIFICIAL IRON ARM
This forerunner of 20th-century prosthetic limbs dates from the late 16th century. It was made by an armourer for a knight who had lost an arm in combat.

exposed the ball-and-socket joint, then they smoothed off the roughened surfaces of the ball-shaped upper end – the head of the femur (thigh bone) – and the bowl-shaped socket in the hip bone, and closed the incisions. In some cases, a polished ball of ivory replaced the head of the femur, but the risky procedure did not catch on.

Finding suitable materials was a challenge. In the 1920s, Norwegian-born US surgeon Marius Smith-Peterson fitted a cup-shaped glass liner into the socket, into which the natural head of the femur fitted. Twenty years later, in Columbia, South Carolina, Austin T. Moore tried the opposite approach – leaving the natural socket and replacing the femoral head, this time with a newly developed cobalt-chromium metal alloy, Vitallium. Meanwhile, in Paris, French brothers Robert and Jean Judet tested a new acrylic-type plastic material for the ball. They mounted the femoral head on a long spike-like stem that fitted into the bone-marrow cavity along the shaft of the femur. They had some successes, but failures too, when the prosthesis came loose, wore away too fast, or fragmented.

War injuries have provided the impetus for improving prosthetic limbs through the ages. During World War II, British doctor John Charnley, who had been elected a Fellow of the Royal College of Surgeons at the age of 25, travelled in the British Royal Army Medical Corps to Northern Ireland, Egypt, and the English county of Kent – where he attended wounded soldiers from the Dunkerque evacuation. He was fascinated by the engineering skills of his army colleagues. They made not only weapons and military equipment, but also artificial arms, hands, legs, and feet for the war-wounded, and surgical equipment for the doctors. Charnley himself invented several devices, including walking calipers (leg braces). Throughout his career, he worked closely with engineers, lathe-operators, machinists, and materials technicians.

After the war, Charnley gained experience in orthopaedics – the branch of surgery concerned with the spine and joints. He studied bone structure and the roles of the different layers of bone in disease and repair. In one daring but ill-advised experiment, he persuaded a colleague to transplant some shards of bone from his own tibia (thigh bone) into different positions, under the skin and next to the bone, to track how they healed. Bone inflammation ensued and he was incapacitated for weeks. In the early 1950s, Charnley, now Consultant

PERCENTAGE OF TOTAL HIP REPLACEMENTS STILL FUNCTIONING AFTER 10 YEARS

90–95%

Orthopaedic Surgeon at Manchester Royal Infirmary, encountered a male patient whose artificial acrylic hip squeaked loudly. This set Charnley thinking about biomechanics – where machines meet living tissues – and factors such as friction, bearing surfaces, and lubrication. "The cart has been put before the horse; the artificial joint has been made and used, and now we are trying to find out how and why it fails," he said. To ease arthritic hips, Charnley experimented with the low-friction material polytetrafluoroethylene (PTFE, better known by the trade name Teflon) and with cement formulations borrowed from dentistry. He tried a metal ball and stem for the femur, fitting it into a PTFE lining in the socket, but the PTFE wore quickly, and its tiny rubbed-off particles caused severe irritation and reaction. More than 200 patients had repeat surgery to limit the damage, and again Charnley experimented on himself, by injecting himself with some of the worn particles so that he could experience the problem at first hand.

Down but not out, Charnley and his team searched for a better and more slippery material to line the hip socket. Salespeople visited with their latest products. In May 1960, supplier V. C. Binns demonstrated gears and other items made from a possible new material – ultra high molecular weight polyethylene (UHMWP). Charnley thought it a waste of time, but biomechanic Harry Craven saw something in it. When Charnley went on a skiing holiday, Craven tested the UHMWP in laboratory wear rigs. The results were impressive. Meanwhile, with characteristic energy, innovation, and desire to help patients, Charnley established a centre to improve hip replacements. The Centre for Hip Surgery, situated in a former tuberculosis hospital at Wrightington, near Manchester, was formally opened in 1961.

In 1962, Charnley began the first trial hip replacements with the metal ball-and-spike head for the femur and a UHMWP socket lining, both cemented in place. Recalling the PTFE disappointments, he was cautious at first. After about five years, promising outcomes spelled the beginning of modern total hip replacement. Charnley devised

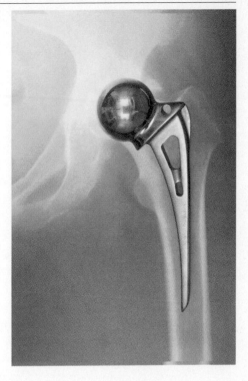

X-RAY OF PROSTHETIC HIP
The metal implant stands out
from the surrounding bone.
Modern hard-wearing metals
used include titanium, stainless
steel, and cobalt chrome.

not just hip hardware but the total package. He devised a type of tent or air enclosure with filtered air, a surgeon's whole-body gown or suit, and a better way of handling instruments, all to minimize the risk of infection. He encouraged post-mortem study of prostheses for joint wear and tear, and other imperfections, and he urged surgeons to record each tiny detail of every operation and its effect on their patient, saying: "A few observations on the human body are often of more value than a large series of experiments on animals... It has rightly been said that every surgical operation is a biological experiment." Charnley was honoured as a Fellow of the Royal Society in 1975, received a knighthood in 1977, and the Gold Medal of the British Medical Association in 1978.

Progress in hip prostheses continues today with stronger, more biocompatible (acceptable to living tissue) materials, ball-and-socket designs that dislocate less easily, improved cements, and "bone-friendly" surfaces, such as micromeshes, foamed metal, or tiny beads that encourage bone tissue to grow into them, creating a stronger bond. This work has benefitted not just artificial hips but the wide range of modern joint prostheses, from finger knuckles, elbows, and shoulders to knees and ankles.

In April 1969, as Charnley hips were marching around the world, a rather more newsworthy prosthetic implant made an entrance. This was the first total artificial heart replacement in a human, for heart-failure patient Haskell Karp in Houston, Texas, inserted by US surgeon Denton Cooley. The device was developed by Argentine heart surgeon and researcher Domingo Liotta. The mechanical heart was intended as a temporary "bridge-to-transplant" – it bought time until a suitable donor heart was found, in this case about 64 hours later. The artificial heart did its job, although the patient died around 30 hours after the natural heart transplant, due to complications including kidney failure and lung infection.

The Liotta heart was, like the real thing, a double pump. The left side received blood low in oxygen from the body and sent it to the lungs; the right side received re-oxygenated blood back from the lungs and pumped it around the body. As in the real heart, valves controlled the blood flow. The heart's pushing power came from air pressure forced along tubes from the external power-control unit. The size of a large washing machine, the unit contained pneumatic pumps, and its console controls altered pressure and rate.

Blood that flows in unusual ways, especially over uneven surfaces, runs the risk of clotting. Even if a clot does not affect the heart, bits of it can sweep into the circulation to block a brain artery (a cerebral embolism), for example, and thus cause a stroke. A major challenge for prostheses that deal with moving blood is to minimize this danger. The original Liotta heart had tubes made from the synthetic plastic-like polymer polyethylene terephthalate (PET, also known as Dacron), which is still used for certain implants such as blood vessels. The polymer has good biocompatibility – the body is unlikely to react against it or reject it. The Liotta heart's chambers were made from Dacron and a silicone-based synthetic rubber called Silastic.

Artificial hearts had been in development for years. Liotta had been researching mechanical pumps to assist the heart since the late 1950s. The focus was on the left ventricle – the most muscular, powerful chamber, which ejects blood into the aorta (the largest artery in the body) to circulate around the body. In July 1963, Liotta and

INTERNAL PACEMAKER
At St George's Hospital in the UK, a senior cardiac technician, Geoffrey Davies, designed this implant in the early 1960s because of problems with infection using external pacemakers.

cardiovascular surgeon E. Stanley Crawford implanted the first left ventricular assist device (LVAD), worked by air pressure. It did not succeed, but work continued and electrically driven VADs have improved greatly since then, with power transmitted wirelessly through the intact skin, rather than along tubes or wires through it. Alongside artificial heart development, the first implantable pacemakers were invented in the early 1960s. A pacemaker regulates the beating of the heart in patients who have a heart block or a malfunctioning sinoatrial node (the part of the heart that initiates the heartbeat). It sends low-energy electrical impulses to stimulate a heartbeat at a suitable rate and rhythm, either on demand or all the time, depending upon the patient's condition.

In 1982, there was a second high-profile heart implant – the Jarvik-7 artificial heart, named after bio-researcher Robert Jarvik. Recipient Barney Clarke survived for 112 days after the operation. Like the Liotta design, the Jarvik-7 was powered by air. The pump-and-control unit – the size of a shopping trolley – accompanied Clarke everywhere. Further designs of artificial hearts followed, and several were approved through the years for temporary and permanent implantation. Several types of implantable heart valves were designed too, including ball-and-cage, leaflet, and tilting disc valves. Animal valves were used too – typically from pigs – and hybrid ones with a metal frame and flexible animal tissue leaflets (animal tissues were treated before use to minimize the risk of rejection).

Human tragedy continues to stimulate the advance of technology and understanding of implants. Injuries from war and terrorim still motivate doctors and scientists to improve prosthetic limbs. Other reasons for implants include replacing body parts that are missing at birth, accidentally damaged or detached, or removed by surgery because of trauma, or diseases such as cancer and arthritis. Modern implants range from the purely cosmetic, such as breast enhancements, to the functional, such as plates that strengthen bones or experimental electronic retinal eye implants that could help people who were born blind or lost their eyesight to see again – a far cry from the earliest, albeit ingenious, false body parts of the ancient world.

Implants and Prostheses

Accident, disease, or other medical conditions can take their toll on the body, and many people have depended on false body parts for thousands of years – and, latterly, on devices implanted within the body (see pp.270–75). Today, developments in materials have increased the durability and comfort of prostheses. Computer technology has since led to greater control and precision in devices as diverse as heart pacemakers and "bionic" hands.

ARTIFICIAL LEG (c.1928)
Before the development of synthetic materials, a lightweight metal alloy such as duralumin was the best material available for a full artificial leg. This example has a mechanism to control the knee and a hand-operated knee lock.

STEEL HAND (c.1890)
Attached to a steel forearm, this artificial hand was designed for someone with a lower-arm amputation. Brass mounts made it possible to move the wrist.

ARTIFICIAL ARM AND HAMMERS (c.1950)
This prosthetic arm was made for a metalworker who had an arm amputated below the elbow. It has a range of hammer attachments that he used in his work.

POWERED LIMBS (c.1964)
Canisters of carbon dioxide gas, triggered by
the user's upper-body movements, powered
artificial limbs manufactured in the 1960s.
A series of cables controlled the movements.

PACEMAKER (c.1970)
A pacemaker sends out
electrical impulses to make
the heart beat regularly.
External pacemakers
appeared in the 1930s, and
implanted ones in the
1950s. They became more
practical with the arrival
of long-lasting lithium
batteries in the 1970s.

ARTIFICIAL HEART (c.2005)
Often used as a temporary measure before a
donor heart is transplanted, artificial hearts
are typically made of titanium and fitted with
batteries that can be charged through the skin.

BIONIC HAND (c.2007)
Bionic hands pick up electrical signals
from the user's arm muscles, and
processors in the hand turn these
signals into precise movements.

Medicine and Care for the Elderly

SIXTY-THREE BECAME THE NEW THIRTY-ONE in the 20th century. In 1900, the global average lifespan was around 31 years; by 2000, it had more than doubled to over 63, and in some wealthier developed nations it exceeded 80 years. The medical advances in that century included safer surgery (see pp.206–213); improved care during pregnancy and childbirth (see pp.214–21); the discovery of antibiotics (see pp.252–59); mass vaccination (see pp.286–93); and new generation medicines. Health threats such as carcinogens, pollutants, and occupational hazards became widely recognized – making it possible to take preventive measures – along with risk factors for heart disease, stroke, and other major killers.

Looked at another way, however, the 20th century was the era when, as a result of increased life expectancy combined with changing diets and lifestyles, age-related diseases came to the fore. Prominent among these are heart and vascular (blood vessel) problems and strokes, cancers, and arthritis, as well as degenerative diseases that include neurological (brain and nerve) conditions such as Alzheimer's (see p.283). In 1900, for example, heart disease was scarce among the general population; by the early 21st century, cardiovascular problems accounted for one in three deaths worldwide. As a result, medicine and care for the elderly have developed into a specialized field.

Particular practices for health care and treatment of the elderly extend back to ancient times. They are mentioned in early Ayurvedic texts in India (see pp.74–81), described in traditional Chinese medicine (see pp.64–73), and recorded in Ancient Greece (see pp.30–39), where Hippocrates noted the way illness affected older patients: "In old persons the heat is feeble, and therefore they require little fuel, as it were, to the flame, for it would be extinguished by much. On this account, also, fevers in old persons are not equally acute, because their bodies are cold". Medieval Arab physicians such as Ibn Al Jazzar and Ibn Sina (see pp.100–105) also documented how disease in the older body differed from that in younger adults. Ibn Sina recommended small meals and certain foods such as fruit and ginger for older people to keep the body "warm and moist".

In 1627, François Ranchin, Professor of Medicine and Chancellor of the University of Montpellier, published *Opuscula Medica*, in which he tackled the question, itself age-old: is ageing a natural progression of the human body, or itself a form of disease or illness? Ranchin proposed that old age was an intermediate condition of decreasing health, in which the body was increasingly prone to disease: "Not only physicians, but everybody else attending old people... realize how noble and important, how serious and difficult, how useful and even indispensable is that part of practical Medicine called Gerocomica, which deals with the conservation of old people and the healing of their diseases". In the same century, Thomas Sydenham, known as the "English Hippocrates", declared "a man is as old as his arteries". Like his Ancient Greek namesake, Sydenham put his patients – young and old – first, encouraging the body's innate healing powers and engendering new attitudes and innovative treatments.

A century later, in 1793, US physician Benjamin Rush stated: "Few persons appear to die of old age. Some of the diseases generally cut the last thread of life". The debate continued about whether ageing was part of the human condition, or a disease in itself. In 1892, however, Heinrich Rosin, a professor at the Albert Ludwigs University in Freiburg, Germany, wrote: "... Extreme old age, with its natural degeneration of resources and the natural decline of organs, is a condition of development of the human body; old-age infirmity is no illness". Interestingly, Rosin was not a medical professor but a lawyer specializing in employment insurance.

While the nature of ageing was still under consideration, in 1849, George Day, Professor of Medicine and Anatomy at the University of St Andrews, Scotland, adopted a more pragmatic approach, publishing *A Practical Treatise on the Domestic Management and Most Important Diseases of Advanced Life*. He described two of what would become known as "geriatric giants": incontinence and impaired intellect-memory (dementia), as well as immobility and instability.

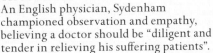

THOMAS SYDENHAM
An English physician, Sydenham championed observation and empathy, believing a doctor should be "diligent and tender in relieving his suffering patients".

Elsewhere, eminent French physician Jean-Martin Charcot was part of a movement in 19th-century France to care for and treat older people in specialized facilities – early versions of what later became geriatric hospitals. He described specific conditions of old age such as senile osteomalacia (softening of the bones), and how the symptoms of disease differ between young and old. On a practical level, he observed that the rectal thermometer gave the most accurate measure of core body temperature in the elderly, whose extremities tended to be cooler due to reduced circulation.

The term "geriatrics" was coined in 1909 by American doctor Ignatz Leo Nascher, writing in the *New York Medical Journal*. "Geriatrics, from [the Greek] *geras*, old age, and *iatrikos*, relating to the physician, is a term I would suggest as an addition to our vocabulary to cover the same field, in old age, that is covered by the term "paediatrics" in childhood". In 1914, he published *Geriatrics: The Diseases of Old Age and Their Treatment*, but little change was made to the care of elderly people for another 30 years.

In Europe, the elderly were still not receiving specialist medical attention either. While hospital and nursing care for other groups improved, older patients – regarded as beyond help – were often relegated to survival conditions, a situation inherited from the old "poorhouse" structures. These abandoned inmates found a champion in Marjory Warren, a Londoner who trained at the Royal Free Hospital School of Medicine, and became Deputy Medical Director of the West Middlesex County Hospital in 1931. Four years later, the neighbouring Poor Law Infirmary and former workhouse, Warkworth House, was incorporated into the hospital. Warren became responsible for more than 700 aged patients, most of whom had no diagnosis or treatment and were regarded as incurable.

With characteristic enthusiasm, Warren took on the patients, their carers, and the system. She recorded how patients underwent a gradual physical and mental decline into institutionalized apathy, with wasted muscles, stiff joints, incontinence, and immobility: "… In this miserable state, dull, apathetic, helpless and hopeless, life lingers on sometimes for years, while those around them whisper arguments in favour of euthanasia".

Warren saw that geriatrics should be its own specialism, and yet ought to be integrated into other branches of medicine and nursing care. She arranged visits from general physicians, surgeons,

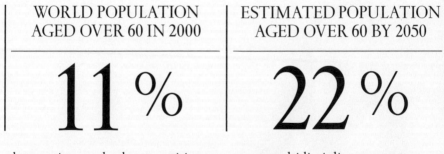

WORLD POPULATION AGED OVER 60 IN 2000	ESTIMATED POPULATION AGED OVER 60 BY 2050
11 %	22 %

pharmacists, and other practitioners; set up multidisciplinary teams of expert nurses, rehabilitation specialists, physiotherapists, occupational therapists, social workers, and chaplains; and brightened the wards. Importantly, in order to gain recognition from the medical establishment, she gathered evidence that all of this worked. Former incurables rallied and many became well enough to leave the wards for less intensive care in family or residential homes: "Whenever possible, they should be retained in, or returned to, their own homes, provided there is sufficient help for their comfort and welfare, and that the home conditions are suitable … Home nursing is therefore an absolutely essential part of the health scheme".

In the US, the American Geriatrics Society was set up in 1942. Founder members included Nascher and Malford W. Thewlis, a New England neuropsychiatrist. (Thewlis was also a renowned conjuror and escape artist who funded his passage through medical college by performing magic shows.) Encouraged by this US development, Marjory Warren stepped up her crusade for geriatrics: she wrote pivotal articles in the *British Medical Journal*, in 1943, and *The Lancet*, in 1946, and, in 1947, she became a founding member of the Medical Society for the Care of the Elderly, which later became the British Geriatrics Society. In the 1950s, geriatric medicine acquired specialty status within Britain's National Health Service. Sadly, Warren herself died in a car accident in 1960, at the age of 62.

To this day, standards and practices of care for the elderly vary throughout the world, often driven by a mixture of tradition and available resources. Many Eastern cultures emphasize respect for the elderly as part of the importance of family life; in these cases, families may be more likely to care for their elderly relatives within the household. Indeed, in some developing countries where healthcare and facilities are limited, there may be little alternative.

DAME CICELY SAUNDERS
A great reformer, Saunders launched the
modern hospice movement. She received
25 honorary degrees and a BMA Gold Medal
before dying in the hospice she founded.

Hospital care of the chronically sick
had been dispensed sporadically
through the centuries, often by
religious orders such as the Knights
Hospitaller. In more recent times,
France led the way, establishing
specialized institutions in the 1800s,
and, in 1879, Our Lady's Hospice
opened in Dublin, Ireland, bringing
new philosophies and standards of
care for the seriously and terminally
ill patients – many of whom suffered
from tuberculosis.

Nearly a century later, in 1967, an innovative new hospice opened
in London, England. St Christopher's Hospice was established by
Cicely Saunders, a former nurse, social worker, and reformer who
launched the modern hospice movement. At the time, many
terminally ill patients were left to die on hospital wards or in the
care of family at home. Once these patients were deemed incurable,
little attention was given to their needs and comfort. Pain relief in
particular was inadequate. Saunders had studied pain control in a
clinical setting and demonstrated that small, regular doses of
morphine and other opioids by mouth could give relief with
tolerable side-effects. Far from accepting that there was no more
that could be done for the dying patients, she always insisted, "there
is so much more to be done".

At St Christopher's, Saunders assembled skilled teams that brought
together a range of disciplines, from consultants and researchers to
pharmacologists and nurses. Her aim was to bring the highest medical
standards to compassionate care of the seriously ill and dying, in a
holistic way. One of the early pain relief projects at St Christopher's
involved comparing the effectiveness of opioids such as diamorphine
for pain relief – most staff had their own opinions about which one
produced better control and fewer side-effects such as drowsiness and

nausea. The small pilot study, followed by a two-year trial involving 700 patients, provided a clinical basis for future use. Saunders also extended the pain concept to "total pain", which included emotional, psychological, and spiritual, as well as physical, sensations.

St Christopher's became the model for the modern hospice movement. Saunders toured, lectured and wrote extensively. She also inspired others, such as Florence Wald, Dean of the Yale School of Nursing, Connecticut, who established hospice care in the US. Saunders, who qualified as a surgeon in the 1950s, received more than 25 honorary degrees and the British Medical Association Gold Medal. She was a Fellow of three Royal Colleges (Nursing, Physicians, and Surgeons) and was made a Dame of the British Empire in 1979. She died in 2005 – at St Christopher's.

Much of the emphasis in hospice care today is on care within the family at home, supported by hospice workers. In the 1980s, the hospice movement also developed the modern concept of palliative care – actions that prevent or relieve patient suffering – which may also be applied to patients who are not terminally ill, in a hospital setting. In a similar way to hospice care, it employs multidisciplinary teams, from pharmacists expert in pain relief to counsellors and faith workers, to ease distress and bring comfort to patients.

Despite the huge progress made in geriatric medicine and care of the dying, new challenges are constantly emerging. In 1906, German psychiatrist and neurologist Alois Alzheimer described the disease that bears his name. It is now the most commonly diagnosed form of dementia, involving memory loss, confusion, mood swings, failing confidence, disorganized thought processes, language difficulties, and social withdrawal. In pathology, Alzheimer's disease is characterized by structures known as plaques and tangles in the brain, involving proteins. The underlying causes are not well understood, and the risk factors are many and varied, from smoking and high blood pressure to whiplash injury.

A century after Alzheimer's description of the disease, more than 25 million people worldwide had been diagnosed with it. By 2012, this number had increased to 40 million; it is rising by 8 million annually, and this rate is itself increasing, with a predicted doubling every 20 years. After the great strides of the 20th century, the "dementia epidemic" and how to care for its sufferers is just one of the new challenges facing the medical profession in the 21st century.

MEDIEVAL HOSPITAL CARE
Nuns care for patients at the Hospital of
Hôtel Dieu in Paris in this 1492 illustrated
manuscript from *Le Livre de Vie Active de
l'Hôtel-Dieu*. In the crowded ward, many of
the emaciated, elderly patients lie two abed.

Vaccination Comes of Age

ALTHOUGH THEY WERE KNOWN TO EXIST, no one had actually seen a virus before 1939 – the year they were first revealed under an electron microscope. Before then, researchers had relied on the light microscope (see pp.150–51), which was not powerful enough to make these tiniest of microbes visible. Bacteria had been observed, but as far as viral infections were concerned – smallpox, rabies, measles, mumps, hepatitis, and influenza, for example – researchers had effectively been working blind. To get some idea of what they were up against, it is worth noting that the average body cell is 25 micrometres (µm) wide, so 15 cells in a row would stretch half of one millimetre – about the width of this "i". The single-celled *Entamoeba histolytica*, which causes a form of dysentery, is approximately this size too. Among the smallest body cells are red blood cells, which are only 7–8 µm across, approximately the size of the adult stage of the *Plasmodium* that causes malaria (see pp.388–89). One of the smallest bacteria, *Mycoplasma pneumoniae*, which is responsible for a form of pneumonia, is just 0.2 µm long, and the largest viruses are of a similar size.

The first viruses to be observed were tobacco mosaic viruses, which infect tobacco plants (see p.228), but people had long known that viruses affect animals and humans too. Pasteur's work with rabies (see pp.196–

205) had already shown that samples, smears, and scrapes of infected tissue could transfer diseases to others. In the mid-1880s, Pasteur's assistant Charles Chamberland made a porcelain filter that had microscopic holes small enough to trap bacteria, but not small enough to stop something else that was passing through and spreading certain diseases. Over the next decade,

SEEING WITH ELECTRONS
A scientist studies a specimen under an electron microscope in the 1930s. The new technology enabled researchers to see viruses by the end of that decade.

extracts of these "filterable agents" were crystallized, but their detailed structure remained a mystery until the 1940s, when studies of crystallized viruses, using X-ray crystallography combined with early electron microscope images, began to shed light on the structure of individual viruses. These revealed the vital differences between viruses and bacteria. Not only did bacteria live in between cells, but most, given suitable nutrients and conditions, could live and multiply independently of other life forms – unlike viruses, which had to invade living cells to replicate. Also, viruses, unlike bacteria, seemed barely to count as "living", since they spent most of their time inactive and only became active to replicate. Crucially, it also became clear that viruses were rarely affected by the antibiotics that killed bacteria (see pp.252–59).

Viruses, bacteria, unmatched transfused blood, transplanted organs, and other items that are foreign to the body have substances called antigens on their surfaces. The body's immune system is constantly on the lookout for these antigens, detecting them with B-cells, a subgroup of the white blood cells called lymphocytes. B-cells produce large, Y-shaped protein molecules known as antibodies. There are millions of antibodies floating in a person's blood, and most of these differ in the chemical structure of their tips, so that when a virus or bacterium invades, some of the antibodies can bind with its antigens. This makes certain B-cells turn into plasma cells – hard-working antibody factories – which rapidly make armies of antibodies that attack the invader or tag it for destruction. Other B-cells become memory cells and remain in the body for years. If the same microbes reappear later, the B-cells recognize them and destroy them before they cause any harm. Immunity means being resistant to an infection. It can occur naturally, or be induced by means of a vaccine (see pp.292–93). Vaccination introduces harmful antigens into the body, so the immune system fights and destroys them, making a person actively immune to the disease. Passive immunity is conferred by injecting ready-made antibodies into the body. This provides rapid protection, but the effects only last for weeks or months, as the antibodies degrade and cannot be replaced.

In the first half of the 20th century, following the pioneering vaccines for smallpox (see pp.152–61) and rabies (see pp.196–205), researchers worked feverishly to develop vaccines for diphtheria, tuberculosis,

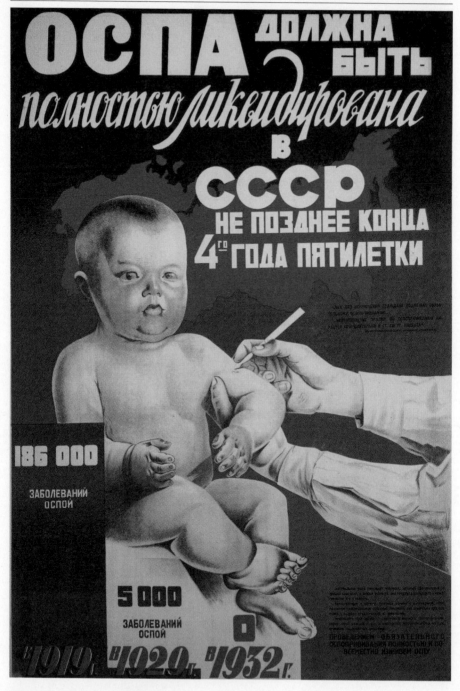

ERADICATING SMALLPOX
A Soviet poster of 1931 urges people to take up vaccination
against smallpox. As suggested by the bar chart at the bottom,
the authorities aimed to eradicate the disease by 1932.

tetanus, polio, whooping cough, yellow fever, and other major infections. Their findings helped to understand antigen-antibody mechanisms and the profound complexities of immunity, which still throw up surprises today.

Diphtheria, the "strangling angel", is a devastating infection that particularly affects children. A tough membrane forms in the throat, causing breathing problems and leading to many fatalities. Diphtheria used to kill millions of people, but by the early 21st century, the number of deaths worldwide had been reduced to a few thousand annually. The bacterium that causes it, *Corynebacterium diphtheriae*, discovered in 1890 by German physiologist Emile von Behring, produces a harmful substance known as diphtheria toxin that gets into healthy body cells and interferes with how they work. The immune system reacts by neutralizing the toxin with a special kind of antibody known as an antitoxin. In the 1890s, early treatment for diphtheria was a ready-made antitoxin extracted from horses. For prevention, there was diphtheria TAT – toxin-and-antitoxin – a combination injection that contained just enough toxin to stimulate immunity, but also enough ready-made antitoxin to prevent the toxin causing the disease. In 1914, the French newspaper *Le Matin* reported that Emile von Behring's latest version of TAT was one of "the Seven Wonders of the modern world [the others being] the aeroplane, wireless, radium, the locomotive, human grafting and the dynamo." Somewhat out of the blue, in 1923, Ramon Gaston, a French vet, then discovered that the preserving chemical formalin altered diphtheria toxin so that it was harmless when injected without the antitoxin, but still triggered immunity. Ramon applied the same chemical to tetanus, establishing the group of vaccines that are correctly called toxoids, as they are based on toxins rather than the microbes, such as *Corynebacterium diphtheriae* in the case of diphtheria, that produce them.

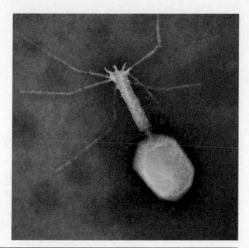

INVISIBLE KILLER
This electron microscope image of a virus shows its 20-sided head, its tail, and tail fibres. The head contains the virus's DNA, which is injected into a host cell during replication.

Another key development in vaccination was the treatment of the poliovirus, a microbe that was first photographed in 1952, the year that the US endured a terrible outbreak of this paralysing infection. As far back as 1905, Swedish physician Ivar Wickman had published the first in a series of studies claiming – controversially at the time – that polio was a contagious disease, spread by physical contact or close proximity. Just three years later, Karl Landsteiner (see pp.242–49) and another Austrian physician, Erwin Popper, had identified the contagion as being viral rather than bacterial; infected material from the spinal cord of a deceased sufferer, filtered to remove bacteria, still transmitted the disease to laboratory monkeys. By 1910, Simon Flexner, Director at the Rockefeller Institute for Medical Research in New York City, had demonstrated that monkeys who recovered from polio had "germicidal substances" (antibodies) in their blood. This suggested that a vaccine of disabled polio viruses might trigger natural antibody production, and thereby lead to immunity.

Although this finding paved the way for research into polio vaccines, early trials did not go well – partly because, in the early 1930s, Australian investigators showed that there was more than one kind of poliovirus. Disaster struck in the mid-1930s when two US projects testing vaccines on more than 20,000 children failed, leaving many dead, paralysed, or suffering from allergic reactions. However, great strides were made in growing polioviruses in the laboratory. It was found that they could grow in human embryonic tissue, thereby reducing the need to use so many monkeys as experimental animals for incubation and testing. The 1954 Nobel Prize in Physiology or Medicine was later awarded to American medical scientist John Enders, and virologists Thomas Weller and Frederick Robbins "for their discovery of the ability of poliomyelitis viruses to grow in cultures of various types of tissue". However, there was a further setback to

THE SALK VACCINE
Medical researcher Jonas Salk developed the first successful polio vaccine, in the 1950s. At the time, the US was suffering its worst ever polio epidemic.

polio research in the early 1950s when work at Johns Hopkins University School of Medicine, Baltimore, by American medical researcher David Bodian and virologist Isabel Morgan, revealed that

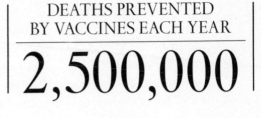

DEATHS PREVENTED
BY VACCINES EACH YEAR

2,500,000

there were three kinds of poliovirus, which meant that a vaccine had to work against all three.

In 1951, Jonas Salk, Director of the Virus Research Laboratory at the University of Pittsburgh Medical School, began growing polioviruses in monkey kidney tissue. The following year, during the US polio epidemic, Salk and his team began human trials of an injected polio vaccine (IPV) based on killed polioviruses. The following year, 1953, Salk tried the vaccine on his wife and three sons, and the year after that, a huge US trial began, involving almost two million children, doctors, nurses, and public health officials. In April 1955, results showed that the Salk vaccine was up to 90 per cent effective against paralytic polio. Russian-born American medical research scientist Albert Sabin and his team at the University of Cincinnati, Ohio, had also been researching a polio vaccine based on weakened viruses, which could be swallowed rather than injected. In the 1950s, the team began trials on millions of children in the Soviet Union, and by 1963, the Sabin vaccine against all three types of poliovirus was in production.

In 1988, an ambitious target was declared by the World Health Organization – the worldwide eradication of polio by the year 2000. The deadline has since been extended, but the impact of the Salk and Sabin vaccines suggests that polio may well become the next disease (after smallpox) to be successfully eradicated. Yet just as smallpox became extinct, with polio and perhaps also diphtheria hopefully to follow, infections such as HIV/AIDS (see pp.328–35) and new, potentially pandemic strains of influenza have entered the stage, opening new battlegrounds in the age-old war between medicine and germs.

How Immunization Works

The most common medical way to immunize people – stop them getting a disease – is by vaccination. A vaccine contains foreign molecules called antigens that trigger the primary immune response, in which the body releases antibodies to kill the infection. The body also produces memory cells that will recognize the invader and leap into action if it strikes again, fighting off any future infection of the disease – the secondary immune response.

PRIMARY IMMUNE RESPONSE
Vaccines contain antigens either in isolation or attached to germs (bacteria or viruses). The germs are weakened or have their living material removed to make them harmless.

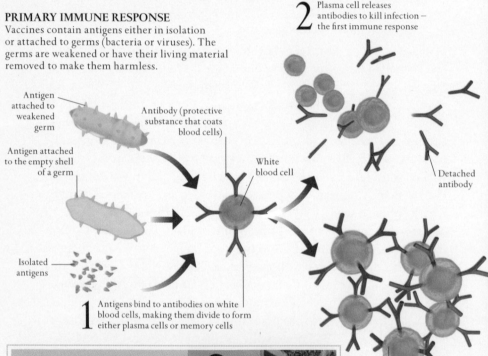

2 Plasma cell releases antibodies to kill infection – the first immune response

Antigen attached to weakened germ

Antibody (protective substance that coats blood cells)

Antigen attached to the empty shell of a germ

White blood cell

Detached antibody

Isolated antigens

1 Antigens bind to antibodies on white blood cells, making them divide to form either plasma cells or memory cells

Vaccination

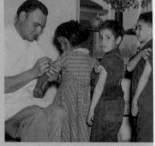

French scientist Louis Pasteur's vaccines for rabies and anthrax, and Spanish physician Jaime Ferrán's cholera vaccine, made a huge impact on human health in the late 19th century. Programmes for vaccinating children have been in place since the mid-20th century.

CHILDREN QUEUE UP FOR VACCINES IN WYOMING, US, IN 1955

3 Memory cells live for a long time and remember the germ. If it invades again, memory cells turn into plasma cells and attack the germ vigorously, before it is able to cause much harm

Inoculation

While vaccination introduces an antigen to trigger immunity, inoculation administers a mild dose of the germ responsible for a disease. Memory cells in the recipient's body will remember the disease if it tries to enter the body subsequently, and produce plasma cells that release antibodies to destroy the germ, just as by vaccination. Inoculation can also be used to produce a disease for research.

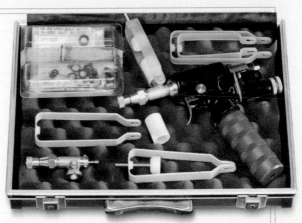

THE MED-E-JET INOCULATION KIT MADE IN OHIO, US, IN 1980, USED A GUN TO FORCE MEDICATION THROUGH THE SKIN AT HIGH PRESSURE WITHOUT THE NEED FOR A NEEDLE

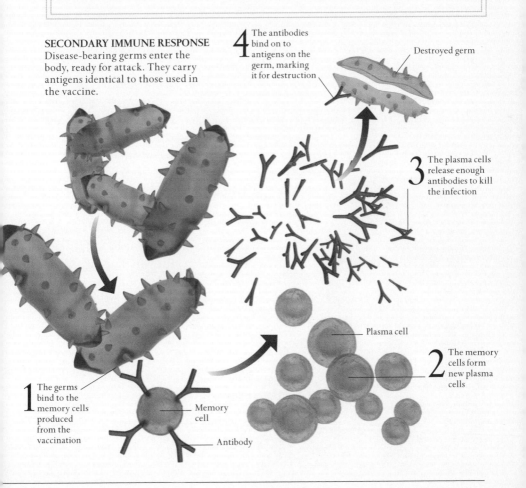

SECONDARY IMMUNE RESPONSE
Disease-bearing germs enter the body, ready for attack. They carry antigens identical to those used in the vaccine.

4 The antibodies bind on to antigens on the germ, marking it for destruction

Destroyed germ

3 The plasma cells release enough antibodies to kill the infection

Plasma cell

2 The memory cells form new plasma cells

1 The germs bind to the memory cells produced from the vaccination

Memory cell

Antibody

The First Transplants

GOOD NEWS RARELY MAKES HEADLINES, but on 3 December 1967, a medical breakthrough – the world's first heart transplant – took the world by storm. Cardiac surgeon Christiaan Barnard and his 30-strong team at Groote Schuur Hospital, Cape Town, South Africa, had spent nine hours on a pioneering operation and saved the life of a 54-year-old patient by giving him the heart of a 25-year-old female donor. In the following days, bulletins on the condition of the patient, Louis Washkansky, dominated world news. Washkansky rallied, but then succumbed to pneumonia because of his suppressed immune system and died 18 days later.

Although the heart transplant was a bolt from the blue to the general public, many medical centres were poised to perform such an operation. The first in the US, for instance, took place just days after Washkansky's. But poor results, mainly from problems linked to rejection, dampened the initial enthusiasm. The following year, 1968, more than 100 procedures were attempted, but the failure rate was unacceptably high. As anti-rejection drugs improved, however, transplant numbers slowly rose again. Today, a heart is transplanted about every two hours somewhere around the world. At some centres, two out of every three recipients are alive ten years later, and one in three after 20 years.

The first human-to-human heart transplant was by no means the first organ transplant. Success with kidneys dated back to 1954, and tissue transplants much earlier. Barnard himself had carried out other transplants, including South Africa's first kidney transplant, just six months before the heart procedure. This taught him how to cope with

CELEBRITY SURGEON
A mere 45 years old, good-looking, and happy in the media spotlight, South African Christiaan Barnard became an overnight sensation for his pioneering heart transplant.

"On Saturday, I was a surgeon in South Africa, little known. On Monday, I was world renowned"

CHRISTIAAN BARNARD

organ rejection, and the recipient, Edith Black, went on to live for more than 20 years. An emboldened Barnard stated: "Everything is ready for a heart transplant. We have the team and we know how to do it." The donor and recipient had to be a perfect match, especially as this first attempt would be closely scrutinized from all angles. The fact that the organ was a heart – the symbol of life – posed new medical, ethical, and social questions about the dividing line between life and death.

When Washkansky arrived at Groote Schuur suffering from congestive heart failure, and was swiftly followed by a car-crash victim, Barnard saw his opportunity. The car accident involved a drunk driver and the donor's mother had been killed. The donor herself had suffered severe head injuries. By modern criteria, she would have been classed as brain-dead, but no such guidelines had been developed at the time (see pp.374–79). She was otherwise fit and healthy, and her heart was still beating. After discussion, the family agreed with Barnard's proposal to donate her heart. A helping injection of potassium hastened the inevitable, stopping the heart while it was still in good condition; the operation began; and the following day, the world learned the astonishing news.

Born in 1922 in Beaufort West, southern South Africa, Christiaan Barnard had graduated from the University of Cape Town Medical School in 1945. He worked in general practice and was so deeply affected by the death of a young boy from a heart-valve defect that he went on to specialize in cardiothoracic (heart-chest) medicine. During a two-year stint in the US, Barnard worked with Professor Owen Wangensteen, Chairman of Surgery at the University of Minnesota, Minneapolis. He watched and learned from Wangensteen and other foremost heart surgeons of the day, including C. Walton Lillehei and Vince Gott. Barnard also came across Norman Shumway of Stanford University, California, who was raising the profile of cardiothoracic surgery and investigating heart-transplant potential.

The first open-heart surgery was carried out with the aid of a mechanical cardiopulmonary bypass (CPB) device, or heart-lung machine (see pp.300–301). CPB dated back to the 1920s, and American John Heysham Gibbon had tested working versions on cats in the 1930s, but no-one used a CPB device during a human operation until 1951, at the University of Minnesota, where Barnard was studying. The heart-lung machine was plumbed into the patient to take deoxygenated blood – from a main vein or the right atrium (smaller upper chamber) – add oxygen to it, and return it to the circulation, via the aorta (the main artery leading away from the heart). There had to be enough force to keep the blood moving through the system. Among the numerous precautions needed were anticoagulants to prevent the blood from clotting as it passed through the tubes and mechanical pump. Although the first open-heart patient did not pull through, success came two years later in Philadelphia, under the auspices of the heart-lung machine's pioneer, Gibbon.

Barnard returned to South Africa in 1958 with a CPB machine. The device was soon in regular use at Groote Schuur Hospital, where Barnard assembled a team capable of the long, complex open-heart procedures he had seen in the US. Barnard himself rose rapidly through the surgical hierarchies. Fascinated by Russian surgeon Vladimir Demikhov's experiments with transplants, including the heart, lungs, and even – horrific to modern eyes – the head, to create two-headed dogs, Barnard developed his own cardiothoracic skills by transplanting dog hearts. Whether dog or human, the existing organ is usually accessed by dividing the sternum (breastbone) in two lengthwise; this saves damaging the ribs, the rib joints and underlying membranes, and the lungs. Sometimes, parts of the atria (the two small upper chambers) are left intact where the main veins join them. The donor heart has these areas removed, then it is fixed in position with sutures along the cut atrial edges.

Barnard's career forged ahead after the epochal operation and he undertook more heart and other transplants. One of his patients from 1971 lived for another 23 years, but this was very much the exception at the time. Despite suffering from rheumatoid arthritis, Barnard continued to operate, and in 1972 he accepted the post of Professor of Surgical Science at his hospital. His personal life was equally eventful. Unlike the staid lifestyle of many senior medical men, Barnard enjoyed jet-setting glamour. With six children by three marriages, he also generated rumours of liaisons with prominent movie stars and other famous women. Barnard retired from surgery in 1983, but continued to act as a consultant and advocate of heart transplants. Controversially, he fronted a campaign to promote a range of anti-ageing skin care products, called Glycel. Countering criticism that he was acting simply for financial gain, Barnard responded: "My father always told me: 'The highest trees get the most wind.' This is something you have to accept." The costly product did not subsequently live up to its claims.

Barnard pioneered not only transplants in which the recipient heart is removed to make way for the donor's, but also procedures where the donor heart "piggybacks" on the recipient's. Throughout his career, he devised many new operations and techniques. Some, especially for children suffering from intestinal and heart conditions, are still practised today. He died in 2001. The Charles Saint Theatre at Groote Schuur Hospital, where Barnard's heart-transplant operation took place, is now the Heart of Cape Town Museum, laid out exactly as it was on 3 December 1967.

While Barnard was preparing for retirement, a quieter revolution in transplant medicine was gaining momentum. From work conducted on vaccinations (see pp.286–93), it was known that the immune system defended the body against material "foreign" to itself, especially invading germs. Transplanted organs or tissues came into this invader category. The transplant was attacked directly by white blood cells, specifically the

CANINE PATIENT
After successful trial operations on dogs, Norman Shumway (left) of Stanford University, California, performed many heart transplants in the US. He persevered when other surgeons gave up amid post-surgical deaths and issues on defining "brain-dead" donors.

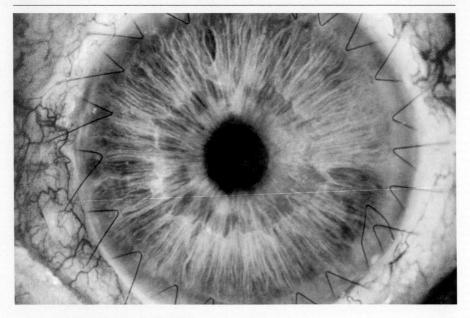

CORNEAL TRANSPLANT
If the cornea (the transparent front of the eye) is
damaged, vision is impaired. The stitches are visible
around this recently replaced cornea, where it
projects like a dome beyond the white of the eye.

recipient's T-cells, and by antibodies manufactured by plasma
cells. For a successful transplant, the answer was therefore to
dampen or weaken the immune response using drugs called
immunosuppressants. Medication had to tread a fine line between
quelling the rejection process enough to allow the transplant to
survive and disabling immunity so much that the body was left wide
open to infection. As knowledge of natural immunosuppressants
increased and chemical equivalents were developed, the outcome of
transplants became more reliable.

In around 1930, the steroid cortisone, a natural body hormone
produced by the adrenal glands, was discovered. Along with another
adrenal hormone, adrenaline, it is part of the body's natural "fight-
or-flight" reaction to stress. Cortisone works as an
immunosuppressant partly by affecting the white cells that produce
antibodies, and in 1949 extracts of the hormoe were first used
successfully to treat the disease rheumatoid arthritis. In 1955, a
related but synthetically manufactured medication, prednisone,
came onto the market. It was followed in 1957 by azathioprine,
which was developed primarily to fight cancers. This drug works by

interfering with cell multiplication, which cancer cells do in an uncontrolled manner (see pp.260–69). White blood cells also multiply rapidly as they mount their immune response.

British surgeon Roy Calne achieved many firsts in transplantation, including the first combined liver-heart-lung transplant in 1987. He was active in testing drugs to counter rejection, and he helped to introduce azathioprine. In the late 1970s, he trialled another promising substance, ciclosporin. Like the antibiotic penicillin (see pp.252–57), it had been discovered in a soil fungus, in this case *Tolypocladium* in Norway. It works primarily by reducing the activity of T-cells, thus diminishing the body's immune response. Ciclosporin was a great advance in anti-rejection therapy and, with several drugs to choose from, heart and other transplant success rates climbed.

The first heart transplant may have grabbed the headlines, but many other organs, especially kidneys, but also the liver, lungs (often done as a combined heart-lung transplant), and pancreatic glands are regularly transplanted too. Tissue transplants are far more common than whole organ changes. They include the cornea (the transparent front of the eye), blood (as transfusions, see pp.242–51), bone marrow, skin, blood vessels, and heart valves. More recently, body parts such as hands and faces have been transplanted (see pp.270–75).

There remain many challenges, especially donor shortages, matching a donor and recipient (identical twins are best, close relatives good, and unrelated strangers problematic), taking organs from living rather than dead donors, obtaining permission in the case of deceased donors, and the hazards of transferring infections such as HIV. Lurking among all these considerations are lucrative organ trafficking and "transplant tourism", in which recipients travel to places where operations are readily available with few questions asked. For all that, the future looks promising. Stem cell research, tissue engineering, and implant technologies (see pp.270–75) may combine to grow healthy versions of diseased organs from the patient's own cells. These could then be inserted back into the patient's body with little or no fear of rejection – perhaps prompting the next dramatic headlines in the transplant story.

A New Heart

The first successful human heart surgery took place in 1895, to treat a stab wound, but it was not until World War II that heart surgery made real advances, when US Army surgeon Dwight Harken removed shrapnel from soldiers' hearts. However, since lack of blood circulation caused brain damage, operations that stopped the heart for more than four minutes were impossible. In the 1950s, the heart-lung machine enabled longer procedures, including heart transplants, pioneered by Christiaan Barnard in 1967 (see pp.294–99). Initially, the recipient's immune system often rejected a new heart. Immunosuppressant drugs were developed from the 1970s to counteract this.

Norman Shumway

Chief heart surgeon at Stanford University's School of Medicine, Norman Shumway performed the first successful heart transplant in the US in 1968. At first, few patients survived for long, but Shumway persisted with the procedure. He found ways of anticipating rejection and adopted new immunosuppressant drugs, notably ciclosporin (derived from a Norwegian soil fungus). His success encouraged other transplant surgeons.

NORMAN SHUMWAY WITH A MODEL HEART

Oxygen-poor blood leaves the patient's heart and enters the machine via a tube

Oxygen-rich blood returns to the body via another tube that leads directly into the aorta, bypassing the heart and lungs

HEART-LUNG MACHINE
ENGLAND, c.1958

Developed by physiologist Denis
Melrose in the 1950s, the heart-lung
machine takes over both the pumping
action of the heart and oxygenation
by the lungs, allowing the heart
to be stopped during surgery.

The patient's blood
is passed through a large
plastic cylinder, where it flows
over rotating discs, while a
stream of oxygen is blown over it

Blood is spread in thin
films over a large surface,
which exposes the red cells
to oxygen for uptake

Transplanting a heart

The surgeon opens the patient's chest
and pericardium (the membrane
around the heart) and attaches the
patient to a heart-lung machine.
The heart is removed by cutting the
great blood vessels (large blood vessels
that carry blood to and from the heart),
leaving only the pulmonary veins in
place, along with part of the left atrium
(the chamber through which blood
enters the heart from the lungs). The
surgeon attaches the donor heart to
the great vessels and the intact part
of the left atrium, starts the heart, and
deactivates the bypass system.

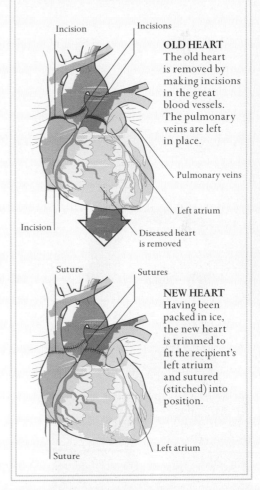

Incision   Incisions

OLD HEART
The old heart
is removed by
making incisions
in the great
blood vessels.
The pulmonary
veins are left
in place.

Pulmonary veins

Left atrium

Incision

Diseased heart
is removed

Suture   Sutures

NEW HEART
Having been
packed in ice,
the new heart
is trimmed to
fit the recipient's
left atrium
and sutured
(stitched) into
position.

Left atrium

Suture

Imaging the Body

MOST BRANCHES OF MEDICINE have been around since Hippocrates of Ancient Greece, Zhang Zhongjing in China, and Charaka of India. How these ancients would marvel at the modern miracle of medical imaging – seeing inside the body without cutting it open. Radiology is the medical specialism that uses imaging to diagnose disease, monitor progress, and carry out therapies. It is a province that mixes biology, biochemistry, and medicine with physics and technology. Its innovators have garnered more than a sprinkling of Nobel Prizes and other accolades, and it is notorious for its dizzying arrays of acronyms – CT, MRI, PET, SPECT, US, and so on.

Imaging technologies have existed for just over a century. First came X-rays, the story of which is well documented. On 8 November 1895, German physicist Wilhelm Röntgen was experimenting with the fashionable electrical gadget of his time – the high-voltage vacuum or Crookes tube. This used electricity to produce "cathode rays", later discovered to be beams of particles called electrons. Röntgen noticed that, although his tube was shielded by cardboard, it made a nearby screen glow – a screen that was coated with a chemical called barium plantinocyanide in preparation for another experiment on cathode rays. Other investigators had noticed this phenomenon with high-voltage tubes, but had not pursued it. Röntgen decided to investigate fully. For several weeks, he feverishly studied the "mysterious rays" coming from the tube, and found that they passed through less dense materials such as paper and card, but not through dense, heavy substances such as metals. Also, as he held objects in their path to see if they cast shadows, he saw that the bones of his hands were projected onto the screen – a phenomenon that had huge medical potential.

WILHELM RÖNTGEN
Known as the father of diagnostic radiology, German physicist Wilhelm Röntgen pioneered the use of X-rays for medical imaging.

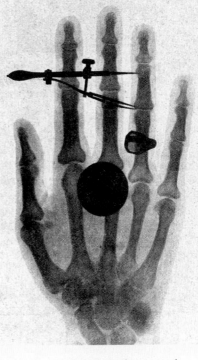

MRS RÖNTGEN'S HAND
In 1895–96, Röntgen took several
X-ray photographs of his wife's
hand, this one complete with two
rings and a pair of drawing dividers.

On December 22, Röntgen placed a sheet of photographic film on the screen and took a photograph of his wife's hand to reveal its bones – prompting her to say: "I have seen my own death!" Röntgen named the rays "X rays", since their nature was unknown, and published his results later that month. In 1901, he was duly awarded the first-ever Nobel Prize in Physics "in recognition of the extraordinary services he has rendered by the discovery of the remarkable rays subsequently named after him" – although the name "Röntgen rays" was soon superseded by that of "X-rays". Soon after Röntgen's discovery, doctors were making the most of the new technology. On January 11, 1896, in Birmingham, UK, surgeon John Hall-Edwards X-rayed a needle embedded in a patient's hand, and on February 3, in Connecticut, US, Professor of Medicine Gilman Frost made an X-ray photograph of the wrist of 14-year-old Eddie McCarthy, who had fractured it two weeks previously. On February 14, back in Birmingham, Hall-Edwards X-rayed a patient before surgery to help guide the operation.

By the start of the 20th century, the use of X-rays had become widespread, and it was noted that the denser a body tissue is, the more it reduces (attenuates) the rays, meaning that bones and cartilage show up best, while softer tissues are hard to see. It was some years before the damaging effects of such radiation became clear, and still more before radiotherapy turned this to an advantage (see pp.260–67). In 1908, Hall-Edwards had to have his left arm amputated due to radiation damage. Nevertheless, radiation doses were reduced and equipment gradually improved, providing images that could be recorded on photographic film or viewed "live", moving on a fluorescent screen. The images on these "fluoroscopy" screens were

RADIATION PROTECTION
A French army radiographer stands in protective clothing prior to using X-ray equipment. The picture was taken in 1918, towards the end of World War I.

extremely pale and dim, which meant that light levels in the examination room had to be kept to a minimum. In the 1950s, electronic image intensifiers and new kinds of cameras made fluorescent screen pictures bright enough to be viewed in normal light and recorded for later study.

Other X-ray techniques had also been developed. As early as 1906, contrast or radio-opaque agents, or "dyes", were in use. These block (are opaque to) X-rays, so they show up clearly on an X-ray image. They can be introduced into the body as liquids, to show the details of hollow structures such as the stomach and intestines. By the 1920s, barium-based compounds were being ingested or introduced via an enema to show the outline of the gut. The same technique was also applied to blood vessels, using iodine-based dyes. Its developer, Portuguese neurologist António Egas Moniz, pioneered cerebral angiography to visualize the blood vessels of the brain, for which he received a Nobel Prize in Physiology or Medicine in 1949.

In 1913, American physicist William David Coolidge invented the "hot cathode" or thermionic X-ray tube to replace the old "cold" Crookes type. Its X-rays yielded clearer, sharper images than those of the Crookes tube, especially of areas deep within the body. In the same year, German surgeon-pathologist Albert Salomon examined 3,000 mastectomy (breast removal) specimens minutely, took X-ray images of them for comparison, and showed how spots on the images correlated with breast cancer growths. His work formed the foundation for mammography, the branch of medicine dedicated to the detection of early signs of breast cancer.

Two other Nobel recipients for medical imaging were Godfrey Hounsfield and Allan Cormack, who received the honour jointly in 1979 "for the development of computer assisted tomography –

commonly known as the CAT or CT scan", a scan being an image that is built up as a series of tiny light units, line upon line. Hounsfield grew up on a farm in Nottinghamshire, England, and from an early age, he invented, tinkered with, and adapted toys and machines, even leaping from haystacks to try out a home-made glider. He continued to pursue his interest in aircraft during World War II, moved into radio and radar, worked in West London for EMI (Electrical and Musical Industries – then an industrial research company as well as a record label). Looking for future projects, he noted: "It was while exploring various aspects of pattern recognition and their potential, in 1967, that the idea occurred to me which was eventually to become the EMI-Scanner and the technique of computed tomography".

Scanning required computers to process the raw data into images, so it did not became a part of mainstream medical procedure until the 1970s. A CT scanner's beam of weak X-rays passes through the patient's body to a detector on the other side, as the whole unit pivots around the patient. The unit then moves along to the next section of the patient's body and repeats the process, and so on. The computer analyses the results and then generates a series of cross-sectional images of the body. This technique is known as "tomography", derived from the term for "drawing slices" in Greek. The cross sections are then compiled to create a full 3D representation of the body that reveals not just the bones and cartilage, but also the full range of soft tissues. Unlike traditional X-ray images, each point of the scan is encoded digitally, which means it can be magnified and manipulated as never before, and communicated electronically far and wide.

Hounsfield's early CT trials in the late 1960s focused on the brain, which could not be seen in ordinary X-rays because it was shielded within the skull. Initially, Hounsfield scanned animal organs with gamma rays, a process that took days to carry out on a large mainframe computer. Switching to X-rays and better scanners greatly reduced this time it took to produce a scan. Hounsfield's team went public on preliminary CTs in 1968, carried out clinical CT head scans in 1971, launched the first EMI scanners in 1972, and moved on to whole-body scans in 1974. Hounsfield volunteered to be the guinea pig for the brain and body scans himself, claiming that he could see his pub lunch of ale and crisps in the latter. At a conference in Bermuda in 1975, he showed off whole-body CT scans of himself – after which, the new scanning technique was accepted by the establishment.

Hounsfield's Nobel co-recipient was South African physicist Allan Cormack, who had published the theoretical basis of CT scanning early in the 1960s. The two men had never met, however, before the Nobel ceremony in Stockholm.

X-rays are a form of electromagnetic radiation, which has a broad spectrum of wavelengths. These wavelengths range from the relatively long radio waves to the ever-shorter microwaves, infrared light, visible light, ultraviolet light, X-rays, and gamma rays. These last, shortest rays are used in what is called nuclear imaging, which is an "inside out" style of medical scanning ("nuclear" deriving from "nucleus" – the central part of the smallest particle of ordinary matter, the atom). Unlike most imaging technologies, which fire radiation into and through the body, nuclear imaging works by introducing substances that emit gamma rays or similar radiation within the body and using external detectors to track their movements. These substances are variously known as radionuclides, radioactive isotopes, radioisotopes, radiotracers, radiotags, and radiolabels.

Radionuclides have unstable nuclei that give off electromagnetic waves (and sometimes particles) as they change into more stable forms. They are incorporated into substances that are introduced into the body by ingestion, injection, or inhalation, and are monitored in specific places. Their first detectors were gamma (or "scintillation") cameras, also known as Anger cameras, after the American physicist Hal Anger who developed them in 1957. One of the most commonly used radionuclide substances is technetium-99m. Discovered in 1938, it became readily available in the 1960s, after a generator to make it was invented by Powell Richards, Walter Tucker, and a team at the US Department of Energy's Brookhaven National Laboratory, Long Island. Technetium-99m reduces by half every six hours, so patient exposure is low, although its radiation is readily detectable by diagnostic equipment. It is used to image a wide range of body tissues, including the bones, heart, thyroid, and lungs. Technetium-99m is usually used as part of a SPECT (single photon emission computed tomography) scan, which, like a CT scan, builds a slice-by-slice 3D image as detectors rotate around the body.

Another electromagnetic imaging technique is MRI (magnetic resonance imaging). MRI too yields a series of slices that disclose soft tissues as well as harder bone and cartilage. It works by magnetically aligning the nuclei of hydrogen atoms in the patient's body – nuclei that otherwise spin and wobble in all directions – and then releasing them to emit radio pulses that are then detected by sensors around the patient's body. Since hydrogen atoms account for two thirds of the body – as a constituent of water (H_2O), carbohydrates, and fats – MRI can picture most parts of the body, including the brain, muscles, connective tissues, nerves, blood vessels, and various types of tumour.

MRI was first investigated in 1946 by Swiss-born American physicist Felix Bloch at Stanford University and American physicist Edward Purcell at Harvard. Early on, they thought of using MRI to image the body's interior, but their main concern was to study the structural make-up of chemicals. In the 1960s and 1970s, American chemist Paul Lauterbur adapted the technique for medical imaging, and used the MRI machine at Stony Brook University, New York, for tests. At the same time, British physicist Peter Mansfield was also working on MRI, establishing how to make images out of the radio pulses emitted by hydrogen nuclei. By the late 1970s, he had produced scans of entire human bodies. Lauterbur and Mansfield shared the Nobel Prize in Physiology or Medicine in 2003 "for their discoveries concerning magnetic resonance imaging". Mansfield went on to develop MRI further with a technique called echo-planar imaging, which allowed images to be taken even faster.

More recently, scanners that combine two or more technologies have been devised. The PET/CT scanner, for instance, reveals both tissue structure – via CT (computerized tomography) – and tissue function – via PET (positron emission tomography). PET has a long history, including advances made in the early 1970s at Brookhaven National Laboratory, US, by James Roberston and Sy Rankowitz, and in Montreal, Canada, by Chris Thompson, Ernst Myer, and Lucas Yamato. Michael Phelps and his colleagues at Washington University, US, constructed the first tomography machines in 1973–74. One of

"Great dicoveries are made accidentally less often than the populace likes to think"

EDWARD PURCELL

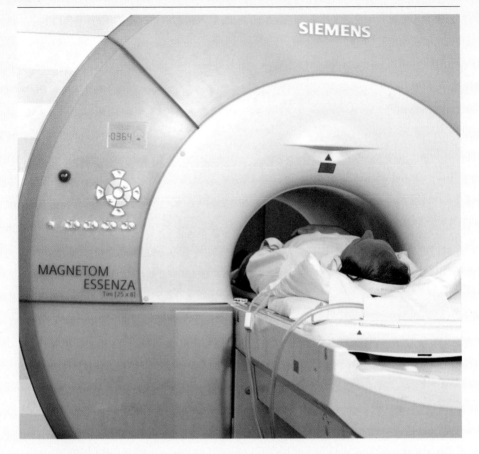

MRI SCAN
A patient lies inside an MRI scanner. The machine is effectively a
large, powerful magnet that acts on various atomic nuclei in the body
to produce images that can be used to assess the patient's condition.

these, PET III, produced the first scans of today's quality, and in 1978,
the first commercial PET scanner, ECAT II (Emission Computed
Axial Tomograph II) went on the market.

Like radionuclide scanning, PET scans require an unstable
radiotracer substance to be introduced into the body, a common
example being a form of glucose. This shoots out particles called
positrons – the opposites of the electrons that "orbit" the atomic
nucleus – and as each positron collides with an opposite electron,
the two annihilate each other in a burst of gamma rays that are
detected by sensors. The most active cells and tissues burn glucose
the fastest, so appear as hot spots on the resulting image. PET scans
reveal how the organs and tissues are functioning, and have a large

ESTIMATED NUMBER OF MRI SCANS
PERFORMED WORLDWIDE ANNUALLY

30 MILLION

number of applications, including cardiology, oncology (cancer treatment), and even in assessing some psychiatric conditions such as schizophrenia or substance abuse. Although PET scans necessarily use radiation, the levels at which it is applied are low, comparatively safe, and do not cause the patient pain or discomfort – although some patients may feel claustrophobic as they lie in the close confines of the scanner. PET scans are also often used in conjunction with other forms of imaging, such as CT and MRI, which illuminate tissue structure. PET is particularly useful for identifying the busily dividing cells in tumours, and a variant of MRI scanning, called fMRI (f for functional), shows brain activity in a similar way.

PET/CT scanners were *TIME Magazine*'s medical invention of the year in 2000. The development of scanning technology has been of huge benefit to patients all over the world, both in terms of diagnosis and in being non-invasive, relatively safe, and comfortable procedures. Radiologists today choose from a wide range of imagers, each of which has its own particular advantages. Ultrasound (US; see p.311), for example, uses sound waves rather than electromagnetic waves to produce an image – this is an extremely safe form of imaging, and is commonly used to examine babies in the womb. The digital pictures of modern scans can be greatly magnified and distributed electronically around the globe for any number of second opinions. Every day, millions of scans identify or rule out problems, help to plan surgery, monitor treatment, and generally save lives – all from outside the body, and without a scalpel in sight.

Seeing Inside the Body

The discovery of X-rays at the end of the 19th century made it possible to see images of the body's interior for the first time, transforming our understanding of its structure, how it works, and how it is affected by illness (see pp.302–309). Increasingly sophisticated types of scan have been developed since then – some for specific organs or tissues, and others for the whole body. They are all invaluable aids to diagnosis, surgery, and treatment.

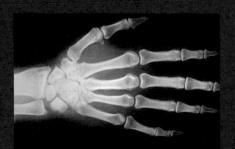

X-RAY
Passing through soft body tissues such as muscle easily, X-rays are blocked by denser tissues such as bones, which therefore show up clearly on the resulting image.

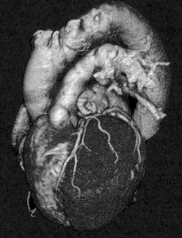

3D CT SCAN
CT (computerized tomography) or CAT scans take X-rays from several different angles at a time. As in this scan of a heart, this builds up three-dimensional images of organs rather than the simple outlines of standard X-ray images.

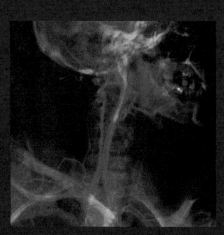

ANGIOGRAM
This type of X-ray uses a special injected dye to highlight a patient's blood vessels, so that doctors can check if they are narrow, blocked, enlarged, or malformed.

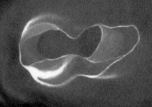

LAYERED CT SCAN
The layered, cross-sectional images produced by a CT scan show all body tissues and can be compiled into a 3D image on a computer. This picture reveals the interior of a narrowed artery.

AREA ACTIVE
WHEN LISTENING

AREA ACTIVE
WHEN SPEAKING

MRI SCAN

Magnetic resonance imaging (MRI)
is a versatile electromagnetic imaging
technique. It creates detailed images of
soft tissues, such as the brain (above),
and is well suited to detecting
cancerous tumours.

PET SCAN

Using a tracer introduced into the body,
a PET (positron emission tomography)
scan shows which areas of an organ are
the most active (the red and yellow
parts of the brain scans above). It is an
effective scan for diagnosing cancer.

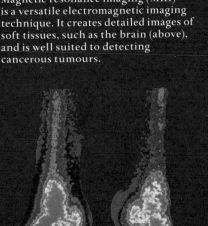

RADIONUCLIDE BONE SCAN

Before a bone scan, radioactive tracer
is injected into a patient and enters the
bones. As the tracer wears off, it gives
off radiation picked up by a camera as
it scans the patient's body.

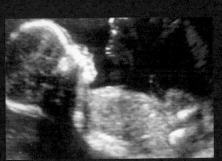

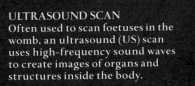

ULTRASOUND SCAN

Often used to scan foetuses in the
womb, an ultrasound (US) scan
uses high-frequency sound waves
to create images of organs and
structures inside the body.

The Birth of IVF

IVF BABIES ARE CONCEIVED OUTSIDE THE BODY, then the fertilized egg is returned to the mother's womb to develop and grow as usual. The first such baby, born in 1959, hardly rocked the world – no doubt because it was a rabbit. However the first human baby born as a result of IVF – Louise Brown, delivered in Oldham, England, on 25 July 1978 – generated global headlines. The event gave hope to millions of couples around the world who were having problems conceiving. It also stirred up a huge ethical debate. Doctors were accused of "playing God" by creating life where there would otherwise be none. Their response was that they did not in fact originate that life; medicine was simply aiding a natural biological process, hence the term "assisted reproduction".

A newborn baby is the end result of a series of complex, delicate processes that take some nine months to complete. These processes start in the female body with the release (ovulation) of a ripe egg cell (mature ovum) from its follicle in one of the two egg-making ovaries. The egg then moves along the fallopian tube towards the womb (uterus). Meanwhile, in the male body, millions of sperm cells (spermatozoa) mature daily in the testicles. During sex, about 250–500 million sperm in their nutrient liquid (seminal fluid) are released into the women's vagina, and some make their way through the cervix into the womb, and onwards into the two fallopian tubes. If there is a ripe egg in one of the tubes, a sperm may fertilize the egg. The fertilized egg (zygote) then continues along the tube into the womb, dividing as it goes – into two cells, four cells, eight cells, and so on, until several days later there is a blackberry-like ball of cells – the early embryo, or morula (see pp. 364–66). The cells of the morula carry on multiplying until they form a hollow cluster of cells called a blastocyst, which then beds down into the lining of the uterus to continue its development. This whole sequence is carefully timed, and each stage relies on the previous one being successfully completed, so a problem anywhere along the line can prevent conception.

IVF, or *in vitro* fertilization, helps an egg and sperm to meet – "*in vitro*" literally meaning "in glass", or laboratory glassware, as opposed to *in vivo*, in the "living tissue" of the mother. In 1978, the original IVF birth was touted as the first "test tube baby", although the actual fertilization can occur in various types of container, such as a beaker, a flask, or a Petri dish (as it was for Louise Brown). After fertilization, development is monitored under the microscope, and, three to five days later, the early embryo, still less than half a millimetre in size, is inserted into the womb – a process that is called embryo transfer.

In up to half of all infertility cases, failure to conceive naturally is caused by deficiencies in the male sperm. It may also be the result of a disrupted female menstrual cycle, which can prevent or limit egg release. This may in turn be due to a lack of, or imbalance between, the hormones that regulate the cycle – in particular oestrogen, progesterone, and follicle-stimulating hormone. Irregularity or absence of ovulation due to hormonal problems may be treated by so-called fertility drugs. One of the first of these was clomifene (trademarked as Clomid and Omifin), which appeared in the 1960s. It works by making the brain think that the body is not producing enough oestrogen, encouraging the body to increase hormone levels, which usually results in ovulation. Another group of fertility boosters are menotropins, which were introduced in the 1970s. These are extracted from the urine of post-menopausal women and contain natural follicle-stimulating and luteinizing hormones, both of which stimulate the growth of eggs in their follicles. One of the menotropins,

THE FIRST IVF BABY
Robert Edwards holds Louise Brown, the first IVF baby. Beside him are the midwife and Patrick Steptoe.

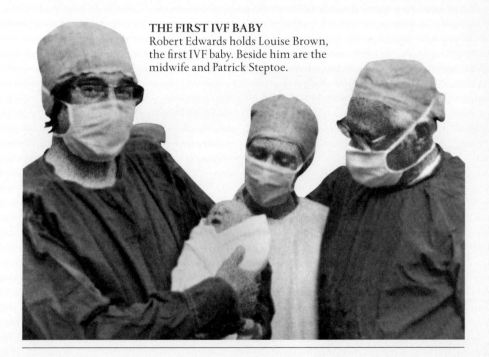

Pergonal, was pioneered by physiologist Robert Edwards and gynaecologist-obstetrician Patrick Steptoe, the duo who achieved the first IVF birth, that of Louise Brown.

Patrick Steptoe grew up near Oxford, trained in medicine in London, and took up a post at Oldham General Hospital in Lancashire, northwest England, where he headed a human reproduction unit. Robert Edwards spent his youth in Yorkshire and Manchester, then studied and furthered his work in various locations around the UK, including Bangor, Edinburgh, London, and Glasgow, and at the California Institute of Technology, before settling at Cambridge University in 1963 to work on developmental biology. Throughout his long alliance with Steptoe, Edwards provided the laboratory and physiological know-how, trying to create conditions that would enable egg and sperm to unite outside the body, while Steptoe developed methods of collecting eggs from women. The pair met in 1968 and began working with patients in 1970. Edwards had already been successful in fertilizing an egg in the laboratory, a process that involved producing a liquid or culture medium in which the eggs and sperm could mingle. This medium had to mimic the temperature and the mixture

PETRI DISH BABIES
Human embryos in a Petri dish at an IVF laboratory in
the US. Fertilization of "test tube babies" can occur
equally well in Petri dishes, beakers, or flasks.

"We had a lot of critics but we fought like hell for our patients"

ROBERT EDWARDS

of the nutrients, body minerals, and other substances found in the fallopian tube, and had to activate sperm cells – the second major challenge for IVF. This involves weakening the "cap" at the front end of the sperm cell so that the sperm can fuse with the egg – a process that happens naturally in the body when the sperm comes into contact with the fluids in the vagina and the uterus.

Steptoe was gaining experience with the laparoscope – a long, slim device inserted through a small incision in the abdominal wall (see pp.350–55) – and developed expertise in removing ripe egg cells from their follicles. He also made use of ultrasound (see p.311), which could be used to display a scanned image of the ovaries, to facilitate egg harvesting. In 1969, he began to offer volunteer women Pergonal and other fertility drugs. This resulted in superovulation – producing several mature eggs. Edwards tried various fertilization media and methods, using sperm donated by each woman's partner. When fertilization was successful, the early balls of cells were examined closely for any abnormalities.

At around this time, there was increasing controversy about the ethics of IVF research in the UK, not only among the public, but also within the medical community, religious bodies, the British parliament, and the establishment generally. Edwards and Steptoe were refused grants and found funding difficult to attract. The team eventually moved to the small Dr Kershaw's Cottage Hospital in Oldham, where they set up clinics and laboratories and moved on to the next phase – transferring an early embryo into the womb. However, failures of various kinds continued to blight the programme, and Steptoe and Edwards reasoned that the fertility treatments given to prospective mothers to bring on controlled superovulation were interfering with the womb, so that it was unable to accept the early embryo several days later. They tried injections of another hormone to help the womb lining maintain its readiness, but this produced mixed results and growing frustration for everyone concerned.

In 1977, after more than 70 failed pregnancies, Edwards and Steptoe reverted to a policy of minimal interference – collecting a single egg that had ripened naturally for ovulation, fertilizing it *in vitro*, monitoring its early development, and transferring it back into the mother, whose womb would be ready as normal. To ensure success, the mothers had to provide a urine sample every few hours to test it for luteinizing hormone, levels of which rose about 36 hours before ovulation. The team also decided to transfer embryos at an earlier stage – when they were only eight cells in size. In November 1977, Lesley Brown, the second patient on the new trial, arrived at Kershaw's. Her menstrual cycle and ovulation were normal, but her fallopian tubes were blocked. Steptoe used his laparoscope to obtain a ripe egg, which was then fertilized with her husband John's sperm. The eight-cell embryo was then transferred back into the womb – and nine months later baby Louise was born.

In 1980, Steptoe and Edwards established Bourn Hall Clinic, near Cambridge – the world's first clinic specializing in IVF. In 2010, Edwards received the Nobel Prize in Physiology or Medicine "for the development of *in vitro* fertilization" (Steptoe was not awarded as he had died in 1988).

The birth of Louise Brown was soon followed by live IVF births around the world: in Australia in 1980, in the US in 1981, and in Sweden and France in 1982. Research teams in these countries began working on diverse ways to improve the process. IVF would still be a time-consuming procedure if it had remained reliant on the single egg ovulated by the mother during each menstrual cycle. During the 1980s, however, better fertility drugs and regimes were produced, enabling more eggs to be released with greater predictability, greatly improving IVF success rates. By the 2010s, these reached one live birth per three treatment sessions for women under 35 years old. Ways of freezing an early embryo for later thaw and transfer to the mother were also established, which meant that a woman could conceive after undergoing treatment that might interfere with her reproductive system. GIFT (gamete intrafallopian transfer) was also developed – a process by which eggs and sperm are put together into the fallopian tube, so that fertilization can take place in the body, as if conception had occurred naturally. By 1990, screening also became available. Properly known as preimplantation genetic diagnosis (P(I)GD, or PGS), screening is a process in which one or more cells of an IVF early embryo are isolated before the embryo is transferred to the womb. These cells are analysed for genetic or chromosomal problems, such as Down's Syndrome, and if they are faulty, the embryo is not

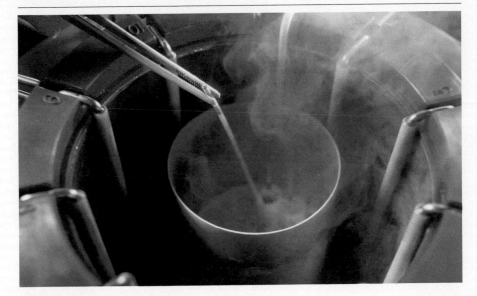

SPERM BANK
A technician removes frozen sperm cells from a tank of
liquid nitrogen. After the sample has thawed, the healthiest
cells are selected, using a computer imaging system, and
are each injected into an egg to form an embryo.

transferred. Another innovation was intracytoplasmic sperm injection
(ICSI). Instead of letting eggs and sperm mingle freely, a single sperm
is selected under the microscope and sucked into an incredibly thin
glass tube, which is then pushed through the outer layers of the egg
cell to insert the sperm. ICSI is useful for men with a very low sperm
count, or when many sperm are malformed or otherwise abnormal.

Meanwhile, the ethical debates continued. In 1984, the Government
of Victoria, Australia, introduced the first legislation to regulate IVF
and associated human embryo research, following a review of the
new practices. As a result of advances in assisted reproduction and
stem cell research (see pp.364–73), most countries have legislated to
regulate related activities. In the UK, the Human Fertilisation and
Embryology Authority (HFEA) was established in 1991 to do this.

In the 35 years since Louise Brown made headlines, some five
million babies around the world have been born thanks to assisted
conception. Who knows what the number will be in another 30 years?
Theoretically, a baby could have four "mothers" (and a "father"): a
same-sex female couple could adopt a baby from a donated egg that
(with help from a sperm) merged to form an embryo that was then
implanted into a surrogate mother.

THE MOMENT OF CONCEPTION
In a process called intracytoplasmic sperm
injection (ICSI), a doctor guides a needle (left)
containing a sperm cell towards an egg cell.
The successful joining of the two marks the
beginning of a human life.

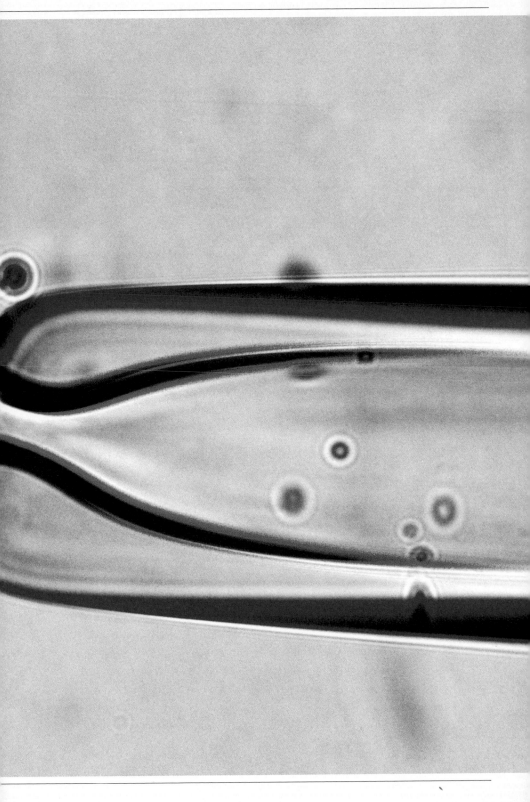

Complementary and Alternative Medicines

IN MANY AREAS OF LIFE, such as music, food, and fashion, one person's "mainstream" is another's "alternative", or yet another's "complementary" – and the same is true of health and medicine. Alternative and complementary therapies include almost any system or philosophy that aims to improve health and wellbeing but is not part of conventional Western medicine. "Alternative" therapies are exactly that – a different, independent option to the mainstream, while "complementary" implies a supplement or aid working alongside established medical practice. A related term is "holistic" medicine, which is directed at the whole patient, taking biological, psychological, and spiritual factors into account, rather than just the "machinery" of the body.

As Western nations recovered after the austerity of World War II, a new era of freedom and prosperity dawned – and by the 1960s, countercultures were blossoming in the arts, religion, and medicine. Newly affordable televisions and air travel exposed people to medical approaches from around the world. Coupled with dissatisfaction with the "production line" philosophy of conventional medicine, with its high-tech machines, invasive surgery, synthetic drugs, and ever-busy practitioners, there was an upsurge of interest in other forms of therapy, especially those of Eastern cultures. During the late 20th century, these attitudes continued to permeate Western society, and the first World Congress of Alternative Medicines was hosted in Rome, Italy, in 1973. The third, held in Sri Lanka, in 1982, announced its goal of providing "Holistic Medicine for all by the year 2000". In 1992, the US National Institutes of Health (NIH) set up the National Center for Complementary and Alternative Medicine (NCCAM), one of its long-term goals being to "enable better evidence-based decision making regarding complementary and alternative medicine use and its integration into health care and health promotion." Perhaps unsurprisingly, by the early 21st century, surveys in Europe and North America showed that half or more of adults consulting conventional general practitioners had also tried some form of complementary or alternative medicine (CAM).

From a conventional Western viewpoint, up to a hundred and fifty therapies have been listed as complementary, alternative, or holistic. Some, such as acupuncture, Ayurvedic medicine, herbalism, kampo, massage, and yoga, have long-standing traditions (see pp.64–97), but many, such as those discussed here, are later, modern inventions. Laser therapy, for instance, was not possible until American physicist Theodore Maiman invented the laser in 1960. Since 1968, lasers have been used conventionally as "light scalpels" that can be aimed with incredible precision to sear through tissues and seal blood vessels to reduce bleeding. Laser treatment to reshape the cornea began in the late 1980s, and laser atherectomy, which unblocks arteries clogged with fatty plaques, was developed around the same time. Lasers are also used for hair removal, lipo/fat reduction, and minor cosmetic procedures such as eye lifts. More controversial, however, is low-level laser therapy (LLLT), a complementary therapy in which specially designed lasers are used to produce deeply penetrating light that is said to stimulate unhealthy tissues and cells to increase their metabolism and to re-energize them. This is said to help healing after surgery or injury, ease pain by releasing endorphins (the body's natural

LASER THERAPY
A patient receives low-level laser therapy for rheumatoid arthritis. The treatment, which reportedly reduces pain, is also used for osteoarthritis, back pain, and chronic joint disorders.

painkillers), improve mobility and function, and even stimulate specific acupoint-type locations to reduce withdrawal symptoms when giving up drugs such as nicotine and alcohol.

Homoeopathy, a technique developed by German physician Samuel Hahnemann in the 19th century, is even more controversial. The guiding principle of homeopathy, which means "same suffering" in Greek, is "like heals like", or the "law of similars". Dating back to Ancient Greece, Rome, and Asia, this doctrine holds that a substance that causes certain effects or symptoms in the healthy body can, in lesser quantities, cure a disease with the same symptoms. For example, a powerful emetic (which brings on vomiting), given in small doses, can be used to treat an illness whose principal symptoms include vomiting. In *Organon der rationellen Heilkunde* (*The Organon of the Healing Art*), Hahnemann argued that sickness was caused by the body being invaded by "miasms" – disease entities that were attracted by negative states of mind – and claimed that many diseases were exacerbated by conventional medicine. This was, in his view, because doctors tended to treat the symptoms of diseases with their opposites, rather than treating the underlying causes (or miasms) with something similar. To counter this, Hahnemann produced a *materia medica* of substances that could be used to combat miasms. He tested hundreds of plant and animal extracts, minerals, and other substances on healthy people, and came to the conculsion, that, counterintuitively, the more a substance was diluted, the more powerful its effects apparently became. He called this process "potentization", and found that it was encouraged by shaking, banging, and vibrating a solution at each stage of its dilution. The end result was often a mixture so weak

HOMEOPATHIST'S MEDICINE CHEST
This French medicine chest, complete with over a hundred homeopathic medicines, dates from the late 19th century.

that only a few molecules of the original curative substance were left. After much experimentation, Hahnemann produced remedies for all kinds of highly specific conditions. For instance, if a headache was made worse by lying down, then Gelsemium was prescribed – if it eased, then Bryonia was recommended.

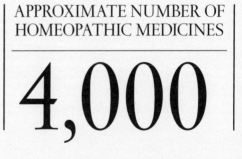

APPROXIMATE NUMBER OF HOMEOPATHIC MEDICINES

4,000

Another influential therapy, known as the Alexander Technique, was developed in the late 19th and early 20th centuries. This was pioneered by Australian actor Frederick Matthias Alexander, who, experiencing breathing problems that affected his stage work, underwent an intense period of self-analysis. During the course of this, he discovered patterns of stress and tension in his face, neck, back, and elsewhere that affected his ability to move freely and speak well. He extended the concept to his mind, and developed patterns of thought, posture, and movement that were designed to bring balance to all aspects of his mind and body. When others consulted Alexander, he devised ways of using his hands to help them relax their muscles, joints, and bones, and taught them about body awareness and coordination, and how to improve their breathing, speech, and general health – all of which he described in his 1932 book *The Use of the Self*.

Around the same time, Daniel David Palmer of Davenport, Iowa, US, was developing the chiropractic discipline. Palmer was a complex character who had had a variety of jobs, including spiritual counsellor and magnetic healer (see p.236), but he had received no formal medical training. In 1895, he manipulated the neck bones of a local patient with long-term hearing problems, and the man regained his hearing. As a manual treatment, chiropractic involves pushing, pulling, levering, and generally manipulating the spinal vertebrae and joints to restore their natural positions and function, thereby helping the nerve and muscle systems and a variety of associated health problems. He conjectured that misaligned spinal joints affected nerves and the general flow of energy around the body, thereby causing a wide range of health problems. Modern chiropractic has refined Palmer's techniques, but its main attention is still on the manipulation of the spine and musculoskeletal system, particularly to relieve lower back and neck pain. Chiropractic is similar to osteopathy, which was founded slightly earlier by US physician and political activist Andrew Taylor Still. The goal of osteopathy is also to activate the body's innate self-healing mechanisms to overcome health problems, by manipulation of muscles and joints.

Another way of balancing the body's energies emerged with the technique of reflexology, which uses "reflexes", or responsive zones on the feet and hands that are believed to correspond to regions and organs of the body. Like many complementary and alternative therapies, this technique has ancient origins and was Westernized only recently, in this case by US ear, nose, and throat surgeon William Fitzgerald, whose work of the 1910s was developed by US physiotherapist Eunice Ingham in the 1930s. At the same time, in Germany, psychiatrist Johannes Schultz developed autogenics (meaning "created by self") – a series of six mental exercises designed to free the individual of stress and worries, so they can focus on their inner being, or spirit. Schultz borrowed elements from Eastern traditions, such as Zen and certain forms of yoga, to help overcome the fight-or-flight instinct encouraged by modern life, and to foster a state of "relax and restore", in which the body can cope better with anxiety, mood swings, insomnia, high blood pressure, muscle tensions, and stress-related health problems.

Two other therapies developed in the 1930s were Bach flower remedies – named after British bacteriologist Edward Bach – and aromatherapy. Bach flower remedies aim to reduce the negative thoughts and feelings that are believed to underlie so many physical disorders. Bach devised a system in which 12 types of negative mental and emotional states – such as fear, uncertainty, lack of interest, loneliness, and depression – could be overcome by the effects of water-based extracts from certain flowers or buds. He called these extracts the 12 Healers, and later supplemented them with the 26 Helpers. Rock Rose, for example, is recommended for states of terror, and Agrimony for concealed worry. Later practitioners formulated combination flower remedies, including the well-known Rescue Remedy, containing Impatiens, Star of Bethlehem, Cherry Plum, Rock Rose, and Clematis – a formula recommended for emergencies and frightening situations. The term "aromatherapy" was coined in 1937 by French cosmetic chemist Professor René-Maurice Gattefossé, although the effects of scents and aromas on the mind and emotions have been appreciated for millennia. Gattefossé developed the use of

LAVENDER OIL
This electron microscope image shows lavender oil droplets
(purple) on the surface of a lavender leaf. Practitioners of
alternative medicine use lavender oil as an antiseptic, an
analgesic, and a chest rub for asthma.

essential oils extracted from flowers, leaves, bark, sap, resins, roots,
and other plant parts, which could be inhaled, massaged into the
skin, or added to bathwater. Garlic oil rubbed onto the abdomen, for
instance, is recommended for digestive problems, chamomile or
rosemary for joint aches, and cinnamon for toothache.

Aside from the dangers of misdiagnosis (which dog all types of
medicine), the question is, do these treatments actually work? Anecdotal
evidence suggests that millions of people have been helped, and all of
the therapies described above now have expert practitioners and official
organizations around the world. What tends to be lacking, from a
conventional point-of-view, is accountable peer-reviewed evidence
derived from controlled trials, and an underlying scientific hypothesis.
The placebo effect does suggest that belief in a cure can effect a cure,
raising the possibility that homeopathy patients, for instance, are
elaborately healing themselves. However, the question of "why" will
always come second to "whether" – and it is likely to be academic to
anyone who benefits from these hitherto mysterious arts.

REVISITING THE APOTHECARY
A 15th-century French apothecary turns plants into medicines. Alternative practitioners in the 20th century sought to reinvigorate the natural remedies of their forefathers, as modern medicine grew ever more reliant on chemicals.

Potential Pandemics

BUBONIC PLAGUE, SMALLPOX, CHOLERA – infections have menaced humankind down the centuries. At their worst, they are pandemics: outbreaks on continental, even global, scales (see pp.180–87). The first and worst pandemic of the 20th century was the three-wave spread of influenza from 1918–19, known as Spanish flu; estimated fatalities ranged from 30 million to more than 100 million people, nearly one in 20 of the world population at the time.

The body's immune system naturally tries to destroy invading microbes and protect the body against future attacks (see pp.286–93). Infecting microorganisms, however, have a nasty habit of mutating (changing) their genes and structures. Different strains can also interact in the body, sharing their existing genes. This means that the immune system may not recognize a new strain as the previous intruder, allowing the infection to take hold. The common cold and influenza viruses are masters of this art, constantly mutating to adapt and evade the defences of the immune system. On a wider scale, microbes that infect one group or species, such as birds or monkeys, may change so that they can transfer to another – such as humans.

Around 1981, US medical establishments recognized that some rare diseases and conditions, such as Kaposi's sarcoma, a skin cancer, and *Pneumocystis carinii* pneumonia (PCP, now called *P. jirovecii*), were

DISCOVERY OF HIV
French scientists Luc Montagnier and Françoise Barré-Sinoussi (left and right) received the Nobel Prize in 2008 for their 1983 discovery of the virus later called HIV. Jean-Claude Chermann (centre) was head of the retrovirology laboratory.

unexpectedly occurring together in certain patients – the first sufferers of what was being referred to by 1982 as Acquired Immunodeficiency Syndrome (AIDS). At that point, the cause was unknown. Then, in May 1983, an article in the journal *Science* reported the discovery of a new virus. It was identified at the Institut Pasteur in Paris by French virologists Luc Montagnier and Françoise Barré-Sinoussi, and called Lymphadenopathy-Associated Virus (LAV). Lymphadenopathy means any disease affecting the lymph nodes (the familiar swollen glands of so many infections), which are part of the immune system, and the virus had been isolated from this source. In April 1984, a related announcement came from a US research team headed by Robert Gallo at the National Cancer Institute, Bethesda. Called Human T-Lymphotropic Virus Type III (HTLV III), Gallo's virus seemed to be related to Types I and II, which had already been discovered and linked to T-cell lymphoma, a type of white blood cell cancer (see pp.260–69). It was suspected, and soon confirmed, that LAV and HTLV III were the same. In 1986, they were renamed Human Immunodeficiency Virus (HIV), the cause of AIDS.

Perceived as a modern plague that could spread like wildfire, AIDS was global news. Its origins were a mystery and it had no cure. It appeared to be linked to certain lifestyles and behaviours, in particular, homosexuality and intravenous drug use. Myths and misconceptions were rife. Governments set up national campaigns to correct fallacies about HIV/AIDS, communicate impartial facts, and encourage precautions to prevent the spread of the disease.

HIV is a retrovirus. Most viruses contain genetic material, DNA (see pp.338–49), inside a protective covering. The virus invades a host cell and tricks it into building more viruses (see pp.228–29). A retrovirus adds a retro (backward) step to this process: it codes its genetic information in a different form and employs a distinctive enzyme to convert it to DNA, which then behaves in the same way as in an ordinary virus. Robert Gallo detected the first evidence of retroviruses in humans in the early 1970s. What HIV does is target the very parts and processes of the body that are designed to repel invaders – the immune system. In particular, it infects and destroys a type of white blood cell crucial to the body's ability to fight germs and make antibodies. As HIV reduces the number of these cells, the immune system is robbed of vital forces. The body's defences weaken, leaving it vulnerable to opportunistic infections and cancerous changes.

HIV UNDER THE MICROSCOPE
The RNA (which encodes genes) is coloured blue in this cross-section of HIV. Its outer coat (also blue) contains a protein that attaches to a T-helper cell (a type of white blood cell).

Retroviruses infect many animals, including birds, cattle, mice, cats, monkeys, and apes. Herein lie clues to the origins of HIV. Researchers began to check through stored samples of blood and other tissues from people whose symptoms and diagnoses matched the HIV/AIDS profile. From 1985, they identified a similar group of viruses known as SIVs (Simian Immunodeficiency Viruses; "simian" meaning monkeys and apes). These occurred in African monkeys and in apes, a group that includes humans and our closest living relatives, chimpanzees and gorillas. By the mid-2000s, intense analysis concluded that HIV had jumped from chimpanzees to humans, probably in West Africa as a result of bushmeat butchering. The jump may have happened in the first half of the 20th century, as the earliest preserved tissue samples testing positive for HIV dated back to 1959 and 1960. From West Africa, the virus travelled in human hosts to Haiti and thence to North America, where sophisticated health care made identification possible. HIV/AIDS has since been detected in every country. By 2010, more than 30 million people had died of it.

In the decade before AIDS emerged, two other significant infections were newly identified. The first recognized case of Legionnaire's disease was in 1976 in the US. It is one of a group of pneumonias – infections that affect primarily the lungs, and especially the millions of alveoli (microscopic air sacs), where essential oxygen passes from air into the blood and carbon dioxide passes out of the blood into the lungs. Pneumonia has many causes, mainly numerous viruses and

ESTIMATE OF PEOPLE LIVING WITH HIV/AIDS

30 MILLION

bacteria. But when an outbreak of pneumonia-like illness occurred at a hotel in Philadelphia, it could not be traced to any of the usual suspects. Delegates at the convention were members of the American Legion, hence the name given to the disease. Eventually, the cause was traced to the bacterium *Legionella pneumophila*. Unlike HIV, this is not a newly evolved germ, but an established, common inhabitant of watery and damp environments. The hotel's air-conditioning system and cooling towers just happened to provide the ideal temperature and humidity for the bacteria to multiply and spread in tiny mist-like water droplets, which were easily breathed in. Most of the convention delegates were middle-aged or older – a group now known to be prone to the infection. Their symptoms appeared a few days later, and local Philadelphia doctor Ernie Campbell noted that several patients had attended the convention. This first outbreak resulted in 220 cases and 34 deaths, so systems were put in place to identify future outbreaks much more quickly. New regulations were also introduced to minimize the risks in equipment such as air-conditioning, heaters, humidifiers, saunas, misting machines, and whirlpool tubs.

Legionnaire's disease is potentially serious but rare, and continues to rumble on at the rate of a few reported outbreaks each year – since its discovery, it has caused small numbers of fatalities in various regions, including Norway, Australia, Spain, and North America. Probably many more cases go unrecognized, especially in areas with less developed health care. Important limiting factors are that Legionnaire's disease tends to occur in certain types of "unnatural" indoor settings and does not spread directly from person to person.

The second infection that was newly identified, also in around 1976, was Ebola virus disease. It was first noted in Sudan and in the Ebola River region of the Democratic Republic of Congo in Central Africa. Extremely serious, it starts, like so many other diseases, with flu-type symptoms, but then progresses to the digestive system, where it causes nausea, vomiting, and diarrhoea; to the nervous system with severe headache, confusion, agitation, seizures, and sometimes coma; and to the respiratory system with breathing difficulties. Haemorrhage or bleeding in the skin and other organs is a characteristic symptom. It is deadly in about two-thirds of cases.

Ebola virus disease is spread primarily by contact with blood and other body fluids, either directly or through contaminated objects. In health centres and hospitals, it can rapidly spread among staff from a patient whose Ebola infection has not been diagnosed. This is why isolation, infection control, and barrier nursing – goggles, masks, gloves, gowns, and thorough equipment sterilization – are paramount.

As with HIV and other viruses, Ebola virus disease probably came from animals, which constitute a reservoir of infection, so that even if all human cases were eliminated at once, people could still be infected in future from close contact with animals. Certain species of fruit bat are the primary and continuing source of the virus. Gorillas, chimpanzees, monkeys, forest antelopes, and porcupines are also recognized sources. Since these creatures are found in few places other than West and Central Africa, and human-to-human transmission can be prevented with intensive precautions, Ebola virus disease is unlikely to be a potential pandemic.

In the mid-1990s, a new strain of avian influenza ("bird flu") was identified in China. It was a subtype of the influenza A virus designated H5N1. At the time, and like its predecessors, it infected only birds, mainly chickens and waterfowl such as geese and ducks. Culling flocks helped to limit these early outbreaks. In the early 2000s, more bird and then human outbreaks spread through China and Southeast Asia, and occasionally elsewhere. By 2012, there were more than 580 cases of bird flu in humans across 15 countries, and almost 350 deaths.

Bird flu moves from infected birds to humans through close contact with feathers, skin, organs, fluids, and droppings (which dry and disperse as dust). Properly handled, cooked food and eggs do not spread the disease. As with other infections, the fear is that the genetic make-up of the virus may alter so that it passes more easily from person to person, triggering a pandemic. In 2013, a different strain, H7N9, was reported to spread more easily from birds to humans, but so far there is no evidence of human-to-human transmission.

Another recent infectious disease is Severe Acute Respiratory Syndrome (SARS). Caused by a type of coronavirus (under the microscope, it looks like a halo or crown – *corona* in Latin), it was named for its effects on the body, which at first resemble influenza. The SARS outbreak in southern China from 2002 to 2003 was both helped and hindered by 21st-century technology, with the internet and electronic communications playing important roles. The disease spread at once via international air travel and global media quickly alerted the world, likening it to Spanish flu. Its cause was rapidly

POLICE PROTECTION FROM SARS
In an effort to contain a SARS outbreak
in 2003, a military policeman, masked
for protection, stands guard outside a
102-ward hospital in Taiwan, the first
to be used solely for SARS sufferers.

identified by the cooperative
efforts of several nations, using the
most advanced medical methods.
Precautions and prevention soon
followed. As a result, the SARS
outbreak was contained to fewer
than 9,000 recorded cases and 800
fatalities, and did not graduate
from epidemic to pandemic.

All these infections continue to cause concern, as do resurgent old
enemies such as new strains of drug-resistant tuberculosis. Another
area for concern is the pox group. Smallpox has gone, declared extinct
in 1980 (see pp.160–61). Since then, smallpox vaccination has ceased,
but it may be that the immunization programme had helped to
protect against the related *Orthopoxvirus* strains, such as mousepox,
monkeypox, and cowpox, which are carried by rats and other rodents.
Just a small change in one of these strains could enable it to pass from
animal to human, and then from one human to another – the ideal
requisites for a pandemic.

Battling HIV and AIDS

HIV (human immunodeficiency virus) is one of the fastest-evolving entities known to medicine – it reproduces lightning-fast, spawning millions of copies of itself in the space of just one day. Producing flu-like symptoms, it leads to a breakdown of its victims' immune system, leaving them vulnerable to life-threatening infection. A recent disease, it probably originated in Africa early in the 20th century, but has nonetheless caused over 30 million deaths, and is still spreading rapidly. There is currently no cure, but antiviral drugs can slow the progress of the disease.

AIDS AWARENESS RIBBON

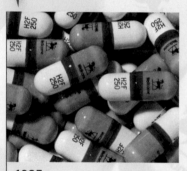

1986 Research in France and in the US identifies the virus that **causes AIDS**; it is confirmed that the retroviruses **LAV** and **HTLV-III** are in fact the same, and the virus is renamed HIV.

1985 Experiments using the antiviral drug **zidovudine** (AZT) reduce replication of HIV, slowing the disease.

1959 The earliest documented case of AIDs occurs in **the Belgian Congo** (Democratic Republic of Congo).

1983 Scientists at the Institut Pasteur in Paris isolate a retrovirus, LAV, that is the **likely cause of AIDS**.

1987 The antiviral drug AZT is made widely available as the **first treatment** for HIV.

1969 The HIV virus is probably **brought to the US** (possibly by a sufferer who travelled from Haiti).

1981 The first cases of the **immunodeficiency syndrome** are identified in New York and California.

1984 A team led by American scientist Robert Gallo **identifies a retrovirus** and calls it HTLV-III.

1982 The disease becomes known as **AIDS**.

RATIO OF THE POPULATION OF SUB-SAHARAN AFRICA WITH HIV

1 IN 20

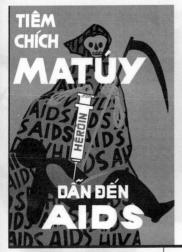

1990S HIV prevention campaigns around the world encourage safe sex and responsible drug use. This poster, showing the figure of death marked "AIDS", and wielding a scythe and a syringe labelled "heroin", is part of a campaign in Vietnam.

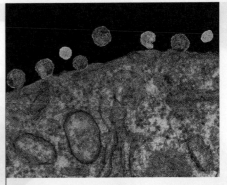

2013 Researchers in the US work on a vaccine that helps the immune system **recognize and attack** HIV.

1990 The Ryan White Care Act provides funds in the US to care for **HIV patients**.

1992 A new drug, Hivid, becomes available for use **in combination** with AZT.

1997 AZT is increasingly prescribed for HIV-positive **pregnant mothers** and reduces transmission to the child.

1998 Human trials of an HIV/AIDS **vaccine** begin.

2004 The US approves the first generic **HIV drug**, paving the way for less expensive medication.

1996 Powerful new drugs called **protease inhibitors** are used against HIV in combination with other drugs.

2000 In response to **widespread ignorance**, 5,000 scientists sign a declaration that AIDS and HIV are linked.

2009 American scientists complete their project to **decode** the entire HIV genome.

2001 US drug companies drop patent claims, enabling European manufacturers to make cheaper, **generic drugs** for use in hard-hit areas of the developing world, especially Africa.

Genes and Future Dreams

2000–PRESENT

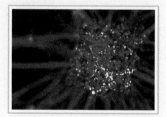

Welcome to a brave new world. Stem cells grow into any tissue or organ for rejection-free implant into their original owner's body. Cloned cells aid them. So does tissue-engineering, with bio-friendly scaffolds that give cells 3D frameworks to help them build spare parts. Nanotechnology delivers molecule-sized machines that melt blood clots with lasers, invade and destroy tumour cells, and attach powerful anti-germ drugs directly on to microscopic invaders. Tailor-made genetic profiling allows doctors to identify detailed risk factors, disease likelihood, and the perfect drug mix for each individual. Gene therapy corrects all manner of inherited defects and treats cell mutations that could lead to cancer. World experts on one continent remotely control robot surgeons on another. The internet gives instant expert diagnosis and prescription. Advanced life-support technologies nurse ailing bodies through the most difficult of disease crises. Anti-ageing treatments, anti-obesity pills, tablets to increase brainpower, even proper cures for baldness and wrinkles – they all work.

Some of these advances are on the way now; some are hopefully not more than a few decades away; others will fall at one hurdle or another. But the 21st century harbours threats, too – the spread of antibiotic-resistant germs; plague pandemics of new infections that have spread from animals; a colossal increase in dementias; more illnesses caused by affluence and old age; spiralling costs and struggles for funding and resources. For medicine, the 2000s may be the century of the greatest extremes and inequalities yet.

Genetics and Medicine

IN JUNE 2000, THE HUMAN GENOME PROJECT announced a breakthrough. For the first time, it had successfully mapped a "rough draft" of the human genome – the entire set of DNA (deoxyribonucleic acid), the genetic material that forms the instructions for building, running, and maintaining a human body. The draft was a phenomenal achievement with immense implications for human biology, health, and medicine, but it was widely misunderstood. It did not identify every gene in the body, explaining how it worked and what it did. To appreciate the relevance of the genome, and the relationship between genetics and medicine, it helps to go back a couple of centuries and explore thebackground of genes and DNA.

Children resemble their parents. Not in all respects, but in general likeness and personality, plus a few very similar family features such as nose shape. The principles of this process, called inheritance or heredity, were laid down by Austrian monk Gregor Mendel, who experimented with pea plants rather than people, and published his results in 1866. He had interbred some 29,000 pea plants that had various contrasting features, such as flowers that were different colours, and had discovered that many parental features were not blended together like some kind of hybrid soup in the offspring, but were passed on in discrete particles or units – now known as genes – that kept their integrity and were inherited in specific patterns over succeeding generations.

In the early 1900s, several biologists rediscovered Mendel's work and quickly brought it to the attention of the scientific community. German biologist Theodor Boveri, who was doing research with sea urchins, and American physician Walter Sutton, who was experimenting on grasshoppers, both independently reached the conclusion that a dividing cell passes sets of chromosomes to each of the new cells, and this is what makes them inherit features and characteristics. Chromosomes had first been identified in the mid-19th century, and were formally described in 1878 by another German biologist, Walther Flemming. Through the light microscope, they appear as thread-like, X-shaped objects when cells prepare to divide. By 1915, American biologist Thomas Hunt Morgan, using fruit flies for experiments, had demonstrated that chromosomes carry

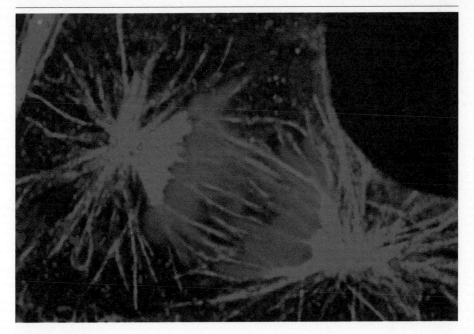

CELL DIVISION
This light-microscope image shows a single cell
dividing into two separate cells. The two sets of
chromosomes can be seen stained red.

hereditary information, and in 1933, he was duly awarded the Nobel
Prize in Physiology or Medicine for "discoveries concerning the role
played by the chromosome in heredity".

What are chromosomes made of? In the 1920s, the answer became
clearer – proteins called histones, as well as the substance we know as
DNA (see pp.348–49). The latter had first been isolated and studied as
"nuclein" by Swiss physician-researcher Friedrich Miescher in around
1870. During the early decades of the 20th century, the building-block
components of DNA were identified in more detail as deoxyribose
sugars, phosphate groups, and four types of component called
nucleotide bases, or simply bases. By the 1940s, investigators had shown
that DNA is a giant molecule and the carrier of genetic information, a
fact that was further confirmed in 1952 by experiments with viruses.
DNA's precise physical structure, however, was still unclear. In 1953,
came the momentous discovery of DNA's double-helix arrangement by
English scientist Francis Crick and US biologist James Watson, aided by
English biophysicist Rosalind Franklin and New Zealand-born Maurice
Wilkins. The finding explained how genetic information in DNA is
carried in the sequence of its bases, which are copied when the cell

divides and then pass to both new cells, including egg and sperm cells, and thus to the fertilized egg and the next generation. It was shown that DNA works in the same way in bacteria, moulds, plants, fruit flies, and other animals, including humans.

At the same time, medical researchers were also studying chromosomes. In the 1920s, research scientists suggested that there were 24 pairs of chromosomes in each human body cell – one of each pair inherited from the mother, and the other from the father. In 1956, with much improved technology, Indonesian-born American cellular geneticist Joe Hin Tjio, working in Sweden, was able to revise this number to the now-accepted 23 pairs, making 46 chromosomes altogether in each body cell. Before long, scientists were discovering that chromosomal abnormalities were responsible for various congenital (present at birth) conditions. In 1958, it was found that people with Down's syndrome have three chromosomes instead of

BUILDING BLOCKS OF LIFE
Geneticists James Watson (left) and Francis Crick
with a model of DNA – the molecule in which
genetic information is encoded.

two on the 21st of the 23 pairs. They are therefore sometimes referred to as "having an extra chromosome".

PROPORTION OF GENES SHARED BETWEEN A HUMAN AND A TREE

50%

Despite these discoveries, pinpointing the mechanics of individual genetic abnormalities and understanding how to mend them, or even knowing how many genes the human body has, was still some way off. What was known for certain, however, was that a gene was a length of DNA that contained the information necessary to make proteins. Some proteins are the structural building blocks of cells and tissues – such as collagen in skin and keratin in fingernails – whereas others are involved in control and coordination: insulin, for example, manages blood glucose, and antibodies counteract microbes. The substances called enzymes that break down food during digestion are also proteins, as are other enzymes that synchronize the mass of chemical changes occurring every second within cells.

Proteins are built from smaller units known as amino acids, which are linked together in sequence. A genetic fault can cause the body to use the wrong amino acid when a protein is made, resulting in a malformed protein. An example of this is an inherited condition called sickle-cell anaemia, in which red blood cells are not the usual doughnut-like shape, but sickle-shaped, which reduces their ability to carry oxygen. In 1949, US scientists Linus Pauling, Harvey Itano, Seymour Jonathan Singer, and Ibert C. Wells published evidence that sickle-cell patients' haemoglobin – the component of red blood cells that transports oxygen and carbon-dioxide around the body – differs from normal haemoglobin. In 1956, the root cause of this condition was pinpointed to a tiny part of the amino acid sequence, in which a different amino acid from usual was present. This was the first discovery of the molecular basis for a genetic disorder.

The Human Genome Project's rough draft was not a catalogue of all the genes and what they did – what it provided was a list of DNA's chemical subunits, or bases. These bases are strung out along the immense length of every coiled DNA molecule, each of which forms one of the 46 chromosomes. DNA has four different types of chemical base : A (adenine), T (thymine), G (guanine), and C (cytosine).

These bases form pairs, and the sequence the pairs form along the double helix carries genetic information that is written out as strings of the four letters: A-T-C-C-G-T-T-, and so on. Crucially, the base on one strand of the double helix can only attach to one other base, which is its partner on the second helix: A always pairs up with T, and G always pairs up with C.

When a cell divides, the double helix splits lengthwise to form two single helices, then each helix builds a new partner strand (see p.348). An A on the existing helix therefore attaches to a T for the new strand. If the next base is C, this links to a new G, and so on. This results in two new double helices, each consisting of one strand of the original double helix plus a new complementary partner strand. Because of base pairing, these two double helices are identical both to each other and to the parent double helix. The genetic information has been copied from the original cell to its two offspring cells. As we have seen, there are only four different kinds of base in DNA, but their numbers are astronomical – more than three billion base pairs are strung out along all the DNA molecules in all the chromosomes of the human genome. And this genetic information is economically packaged. Joined end to end, the set of DNA molecules would stretch over 2m (6ft), yet they are tightly coiled and folded into a cell so small that 500 of them could fit on a pinhead.

The Human Genome Project began in 1990 and aimed to sequence all the DNA bases in the main parts of the genome. It was declared complete in April 2003, and the information was made freely available online to the public, including research scientists, doctors, drug companies, biotechnologists, life insurance companies, mortgage lenders, and lawyers. There would be other far-reaching effects – understanding in greater detail how genes actually work, unravelling what happens in genetic or inherited diseases and conditions, and finding out how and why the DNA in some cells in the body changes or mutates to produce tumours, for example. The project's Ethical, Legal, and Social Implications (ELSI) programme considered the consequences of this knowledge, especially its application to human health and medicine. The "rough draft" published in June 2000 listed sequences for

THE HUMAN GENOME
A scientist working on the Human Genome Project in 1998 at Washington University in the US uses ultraviolet light to study strands of human DNA.

SCANNING THE GENOME
A technician working at the California Institute of Technology uses a circular scanner to read sections of DNA radiograms for computer analysis.

about 85 per cent of the bases – 25 per cent to such a high degree of accuracy that they were regarded as finished, and more than another 50 per cent very nearly so.

One particular area of genome study is that of SNPs (single-nucleotide polymorphisms), pronounced "snips". These are variations in the location of a particular base. For example, one person may have base A at a certain location on a particular chromosome, while another person might have base C. In fact, SNPs occur on average once every 100–300 bases along the whole human genome. They are part of what makes each human genetically unique (apart from identical twins). Many SNPs have no effect on health, but some do. One SNP results in sickle-cell disease, as mentioned above, and we now know that the change or mutation occurs within a gene called HBB, which contains instructions for a part of haemoglobin. The chromosome on which it occurs is about 134 million base pairs long, has around 1,500 genes, and is involved in more than 150 genetic disorders and other health problems. As details such as these become known for genetic disorders, the hope is that they will lead to better treatment and possible cures.

SNPs help to track inherited disorders through family lines, even if the SNPs themselves are not directly responsible for the disorder. Those that are located near or among the mutated sequences can act as "markers" to determine patterns of heredity. SNPs and similar changes in genes are also linked to more general phenomena, such as reaction to environmental factors such as inhaled toxins; response to certain drugs and foods; and the chances of developing particular diseases – even complex diseases such as cancers. For instance, in 2010, the gene APCDD1 was linked to a form of hereditary hair loss. In 2011, the loss of a group, or cluster, of 27 genes was linked to autism-like features. In 2013, a research consortium reported finding another seven positions, or loci, in the genome linked to age-related macular degeneration, which is the main cause of sight loss in the elderly.

As we learn more about genes, what they do, and how they go wrong, the question arises: can we treat genetic conditions by introducing normal DNA into the body to enable it to produce a substance, such as an enzyme or a hormone, that is otherwise missing or abnormal? Introducing normal DNA into body cells is known as "delivery", and one such method exploits viruses (see p.228–29). When a virus invades a cell, it hijacks the cell's production machinery, then uses its own genes to make more viruses. In gene therapy, the virus is used to deliver normal human genes into the cell. A virus used in this way is known as a "virus vector". The vector technique has been widely used in other areas of biological sciences since the 1970s, to make genetically modified bacteria and crops, for example. Another form of gene therapy is to insert the correct genes as "naked" lengths of DNA. One such technique, electroporation, involves applying an electric field to a cell in short, sharp bursts, to create pores in the cell's outer skin through which much larger molecules or substances than usual can be admitted – including drugs to destroy a tumour, or lengths of DNA to repair a genetic condition. Electroporation has been performed both on cells floating in laboratory liquid (*in vitro*) and on living tissue that is accessed by tiny probes inserted into the body (*in vivo*). Inserting genes into cells like this is known as gene electrotransfer. Another way of delivering the DNA is to wrap it in fatty substances to form artificial bubbles, or vesicles, known as liposomes, which are then injected into the cell. This method is used to treat cancers. The healthy DNA stimulates the natural cancer-

"What more powerful form of study of mankind could there be than to read our own instruction book?"

FRANCIS S. COLLINS, US GENETICIST

suppressing genes already present in the genome, which for some reason are not working. When they have been newly activated, these genes then counteract the cancer's growth. Liposome delivery has also been researched for the inherited condition of cystic fibrosis. Whichever method is used, the aim is to get as many normal genes into as many cells as possible, and to ensure that they remain active for as long as possible.

In 1990, gene therapy came of age when a four-year-old girl was treated for a rare enzyme disorder known as ADA deficiency (adenosine deaminase deficiency). However, faith in the new treatment was damaged in 1999, when Jesse Gelsinger died in Philadelphia, US. Gelsinger, who was only 18 years old, was participating in clinical research for a genetic disorder that renders the liver unable to deal with ammonia, a waste product created when proteins are broken down. Virus vectors were used to introduce normal copies of the gene, but Gelsinger's immune system reacted in a catastrophic manner. He developed brain damage, went into a coma, and died four days later. Subsequent investigations revealed that the organizers of the trial had not informed Gelsinger and his family about previous reactions to the treatment. This was followed by news that other gene therapy trials had failed, with more than 600 reports of "adverse events", including deaths. These tragedies were severe blows to gene therapy, but as time has gone by, the numbers of clinical trials have increased.

One area in which gene therapy is flourishing is vaccination – the introduction of harmless versions of a disease-causing microbe or its products into the body (see

LIPOSOME CLUSTER
This scanning electron micrograph shows liposomes – bubbles made from the same material as cell membranes – used to deliver DNA into patients.

pp.286–93). The body's immune system recognizes the foreign substances, called antigens, and mobilizes defences against them. DNA vaccination goes a step further and introduces artificially made genes that carry instructions to make the antigens. When the antigens are produced, the body's defence mechanisms swing into action. Such vaccines have been under trial since the 1990s, and their targets include tuberculosis, HIV (see pp.334–35), and malaria (see pp.388–89). DNA vaccination could help in eradicating these diseases, as could genetic studies such as those investigating why sickle-cell disease protects people against malaria.

During the 1980s, estimates of the total number of genes in the human genome usually exceeded 100,000. As the Human Genome Project progressed, scientific consensus reduced this total to 60,000–70,000, then to 40,000–50,000. In 2013, around ten years after the project finished, most estimates were in the area of 20,000–25,000 – a number that, 20 years earlier, would have seemed impossibly small for an organism as complex and sophisticated as a human being. Furthermore, most of the DNA in the human genome does not actually represent the genetic code as such. The base sequences that we call genes, known as coding DNA, account for less than two per cent of the genome. The rest, non-coding DNA, was assumed to be an array of harmless leftovers or accidental copies – what is sometimes labelled "junk DNA". Recently, it has become clear that large portions of this DNA are in fact not "junk" at all and contain instructions for making substances and molecules that control if, when, and how genes work (see pp.364–73). This has huge implications for the study of genetic disease and designing gene therapies for the future.

The Genetic Code

All living beings are made of complex chemicals called proteins. The substance in a cell's nucleus that controls how these proteins are produced – and therefore determines the similarities and differences between individuals – is DNA (deoxyribonucleic acid). DNA has a regular structure. It was identified as a double helix – like two intertwined coil springs – by James Watson and Francis Crick in 1953.

DNA is present in every living cell, and contains a set of instructions – genes – that control inherited characteristics. As an organism grows, its cells divide in such a way that every cell has a copy of the DNA instructions for making protein. So, genes are consistent within an individual, but vary from one individual of the same species to another. Unravelling the genetic code – how genes influence the body's chemical make-up – continues to occupy scientists (see pp.338–47), and is leading to a greater understanding of diseases and genetic disorders.

Friedrich Miescher

Swiss scientist Friedrich Miescher began studying the proteins in white blood cells soon after qualifying as a physician in 1868–69. In the nuclei of the cells, he found a substance that contained phosphates and other elements that are not usually found in proteins. Miescher named this mysterious substance "nuclein", because it occurred in the cells' nuclei, and this term is still part of the substance's modern name: deoxyribonucleic acid (DNA).

FRIEDRICH MIESCHER BECAME PROFESSOR OF PHYSIOLOGY AT THE UNIVERSITY OF BASEL IN 1871

DOUBLE HELIX

DNA is a long-chain molecule made up of repeated building blocks called nucleotides (see top right). How the nucleotides are arranged influences the composition of proteins.

Complementary base pairs of nucleotides are arranged in a specific order that is replicated before cells divide

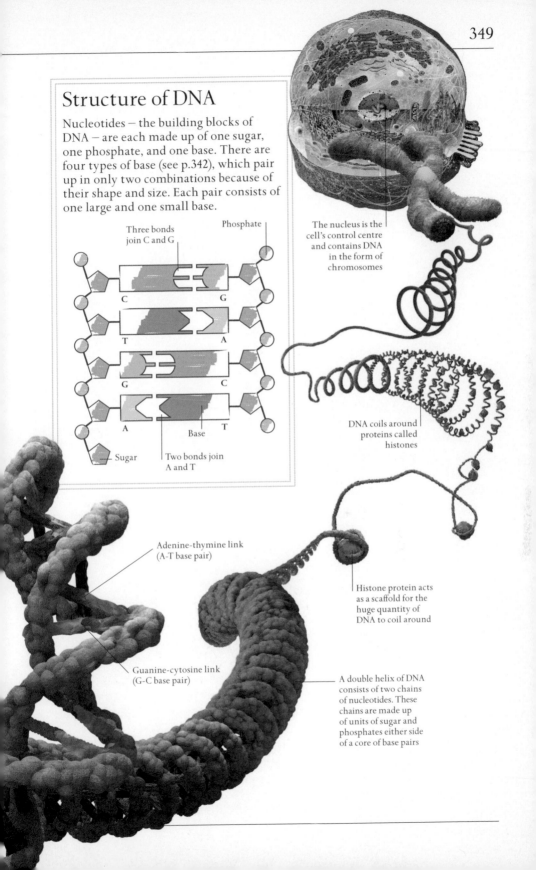

Structure of DNA

Nucleotides – the building blocks of DNA – are each made up of one sugar, one phosphate, and one base. There are four types of base (see p.342), which pair up in only two combinations because of their shape and size. Each pair consists of one large and one small base.

Three bonds join C and G

Phosphate

C — G

T — A

G — C

A — T

Sugar

Base

Two bonds join A and T

The nucleus is the cell's control centre and contains DNA in the form of chromosomes

DNA coils around proteins called histones

Adenine-thymine link (A-T base pair)

Guanine-cytosine link (G-C base pair)

Histone protein acts as a scaffold for the huge quantity of DNA to coil around

A double helix of DNA consists of two chains of nucleotides. These chains are made up of units of sugar and phosphates either side of a core of base pairs

Robots and Telemedicine

ON A FUTURE BATTLEFIELD, an armoured truck arrives near the front line – a military surgical unit, ready for action. Inside is a miniature operating theatre packed with diagnostic and surgical equipment. Each wounded patient brought in is hooked up to monitors for detailed assessment – then fast, expert treatment, including surgery, is delivered to almost any part of the body by top consultants in virtually every branch of medicine. Yet the unit carries only a few, albeit highly trained, personnel. The medical experts are far away, providing their services remotely via super-fast satellite communications and robotic operating technology. This is one scenario for telesurgery, itself a branch of telemedicine – medical care from a distance. Telemedicine is just a tiny part of a revolution in medicine that is being powered by computing and information technology – a revolution that began in the early 20th century and is still gaining momentum.

In 2001, telesurgery was carried out for the first time across the Atlantic. Surgeons in New York joined the patient and operating team in Strasbourg, France, by fast fibre-optic link. Guided by cameras showing close-ups of the operating area, along with patient monitor read-outs and two-way audio, surgeons in New York operated a remote surgical console, the movements of which were copied in Strasbourg by robotic effector arms and equipment. The 68-year-old female patient underwent laparoscopic cholecystectomy – removal of the gall bladder through a minimal incision. Since this was chiefly a pioneering trial to demonstrate telesurgery's potential, a highly experienced medical team stood by in France in case of problems. Among the challenges facing the telesurgeons was making the robotic manipulators copy the surgeon's movements in almost real time across a distance of nearly 7,000km (4,350 miles). Tests had shown that a time lag of more than 250–300 milliseconds (about one quarter of a second) from the operator's movement to the robot arm/camera and back to the operator's visual display could make the surgeon feel detached and disorientated. The NY–Strasbourg–NY lag was an acceptable 155 milliseconds. Also vital was an isolated communications link that, unlike usual worldwide web traffic, would not slow down or be interrupted, and which could also carry the amounts of data needed for robot control, medical monitoring, and two-way audio and visual communication. The whole operation took less than an hour, and the patient went home two days later. The milestone event was dubbed the "Lindbergh Operation", after the first solo, non-stop transatlantic flight in 1927 by Charles Lindbergh. Director of the European Institute of Telesurgery Professor Jacques Marescaux, who conducted the operation remotely from New York, said: "It lays the foundations for the globalization of surgical procedures, making it possible to imagine that a surgeon could perform an operation on a patient anywhere in the world".

The Lindbergh Operation employed a remote three-arm robotic system called ZEUS, which was controlled by the motions of the surgeon's hands. Two of ZEUS's arms held surgical instruments, including a laparoscope, while another held a laparoscope positioner called AESOP (Automated Endoscopic System for Optimal Positioning). A laparoscope is a long, slender tube that can carry a light, a camera, and various surgical tools – including forceps, grabs, crushers, blades, and cautery tips. It is inserted into the patient through a small incision made in the abdominal wall. A laparoscopy is an example of minimally invasive surgery, or MIS – otherwise known as "keyhole surgery" – which, compared to the traditional method of making a large incision, greatly reduces tissue disruption, blood loss, post-operative pain, recovery time, and scarring. AESOP was designed primarily to help the surgeon guide the laparoscope, and as such, it was an early stage of computer-assisted robotic surgery. Following AESOP and ZEUS came the da

Vinci system in 2000. Using NASA's space technology adapted initially for battlefield conditions, the da Vinci system has three or four robotic arms. One carries a laparoscope and

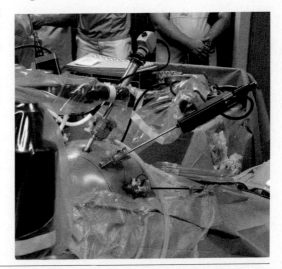

THE LINDBERGH OPERATION
Doctors stand by as the remotely controlled arms of the ZEUS surgical robot perform a laparoscopic cholecystectomy during the historic Lindbergh Operation of 2001.

REMOTE HEART SURGERY
A surgeon operates the arms of
a da Vinci robot during the first
organ transplant performed using
such a system. The operation took
place at Guy's and St Thomas'
Hospital, London, in 2004.

twin cameras for 3D visual display, while the others hold various
surgical instruments. Its arms and wrists exploit so many pivots
and swivels that they have a greater range of movements than those
of any human. The surgeon uses hands, feet, head, and voice to
control the laparoscope, instruments, visual display, lighting, and
other features.

Hundreds of thousands of procedures are carried out yearly by da
Vinci, although most of these are not conducted over vast distances
– the operator and console are usually next to the patient's bedside.
This computer/robot interface is prohibitively expensive for many
medical centres, but is said to have benefits over direct manual
manipulation. For instance, it helps to reduce the normal small hand
vibrations of even the most experienced surgeon. It
can "gear down" motion so that a large hand movement produces a
much smaller robot version, thereby improving precision for
microsurgery. The system helps to detect and negate rare accidental
slips, and the surgeon can sit in a comfortable, efficient position
that minimizes fatigue. It also allows the surgeon to trial manoeuvres
on the console; the system takes details from the actual patient
and adapts them using a database to display predicted results on a
virtual patient. If all is well, the surgeon then orders the manipulators
to perform the manoeuvre.

During the 2000s, telesurgery reached a new level of sophistication – touch sensitivity, or haptic feedback. Arrays of sensors detect the smallest of vibrations passing through the operating instruments, yielding information such as tissue resistance and fluid slipperiness. This is fed back in the form of resistance in the surgeon's controls, effectively allowing the surgeon to feel what is happening.

Computerized robot-assisted surgery has a growing list of applications. Hysterectomy (womb removal) and other gynaeological procedures, heart valve and coronary artery bypass, the removal of tumours, and neurosurgery have all been carried out in this way and forms of telesurgery in which patient and surgeon are far apart are on the increase. Telementoring and teleteaching allow experienced surgeons to advise, monitor, and even assist trainees around the world as they practise on animals or computer-simulated virtual patients, or even (given all the safeguards) with real-life patients. Surgeons can also watch and support each other, discuss individual cases, and pool their knowledge.

Telesurgery is the high-tech end of the increasing use of computers in medicine. In many places around the world, computers work away in the background helping physicians and patients. They analyse and visualize molecules and compounds that have potential as new drugs, and coordinate data on drug effectiveness and side-effects. They crunch numbers to track outbreaks of infection, and link cause and effect for epidemiologists (see pp.180–87). They sharpen, colour, and interpret images from scanners that also rely on computer power, and suggest diagnoses based on these. Computer-automated medical history questionnaires help doctors use their time more efficiently, and evidence shows that patients answer a machine more honestly than they do a human doctor, especially on sensitive topics, such as alcohol or drug intake and sexual relationships. From alerting the family doctor to the side-effects a medicine might have on a particular patient, to performing a life-saving operation on an astronaut via a telesurgeon here on Earth, these electronic devices may one day supplant human doctors. In the meantime, medicine – certainly surgery – is becoming hard to imagine without them.

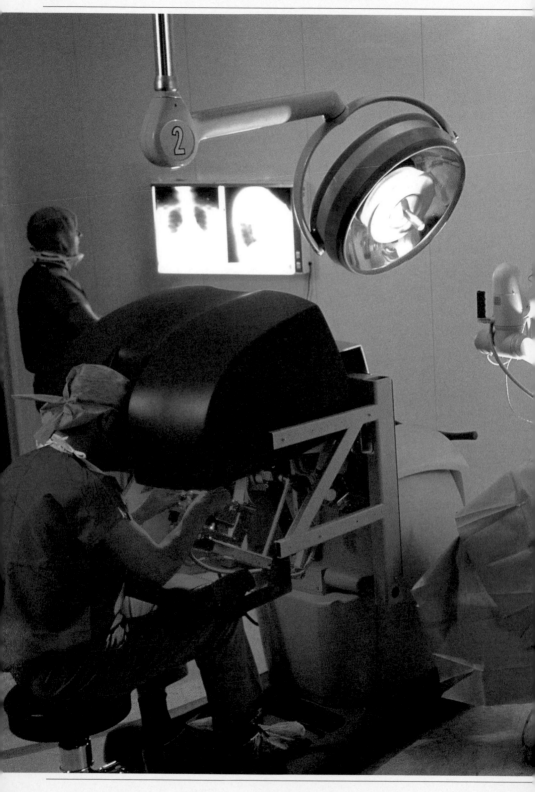

ROBOTIC SURGERY
A surgeon (left) performs minimally invasive surgery (MIS, or "keyhole" surgery), on a patient's heart using a remotely controlled da Vinci robot. The surgeon views a three-dimensional image of the operation site on his screen.

Emergency Medicine

"**IT'S A MAJOR INCIDENT.** Alert all first responders, paramedics, and other EMTs. Scramble the air ambulance. Contact ER, A&E, ICU, CCU, HDU. Make ready for triage, SCA, MI, CAB, CPR, defib, and AED. We'll do BP and other vital signs, sats…" Medicine is full of acronyms, abbreviations, and jargon. One of the branches richest in these is emergency medicine, or EM – partly, it is said, to shorten speaking, reading, and writing in this area of medical care where time is most precious.

It has been a long journey from the emergency procedures carried out on the battlefields of Ancient Rome, Persia, and China (tightening tourniquets near wounds, or roughly sewing gashes with a dagger and threads ripped from clothing) to today's sophisticated EMS (emergency medical services). Progress in emergency medicine has accelerated rapidly, especially since the 1980s, thanks to instant communications via mobile phones and the internet, the increasingly rapid transport of patients and personnel by fast cars, helicopters, planes, and speedboats, and the use of computers in diagnosis and treatment plans. There has also been an increasing move towards professionalization, away from panicky amateurs trying out partly forgotten first-aid techniques, to the latest highly trained and qualified, constantly updated experts in the field. The precise terminology varies among countries and regions, but there is now a wide spectrum of authorized emergency medical personnel, ranging from casual, licensed first-aiders to first responders, basic and

BATTLEFIELD SURGEON
Baron Dominique Jean
Larrey, surgeon-in-chief
of Napoleon's army, gives
emergency aid to a soldier at
the Battle of Hanau in 1813.

advanced EMTs (emergency medical technicians), and paramedics. It also includes medical centre and hospital ED (emergency department) and ER (emergency room) staff, such as nurses, junior doctors, and senior consultants.

As an official branch of the medical system, emergency medicine is relatively young. Its first hospital specialists were appointed in the 1950s. Prior to this, staff from other specialisms did their rota duties in Casualty or A&E (Accident and Emergency). Fully recognized emergency medicine departments were established in major hospitals in the US, Europe, Canada, Australia, and Japan from the 1970s. The US's *American Journal of Emergency Medicine* began in 1983; issue 1 of the UK's *Emergency Medicine Journal* was published in 1984; and by 2010 a major survey showed that around one third of the world's nations recognized emergency medicine as a formal speciality.

Where did it all begin? During the First Crusade (1096–99), European armies organized groups such as the Knights of the Order of St John of Jerusalem (Knights Hospitaller), who specialized in giving first aid to soldiers wounded in battle and helping pilgrims in need of medical treatment. One of the UK's leading first-aid organizations, St John Ambulance, traces its origins to this time. Such orders continued through the Late Middle Ages and into the Renaissance, especially across Europe (see pp.126–31). In the early 19th century, battlefield surgeon Baron Dominique Jean Larrey and his advisors pioneered the concept of the ambulance in the form of rapid horse-drawn transport for the wounded in Napoleon's armies. They arranged for medically trained personnel to man front-line units, and set up early versions of combat medical care facilities or field hospitals. Larrey's teams refined the idea of triage – the process of quickly assessing and prioritizing patients in the face of overwhelming casualties. Those who could probably be saved by treatment were prioritized, ahead of those who would probably recover without treatment, and those who were likely to die even with treatment. Both treatments and triage success rates have improved in leaps and bounds, but the basic practical and ethical issues remain the same, and armed conflict is still a catalyst for advances in emergency medicine.

Today, one of the most common treatments in emergency medicine is mouth-to-mouth ventilation, or rescue breathing. The practice has a long history, being mentioned in antiquity and the Middle Ages, but it was only in the 18th century that it became commonplace. In 1744, Scottish surgeon William Tossach recorded

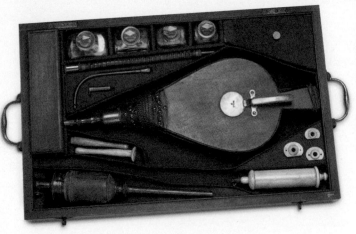

RESUSCITATION KIT
This 19th-century apparatus for blowing tobacco smoke into the lungs of a patient was used to revive people whose hearts had ceased beating and who had stopped breathing.

one such instance when he had revived a comatose coal miner: "There was not the least pulse in either heart or arteries, and not the least breathing could be observed... I applied my mouth close to his, and blew my breath strong as I could; but having neglected to stop his nostrils all the air came out at them; wherefore taking hold of them with one hand... I blew again... raising his chest fully with it... immediately I felt six or seven very quick beats of the heart". The practice spread across Europe and North America in the 1760s and 1770s as "rescue organizations" were established – largely in response to the number of people who died falling through ice on frozen rivers in winter. Ventilation was sometimes performed using a bellows (which might be used to blow tobacco smoke rather than air), but the mouth-to-mouth method proved to be more effective.

This is how one of emergency medicine's best-known, most high-profile techniques evolved – CPR (cardiopulmonary resuscitation). In the early 1900s, the "cardio" part of the process – ECC (external chest compression) – was added to the "pulmonary" component of assisted breathing. Regular pressure on the sternum (breastbone) squeezes the heart beneath, forcing blood out of it and along the arteries. Valves in the heart and main veins (see p.134–43) maintain some kind of one-way circulatory flow and distribute at least some oxygen to the vital organs – critically, to the brain. By the 1960s, CPR was on a more scientific footing and was recommended not only for victims of drowning, but also for medical emergencies such as SCA (sudden cardiac arrest), in which the heart suddenly stops beating. SCA has a variety of causes, including the common form of heart attack – when a piece of fatty deposit called atheroma inside an artery detaches and causes a blood clot in the arteries supplying the heart muscle, leading to myocardial infarction (MI), death of the heart muscle. SCA is one of the main reasons that emergency medicine is summoned.

CPR is part of a protocol called "ABC" for the treatment of an unconscious casualty who has no detectable breathing or pulse. The acronym ABC stands for airway, breathing, circulation: A, ensure that the airways down into the lungs are unobstructed; B, assist breathing by mouth-to-mouth; C, encourage circulation by chest compressions. Each step is needed for the next to succeed – there is no point in giving assisted breathing, for instance, if the airway is blocked, such as by vomit. ABC was developed during the 1950s by physicians Peter Safar and James Elam in the US. Safar wrote *ABC of Resuscitation* (1957) and Elam produced *Rescue Breathing* (1959). In 2010, the American Heart Association (AHA) and other US experts recommended changing ABC to CAB (except for new babies), and upping the compression rate from 60 to 100 per second. This shifted the very first casualty-side task away from checking the airway and assisted breathing to compressions and maintaining circulation. The AHA explained: "In the A-B-C sequence chest compressions are often delayed while the responder opens the airway to give mouth-to-mouth breaths or retrieves a barrier device or other ventilation equipment. By changing the sequence to C-A-B, chest compressions will be initiated sooner and ventilation only minimally delayed until completion of the first cycle of chest compressions (30 compressions should be accomplished in approximately 18 seconds)". Applying compressions first delays the start of assisted breathing by less than 20 seconds, and most people can hold their breath for longer than this. Another recent trend is to ignore assisted breathing and to concentrate on chest compression once the airway is clear, since the compressions give some air movement into and out of the lungs.

A variant of CAB/ABC adds D for "defib", or defibrillation – administering carefully controlled electric shocks through the chest and heart, in an attempt to jolt the heart's electrical control system back into action (see pp.362–63). Cardiac defibrillators have existed for more

"For the service of mankind"
ST JOHN AMBULANCE MOTTO

than a century, although they were initially intended for animal research only. The first hospital use of defibrillators took place in 1947, on hearts exposed during open-chest surgery. Defibrillation was applied to closed chests from the mid-1950s, using electrode "paddles" that were pressed against the skin. Over the following decade, portable defibrillators appeared and were soon being carried by most ambulances and emergency medical transports. In the 1970s, in Portland, Oregon, US, physician Archibald Warren "Arch" Diack and his collaborators devised the first of the devices now known as AEDs, or automated external defibrillators. In Britain, early versions, trialled in the 1980s, were known as Heart Aid. Electronics made AEDs smaller and easier to use, so that after they were connected to the patient, emergency diagnosis could be made and suitable treatment applied. AEDs can now be used with minimal or even no training, and are installed in all manner of premises, from offices and factories to shopping malls, swimming centres, and gyms.

As well as defibs and other hardware, many drugs are available for emergency patients. For example, a thrombolytic, or "clot-buster", drug can dissolve and disperse a thrombus, or blood clot, to restore blood supply. Clots are involved in many medical emergencies, including myocardial infarction, stroke, and deep-vein thrombosis. As far back as 1933, William Smith Tillett at Johns Hopkins University, Baltimore, USA, discovered that certain bacteria make a clot-dissolving substance, which he called streptokinase. In the late 1950s, this was given to patients with sudden or acute MI, though due to unclear data on its side effects it only came into restricted use in the 1970s, and general use in the late 1980s. Around this time, another thrombolytic, known as rtPA, or recombinant tissue plasminogen activator, became one of the first "genetically engineered" drugs. It was derived from a natural clot-dissolver in the body, tPA, discovered in the 1940s. Administered as soon as possible, these and other clot-busters now save lives and reduce lasting damage in untold numbers of people each year.

Hospital emergency assessment is well rehearsed and rapid. Traditionally, the four main vital signs that are checked are body temperature, heart rate (pulse), BP (blood pressure), and breathing or respiratory rate. Some assessment schemes add pupil response, pain experience, and "sats" – blood oxygen saturation, or the percentage of oxygen carried by the blood. Along with pulse rate, sats is non-invasively, conveniently, and continuously measured by a pulse oximeter; a small

THE GOLDEN HOUR
Paramedics rush to an emergency room, having
spent the transportation time assessing the patient's
condition and delivering preliminary treatment.

clip-on sensor on a fingertip or ear lobe uses light of specific wavelengths
to detect how much of the haemoglobin in red blood cells is in the form
of oxyhaemoglobin, which contains oxygen. Emergency patients in
most need may be cared for in an ICU (intensive care unit), a CCU
(critical care unit), or a similar department – the exact names for them
vary from one place to another. For example, a life-threatening heart
condition may demand the Cardiac Intensive Care Unit, CICU, while
new babies are in units for Neonatal Intensive Care, NICU.

Lodged in popular consciousness is the notion of the "Golden
Hour" – the theory that emergency treatment will have the greatest
chance of success if it is administered within the first 60 minutes after
a trauma. This has since led to the Platinum Ten Minutes – the time
it should take for EMTs or paramedics to assess, treat, and instigate
transport of an emergency patient. In a sense, this is the paramedic's
share of the Golden Hour. As ambulance crews become more highly
trained, and their equipment becomes increasingly extensive and
sophisticated, the chance to save life and improve eventual outcome
shifts to the very first minutes of emergency medical care.

A Shock to the System

When a person has a heart attack, the muscles of the heart often contract randomly, a symptom known as ventricular fibrillation. In the late 19th century, scientists discovered that they could stop fibrillation and resuscitate their subject – a dog – by applying an electric shock to its heart. In 1947, this technique was first used on a human. American surgeon Claude Beck successfully used a combination of electrical current and internal cardiac massage to resuscitate a child who had gone into cardiac arrest during an operation. In the 1950s, external defibrillators became available, which worked without the need to open up the patient's chest. Some modern units are able to calculate the patient's heart rhythm automatically, so can be used in emergencies by people with little or no training.

Trial and error

Before the 20th century, doctors tried many methods of getting a patient's heart to start beating again, from bloodletting to tickling the throat. Breathing into the mouth and pressing the abdomen were advocated in the 18th century, but not widely used. This was the forerunner of modern cardiopulmonary resuscitation (CPR), used from the early 1960s, which keeps the brain alive with artificial blood circulation using mouth-to-mouth ventilation and chest compression.

FRENCH COUNT GASTON DE FOIX DYING OF A CARDIAC ARREST IN 1391

type 180 C

④

defibrillate

DANGER HIGH VOLTAGE

①

patient

CARDIAC RECORDERS LTD. LONDON E

The electrodes are held in paddles with insulated plastic handles to protect the operator

DEFIBRILLATOR
1970–80
By the 1970s, portable defibrillators with a rechargeable power pack were available. Their compact size made them useful to emergency services and hospitals.

Voltage and battery indicator

Battery test and capacitor charge switch

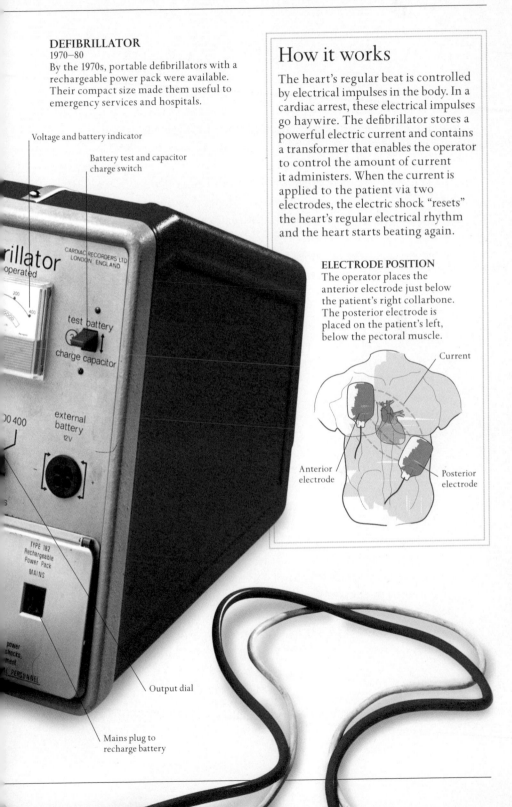

CARDIAC RECORDERS LTD
LONDON, ENGLAND

rillator
operated

200
400

test battery

charge capacitor

00 400

external battery
12V

TYPE 182
Rechargeable
Power Pack
MAINS

power
shocks,
ment
L PERSONNEL

Output dial

Mains plug to recharge battery

How it works

The heart's regular beat is controlled by electrical impulses in the body. In a cardiac arrest, these electrical impulses go haywire. The defibrillator stores a powerful electric current and contains a transformer that enables the operator to control the amount of current it administers. When the current is applied to the patient via two electrodes, the electric shock "resets" the heart's regular electrical rhythm and the heart starts beating again.

ELECTRODE POSITION
The operator places the anterior electrode just below the patient's right collarbone. The posterior electrode is placed on the patient's left, below the pectoral muscle.

Current

Anterior electrode

Posterior electrode

Stem Cell Therapy

A PLANT SEED SENDS OUT A SHOOT, which grows into a stem. From this seemingly mundane, unremarkable structure, the sophisticated, specialized parts of the plant gradually develop – buds, side shoots, leaves, and delicate, intricate flowers. The stem analogy works quite well for the so-called stem cells of humans and other animals, and plants. A stem cell is a "general-purpose" cell. It has not yet developed any features for a specialized function – unlike nerve cells (neurons), for example, which typically have branches (dendrites) and a longer axon (a special cellular extension) and are specialized to transmit and receive nerve impulses; or red blood cells (erythrocytes), which are disc-shaped and packed with haemoglobin to carry oxygen. Stem cells do, however, have distinguishing characteristics. They can self-regenerate – keep up their numbers by splitting or dividing to make more cells like themselves – and in certain conditions, they can make many other kinds of specialized cell.

In a sense, the ultimate stem cell is the zygote – an egg cell that has been fertilized by a sperm cell. It divides into two, then four, and so on. At first, its offspring cells all look similar, making a blackberry-like ball known as a morula. The offspring cells continue to multiply and form a hollow ball of cells called a blastocyst. Cell division continues, but now the various cells begin to specialize, so that they no longer look alike and work differently from each other – a process called differentiation. Next, during the embryo stage, thousands of multiplying cells make millions of specialized cells that eventually constitute the body's 200-plus kinds of tissue. By the time cells are fully specialized, and have become nerve cells or red blood cells, for example, they usually cannot change any further, or even renew themselves by dividing to produce more of their kind. They are, as it were, at the "end of the line", and can only carry out their particular jobs and then die. This is because most cells, and specialized cells in particular, have a limited lifespan. A red cell in the blood, for example,

HUMAN STEM CELLS
These early embryonic stem cells all look alike.
As they continue to multiply, they will give rise
to millions of specialized cells that will form every
type of tissue in the human body.

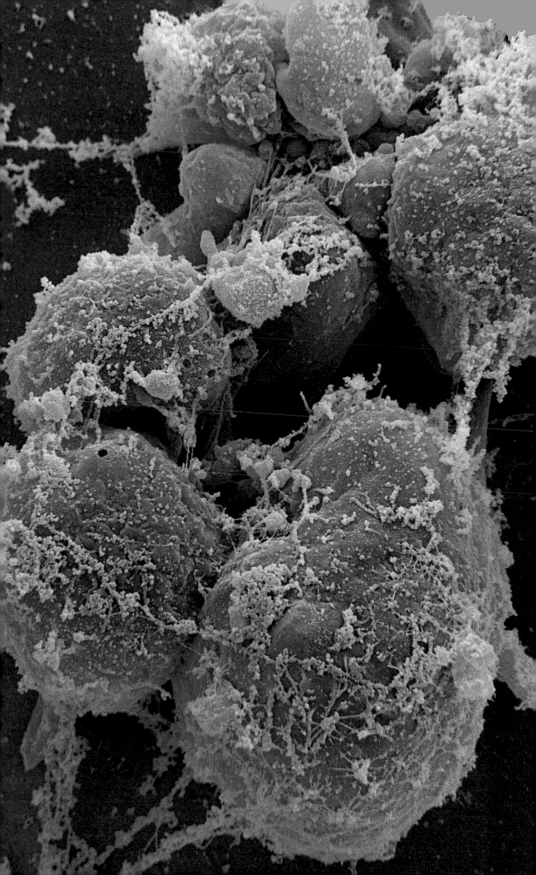

lives for around three months, and a cell in the lining of the intestine lasts for less than a week, so new cells must be made to replace them. New red cells, for instance, are produced at the rate of three million every second. This is the job of stem cells in the adult body. Unlike the original zygote, they are not able to form any kind of cell or tissue, but have a more limited function – to create a set of related cells. The stem cells for blood are known as haematopoietic stem cells. They are found mainly in bone marrow, and they keep dividing, supplying lines of descent for the dozen or more different kinds of blood cell in the circulation – red cells, platelets (which help blood clot), and numerous kinds of white cell in the body's immune system that fight disease and invading microbes. Because haematopoietic stem cells exist throughout a person's life, and not just during the embryo stage, they are known as adult (somatic) stem cells. So there are two broad categories of stem cells: embryonic stem cells, and adult stem cells.

A stem cell's degree of flexibility – the numbers and types of specialized cell it can create – is known as its potency. The fertilized egg cell, and the cells it makes in the morula stage of development, are known as omnipotent stem cells. These can generate all the types of cell in the body, plus the supporting cells and tissues that the embryo needs in order to grow and develop, such as the placenta, the umbilical cord, and the surrounding membranes and fluids in the womb. Next are the so-called pluripotent stem cells, which generate every type of body cell, apart from the tissues in the womb (so a single pluripotent stem cell could not create a human being by development in the womb). Multipotent stem cells are more limited, as they can make a range of related cells, but none that are too dissimilar. Haematopoietic stem cells, for example, create various kinds of blood cell, but cannot make muscle cells, liver cells, etc. Unipotent stem cells, or precursor cells, are even more limited and can only make one kind of specialized cell.

So, stem cells range from those with extensive potential but little differentiation, to those that are very specialized but have almost no potency. Why do some cell lines differentiate, while others remain as stem cells? Nearly all human cells have, in their genetic material or DNA (see pp.348–49), the entire human genome – the full set of 20,000–25,000 genes that form the instructions for building and running a human body (see pp.338–47). Differentiation, or becoming specialized, does not apparently involve losing or destroying some

DIFFERENTIATION

Omnipotent stem cells – those in a fertilized egg or early embryo – can develop into multiple types of cells in the body.

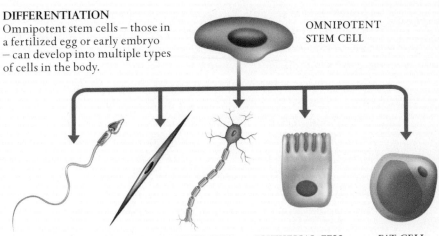

OMNIPOTENT STEM CELL

SPERM CELL   MUSCLE CELL   NERVE CELL   EPITHELIAL CELL   FAT CELL

genes and creating or duplicating others. All the genes remain intact, but only some subgroups of genes in the full set are "switched on". In a nerve cell, for instance, the genes needed to create nerve cells and make them work are active but the rest are not; in a bone cell, the genes that create and maintain bone tissue work, but the others do not. In a stem cell, these subgroups of specialized genes are not switched on, but are held ready for activation at a future date. What *are* working are the genes that make the cell keep dividing and making copies of itself. The key to the medical use of stem cells lies in knowing how to manipulate different subgroups of genes so that they can be turned on and off as and when they are needed.

After the atomic bomb attacks on the Japanese cities of Hiroshima and Nagasaki in 1945, it was found that exposure to radiation caused damage to the blood and immune system. White blood cells were not renewed, and the numbers of platelets, needed for blood to clot, were reduced. This led to experiments with mice that traced the source of new, healthy blood cells to the bone marrow – and to haematopoietic stem cells. Several medical disorders can also have an affect on haematopoietic stem cells, disrupting their busy production lines of new blood cells. These include aplastic anaemia, which damages the bone marrow and its haematopoietic stem cells, and various forms of leukaemia – cancers that affect white blood cells, making them either multiply too fast or fail to do their jobs, crowding out or destroying other, normal cells. Radiation or drug treatments can destroy these wayward cells, but – like atomic bomb radiation – such treatments also kill off the all-important haematopoietic stem cells.

Could transplanting haematopoietic stem cells treat such problems? If marrow were taken from one person's bone and put into a patient, would the stem cells "take" and replenish the patient's specialized blood cells? This procedure, known as haematopoietic stem cell transplantation (HSCT), or a bone marrow transplant, was first performed in 1956 by Dr E. Donnall Thomas and his team at the Mary Imogene Bassett Hospital, New York. The subjects were identical twins, one of whom had leukaemia. Being identical twins, the problem of rejection – of substances regarded as foreign to the body being attacked by the recipient's immune system – did not occur. This was, in effect, the first successful trial of a new class of treatments called stem cell therapies – and, in 1990, Dr Thomas was duly awarded the Nobel Prize in Physiology or Medicine for "discoveries concerning organ and cell transplantation in the treatment of human disease".

Developing HSCT involved overcoming many obstacles, including rejection, which was countered by a process called immuno-suppression. Thanks to this, the first transplant between non-identical siblings was made in 1968, and between unrelated but tissue-matched donors and recipients in 1973. Today, there are several forms of HSCT, many of which involve giving the patient back his own haematopoietic stem cells that were gathered and stored before a course of chemotherapy or radiotherapy eradicated the diseased cells in the bone marrow. Haematopoietic stem cells are then reintroduced into the marrow and restart blood cell production. HSCT from one person to another follows the same procedure, but involves

"There is no disagreement among scientists over the need to aggressively pursue [stem cell research]"

DR DOUGLAS MELTON,
HARVARD STEM CELL INSTITUTE

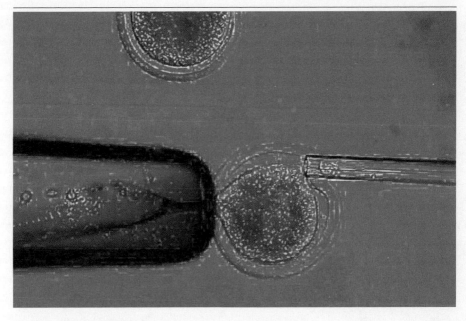

NUCLEAR TRANSFER
An adult stem cell is injected into a human egg that has
had its nucleus removed. This creates a new, "cloned"
human embryo from which stem cells can be harvested.

suppressing the immune system to prevent rejection. In both cases, the haematopoietic stem cells can be obtained from the donor's blood by passing it through a device that removes white cells by spinning the blood very fast in a centrifuge, so that the different fluids and cells separate into different layers. The stem cells can also be taken from the donor's marrow, which is drawn out through a wide needle inserted into a big bone, often the hip bone or pelvis. More recently, stem cells have also been sourced from umbilical cord blood.

HSCT is still the most common therapy involving stem cells, but in this fast-moving area of medicine it is hoped that stem cells in general will have many uses. Studying how and why embryonic stem cells work sheds light on the way the early human embryo develops, which in turn provides insights into congenital problems such as spina bifida and certain heart malformations. Serious medical conditions, such as cancer, arise from cells that multiply abnormally, and fail to differentiate as they should. Again, stem cell research may help to identify how and why the "wrong" genes are active in these cells, and so lead to treatments. Stem cell research can also provide more ways of testing potential medicinal drugs and toxic chemicals. For many years, certain types of cell grown in laboratory culture have

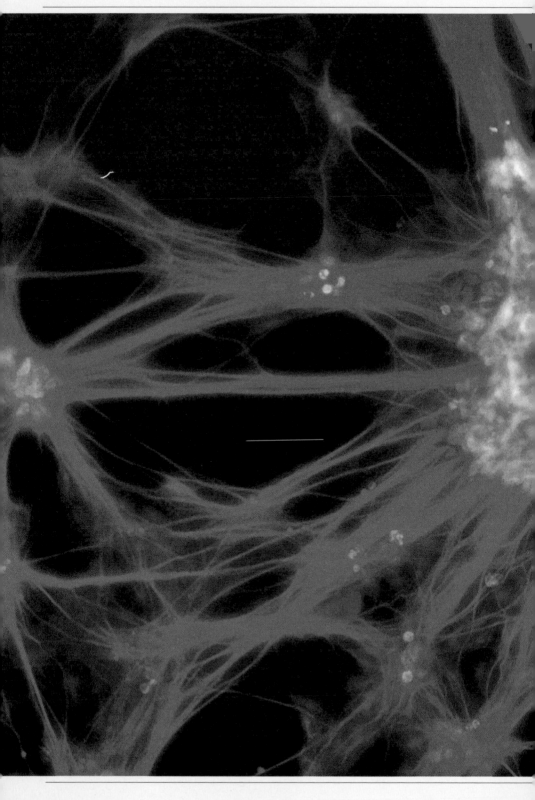

NEURAL STEM CELLS
This fluorescent light micrograph shows neural stem cells migrating from the culture in which they are growing. Neural stem cells can develop into nerve cells, or support cells that could be used to replace damaged or lost brain cells.

been exploited to screen drugs for their effects, both wanted and unwanted. Some lines of cancer cells were cultivated like this in the 1950s, and have been central to the development of new anti-tumour drugs. Various kinds of stem cell are being added to this armoury of cultured cell lines, including induced pluripotent stem cells, or iPSCs.

As explained earlier, a pluripotent stem cell in an embryo can proliferate to make any tissue of the body, except those external to the embryo, such as placental tissue. The iPSC is usually a mature, specialized cell taken from an adult body. When subjected to certain conditions and substances in the laboratory, it is persuaded to regress to the pluripotent state, as though it were in an early-stage embryo. Human iPSCs were first obtained in 2007 by processing or "reprogramming" adult cells called fibroblasts, which make a variety of structural components, including fibrous proteins such as collagen for the body's connective tissues. In 2012, Japanese doctor and researcher Shinya Yamanaka and British stem cell researcher John Gurdon received the Nobel Prize in Physiology or Medicine "for the discovery that mature cells can be reprogrammed to become pluripotent". Also in 2012, iPSCs were generated from cells shed from the inner lining of the kidney. Instead of needles, scalpels, or similar invasive techniques, all this required was a urine sample.

The exciting aspect of iPSCs is that they can be manipulated in the laboratory so that they start to develop into specialized cells, much as if they were embryonic stem cells. The cells can be induced to form

the particular types of cell and tissues that are needed to treat disease in the patient, the owner of the originating cells. If specialized cells and tissues came from embryonic stem cells transplanted from someone else, they might be rejected because the embryo would be from a genetically different individual. The solution is to take

COLD STORAGE
Stem cells, which hold the promise of new cell-based therapies for critical medical conditions, can be stored until they are required. This is done by immersing them in liquid nitrogen to freeze them.

adult specialized cells from the patient, make them revert to the embryo-like stem cell condition as iPSCs, then induce them to develop into the cells or tissues required for the patient's treatment and put them back into the patient.

Haematopoietic stem cells are not the only kind of adult stem cell. By the 1960s, mesenchymal stem cells (bone marrow adult stem cells) had been identified. These can generate bone, cartilage, fat, and many other types of tissue. More types of adult stem cell have since been discovered, each able to multiply to replace itself and make lines that can become specialized cells. These stem cells have been found in skin, blood vessels, muscles, heart, teeth, intestines, the liver, ovaries, and testes. Even the adult brain, with its highly specialized nerve cells, is now known to house stem cells that can generate the three main types of cell in its tissues. Many adult stem cells remain dormant until they are needed to divide and replenish cells, both as part of normal cellular renewal and in the event of injury or disease. Like iPSCs, adult stem cells seem to be excellent candidates for stem cell therapies, but they are small in number, are difficult to propagate outside their natural environment, and making them differentiate to order is problematic. There are, however, promising signs of early progress in adult stem cell treatments for skin burns and damage to the cornea (the domed "window" at the front of the eye).

Will stem cell technology lead to growing "spare parts" and even whole organs for implantation? There is a long way to go before a patient can donate a few cells that are then grown into a new heart, liver, eye, or mending patch for the spinal cord. There are also legal and ethical questions such as who, if anyone, should control patents for manipulating stem cells. Nevertheless, treatments involving iPSCs and adult stem cells are currently being proposed for hundreds of conditions, including Alzheimer's disease, baldness, certain cancers, cerebral palsy, coeliac disease, defects of hearing and sight, diabetes type 1, heart failure, infertility, Parkinson's disease, rheumatoid arthritis, spinal cord injury, stroke, systemic lupus erythematosis, and tooth decay – a lengthening list that already represents a revolution in medical treatment.

Dignity and Death

THE PASSING OF HUMAN LIFE IS INEVITABLE. It is usually coloured with sadness, and sometimes with tragedy. If it happens within the medical care system, it can also be complicated. However, everyday meanings, philosophical concepts, and scientific definitions of death have changed over time, and differ from place to place.

Religious faiths, for example, often incorporate the notion of an afterlife, which renders death a mere transitional stage between this world and the next. According to this idea, the immortal soul adopts a human form at birth, and at death it moves onwards, and perhaps upwards or down, depending on its behaviour on Earth. The Ancient Egyptians regarded death as a temporary state before revival. The deceased first entered the dreaded realm of the underworld, where, overseen by the god Osiris, he or she was assessed by a 42-member judging panel, perhaps aided by Anubis, the jackal-headed god of mummification and the afterlife. In a ritual called "weighing the heart", a set of scales balanced the deceased's heart against a feather,

the goddess Maat's symbol of justice and truth. If the scales showed that good prevailed, the deceased was then allowed to move on to the Field of Rushes – a paradise of everlasting bliss. However, if bad deeds predominated, then the heart was fed to Ammit, Devourer of the Dead, and the rest of the body was consigned to Seth, god of doom, gloom, darkness, disorder, and chaos.

The idea that the heart is the essence of a person's life predates Ancient Egypt, and flourished throughout antiquity to the Middle Ages and beyond. In the 11th century, Arab philosopher-physician Ibn Sina (see pp.100–105) described the soul as acting via the heart to regulate the body's sensitive, vegetative, and physical "spirits". Regular breathing was also regarded as necessary for life, and when either breathing or heart activity ceased, the individual was declared dead. These criteria for judging the moment of death prevailed in scientific medicine until the early 1920s, yet as far back as the 12th century, Jewish scholar, teacher, and physician Musa ibn Maymun (also known as Maimonides) suggested that there was another element to take into account. He noted that when a person is decapitated, their heart and lungs still work for a short time, but it

WEIGHING THE HEART
Jackal-headed Anubis weighs a dead man's heart on a set of scales in the Egyptian underworld. Ammit, the Devourer of the Dead, waits beneath the scales, while Osiris (right) delivers judgment.

"The boundaries which divide Life from Death are at best shadowy and vague"

EDGAR ALLEN POE

would be wrong to say that they were still alive. Foreshadowing the notion of "brain death" that arose some eight centuries later, he suggested that a central controlling mechanism for movement had been removed, and that this signified death.

During the late Middle Ages, and up to the 19th century, this idea that you could be dead according to your lack of heartbeat and breathing, and yet still alive, became popular as stories arose of people being incorrectly presumed dead and buried alive. This most serious of misdiagnoses became a staple of horror fiction and supposed true-life tales. In 1844, American author Edgar Allen Poe published *The Premature Burial*, in which the central character is obsessed with waking up after being mistakenly entombed while unconscious from catalepsy. This short story fed into contemporary fears and led to safety coffins and crypts being equipped with signals or devices with which the recovered occupant could alert the outside world. In some designs, the unlucky "corpse" pulled a rope attached to a bell or flag.

In 1952, a polio epidemic gripped Denmark. Some patients were so badly affected by the disease that their breathing muscles were paralysed and they died of suffocation. In an attempt to save lives, Danish anaesthetist Bjorn Ibsen adapted existing "iron lung" mechanical ventilation equipment. The iron lung exposed polio sufferers to negative air pressure to stimulate breathing, but Ibsen changed the air pressure to positive, forcing air into a patient's lungs with the assistance of the drug sodium thiopental. Death rates for patients treated with this equipment fell from more than 80% to less than 20%, and Ibsen went on to establish the world's first dedicated medical and surgical intensive care unit (see pp.356–63).

His work was also used to help patients with such severe brain damage that it prevented them from breathing. Physicians studying such comatose patients included Pierre Mollaret and Marcel Goulon of the Claude Bernard Hospital, Paris. A coma is usually defined as a state of unconsciousness, lasting several hours or more, from which a person cannot be roused. In 1959, Mollaret and Goulon devised the term *le coma dépassé*, or "irretrievable coma", to describe deep unconsciousness combined with little or no sign of electrical activity in the brain. In a state of irretrievable coma, the heart might beat – or stop, then be restarted by defibrillation (see pp.362–63) – and the lungs might breathe, but the brain has no hope of recovery. This limbo between life and death, in which the heart and lungs are working, but the brain is not, is known as "brain death" – a state in which, thanks to improved life-support machinery, a body can be kept functioning for hours, days, or even weeks.

Further studies of terminally ill patients led to the convening of an ad hoc committee to examine the definition of death at Harvard Medical School, US, in 1968. Its report discussed not just death, but also the delicate subject of organ donation. Commenting on the condition of irreversible coma, which was recommended to indicate that death had occurred, Chairman Henry Beecher added: "Can society afford to discard the tissues and organs of the hopelessly unconscious patient when he could be used to restore the otherwise hopelessly ill, but still salvageable individual? ... It is best to choose a level where although the brain is dead, usefulness of other organs is still present".

This shifted the criteria for death from cardiorespiratory symptoms (meaning lack of circulation

IRON LUNG
This mechanical ventilator was adapted in the 1950s to provide positive pressure to enable patients with brain damage to breathe. It was later modified to become the first life-support machine.

NUMBER OF YEARS OF THE LONGEST COMA EVER RECORDED

42

or breathing) to symptoms based on the non-functioning of the brain and nervous system.

In 1970, Kansas became the first US state to incorporate brain death into its legal definitions. In Europe, Finland followed in 1971. Within a couple of decades, most nations with advanced medical care routinely used brain-based criteria to declare that a person was officially dead – at which point the "harvesting" of tissues and organs for transplantation could begin. Brain death criteria vary from country to country, but they may include irreversible coma, lack of certain reflexes based in the brainstem (see below), the absence of unassisted breathing or responsive movements, and lack of significant electrical activity as shown by the EEG trace. The cause of all these features is also taken into account and is checked again after a suitable interval. At least two qualified physicians must be involved, and should have the agreement of their nursing and support staff.

Medicine is rarely cut-and-dried. Even when other organs still function on life support, a dead brain can be used as a sign of an individual's demise – but which part of the brain? The whole brain, the brainstem, or the higher brain (the neocortex)? Traditional signs of life include spontaneous breathing, response to stimuli such as spoken words or pain, and automatic reflexes, such as the pupil of the eye constricting in bright light. These indicate that several parts of the brain are functioning, and their absence, along with lack of electrical activity, can be taken as evidence of whole-brain death. Centres for maintaining breathing, heartbeat, and other basic functions are based in the the brainstem, the lowest part of the brain, just above the upper spinal cord. This region is also responsible for consciousness, helps to regulate body temperature and blood pressure, and coordinates actions such as swallowing, coughing, sneezing, and eyeball movement. When the brainstem does not work, many or all of these vital functions cease. The neocortex, or higher brain, includes the familiar, large wrinkled domes at the top, the cerebral hemispheres. This is where most sensation and mental activity occurs. If the higher brain stops functioning, lower parts such as the brainstem may continue to provide breathing, heartbeat, and life-support for the organs — but consciousness, personality, and other attributes that make a human body into an individual person cease.

As medicine adopted the idea of brain death, further grey areas between life and death were identified. These included persistent vegetative state, a term introduced in 1972 by US neurologist Fred Plum and Scottish neurosurgeon Bryan Jennet to describe a hybrid state between full consciousness and coma. Patients in this state are not totally inactive and unresponsive; they may perform reflex actions, such as sleeping and waking, gripping people's hands or objects, and making facial movements, but they remain unaware of their surroundings and bodily sensations. If the condition lasts for more than a certain number of months, the person is said to be in a permanent vegetative state. Another state of limbo, identified in 1966, is locked-in syndrome (LIS), also established by Fred Plum, with US neurologist Jerome Posner, another specialist in impaired consciousness. In this condition, a patient can receive and assimilate stimuli such as sounds, sights, smells, and touch, but has extensive muscle paralysis and cannot speak or make any movements, except perhaps with their eyeballs or eyelids. Posner summarized: "In the locked-in state, patients look unconscious but are conscious".

Fred Plum was an early supporter of the "living will" proposed in 1969 by US lawyer Louis Kutner — a document compiled by a person still of sound mind to instruct how they should be treated if they later become unable to make informed, important decisions about their health. This leads to another extremely complex medico-legal area for physicians and patients: the wish to die, quality of life and maintaining dignity, being allowed to die, DNR (do not resuscitate) and AND (allow natural death) notices, withholding treatment or nutrition, the wishes of partners and close relatives, assisted suicide, when to switch off life-support, euthanasia, and the possibility of tissue and organ donation. Here, clinical considerations become increasingly entangled with ethical, legal, and religious concerns. At the moment, voluntary euthanasia is legal only in Belgium, Luxembourg, and the Netherlands, and assisted suicide only in Switzerland and some US states. In most countries, the question of who should have the power to make such life-or-death decisions is part of an ongoing debate that shows little sign of being resolved.

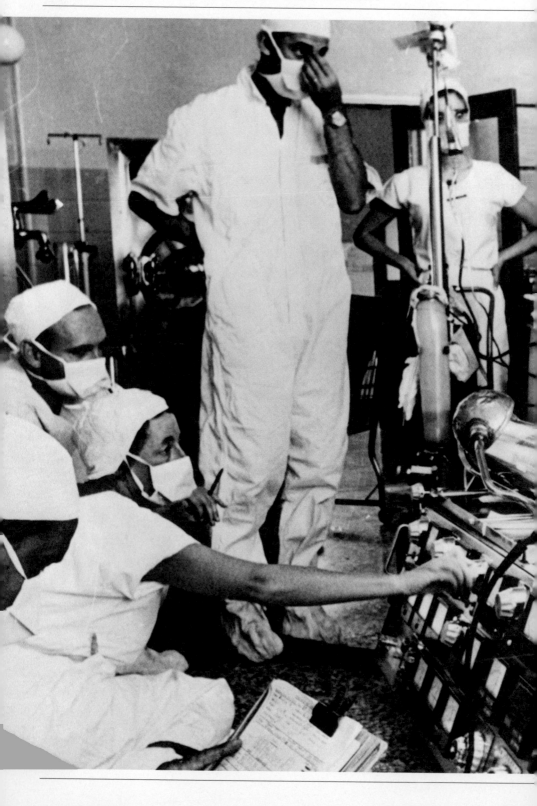

KEEPING PATIENTS ALIVE
In some operations, such as open-heart surgery, the heart has to be stopped. To keep the patient alive, a heart-lung machine is used. Often referred to as the "pump", this does the work of the heart and lungs during the operation.

Medicine in the Third Millennium

LOOKING BACK TO THE PAST shows how tricky it is to predict future challenges. Halfway through the 20th century, no one knew of Ebola (discovered in 1976), the *Helicobacter pylori* microbes of digestive ulcers (1982), HIV/AIDS (1983), or SARS (2002). Until 1977, Alzheimer's disease was a diagnosis reserved for early-onset dementia, and a term unfamiliar to most of the public. IVF (achieved in 1978) was a twinkle in the eyes of a few researchers. With scanners yet to come (1958), the only body-imaging methods were standard X-rays. Kidney transplants had just begun (1950), and antibiotics were prescribed with almost no regard for the possibility that microbes might develop resistance. What will come to pass, either good or bad, in another century?

Among medicine's "ticking time bombs" is increasing antibiotic resistance. Antibiotics revolutionized not only treatment of infectious diseases, but also surgery (see pp.252–57) and other areas of medicine. However, microbes adapted so rapidly that within three years of the first "designer antibiotic", meticillin, being introduced in 1959, MRSA (meticillin-resistant *Staphylococcus aureus*) appeared. Dozens of other new bacterial strains have since joined the ranks of superbugs. In Europe, the number of strains of *Neisseria gonorrhoeae* – the cause of the sexual infection gonorrhoea – that are resistant to the main antibiotic used to treat it doubled between 2009 and 2010. *C. diff* (*Clostridium difficile*), a bacterium in the gut that causes diarrhoea, is another rising demon, with strains resistant to fluoroquinolone antibiotics appearing in the mid-2000s.

INFLUENZA OUTBREAK
A commuter in Tokyo, Japan, wears a surgical mask to help protect herself from infection during an influenza outbreak.

Increasingly resistant strains of microbes are appearing ever more frequently across the globe – a disaster, given that antibiotics are fully integrated into all of our medical systems. Gene manipulation, genetic engineering, and the creation of GMOs (genetically modified organisms) for agriculture, livestock, and even for dispersing oil slicks, are another potential source of new harmful microbes. Scare stories about artificially created "supergerms" that are resistant to any known antibiotics or other drugs occasionally make their way into the news.

Tackling the ominous peril of antibiotic resistance requires action on several fronts. In 2001, the World Health Organization (WHO) published its Global Strategy for Containment of Antimicrobial Resistance, in which it stated: "Many countries have expressed growing concern about the problem of antimicrobial resistance... Despite the mass of literature... there is depressingly little on the true costs of resistance and the effectiveness of interventions. Given this lack of data... actions need to be taken now to avert future disaster". Inventing new, more powerful antibiotics might seem the obvious answer, but developing any new drug is an immense task. For the near future, the estimated overall cost of producing new antibiotics – adjusted to include failures – is in excess of £3 billion (approaching US$5 billion), and some estimates are double this figure. Even if this strategy is successful in the short term, it only delays the inevitable as microbes adapt and become resistant to the new antibiotics. Doctors regularly receive new prescription guidelines that take into account the rise in antibiotic resistance, and WHO emphasizes that better patient education is vital for the future. Take antibiotics or other drugs exactly as prescribed; do not skip doses; complete the course even if you are already feeling better; do not share prescriptions or save leftovers until next time; vitally, do not demand medication when a doctor says it is not needed; and follow the best hygiene and preventative measures such as handwashing, careful food preparation, and the use of insect nets and repellents. This rudimentary advice has been with us for half a century, but somehow it is still not ingrained.

Information technology and communications networks developed during the last few decades continue to bring great changes in medical decision-making. Evidence-based medicine, or EBM, systematically appraises the available clinical research and uses it to help deliver

PHARMACEUTICAL PRODUCTION LINE
Workers package drugs at a pharmaceutical
production line in China – the third-largest
prescription drugs market in the world.

optimum care to patients. The evidence comes from a clinician's
personal experience and that of colleagues, from informed reasoning
and intuition, and especially from information published in medical
and clinical databases. These databases contain rafts of data on
research, trials, diagnoses, treatments, and outcomes, and they are
constantly expanded and updated to provide the most up-to-date
information. EBM helps doctors to weigh up risks and benefits in
light of a sound scientific context, and then to propose the most
appropriate action for the patient. Woven into EBM are not only
statistics for morbidity (incidence of illness and disease) and mortality
(death), which are relatively easy to quantify, but also more complex
measures, such as quality of life. The basic principle is to treat a
patient where on balance there is evidence of benefit, and not treat
where there is no such evidence.

Regarding hi-tech future hardware, the smart cellphone – that
most ubiquitous of devices – is lined up to take a starring role. From
2012, apps have been available that record heart rate and rhythm (a
simple ECG) and send data to a medical centre for expert evaluation.
The medical use of smartphones is expected to rise exponentially in

the coming decades, with sensors and apps designed to analyse breathing, blood pressure, and oxygen sats (see p.360–61), take images of possible skin cancers, and – by the detailed analysis of vocal sounds – even to alert users to conditions such as Parkinson's, motor neurone disease, and Alzheimer's. However, the biggest advances are expected to come from the science of nanotechnology, which is poised to transform many areas of medicine. The "nano" level is considerably smaller than the "micro" level of body cells, and deals with individual molecules and even atoms at scales of thousandths of one millimetre. In the wondrous new world of nanomedicine, "quantum dot" nanoparticles are already being designed that can be absorbed by particular tissues, such as those of a tumour, and then show up brightly with astonishing detail on a scan tuned to their wavelength. Nanocapsules have also been produced with coatings that break down to release the drug inside them when they reach the appropriate environment inside a damaged body part. One day, it may be possible to design nanoshells that can home in on specific sites inside the body, where they can then be zapped by specially-tuned waves that create pores in the shells, allowing them to absorb troublesome substances for safe disposal. Perhaps the high-point of this technology will be the creation of nanobots (nanoscale robots) that can carry out simple mechanical actions such as reconstructing damaged tissue and removing fat deposits.

Tissue engineering exists at the interface between the living and the non-living. Living cells and artificial bio-friendly materials are put together to produce new tissues and even whole new organs. Cells respond to many features in their environment – not just temperature, chemicals, and nutrient concentration, but also physical factors, such as contact with each other and with a suitable surface or shaped framework. A combination of congenial chemical and physical conditions, specific growth factors and hormones, and a suitable bio-scaffold on which they can crawl and form layers and patterns, allows them to multiply and develop as directed, into a tissue, or several tissues with a 3D architecture, or even a whole new organ. Transplant

YEAR OF THE FIRST STEM CELL-GROWN ORGAN TRANSPLANT

2011

patients suffer from lack of donors (see pp.294–301), so organ engineering could plug this gap, especially using induced pluripotent stem cells, or iPSCs (see pp.364–73). Research on embryonic layers of cells that form an organ as complex as an eye indicates that if cells are treated appropriately, they know what to do: they multiply, move, specialize, or differentiate, and self-arrange. Maybe iPSCs can be coaxed to grow, on bio-scaffolds, into whole organs such as kidneys, livers, and hearts, and then be reintroduced into the bodies from which they came, thereby avoiding the problem of rejection encountered during transplantation from a donor.

Another developing technology is 3D printing. This technique is currently used by engineers to make 3D models and prototypes, but one day it could be adapted to print living cells rather than inorganic composites. Shaped layers of cells could be built into tissues that could eventually form a whole organ. Currently, researchers are looking into the possibility of fashioning layers of cells over burns or wounds to encourage faster healing. One day, it may even be possible to access the body's interior with an endoscope that can also print cell layers from its tip to build up tissues in situ.

Other frontiers of progress are less concerned with new technology than with extending established medical practices. Immunization research, for example, is working on vaccines against malaria (see pp.388–89), HIV (see pp.334–35), and other diseases, while cloning may have ever more helpful applications. Another great advance is genetic profiling, which may lead to personalized medicine. For example, an individual's genome may be identified as carrying a sequence of genes that predisposes them to a specific cancer – information that allows the person to take preventative measures, such as altering their diet or avoiding exposure to particular carcinogens (cancer-triggering substances). Should the malignancy appear, the anti-cancer drug known to be most effective in such situations could then be prescribed. Ultrasound technology has also been adapted to perform surgery, rather than simply to make diagnoses. The sound waves are focused onto a particular target and are used to disrupt or destroy tissues such as tumours. There is no need to make an incision; the waves come from outside the body and are aimed to come together with maximum power at a precise point. Known as HIFU (high-intensity focused ultrasound), this is one of several areas exploring the use of concentrated energy to replace traditional surgery.

BIONIC HAND
Recent technological advances have led
to the i-LIMB ultra revolution – making
it possible to create a prosthetic hand that
has an unparalleled degree of flexibility.

As the world and its nations evolve,
medicine responds to changing
needs. Cutting-edge research flags
the possibilities, which are then
reduced to what is practicable.
Targets shift and fresh innovations
leapfrog the previous year's advances,
and at each stage politicians, interest
groups, and society in general have
their say. Medicine is always bound
up with ethical issues and the trials
and tribulations of legislation and
litigation. It is a long, laborious, and
costly business, but the current wave
of innovation – including gene therapy, tissue engineering,
personalized medicine, bloodless and fast-healing surgery, organ
culture, and pills for obesity, hair loss, and almost anything else – is
set to have an impact similar to that of immunization, anaesthesia,
antibiotics, electronic imaging, and fertility control combined. With
continued perseverance, we may yet find that the best medicines are
waiting to be discovered.

Mosquito-borne Malaria

Malaria is a dangerous tropical fever, caused by a parasite transmitted by mosquitoes – a person can be infected from a single bite, and if not treated quickly, it can be fatal. Each year, 10 per cent of the global population contracts malaria, and it is still one of the modern world's deadliest killers. Drugs can provide effective treatment, but are not always available in the tropical and subtropical parts of the world that are most badly affected.

MALARIA-CARRYING MOSQUITO

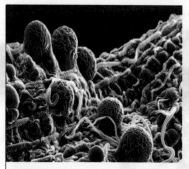

1906–10 The systematic use of mosquito screens and draining standing water reduces malaria cases among workers on the **Panama Canal**.

1880 French army surgeon Charles Louis Alphonse Laveran discovers microscopic **parasites** in the blood of a malaria sufferer.

1632 Jesuit missionary Barnabé de Cobo brings **cinchona bark,** used medicinally, from Peru to Spain.

1820 French chemists Caventou and Pelletier isolate **quinine**, the active ingredient in cinchona bark.

1885–86 Camillo Golgi, an Italian scientist, shows that there are **different forms of malaria**, with varying periods of fever.

1898 A team working in Rome establishes that human malaria is **transmitted** by mosquitoes of the genus *Anopheles*.

1712 Italian physician Francesco Torti announces that cinchona bark is effective against **"intermittent fever"** (malaria).

C.1850 Attempts are made to develop **synthetic quinine** to bring down the cost of anti-malarial treatment.

1897 British medical officer Ronald Ross shows that malaria can be transmitted by **mosquitoes**.

1902 Ross is awarded the **Nobel Prize** for Medicine in recognition of his work.

ESTIMATED ANNUAL DEATHS FROM MALARIA

700,000

1939 A malaria outbreak occurs in Italy; **fumigation** is used in an attempt to curtail it.

1940S Posters urge British **wartime troops** posted abroad to take precautions against mosquito bites in countries where malaria is a risk.

I'M LOOKING FOR YOU

FEVER MALARIA

PROTECT YOURSELF AGAINST MOSQUITOES

1946 The US **Communicable Disease Center** (CDC) is founded to work on controlling malaria in the US.

1951 As a result of the CDC's work, malaria is **eliminated** from the US.

1972 DDT is banned in the US because of the **environmental impact** of spraying. Alternative pesticides such as pyrethrins are adopted.

2007 World Malaria Day is instituted every 25 April to encourage investment in malaria containment and even **eradication** of the disease.

1939 Working in Switzerland, Paul Müller discovers the insecticidal property of the chemical **DDT**.

1930S German company I.G. Farben produces a **synthetic substitute** for quinine.

1955 World Health Organization sets out to eliminate malaria **worldwide** using insecticides and drug treatment.

1981 Chinese pharmacologist Tu Youyou presents her findings that **artemisinin** is an effective anti-malarial treatment.

1980S Rapid **diagnostic tests** for malaria are developed.

Glossary

AGONIST DRUG A drug that simulates a natural substance and replicates its effects in the body.

ALTERNATIVE MEDICINE Systems of health, diagnoses, and treatments that are outside the mainstream of science-based medicine.

ANAESTHESIA Drug-induced loss of sensation, including of touch and pain, either in a part of the body (local anaesthesia) or in all of the body (general anaesthesia).

ANALGESIA Pain relief.

ANTAGONIST DRUG A drug that blocks the action of a natural substance in the body.

ANTIBIOTIC A substance that kills, stops the growth of, or somehow neutralizes bacteria and certain other harmful microbes.

ANTIBODY A substance in the blood that kills, neutralizes, or identifies any foreign material, such as microbes and transplanted tissues.

ANTIGEN Foreign material that provokes the production of antibodies.

ANTISEPTIC A substance that kills or renders harmless microbes; especially used on the skin and surgical instruments.

ARTERY A blood vessel that carries blood away from the heart.

BACTERIUM A type of microbe that is too small to see and lacks a nucleus.

BIOPSY The taking of a sample of fluid or tissue for analysis.

BLOOD PRESSURE The pushing force of blood as it flows around the circulatory system.

BLOOD TYPE/GROUP An individual body's specific combination of antigens on red blood cells and antibodies in blood fluid (plasma).

CANCER A group of diseases characterized by cells that multiply fast, out of normal control, and fail to carry out their usual functions.

CARDIOVASCULAR SYSTEM The heart, blood vessels, and blood.

CELL A microscopic living unit, or "building block", of the body. The human body has over 250 different kinds of cells.

CHEMOTHERAPY Drugs used against cancers and certain other disorders.

CHROMOSOME A thread-like strand of DNA that carries the genes in which hereditary information is encoded. The human body is made of 46 chromosomes.

CIRCULATION The passage of blood through the heart and blood vessels.

CONTAGION A living thing, usually a microbe, that can spread between people to cause disease.

CT/CAT SCANNING Computerized (axial) tomography scanning, a form of computerized scanning that uses weak X-rays to visualize thin, 2D, slice-like images through the body and combines them to make 3D images.

DIASTOLIC In the heartbeat cycle, the lowest measure of blood pressure, as the heart relaxes.

DNA Deoxyribonucleic acid. A long, thin, double-helix molecule in which genetic information is encoded.

ELECTROCARDIOGRAM (ECG) A display or recording of the electrical activity of the heart, especially its muscle action.

ELECTROENCEPHALOGRAM (EEG) A display or recording of the electrical activity of the brain, especially its nerve impulses.

ENDOCRINE SYSTEM The body's chemical messengers (hormones), which control the activity of many tissues and organs, and the endocrine glands that produce them.

ENDOSCOPE A viewing instrument inserted into the body through a natural orifice, or a surgical incision that can often also carry out procedures such as sample-taking.

ENZYME A substance that speeds up or slows down the rate of chemical changes in the body, such as when food is digested.

EPIDEMIC An outbreak of a contagious disease that spreads widely and rapidly.

EPIDEMIOLOGY The study of diseases, how common they are, their causes and effects, and how they can be controlled.

GENE An instruction in chemical form for making a substance or controlling a process in the body.

GERM A harmful microbe, such as a virus, bacterium, fungal spore, or protist.

HISTOLOGY The study of cells and tissues, especially under a microscope.

HORMONE A substance produced in an endocrine gland that circulates in the blood and controls a biological process or activity.

IVF In vitro fertilization; the joining together of an egg and a sperm outside the body.

IMMUNE SYSTEM A defence network, including lymph fluid, lymph nodes, thymus, spleen, and white blood cells, which protects the body against infections and other diseases.

IMMUNIZATION Rendering an individual resistant to attack from microbes that would otherwise cause an infectious disease.

IMMUNOSUPPRESSANT A substance that reduces the workings of the immune system.

IMPLANT An item surgically inserted into the body. The implant may be living (e.g. bone marrow cells), mechanical (e.g an artificial hip joint), electronic (e.g. a heart pacemaker), or a combination of all three.

IN VITRO Literally "in glass". In a laboratory container, such as a test tube, as opposed to in living tissue.

IN VIVO Literally "in living tissue". Inside the body, as opposed to in a laboratory container.

INFECTION A disease caused by invading microbes, such as bacteria, viruses, protists, or similar life-forms.

INOCULATION The placement of a vaccine, antigenic substance, or serum into the body, usually for the purposes of immunization.

LAPAROSCOPE A type of endoscope inserted into the abdomen.

LESION An abnormality, such as an ulcer or tumour, in a tissue or organ.

MRI Magnetic resonance imaging – a form of computerized scanning that uses a powerful magnetic field and radio pulses to visualize thin, 2D, slice-like images through the body, and combine them to make 3D images.

METABOLISM The sum of all the chemical processes in the body, from digesting food to using energy for muscle action.

METASTASIS The spread of cancerous cells from one part of the body to another.

MICROBE A tiny life-form visible only under a microscope.

MITOCHONDRIA Sausage-shaped organelles inside cells that make energy available for the cell to live and function.

MUSCULOSKELETAL SYSTEM The body's muscles, bones, and joints.

MYOCARDIAL INFARCTION Loss of blood supply to heart muscle, causing damage or death to the muscle cells; a common form of heart attack.

NERVOUS SYSTEM The brain, spinal cord, and body-wide system of nerves.

NUCLEOTIDES Chemical subunits of DNA and RNA that function as "code letters" for genetic information.

NUCLEUS The part of a cell in which genetic information is stored.

OBSTETRICS The branch of medicine concerned with pregnancy, childbirth, and postnatal care.

ONCOLOGY The branch of medicine concerned with cancers and similar diseases.

PANDEMIC A very large-scale outbreak of a disease, which affects a huge region.

PATHOGEN A harmful microbe, such a virus, bacterium, fungal spore, or protist.

PET Positron emission tomography, a form of computerized scanning that uses rays given off by substances put into the body to identify very busy (metabolically active) cells and tissues.

PLASMA The liquid part of the blood that holds the blood cells in suspension.

PLATELETS Cells in the blood that are vital to the blood-clotting process.

PROSTHESIS An artificial item used as a substitute or replacement body part.

PROTEINS Chemical substances made from subunits called amino acids that form essential structural and functional parts of the body, from hair and nails to enzymes.

RNA Ribonucleic acid. A long, thin, helical molecule with many functions in the body, including protein production and gene control. Some viruses use RNA to carry genetic information.

RED BLOOD CELLS Doughnut-shaped blood cells that carry oxygen from the lungs to tissues, and carbon dioxide from tissues to the lungs.

RESPIRATORY SYSTEM The parts of the body responsible for breathing: the nose, throat, windpipe (trachea), the main lower airways (bronchi), and the lungs.

STEM CELL A non-specialized cell that is able to specialize, or differentiate, into particular types of cell, such as nerve cells, muscle cells, or skin cells.

STETHOSCOPE A device for listening to body sounds such as breathing, heartbeat, blood flow, and bubbling gases in the intestines.

SUTURE A closure, or "stitch", for holding ruptured tissues together.

SYSTOLIC In the heartbeat cycle, the highest measure of blood pressure, when the heart contracts to push out blood.

TRANSFUSION The transferral of blood, or parts of blood such as plasma or red blood cells, from one body to another.

TRANSPLANT The transferral of cells, tissues, or organs from one body to another, or from one site to another in the same body.

TUMOUR A growth or lump of abnormal cells that may be benign (non-cancerous) or malignant (cancerous).

ULTRASOUND Sound waves of such high frequency that they are inaudible to humans. An imaging technique based on bouncing such waves off living tissue.

VACCINATION Giving a vaccine to cause future immunity, or protection against, infectious diseases.

VACCINE A preparation of weakened or neutralized germs and/or their harmful products that makes the body become immune to those germs.

VARIOLATION An early form of vaccination against smallpox that uses smallpox itself.

VEIN A blood vessel that carries blood towards the heart.

WHITE BLOOD CELLS Blood cells that protect the body by counteracting invading germs and other foreign matter.

VIRUS The smallest type of harmful microbe, consisting of genetic material wrapped in a protective coating. Viruses can only multiply by invading living cells.

X-RAYS Electromagnetic waves that have a very short wavelength and so can penetrate through many materials, including most living matter; images made by the use of such waves.

Bibliography

Many hundreds of information sources and references, both primary and secondary, and printed, digital and online, were used in compiling this book. A very brief selection is included below. For a fuller listing, please contact the author.

GENERAL PRINTED SOURCES

Roberta Bivins, *Alternative Medicine? A History*, Oxford University Press, 2007

William Bynum and Helen Bynum, eds, *Great Discoveries in Medicine*, Thames & Hudson, 2011

James Le Fanu, *The Rise and Fall of Modern Medicine*, Little, Brown Book Group, 2011

Mark Jackson, ed, *The Oxford Handbook of the History of Medicine*, Oxford University Press, 2013

Peter E. Pormann, *Medieval Islamic Medicine*, Georgetown University Press, 2007

Roy Porter, ed, *The Cambridge Illustrated History of Medicine*, Cambridge University Press, 2006

Larry Trivieri, John W. Anderson, Burton Goldberg, eds, *Alternative Medicine: The Definitive Guide* (second edition), Celestial Arts, 2013

GENERAL ONLINE SOURCES

American Association for the History of Medicine
www.histmed.org

Department of History and Philosophy of Science, University of Cambridge
www.hps.cam.ac.uk/medicine

European Association for the History of Medicine and Health (EAHMH)
www.eahmh.net

Traditional Medicines
ca.traditionalmedicinals.comsystems_of_THM

University College London – UCL Centre for the History of Medicine
www.ucl.ac.uk/histmed

US National Library of Medicine, National Institutes of Health
www.nlm.nih.gov/hmd

Wellcome Library, History of Medicine Collection
wellcomelibrary.org/about-us/about-the-collections/history-of-medicine-collection

Wellcome Unit for the History of Medicine, University of Oxford
www.wuhmo.ox.ac.uk

HOSPITAL AND HEALTH CENTRE ARCHIVES AND ARTICLES

Bethlem Royal Hospital Archives and Museum Service
www.bethlemheritage.org.uk

Groote Schuur Hospital
www.gsh.co.za/christiaan-barnard

Johns Hopkins School of Medicine
webapps.jhu.edu/jhuniverse/academics/schools/school_of_medicine

Massachusetts General Hospital
www.massgeneral.org/history

Papworth Hospital
www.papworthhospital.nhs.uk/content.php?/about/history

St Christopher's Hospice
www.stchristophers.org.uk/about/history

Wrightington Hospital
www.wwl.nhs.uk/Internet/Home/wrt/john_charnley.asp

ORGANIZATIONS, MUSEUMS, AND EXHIBITIONS

American Cancer Society (History of Cancer)
www.cancer.org/cancer/cancerbasics/thehistoryofcancer/index

Aphorisms by Hippocrates
classics.mit.edu/Hippocrates/aphorisms.html

Cancer Research UK
www.cancerresearchuk.org/cancer-info/cancerandresearch/progress/a-century-of-progress

Elizabeth Garrett Anderson Hospital for Women
www.english-heritage.org.uk/discover/people-and-places/womens-history/women-and-healthcare/elizabeth-garrett-anderson-hospital-for-women

Florence Nightingale Museum
www.florence-nightingale.co.uk

Galen and Greek Medicine
www.greekmedicine.net/whos_who/Galen.html

Human Fertilisation and Embryology Authority (HFEA)
www.hfea.gov.uk/history-of-ivf.html

Institut Pasteur
www.pasteur-international.org/ip/easysite/pasteur-international-en/institut-pasteur-international-network/history-in-movement

Nobel Prize Foundation
www.nobelprize.org/nobel_prizes/medicine

Robert Koch Institute
www.rki.de/EN/Content/Institute/History/history_node_en.html

Royal College of Midwives
www.rcm.org.uk/midwives/by-subject/midwifery-history

Royal College of Nursing
www.rcn.org.uk/aboutus/our_history

Royal College of Physicians
www.rcplondon.ac.uk/about/history

Royal College of Surgeons
www.rcseng.ac.uk/museums/hunterian/history

Stem Cells (National Institutes of Health)
stemcells.nih.gov/Pages/Default.aspx

World Health Organization (WHO)
www.who.int/research/en

Index

Page numbers for illustrations are in italics.

Acknowledgments

Dorling Kindersley would like to thank the following for their help on this book:

Philip Wilkinson for additional text; Satu Fox for editorial assistance; Katie Cavanagh, Stephen Bere, and Peter Laws for design assistance; Margaret McCormack for indexing.

The publisher would also like to thank the following for their kind permission to reproduce their photographs:

(Key: a-above; b-below/bottom; c-centre; f-far; l-left; r-right; t-top)

2–3 **Getty Images:** De Agostini . **5 The Bridgeman Art Library:** Musée d'Histoire de la Médecine, Paris, France / Archives Charmet. **9 Science & Society Picture Library:** Science Museum. **12 Science Photo Library:** S. Plailly / E. Daynes. **15 Science Photo Library:** Mauricio Anton. **16 akg-images:** Florilegius; **17 Getty Images:** Gamma-Rapho. **19 Getty Images:** The Bridgeman Art Library. **20–21 Science & Society Picture Library:** Science Museum (c). **20 Science & Society Picture Library:** Science Museum (bc, bl). **21 Alex Peck Medical Antiques:** (r). **22 Getty Images:** G. Dagli Orti / De Agostini (br). **24 Getty Images:** De Agostini. **25 akg-images:** Francis Dzikowski. **26 Science & Society Picture Library:** Science Museum. **28–29 akg-images:** Bildarchiv Steffens (b). **28 Getty Images:** Marwan Naamani / AFP (bl). **29 Getty Images:** De Agostini. **31 Corbis:** Gianni Dagli Orti. **32 Getty Images:** De Agostini. **34–35 Scala, Florence:** White Images. **37 Getty Images:** A. Dagli Orti / De Agostini. **38 Corbis. 40 Corbis:** Ken Welsh / Design Pics. **42 akg-images:** Nimatallah. **44 Corbis:** Araldo de Luca. **45 Getty Images:** A. De Gregorio / De Agostini (tr). **46—47 Courtesy of Historical Collections & Services, Claude Moore Health Sciences Library, University of Virginia. 49 akg-images:** Erich Lessing. **51 Science Photo Library:** Jean-Loup Charmet (t). **53 The Art Archive:** Biblioteca Augusta Perugia / Gianni Dagli Orti. **54–55 (background) Getty Images:** Photo12 / UIG; Wellcome Library, London: (c). **54 Corbis:** (c); Science Photo Library: (cla). **55 Corbis:** Dr. Robert Calentine / Visuals Unlimited (cr); **55 Science Photo Library:** Eye of Science (c). **57 akg-images:** Erich Lessing. **59 Scala, Florence:** Ann Ronan / Heritage Images. **60 akg-images:** IAM. **62-63 Getty Images:** Josef Mensing Gallery, Hamm-Rhynern, Germany / The Bridgeman Art Library. **64 akg-images:** R. u. S. Michaud. **67 Wellcome Library, London. 69 Scala, Florence:** Digital Image Museum Associates / LACMA / Art Resource NY.

70–71 akg-images: Erich Lessing. **73 Ancient Art & Architecture Collection:** Heojun Museum / EuroCreon. **74 Getty Images:** Musee Guimet, Paris, France. **76 akg-images:** British Library. **79 akg-images:** R. u. S. Michaud. **80–81 The Bridgeman Art Library:** Luca Tettoni. **83 Getty Images:** Universal History Archive / UIG / The Bridgeman Art Library. **84 akg-images:** Rabatti Domingie. **85 Getty Images:** The Bridgeman Art Library. **87 The Bridgeman Art Library:** Collection of the Lowe Art Museum, University of Miami / Gift of the Institute of Maya Studies. **88 The Bridgeman Art Library:** Collection of the Lowe Art Museum, University of Miami / Gift of the Estate of Ann M. Grimshawe (cl); Getty Images: UIG via (bl); Science & Society Picture Library: Science Museum (tr). **89 The Bridgeman Art Library:** Werner Forman Archive (cr); Corbis: Werner Forman (cl); Getty Images: Werner Forman / UIG (crb); Science & Society Picture Library: Science Museum (clb, tl, tr). **90 Getty Images:** Robert Harding World Imagery. **92 Corbis:** Bowers Museum (tl). **93 Alamy:** Zev Radovan / BibleLand Pictures. **94–95 Getty Images:** Hulton Archive. **97 akg-images:** africanpictures. **98 Getty Images:** M. Seemuller / De Agostini. **100 Wellcome Images. 103 Getty Images:** De Agostini. **104 akg-images:** Erich Lessing. **106–107 akg-images:** British Library (c). **106 The Bridgeman Art Library:** Bibliotheque Nationale, Paris, France / Archives Charmet (bl). **107 The Art Archive:** Saint Stephen's Cathedral Vienna / Dagli Orti (br, ca, cb,cr). **109 The Art Archive:** Bodleian Library Oxford. **110 Getty Images:** De Agostini. **112–113 akg-images:** Erich Lessing. **114 Scala, Florence:** Ann Ronan / Heritage Images. **115 Wellcome Images. 116 Getty Images:** Universal History Archive. **118 Corbis. 121 The Bridgeman Art Library:** Christie's Images. **124–125 The Bridgeman Art Library:** Musee des Beaux-Arts, Marseille, France. **126 akg-images. 129 The Art Archive:** Museo del Prado Madrid / Gianni Dagli Orti. **130 The Bridgeman Art Library:** British Library, London, UK / © British Library Board. All Rights Reserved. **132–133 Science & Society Picture Library:** Science Museum (c). **132 Wellcome Library, London. 133 Getty Images:** Visuals Unlimited, Inc. / Scientifica (bl); **Science & Society Picture Library:** Science Museum (br, ca); **Wellcome Library, London. 134 Wellcome Library, London. 137 The Bridgeman Art Library:** Bibliothèque des Arts Décoratifs, Paris, France / Archives Charmet. **139 Wellcome Images. 141 Wellcome Images. 142–143 akg-images:** Album / Oronoz. **144 Getty Images:** Hulton Archive. **145 Getty Images:** De Agostini.

149 Corbis: Bettmann. 150 Science & Society Picture Library: Science Museum (br, cr, l, tr); Wellcome Images: (br). 151 Science & Society Picture Library: Science Museum (b, r). 152 Science & Society Picture Library: Science Museum. 153 Science Photo Library: NYPL / Science Source. 154 Wellcome Images. 157 Wellcome Images. 160–161 (background) Corbis: Bettmann. 160 Science Photo Library: NYPL / Science Source (cl); Science Photo Library: CCI Archives (cla); Wellcome Library, London: (cr). 161 Getty Images: Leemage (cl); Getty Images: Lynn Pelham (cr); 162 Corbis: Bettmann. 165 Getty Images: Werner Forman / UIG. 166 The Bridgeman Art Library: Biblioteca Universitaria, Bologna, Italy / Archives Charmet. 168 Getty Images: Time & Life Pictures. 169 Getty Images: Hulton Archive. 170–171 Wellcome Library, London. 173 Wellcome Library, London. 175 Wellcome Library, London. (t); 176 Science & Society Picture Library: Science Museum. 178 Science & Society Picture Library: Science Museum (br, cr, l); Science & Society Picture Library: SCM (cl). 179 Science & Society Picture Library: Science Museum. 181 U.S. National Library of Medicine, History of Medicine Division. 182 Science & Society Picture Library: Science Museum. 184 Alamy: Neil Setchfield. 186–187 Wellcome Library, London. 188 Getty Images: Time & Life Pictures. 190 Getty Images: Universal History Archive. 193 Getty Images: Universal History Archive. 194–195 Science & Society Picture Library: Science Museum (c). 194 Mary Evans Picture Library: INTERFOTO / Bildarchiv Hansmann. 196 Getty Images: Roger Viollet Collection. 199 The Art Archive: Eileen Tweedy (t). 201 Getty Images: BSIP / UIG. 202 The Bridgeman Art Library: Musée Pasteur, Institut Pasteur, Paris, France / Archives Charmet. 204–205 (background) U.S. National Library of Medicine, History of Medicine Division. 204 Wellcome Library, London: (cl); Science Photo Library: Dr P. Marazzi (cla); Corbis: Bettmann (cr). 205 Corbis: Dr. Fred Murphy /Visuals Unlimited (cl); Science Photo Library: Simon Fraser (cr). 206 Science & Society Picture Library: Science Museum. 209 Corbis: Bettmann (t). 210 Science & Society Picture Library: Science Museum. 211 Science & Society Picture Library: Science Museum. 212–213 The Bridgeman Art Library: Deutsches Historisches Museum, Berlin, Germany. 214 U.S. National Library of Medicine, History of Medicine Division. 216 Wellcome Library, London. 217 Wellcome Library, London. 218–219 U.S. National Library of Medicine, History of Medicine Division. 221 Wellcome Library,

London. 222 Corbis: Bettmann. 224 Getty Images: Universal History Archive. 227 Wellcome Library, London. 228 Science Photo Library. 229 Corbis: Visuals Unlimited (ftr, tc, tl); Corbis: Dennis Kunkel Microscopy, Inc. / Visuals Unlimited (tr). 231 Getty Images: Hulton Archive. 232 Science & Society Picture Library: Science Museum. 233 Getty Images: Buyenlarge. 234 Scala, Florence: White Images. 237 Corbis. 238–239 Corbis: Burstein Collection. 240 Science Photo Library: Dept. of Microbiology, Biozentrum. 242 Getty Images: Universal History Archive. 245 U.S. National Library of Medicine, History of Medicine Division. 247 Science & Society Picture Library: Science Museum. 249 Corbis: Bettmann. 250–251 Science & Society Picture Library: Science Museum (c). 250 U.S. National Library of Medicine, History of Medicine Division (bl). 253 Getty Images: Davies. 254 Science & Society Picture Library: Science Museum. 257 Library of Congress. 258 Corbis: Bettmann. 261 Alamy: BSIP SA. 262 Getty Images: Esther Bubley / Time & Life Pictures. 265 U.S. National Library of Medicine, History of Medicine Division. 267 Alamy: ZUMA Press, Inc. 268 Wellcome Images: Yorgos Nikas, (bl); Wellcome Images: K. Hodivala-Dilke & M. Stone (br); Wellcome Images: Annie Cavanagh (cl); Wellcome Images: Steven Pollard (cr). 269 Science Photo Library: Steve Gschmeissner (br); Wellcome Images: Anne Weston, LRI, CRUK (bl, tl); Wellcome Images: Dr. Yi Feng, University of Bristol (tr). 270 Science & Society Picture Library: Science Museum. 273 Getty Images: Steve Allen. 274 Science & Society Picture Library: Science Museum. 276 Science & Society Picture Library: Science Museum (bl, cr); Wellcome Library, London: (cl). 277 Science Photo Library: James King-Holmes (br); Science & Society Picture Library: Science Museum (bl, t); Wellcome Images: (cl); 279 Getty Images: Universal History Archive. 282 Courtesy of St Christopher's Hospice, London. 284–285 The Bridgeman Art Library: Musée de l'Assistance Publique, Hopitaux de Paris, France / Archives Charmet. 286 Corbis. 288 U.S. National Library of Medicine, History of Medicine Division. 289 Science Photo Library: AMI Images. 290 Getty Images: Archive Photos (br). 292 Getty Images: Evans / Three Lions. 293 Science & Society Picture Library: Science Museum. 294 Getty Images: Charles H. Phillips / Time Life Pictures. 297 Corbis: Bettmann. 298 Corbis: Mediscan. 300–301 Science & Society Picture Library: Science Museum (c). 300 Corbis: Bettmann (bl). 302 Science & Society Picture Library: Science Museum. 303 Getty Images: Universal History

Archive. **304 Wellcome Library, London:** (tr). **308 Science Photo Library:** Arno Massee. **310 Corbis:** Zephyr / Science Photo Library (cr); **Getty Images:** Dirk Freder (cl); **Science Photo Library:** Zephyr (br); **Science Photo Library:** CNRI (bl). **311 Alamy:** Chad Ehlers (br); **Science Photo Library:** GJLP (bl); **Science Photo Library:** Wellcome Dept. of Cognitive Neurology (tr); **Wellcome Images:** Mark Lythgoe & Chloe Hutton (tl). **313 Getty Images:** Gamma-Keystone. **314 Rex Features:** Sipa Press. **317 Science Photo Library:** Colin Cuthbert. **318–319 Rex Features:** Image Broker. **321 Corbis:** Hero Images. **322 The Bridgeman Art Library:** Société d'Histoire de la Pharmacie, Paris, France / Archives Charmet. **325 Science Photo Library:** Thierry Berrod / Mona Lisa Production. **326–327 Scala, Florence:** White Images. **328 Getty Images:** Michel Clement / AFP. **330 Getty Images:** BSIP / UIG. **333 Getty Images:** Patrick Lin / AFP. **334–335 (background) Science & Society Picture Library:** Science Museum. **334 akg-images:** Paul Almasy (cr); **Corbis:** Wavebreak Media Ltd. (cla); **Science & Society Picture Library:** Science Museum (cl). **335 Wellcome Library, London:** (cl, cr). **336 Science Photo Library:** Riccardo Cassiani-Ingoni. **339 Corbis:** Thomas Deerinck / Visuals Unlimited. **340 Science Photo Library:** A. Barrington Brown. **343 Corbis:** Karen Kasmauski.

344 Corbis: Tek Image / Science Photo Library. **346 Science Photo Library:** David McCarthy. **348 Alamy:** INTERFOTO. **351 Corbis:** epa. **352 Rex Features:** Intuitive Surgical. **354–355 Science Photo Library:** Peter Menzel. **356 The Bridgeman Art Library:** Musée du Val-de-Grace, Paris, France / Archives Charmet. **358 Science & Society Picture Library:** Science Museum. **361 Getty Images:** DreamPictures. **362–363 Science & Society Picture Library:** Science Museum (c). **362 Wellcome Library, London:** (c). **365 Corbis:** David Scharf / Science Faction. **369 Corbis:** epa. **370–371 Science Photo Library:** Riccardo Cassiani-Ingoni. **372 Corbis:** Dan McCoy, Rainbow / Science Faction. **374–375 The Art Archive: British Museum / Jacqueline Hyde. 377 Corbis:** SuperStock. **380–381 Corbis:** Hulton-Deutsch Collection. **382 Getty Images:** Adam Pretty. **384 Corbis:** Yang Liu. **387 Getty Images:** Jeff J. Mitchell. **388–389 (background) Getty Images:** BSIP / UIG. **388 Science Photo Library:** (cr); Wellcome Images: Hugh Sturrock (cla); Wellcome Library, London: (cr). **389 Corbis:** Studio Patellani (cl); Wellcome Library, London: (cr).

All other images © Dorling Kindersley
For further information see: www.dkimages.com